Ethics and values in psychotherapy

The role of ethics and values within psychotherapy is an important and sometimes contentious one; yet discussion has often taken place in isolation from traditional ethical theories. However, traditional ethical theory does not address questions of practice in psychotherapy.

Covering the intellectual and social context, the means and ends of therapy and the role of therapy in society, this book draws upon philosophy's understanding of ethics and the psychological literature to focus on the role of the therapist as ethicist, and examines how the ethical convictions of both therapists and clients contribute to the practical process of therapy. *Ethics and Values in Psychotherapy* will be welcomed by all those who have an interest in the increasingly important issue of professional ethics and values within psychotherapy.

Alan C. Tjeltveit, who has a Ph.D. in clinical psychology, completed a clinical internship at the University of Minnesota. A psychotherapist since 1978, he has taught undergraduate and graduate students, contributed articles to *Clinical Psychology Review* and *Psychotherapy* and chaired a psychological association ethics committee. He is Associate Professor of Psychology at Muhlenberg College in Allentown, Pennsylvania, where he maintains a clinical practice.

Ethics and values in psychotherapy

Alan C. Tjeltveit

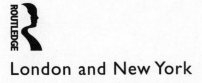

London and New York

First published 1999
by Routledge
11 New Fetter Lane, London EC4P 4EE

Simultaneously published in the USA and Canada
by Routledge
29 West 35th Street, New York, NY 10001

Typeset in Garamond by Routledge
Printed and bound in Great Britain by
TJ International Ltd, Padstow, Cornwall

British Library Cataloguing in Publication Data
A catalogue record for this book is available from the British
Library

Library of Congress Cataloguing in Publication Data
A catalogue record for this book has been requested

ISBN 0–415–15663–7 (hbk)
ISBN 0–415–15664–5 (pbk)

To Maria

Contents

PART IV
Change in psychotherapy: ethical facets 153

PART V
Implications 229

Preface

Murder mysteries accompany me on long trips. I like people who find clues that others miss, who patiently put together a case, who pay attention to all the important evidence, who look beyond the obvious, who think clearly and well.

To think well about the ethical character of psychotherapy we need, I think, to be like those sleuths. Although the mystery of therapy has to do with positive human change, not murder, complexities abound, and the skills of the detective can help us to understand and make good decisions about ethics and values in psychotherapy.

Abundant clues await those who want to think more deeply than "Therapy is not value-free." New evidence from a variety of sources can be used by people who want to explore how – for good and ill – the ethical convictions of therapist, client, and culture invigorate therapy. The empirical finding that therapists influence client values, research on therapy in general, the increasingly sophisticated psychology of moral development, the retrieval and application to psychology of Continental philosophical traditions, cross-cultural psychological investigations, and the careful historical work that is reshaping our understanding of psychology and psychotherapy all provide evidence that is essential to a satisfactory solution to the mystery of the role of values in therapy.

Emerging developments in ethics provide crucial clues as well: the rise of a transdisciplinary bioethics that links together academic philosophy and the clinical setting, ethical analyses of psychotherapy, evolving standards of professional ethics, the vigor and creativity of feminist ethics, the development of revivified and psychologically nuanced forms of virtue ethics, cross-cultural ethical studies, and analyses of how culture shapes ethics and therapy. Finally, careful work on the definition of "values" and the increasing involvement in therapy of those who pay for therapy (e.g. insurance companies, governments, and managed care organizations) provide us with new perspectives from which to consider the evidence.

To make progress in unraveling the mystery of the ethical character of therapy, we need to move, I think, beyond obvious solutions and think deeply about those various strands of evidence. Accordingly, this book joins together what many would sunder – the practical and the theoretical. Psychotherapists and others who dislike the philosophical may thus think it too theoretical; philosophers, in turn, may find it too practical and insufficiently philosophical. But I think it is in the balance of the practical and the theoretical that we can discover the best answers, even if those answers fall far short of perfection or certainty.

My interest in ethics, values, and psychotherapy began in graduate school. A seminar with Neil Clark Warren and David Allan Hubbard played a pivotal role. I am grateful for their assistance and encouragement, and that given to me at the time (and since) by Hendrika Vande Kemp, H. Newton Malony, Lewis Smedes, Don Browning, and Paul Meehl. My ideas evolved through five years of full-time clinical practice, work on a hospital Bioethics Consultation Team, seven years of service on a psychological association ethics committee, teaching and supervising undergraduate and graduate students in psychology (including a seminar on Values and Psychotherapy I team-taught with C. Stephen Evans), and conducting empirical research on values in collaboration with my students. I have benefited from working in a scientifically-oriented department that shares a cozy building with an excellent philosophy department. Teaching in a liberal arts college encourages me to think from a variety of disciplinary perspectives and reinforces my belief in the importance of the liberal arts, of scholarly breadth and integration. Active participation in conferences and numerous e-mail exchanges with an informal group of researchers investigating the role of values in therapy has also been very helpful. And personal support and increasing theoretical and philosophical sophistication have been the fruits of my involvement with the American Psychological Association's Division of Theoretical and Philosophical Psychology.

Muhlenberg College has supported me with several summer research grants and a year-long sabbatical to work on this project, for which I am deeply grateful. I am also thankful to the librarians at Muhlenberg and Abbott Northwestern Hospital for faithfully tracking down books and journal articles in accord with my repeated requests.

I am particularly grateful to Sam Knapp, who read the entire manuscript, and to Christine Sistare, Daniel Wilson, Larry Hass, Ed Lundeen, Stanton Jones, Deborah Heggie, George Howard, Isaac Prilleltensky, Gary Schoener, students in several classes, and anonymous reviewers, who read portions of it. The usual caveat applies: I have benefited from their wise counsel, but have sometimes chosen to disregard it. I am also grateful to my therapy clients and my students, from whom I have learned much. Finally, I am most thankful to my wife, Maria, whose arrival in my life – at the beginning of the sabbatical supposedly devoted entirely to writing this book – proved to be a great distraction. And my greatest delight.

Part I

Developing a better understanding of the ethical character of psychotherapy

Introduction

Psychotherapy, once viewed as value-free, is now widely acknowledged to be value-laden. But what does it mean that psychotherapy is value-laden? In what ways is it laden? With which values? Can those values be eliminated from therapy? If not, with which values *ought* it be laden? Put another way, how can we best understand and address the ethical dimensions of psychotherapy?

When a client comes to a psychotherapist with complaints of sadness and meaninglessness and says "I feel absolutely horrible. What should I do?" the therapist's response invariably represents some ethical position; it is value-laden. As Bergin put it, "Values are an inevitable and pervasive part of psychotherapy" (Bergin 1980b: 97).

Challenges immediately confront such assertions. But when we face them squarely and thoroughly, we can better understand the complexity of psychotherapy's ethical dimensions and the field can move beyond its present impasse in understanding and addressing values in therapy.

Setting the stage

The challenges to the claim that psychotherapy is invariably value-laden have much validity. Because they raise key questions, highlight some of the debate to come, begin to clarify the reasons for the current impasse, and help to clarify the central thrust of this book, six of those challenges warrant brief consideration at the outset.

Psychotherapy is inconsequentially value-laden

Some psychotherapists deny that *all* therapy is value-laden. They hold that some or most therapy is not; therefore, therapists rarely function as ethicists. Although acknowledging that some therapist responses to the sad client's entreaty would clearly be value-laden (e.g. "You should honor the sacred commitment you made on your wedding day, return to your spouse, and begin paying some attention to your obligations to your children"), they argue that other responses are ethically "neutral" (e.g.' "Sounds like you're really feeling sad. How long has this been going on?"). This challenge thus raises some key questions that need to be addressed to develop a full-fledged understanding of values in therapy: to what extent is therapy value-laden? doesn't value-free therapy (or minimally value-laden therapy) remain an important ideal, albeit one not achieved by inexperienced or inexpert therapists? Another issue will also need to be considered: are there implicit values in therapy (even in "neutral" responses in therapy), values that are rarely examined, values perhaps subtly conveyed in the language, symbols, stories, and institutions of psychotherapy, values perhaps so widely or deeply held in a particular culture that they remain unnoticed?

Psychotherapy involves only mental health values

Other psychotherapists acknowledge that therapy is value-laden but assert that it is (or ought to be) laden primarily with values that contribute to therapeutic goals, that is, with values that contribute to improved psychological functioning. Strupp, for instance, distinguishes between essential therapeutic values (e.g. "People have the right to personal freedom and independence"), which are essential to the therapeutic endeavor, and optional and idiosyncratic values, which are not (Strupp 1980: 397–8). If psychotherapy is viewed in terms of essential therapeutic values and therapists practice in accord with them, he argues, "the issue of indoctrination or the alleged dangers of a laissez-faire stance are largely inconsequential" (Strupp 1980: 400). Accepting Strupp's distinction raises two questions: which values are "essential therapeutic values"? to what extent do therapists' optional values (e.g. their deepest convictions about human flourishing) influence the outcome of therapy?

This challenge raises a vitally important, very complex issue: the relationship between values and the goals of therapy. To make my position clear (arguments will be developed later), I propose the following thesis: *a central reason for the inevitability of therapy's value-ladenness is that all therapy involves value-laden goals.* As Bergin notes, "as an applied field, psychotherapy is directed toward practical goals that are selected in value terms" (Bergin 1980b: 97). So, for instance, if we want to understand "essential therapeutic values," we need to examine therapeutic goals very closely.

This raises some key questions: what is the goal of psychotherapy? if it is "mental health," or "improved" or "ideal" psychological functioning, what do those terms mean? to which values or ethical positions (if any) does endorsement of a therapeutic goal commit a therapist?

Discussion of therapy goals is often difficult, for several reasons: the terms therapists use to express therapy goals (e.g. "mental health," "behavior change," and "self-actualization") vary widely. Therapists use the same terms in significantly different ways. And many therapists individualize the goals they set for clients – so goals in a particular therapeutic relationship depend on the nature of the problem, the client's stated goals, client characteristics (including client personality and personal and social strengths), financial considerations (character reconstruction is rarely a goal for a managed care client of modest means), the stage of therapy, and so forth. As an example of the second difficulty, two significantly different meanings of mental health (and related terms) need to be distinguished: freedom from serious psychological dysfunction, and positive mental health. In general, greater consensus has developed regarding values tied to the former than to the latter. For instance, in working with a severely depressed client a therapist may establish the therapeutic goal of decreased depression. That goal involves a value ("It is good to be free from severe depression") about which there is wide agreement in society. However, mental health professionals disagree, at times sharply, about the meaning of mental health understood as ideal human functioning. In 1958, Jahoda sought – without success – to find agreement among therapists about the meaning of "positive mental health." And it is likely that there is even less agreement now.

Introducing different perspectives on mental health (including those of non-therapists) makes even more complex the tasks of defining concepts of mental health[1] and clarifying the values (if any) tied to such definitions. Stiles, Shapiro, and Barkham suggest that, "stakeholders – individuals or groups, therapists, clients, families, or others in society – may have different perspectives, interests, and values regarding psychotherapeutic outcomes" (Stiles, Shapiro, and Barkham 1993: 116).[2]

Adopting cross-cultural perspectives makes clarifying, evaluating, and justifying the values tied to therapeutic goals (and thus to therapy itself) even more daunting, because some argue that traditional therapy goals reflect Western cultural values. And so, those goals may or may not be transportable to other cultural settings. Any claims that they represent *the* essence of psychotherapy and ideal human functioning may thus need rethinking. To give one example, consider autonomy, a value Strupp (1980) considers an essential therapeutic value and which 96 percent of the US therapists surveyed by Jensen and Bergin endorsed as "important for a positive, mentally healthy life-style" (Jensen and Bergin 1988: 293). Varma noted that in India "there is a greater degree of mutual interdependence" than in the West. Thus, he argues:

> it is questionable how far Western psychotherapy with its high emphasis on autonomy and individual responsibility can be prescribed for members of such a society; and accordingly what modifications are required in the rules and practice of conventional psychotherapy.
>
> (Varma 1988: 145)

Western feminists (e.g. Adleman 1990; Ballou 1990; Feminist Therapy

Institute 1990; Lerman and Porter 1990) have also criticized dominant values in therapy, challenging the sexist values implicit in traditional therapies and codes of ethics.

These considerations raise several questions: with which values are therapy goals laden? to what extent is it possible for therapists to free clients from their presenting problems without also changing them in directions valued by the therapist? how do various concepts of mental health represent answers to classic ethical questions concerning what is good, what is virtuous, and what is right? which therapy goals are best? and why?

To sharpen the terms of the debate, let me state an assertion, a qualified version of which I will defend in this book: *any therapeutic goal held by therapists, clients, or third parties (e.g. insurance companies or government funding sources) represents a commitment (implicit or explicit, limited or extensive) to some value(s) and some working ethical theory.*

Some psychotherapists suggest that the problems of values in psychotherapy goals can be solved by adopting, to the widest extent possible, the consensus among therapists regarding essential therapeutic values (while of course continuing to allow ample room for individual differences among therapists regarding *non*essential therapeutic values). This seems plausible. And I will argue that it is essential, as a matter of public policy, that a society should develop *some* measure of basic agreement about the goals of therapy (in part to justify why insurance companies, managed care entities, governments, and other third-party payers should continue to pay increasing amounts for "mental health" coverage). But I will also argue that the articulation and development of a consensus needs to occur much more explicitly, and involve *all* stakeholders in therapy, not just third-party payers.

At a deeper level, however, those psychotherapists who rely solely on consensus to define the goals of therapy may adopt a decidedly conservative ("when it comes to therapy goals and values, therapists should believe what our elders passed on to us") and profoundly problematic position. One of the marks of the scientist, indeed of any well-educated person, is the ability to question received tradition and to use reason and evidence to formulate an argument, either supporting or rejecting a particular intellectual claim. The goals of therapy in particular, and the whole set of questions having to do with ethics and values in therapy in general, require this kind of rigorous intellectual scrutiny. The fact that therapists do endorse certain values does not establish that those values are best, are correct, or should be endorsed. That is, we cannot move directly from a fact about an existing consensus to the claim that those values should be adopted; we cannot move in any straightforward way from assertions about what *is* to assertions about what *ought* to be.

Accordingly, whether or not there is a consensus (and the evidence is mixed; see Consoli 1996; Haugen, Tyler, and Clark 1991; Jensen and Bergin

1988; E. W. Kelly 1995a), we must still ask *why* therapy should be devoted to a particular goal or goals, and not to other goals, and what ethical justification (if any) can be provided for such goals.

From Strupp's perspective, psychotherapists addressing such questions face a dilemma: "We don't know how to research the problem" of values in therapy (Strupp 1980: 397). While we should not underestimate the difficulties of arriving at ethical knowledge, if someone interpreted Strupp to mean we are unable to make *any* ethical assertions, I would think that person unduly pessimistic. Psychotherapists have, in fact, always answered ethical questions – by drawing upon consensus, training, experts, experience, intuition, rational arguments, science, and so forth. Furthermore, pessimism that paralyzes efforts to reflect deeply about therapy's value-ladenness has contributed substantially to the present impasse in the field of values and therapy. While definitive solutions will likely remain elusive, I think progress *can* occur in the ethical arena. The challenge is to determine the best, or the best possible combination, of those approaches to address a particular ethical question. Accordingly, in Chapters 4, 5, and elsewhere, I will defend the thesis that *it can be fruitful for therapists to think about ethical convictions and ethical theory (e.g. to think about the reasons for holding certain ethical convictions as opposed to others)*. From this thesis (which stands in stark contrast to the philosophical stance adopted – at times after careful reflection – by many in psychology) follows a second: *since ethics and values inevitably play a role in psychotherapy, therapists need to think well about the ethical theory and values with which therapy is laden*. In accord with those theses, this book addresses how to think well ("how to research") the problems of ethics and values in therapy.

Clients alone should choose therapy values

Other critics of the idea that therapy is value-laden raise a (related) challenge: therapists do not, and ought not to, determine goals or values in therapy but, rather, simply serve the goals and values clients themselves choose. This position could, of course, lead to the conclusion that there are as many legitimate therapeutic goals (or notions of mental health) and values as there are clients. While this position has considerable intuitive appeal, and substantial merit, it faces several intellectual challenges.

This position is not, finally, a claim that therapy is value-free, but an argument that therapy involves, or should involve, a particular value or set of values (e.g. the value that all client goals are good or acceptable, that it is best or most good for clients to choose their own values, or that it is wrong for therapists to impose their values on clients). It is thus not a claim that therapy is value-free, but that therapy should be delimited to a narrow range of values – those chosen by clients and those supporting client choice of therapy goals. The argument is defensible, but it raises its own set of questions: why should we adopt this position? how can its "essential thera-peutic values" be justified?

A practical issue must also be faced. When third parties (government agencies or corporations, acting directly or through insurance companies or managed care entities) pay for therapy, they increasingly want a say in deter-mining therapy goals. Taxpayers and retirees may well wish to pay only for therapy to reduce serious psychopathology. Government funding (provided by taxpayers) and insurance companies (who serve corporations, whose stock is often owned by pension funds, upon which the elderly rely for their income) may thus limit their support for psychotherapy. Accordingly, only the wealthy may be able to afford therapy intended to reach *any* goal clients choose.

In addition, those arguing that clients alone appropriately choose therapy goals must wrestle with the possibility that some clients might choose therapy goals many would consider undesirable or unacceptable. A client goal may conflict, for instance, with the "essential" therapeutic value of client autonomy. Suppose a new client states, "I came to therapy because I want to feel better. Now, I don't want to change how I lead my life, but I want you to make me feel better." Or, "My goal for therapy is for you to tell me what to do." Few therapists would accept those client goals, because they conflict with therapist values about proper therapy goals, with values thera-pists believe necessary for the development of ideal psychological functioning, or both.

The issue of how to handle other types of questionable client goals was raised in connection with a case discussed by R. J. Kohlenberg (1974). In accord with a male client's wishes, Kohlenberg successfully decreased the client's behaviors associated with child molesting and increased his sexual arousal to adult males. In a commentary on the case, Strupp (1974) raised the question of whether, had the client sought treatment for his ineffec-tive prowling behavior (which meant little sexual contact with young boys), Kohlenberg would have used assertiveness training to increase the efficacy of the client's prowling behavior, and thus increased his sexual success with young boys. Strupp suggested that Kohlenberg's likely unwillingness to do so would have stemmed from Kohlenberg's and society's values, which, in that instance, would have (appropriately) super-seded the client's goal. Similarly, Garfield (1974) posed the question of how Kohlenberg would have responded if the client's goal had been the elimination of the discomfort and stress he felt about being sexually involved with boys, if the client had aspired to guilt-free pedophilia. Garfield concludes that therapists must make a judgment about how "desirable" client goals are. The comments of Garfield and Strupp suggest that the doctrine, "Client goals are always to be pursued," warrants at least some qualification.

Finally, even when client goals are accepted, other values may also be present in therapy, those tied to the means by which the client's ends are pursued. For instance, leaving aside practical considerations related to the transmission of the HIV virus, therapist values may permit (or encourage) the use of sexual surrogates to treat client sexual problems (the elimination of which is an end endorsed by the client). But the client may have moral objections to that particular means. To use Rokeach's (1973) language, even when therapists and clients agree about terminal values in therapy, they may disagree about instrumental values.

Psychotherapy ought to be based on science, not values

Others who challenge the idea that therapy is value-laden argue that the idea represents a fundamental misunderstanding of the nature of therapy. Therapy is a scientific rather than an ethical endeavor, stemming solely from scientific findings about diagnosis, etiology, empirically validated behavioral interventions, efficacious treatments, and the like.

I believe that psychotherapy is, or at least ought to be, based in part on scientific findings. For example, attempts to discover empirically the relationship among the (self-reported) values of therapists and clients and therapeutic outcome – as in the sustained research program of Beutler and colleagues (e.g. 1970, 1981; Consoli and Beutler 1996) – are legitimate and essential. To the extent we thereby discover the values, or therapist–client value matches, that produce optimal client improvement, therapists should alter what they do accordingly.

But even if science produces unequivocal empirical findings that would permit definitive prescriptions for therapist behavior regarding values and other therapeutic techniques (and so far it has not), other questions remain: which outcome measure should we employ in measuring "optimal client improvement"? which definition of mental health should we adopt? To reiterate points just made, full agreement about the meaning of mental health (outcome), especially when viewed broadly as ideal human functioning, does not exist. And all therapy goals rest on values. Accordingly, in and of itself, empirical research cannot definitively or exhaustively address the ethical questions of ideal therapy goals or the proper means by which therapy is carried out. Attempts to "solve" the problem of values in therapy on an entirely scientific basis may thus rest on a value-laden definition of mental health. Such attempts will likely contribute to our understanding of the problem, but not, finally, solve it.

This by no means entails a rejection of science, however. One can hold that empirical findings are very helpful, indeed, essential, without also accepting the philosophical claim that science alone can produce knowledge about ethics, values, and the ethical dimensions of therapy. I can summarize my dialectical position in two theses:

Science alone will not resolve the ethical questions raised by the presence of values in therapy.

The ethical questions raised by the presence of values in therapy cannot be adequately resolved without relying upon pertinent scientific findings.

I thus reject the notion that we must choose *either* science *or* ethics to address values in therapy. That notion, and the related differentiation between philosophy and science, bears close scrutiny, in part because, as Koch noted, "psychology is necessarily the most philosophy-sensitive in the entire gamut of disciplines that claim empirical status" (Koch 1981: 267). And Leahey observed that "psychology, more than any other science, occupies treacherous middle ground between *is* and *ought*" (Leahey 1992: 470).

My claim is that we need to move beyond arguments about whether questions of values in therapy are to be solved by scientific or by philosophical means, and focus on how to draw upon *both* scientific *and* philosophical questions to understand the ethical dimensions of therapy. Accordingly, I believe that the ethical questions raised by the presence of values in therapy cannot be adequately resolved without relying upon pertinent scientific findings. And that *progress in understanding values and ethics in therapy requires in-depth philosophical reflection.*

Sorting out the respective contributions of scientific methods and philosophical reflection is, to be sure, knotty and controversial. But I am convinced that psychologists' profound resistance to philosophical reflection (in Chapter 6, some of the historical reasons for this resistance will be explored) has contributed substantially to the failure of mental health professionals to develop a more intellectually satisfying understanding of ethics and values in psychotherapy.

It is meaningless to claim that values or ethical assertions in psychotherapy can be true or correct

Logical positivists and others raise an additional challenge to the claim that therapy is value-laden, indeed, to *any* discussion of the ethical character of therapy. One version of this type of position, which I will call the positivist ethical theory, makes assertions like the following:

Since there can be no truth-value attributed to ethical statements, it is cognitively meaningless to claim to understand values in therapy, or to discuss which values *ought* to be present. For instance, it is meaningless to argue that it is *good* for a client to move in a healthier direction. We can only say we *prefer* the client to do so. The values of the mental health professional about therapy goals thus carry no more epistemic weight

than those of a garbage man, physicist, or cult leader. Not even experience or science permits us to draw conclusions about the goodness of
therapy goals or about which values ought to be present in
psychotherapy.

Other ethical positivists would concur that it is pointless to discuss
which values ought to be in therapy. But they would nonetheless argue
that the empirical investigation of "values" (where "values" is a descriptive
term referring to beliefs or feelings about matters commonly considered to
be "ethical") is a meaningful activity, indeed, that it is an essential task,
one for which the scientific method is well suited. This disagreement likely
stems, in part, from the issue to which Chapter 5 is devoted – the multiple
definitions of "values." If both types of positivists agree that "values" is a
strictly ethical term (so values have to do with goodness, rightness, obligation, virtue, and the like, and thus can be correct or incorrect), then both
would likely agree that a claim to explain "values" is meaningless –
because "values" cannot be investigated empirically. However, if one party
assumes everyone uses values in a strictly *ethical* sense, but the second party
assumes everyone employs it as a *descriptive* term, communication will be
impaired.

(This illustrates a major reason for the impasse reached by those striving
to understand and address values in therapy: the profound ambiguity of the
term "values." From this follows a thesis that will be addressed in Chapter 5:
*definitional disparities and conceptual confusion regarding the term "values" have
greatly impeded progress in understanding and addressing values in therapy and the
ethical dimensions of therapy.*)

However, positivists who assume it is meaningful to study values empirically and positivists who assume it is not both concur in believing that it is
meaningless to make assertions about goodness or obligation. Based on that
philosophical position, they claim that it is cognitively meaningless to ask
what values *ought* to be pursued in therapy. Their claim raises further questions: on what philosophical grounds do its adherents support it? how do
therapists adopting this philosophical position address the logical and other
objections to the positivist theory of ethics, objections that have led almost
all philosophers to reject it? how do such psychotherapists work with clients
whose cultural, subcultural, religious, or personal philosophical beliefs are at
variance with that ethical theory?

In summary, the positivist ethical stance does not mean that philosophical positions regarding values in therapy are avoided in favor of science, but
rather that a particular philosophical position is adopted, often implicitly
and sometimes in a way that is hidden from clients. Others committed to
science support alternative ethical theories, arguing that a commitment to
science does not require a therapist to become an ethical positivist.

Psychotherapy is not value-free. So what?

The final response to the claim that therapy is value-laden is perhaps not aptly described as a challenge to the claim. Rather, the response is one of boredom:

> Yes, of course therapy is value-laden. The solution to "the problem" is very straightforward: Therapists need to be aware of their own values and not impose them on clients. So these issues are not, finally, difficult at all. Or very interesting.

Or, "Yes, I know therapy is value-laden. So what?"

This position deserves consideration; superficial analyses, which have abounded in this arena, warrant such ennui. Flawed analyses of ethics, values, and therapy will result in the conclusion that the issues are boring and the answers simple. I am convinced, however, that those who examine these issues carefully will be struck, not with the simplicity of the issues, but with their extraordinary complexity, and with the barren superficiality of "simple" explanations of them. As H. L. Mencken noted, "For every complex problem there is a simple answer. And it is wrong" (cited in Smith and Anderson 1989: 1154).

Some psychotherapists would agree that the issues are complex, but nonetheless assert that the solution is simple. Because of what they see as the opacity of the problems (rather than their simplicity) and because they argue it is pointless to ask questions like "with which values ought therapy to be laden?", these psychotherapists propose a simple, practical solution: therapists need to be aware of their values and not impose them on clients.

Both the view that the problem is simple and the view that the issues are hopelessly complex may thus lead to the same conclusion: the solution is simple. Contrariwise, I will argue that making progress is extraordinarily difficult, in part because therapist awareness of their own values is neither a simple nor a sufficient solution. For example, it is likely that therapists sometimes influence the values of clients and of society, whether or not they are aware of their values or intending to change the values of others, and even if they are not "imposing" values on others. This raises ethical problems, which I can articulate in the form of a thesis:

> *The conversion of a client's values and ethical theory to those of his or her therapist is, prima facie, unethical.*

Because we *do* influence the values of others, I will argue, we have a professional responsibility to reflect with great care on the values and ethical theories we hold, lest our value influence be less than optimal.

Accordingly, more sophisticated analyses of values and ethics in therapy need to be developed, both to understand adequately the ethical dimensions of therapy and to permit practice consistent with the highest possible professional standards.

Developing more sophisticated analyses does require awareness of one's own values (the "half-truth" in the "simple" solution). But it is also vitally important that psychotherapists critically examine values and ethical theory, their own and those of others, and especially those held by clients. This means thinking about alternative analyses of values and ethics (including the best ethical answers from across the centuries and from other cultures), exposing one's own beliefs to rational scrutiny, and entering into dialogue with those holding other views. It also requires a careful "unpacking" of the various uses of "values." Scientific (including biological, psychological, sociological, and anthropological), cultural, religious, philosophical, and literary perspectives on values and ethical theory may add depth to our understanding of values and ethics in general, of our own values and ethical positions, and of the values and ethical positions of clients. These tasks are multi-faceted and intricate, requiring us to explore philosophically-laden waters many experience as deep and murky.

Some will no doubt be bored by such an exploration. Some will no doubt continue to assert that such explorations are pointless, and the only solutions simple. This book is written for people open to the possibility that progress in understanding and addressing values and ethics in therapy *can* occur, albeit progress which is likely to produce answers that are neither simple nor definitive.

In conclusion, when the various challenges to the idea that therapy is value-laden are examined closely, it becomes evident that we need more sophisticated analyses of the ethical character of psychotherapy. Because when a therapist moves into a realm beyond what is consensually agreed to be therapeutic, when a therapist operates out of a school of therapy associated with particular values, when a therapist selects a goal for therapy (however consensual), when a therapist concurs with a goal a client selects, when a therapist adopts a position about the relationship of science and ethics, when a therapist adopts a position about the meaningfulness and/or truth of an ethical position, when a therapist concludes that understanding and addressing values in therapy is a simple matter, and when a therapist makes a response to a sad client who wants to know what he or she should do, that therapist is engaging in a value-laden activity, that therapist is functioning as an ethicist.

Therapists need to palpate the ethical structure of psychotherapy more sensitively, to understand the various dimensions of values in therapeutic relationships more adequately. Accordingly, it is to a *constructive exploration* of values and ethics that this book is devoted, "constructive" because I think we can make progress in understanding and addressing values and ethics, and "exploration" because we must enter complex, murky waters with no promise that we will obtain certain answers. It is to an overview of the ways in which I will proceed with this exploration that I now turn.

Ethics, "values," and psychotherapy intertwined: an overview

To maximize progress in understanding and addressing values and ethics in therapy, I am convinced that we need to combine traditional scientific and nontraditional approaches. In the discussion to follow, I will thus rely more heavily on scientific findings and methods than philosophers customarily do. I will also address issues, such as philosophical and religious issues, that are foreign to many psychotherapists. And I will use methods, including those that are philosophical, cultural, and historical, that are unfamiliar to many psychotherapists. I use that full range of methods because I am convinced that an in-depth understanding of the thorny issues of values and ethics in therapy requires doing so.

Because of the many complexities entailed in addressing ethics and values, because key terms like "ethics" and "values" are used in divergent ways, and because of the philosophical nature of many of the issues involved, the first section of the book will be devoted to in-depth clarification of several key concepts. In Chapters 2 and 3, I will address the multiple meanings of "ethics" and "ethicist," clarifying what I mean by those terms and by my claim that therapists function as ethicists. In addition to clarifying my meanings of these terms, I will also argue that psychotherapists need to draw upon the traditions and analytic approaches of philosophical ethics and to develop increased ethical sophistication.

In Chapter 4, I will discuss ethical theory, a summary term for a wide range of theoretical issues pertaining to the intellectual foundations of, or justificatory discourse regarding, specific values, codes of professional ethics, and a variety of other ethical dimensions of the practice, theory, research, institutions, and discourse of psychotherapy. In that chapter, I will tackle issues such as the meaningfulness of making assertions like "Therapists ought not have sexual relations with their clients," how one arrives (if at all) at ethical knowledge, ethical principles, the basis of moral obligation, and the relationship of religion to values and ethical theory. That *therapists* need to consider these issues (especially religion) is, of course, controversial. I will argue, however, that examining these intellectual dimensions of ethics and values in therapy provides an essential perspective on the ethical character of therapy. For instance, even though many (and perhaps most) therapists are not religious, some of their clients are likely to be. Because ethics and values are inextricably tied to religion for some clients (though obviously not for all), fidelity to clinical reality, and any *comprehensive* explanation of values in therapy, must thus touch upon religion. To sharpen the terms of the debate, I argue that:

Since some therapists and many clients base their values, and their ethical theory, in some substantial measure on their religious convictions, no account of ethics and values in therapy that claims to be adequate and comprehensive can ignore religion.

Due attention will, of course, be paid to empirical research regarding religious demographics and correlates of religiousness.

The discussion of ethical theory in Chapter 4 will make more fruitful the discussion of the meanings of "values" in Chapter 5. When the significant differences between various definitions are clear (involving deep-seated differences in ethical theory and underlying metaphysical and epistemological assumptions), the psychological and philosophical literature on values and ethical theory will make much more sense.

Chapters 6 and 7 will be devoted to a discussion of some of psychotherapy's key historical, intellectual, and social contexts. Therapists have long known the importance of their clients' familial, social, cultural, and other contexts, and have become increasingly sophisticated in assessing those contexts. In these chapters, I will look at some contexts relevant to an understanding of therapy's values and ethical dimensions. I will focus on the intellectual and social contexts out of which contemporary psychotherapy grew, considering how these contexts both shape and obscure therapy's ethical dimensions. I will focus on how the ethical, scientific, clinical, and business contexts of psychotherapy relate to ethics and values in therapy. This will permit a more rigorous and comprehensive intellectual evaluation of the ethical dimensions of therapy.

With the conceptual tools discussed in Chapters 2 through 5 and an understanding of some of the historical, intellectual, and social contexts of psychotherapy (discussed in Chapters 6 and 7) at our disposal, we can turn to a more focused discussion of psychotherapy, addressing what happens when a sad client asks a therapist, "What should I do?" The ethical dimensions, or value-ladenness, of therapy process and outcome will be discussed in Chapters 8 and 9, respectively. I will examine the ethical dimensions of psychotherapeutic techniques and processes, and the values contained (usually implicitly) in therapy goals and evaluations of outcome. Both descriptive and evaluative dimensions of process and outcome will be addressed, with some key concepts from the empirical research literature analyzed in terms of the ethical considerations discussed in the first six chapters.

In the last section of the book, I will draw some implications that follow from thinking about therapy as value-laden and the therapist as ethicist. I will do so under three headings: the need for a more adequate public philosophy about the optimal role of psychotherapy in society; rethinking professional ethics; and the challenge facing therapists who want to perform well a task to which their craft commits them (but for which they are rarely well-trained), the task of being an ethicist, of addressing well the ethical character of psychotherapy.

I will address the issue of a public philosophy for psychotherapy in Chapter 10 for two reasons: ideas and agreements within a society about psychotherapy represent another ethical dimension of psychotherapy which warrants examination; and current societal ideas about therapy still tend to assume that therapy is value-free. Since it is not, but the existing societal contract about therapy assumes it is, the role of therapy in society and the societal contract about therapy need rethinking, a task that is particularly challenging in societies in which there is little ethical agreement.

Given therapy's value-ladenness, professional ethics also needs to be reconsidered, especially since the working assumptions of many mental health professionals (and perhaps some of the framers of professional codes of ethics) still reflect a belief in value-free therapy, a positivist ethical theory, or both. The central issue is this: in light of the pervasively ethical character of psychotherapy and the wide diversity of contemporary ethical convictions, how do therapists responsibly function as ethicists?

I will conclude in Chapter 12 with a discussion of how therapists and other therapy stakeholders can address most effectively the full range of ethical questions to which therapy is tied and make better choices about the ethical character of psychotherapy. That is, I will discuss how therapy stakeholders, including therapists, can best function as ethicists.

I should add that, by focusing on how therapists function as ethicists, I do not intend to claim that the psychotherapist is only an ethicist, always an ethicist, or primarily an ethicist. Psychotherapy is also an economic activity. So we can analyze it in the terms of the discipline of economics. But it does not follow that therapy can be reduced to strictly economic terms. Or that it ought to be. The ethical dimension of therapy is but one of many dimensions of therapy, albeit one of its often unspoken, unacknowledged, and understated sides. If, however, the ethical dimensions of therapy and the role of the psychotherapist as ethicist ought not be exaggerated, neither ought they be denied or ignored.

I am convinced that an acknowledgment that therapists function as ethicists does not, and ought not to, sanction therapist dogmatism or therapeutic moralism. I believe a mature approach to values, ethics, and therapy will be humble and tentative. I agree with Caplan who, when considering whether it might jeopardize modesty to assert that ethical expertise exists, asserted, "it is those who lay claim to the mantle of expertise who best understand how little is known or understood with certainty about morality" (Caplan 1989: 83). The challenge thus facing therapists is this: while avoiding despair and dogmatism, what *better* answers about ethics, values, and therapy can we discover?

To begin answering that question, to start clarifying the ways in which psychotherapists are, for good and ill, ethicists, I will first examine the meanings of "ethics" and "ethicist."

2

Ethics

Challenging, inescapable questions

The phrase "psychotherapist as ethicist" has a decidedly odd ring. While generally considered to be ethical, psychotherapists are not customarily considered to be ethicists. What does it mean to claim that therapists are ethicists?

In large measure, this book is devoted to an exploration of that question. But clarity requires a preliminary discussion of the many meanings of "ethics" and "ethicist." Because ethicists address issues pertaining to ethics, I will first address ethics.

Dimensions of ethics

Ethics has to do with a wide range of questions about what is good, right, and/or virtuous and with questions of value (in some uses of "value"). As Slote noted, "Over the millennia, thoughtful people and philosophers have asked what kind of life is best for the individual and how one ought to behave in regard to other individuals and society as a whole" (Slote 1995: 721). These perennial ethical questions, although perhaps not fully answerable, cannot be avoided entirely. To address them, we need to examine six distinguishable but intertwined dimensions of ethics: professional ethics, theoretical ethics (i.e. philosophical ethics or moral philosophy), clinical ethics, virtue ethics, social ethics (including regulatory and policy ethics), and cultural ethics. All pertain to psychotherapy.

To ground the discussion in this and the following chapter, consider this case:

> Mike, a 37-year-old depressed computer programmer, enters therapy. In the third session, his therapist learns that Mike has been having a series of affairs, about which he has some guilt, balanced against his feeling that having the affairs is his right as a male because his wife occasionally declines his sexual advances. His wife is unaware of these affairs, and he lies to prevent her from learning of them. Mike has met several of his paramours through his extensive involvement with a progressive

community organization that challenges injustices faced by the poor in the community's impoverished, largely minority, inner-city neighborhoods. Intrigued by his line of reasoning justifying extra-marital involvements and by the labyrinthine logistics required to sustain multiple surreptitious affairs, Mike's therapist (whose own marriage is none too fulfilling) mentions the case to his buddies on the golf course. Seeing their fervent interest, he entertains them with numerous illustrative anecdotes, which permits one of the golfers to identify the client as one of his employees. Mike is terminated from therapy when he reaches the six-session psychotherapy limit set by his Health Maintenance Organization (HMO). Although the therapist failed to pick up on his alcohol abuse, Mike leaves therapy feeling much less depressed ("You're right. I get depressed whenever I say 'should' to myself. I'll just stop doing that.").

Professional ethics

Several professional ethical issues are readily apparent: the therapist's violation of confidentiality, the influence of the therapist's apparently unresolved marital issues on his handling of the case, and (possibly) the therapist's failure to screen for alcohol abuse and to request additional sessions from the client's HMO.[1] One way to conduct an ethical analysis of psychotherapy is to employ codes of professional ethics: therapists' behaviors would be examined in terms of their profession's ethical standards.

Codes of professional ethics (e.g. American Association for Marriage and Family Therapy 1991; American Psychiatric Association 1993; American Psychological Association 1992; National Association of Social Workers 1993) set the standards that govern members of the profession in their interactions with clients. As Haas and Malouf note, professionals "take on special duties to persons who enter professional relationships with them" (Haas and Malouf 1995: 2). Those who enter a profession agree to abide by the standards set forth in the profession's code of ethics (Ozar 1995). Such codes, and the ethical assertions they make, are ancient. The Hippocratic Oath, for instance, dates back at least 1900 years, with literature articulating the ethics of Greek doctors appearing as early as the fifth century BC. "The popular ideal of the physician," Amundsen notes, "was a dedicated, unselfish, and compassionate preserver or restorer of health – and, sometimes, inflicter of health-giving pain – always committed to the good of the patient" (Amundsen 1995: 1510).

That classic exemplar of professional ethics – medical ethics – has been thoroughly scrutinized in recent years. In response to the plethora of new ethical issues produced by an explosion of medical advances, some serious problems with medical ethics in particular, and with professional ethics in general, have been identified by physicians, moral philosophers, theologians, and others (Veatch 1989b). And they have also established the extensive, rapidly growing, multi-disciplinary field of bioethics, which incorporates medical ethics but is much broader, including all of the life sciences, philosophy, law, theology, and the social sciences (Callahan 1995; Reich 1995b). Callahan suggests that bioethics consists of four distinguishable "general areas of inquiry...[which] can be distinguished even though in practice they often overlap and cannot clearly be separated" (Callahan 1995: 250).

Because considering those four dimensions of ethics, in conjunction with professional ethics, permits a richer ethical analysis of psychotherapy, because doing so permits us to address the challenges posed to professional ethics in general (Veatch 1989b), and because I think we can learn by exploring the analogy between the ethical issues faced by the physician and the ethical issues faced by the psychotherapist (obviously so for the psychiatrist), I will extend to psychotherapy a modified version of Callahan's (1995) four-fold consideration of ethics. I will consider in turn professional ethics, philosophical ethics, clinical ethics, virtue ethics, social ethics, and cultural ethics.

But before I do so, I want to point out several areas of discontinuity between professional ethics (narrowly construed[2]) and the broader ethical issues raised in philosophical ethics, clinical ethics, virtue ethics, social ethics, and cultural ethics.

Codes of professional ethics are generated, in the first instance, from within the profession rather than from the kind of multi-disciplinary effort common in bioethics. Although those writing about professional ethics sometimes draw upon the thinking of philosophers and others (e.g. K. S. Kitchener 1984, 1986), the primary responsibility for developing professional codes of ethics rests within the profession itself. This has been challenged in two ways: Veatch (1989b) and others have argued that clients (the purported "partners" in the psychotherapeutic endeavor) and other key stakeholders should participate in the development of professional ethical standards. And governmental agencies have mandated changes in professional codes of ethics, for example when the US Federal Trade Commission required changes, first in the American Medical Association's code of ethics, then in the ethical code of the American Psychological Association (APA) (modifying the prohibition against some forms of advertising and referral fees, APA 1992; Bersoff 1995; Canter et al. 1994: Koocher 1994).

Second, professional ethics is narrower in scope than other dimensions of ethics. Professional ethics applies only to the members of a particular discipline and only to the role-specific functions of the professional (Bassford 1990). Professional ethics is also code-focused. Such codes, occasionally revised, outline the professional's obligations and, in some instances (e.g. APA 1992), outline ideal behaviors to which a therapist is to aspire (Canter et al. 1994). In addition, codes of professional ethics do not pertain to the ethical analysis of clients (e.g. whether it is good for Mike to combat injustice or wrong to lie to his wife).

Finally, codes of professional ethics do not generally contain a rationale for the principles and standards they contain. Psychologists, for instance, are told that "Psychologists do not engage in sexual intimacies with current patients or clients" (APA 1992: 1605), but the *reasons* for that prohibition are not included in the code.

Accordingly, although a full-fledged analysis of the ethical dimensions of psychotherapy must include codes of professional ethics, stopping with them would mean ignoring many important questions. An analysis of the therapy Mike received that relied solely upon professional codes of ethics would not address the following issues:

ethics in general: Mike's own standards of right and wrong (injustice is wrong; infidelity is okay when one's wife doesn't "put out").

theoretical ethics: the intellectual grounding for mandating, for instance, that Mike's therapist maintain client confidentiality (the reasons for that ethical standard).

clinical ethics: the practical clinical challenge of

   (a) optimally reducing Mike's depression (that is, in the best possible, or "most good," way) and

   (b) working in partnership with Mike so he changes in the best possible ("most good") direction

within six sessions, doing so in the context of: Mike's lying to his wife; possible physical harm to Mike, his wife, and his other sexual partners stemming from the uncertain HIV status of Mike and the women with whom he is sexually involved; Mike's (sexist) assumption that it is his right to have affairs if his wife declines his sexual advances; and his assumption that the key to eliminating depression in his life is to eliminate his use of "should" (which could be understood as eliminating from his life any binding moral obligations).

virtue ethics: enduring, trans-situational moral and nonmoral ethical characteristics of therapists, clients, and other therapy stakeholders (e.g. integrity, honesty, warmth, and empathy).

social ethics:

   • the impact on society if all psychotherapy clients eliminate all "shoulds" from their lives in order to achieve individual well-being

   • ethical issues, such as harm to individuals and the general welfare, stemming from HMOs terminating clients after six sessions (regulatory and policy aspects of social ethics).

cultural ethics: the influence of culture on the ethical beliefs of:

> Mike
> his therapist
> the present reader of this book, and
> the author of this book

To address these and other ethical issues, we need to move beyond professional ethics and draw upon the five other overlapping dimensions of ethical reflection.

Theoretical ethics

Psychotherapists and others engaged in theoretical ethics address the intellectual foundations of ethics. To refer to such philosophical or theoretical reflection, Pojman offers the following definition of moral philosophy:

> the systematic endeavor to understand moral concepts and to justify moral principles and theories. It undertakes to analyze such concepts as "right," "wrong," "permissible," "ought," "good," and "evil" in their moral contexts. Moral philosophy seeks to establish principles of right behavior that may serve as action guides for individuals and groups. It investigates which values and virtues are paramount to the worthwhile life or society. It builds and scrutinizes arguments in ethical theories and seeks to discover value principles (e.g. "Never kill innocent human beings") and the relationship between those principles (e.g. does saving a life in some situations constitute a valid reason for breaking a promise?).
>
> (Pojman 1995b: 2–3)

Although theoretical ethics (or ethical theory or moral philosophy) can address the foundations of professional ethics (e.g. Blackstone 1975; Camenisch 1983; Freedman 1978; Goldman 1980), it applies as well to the full range of ethical issues. A flavor of the type and range of such theoretical ethical issues can be seen in the following examples:

> If Mike is well-advised to eliminate "shoulds" from his life, why?
>
> What justification can be given for Mike's belief that society ought to treat minorities justly?
>
> On what grounds could a therapist claim that "All moral assertions are relative to individuals or cultures, so no universal moral claims can be made"?

What reasons justify the psychotherapeutic professions' claim that "Ethical psychotherapists *should* normally uphold client confidentiality"?

Although a more complete discussion of such theoretical issues will be provided in Chapter 4, one debate within theoretical ethics warrants consideration here, because it bears on the discussion in Chapter 3 about who can be considered an ethicist. The issue in dispute is the disciplinary home for the grounding for ethics. Bioethicists debate whether the foundations of bioethics "should be looked for within the practices and traditions of the life sciences, or whether they have philosophical or theological starting points" (Callahan 1995: 250). With regard to psychotherapy, the question is whether the basis for professional and other ethical issues should be founded within philosophy *or* within the disciplinary homes of psychotherapists, that is, within psychology, medicine, social work, and so forth.

The traditional origin myth of American psychology's code of ethics clearly places its genesis within psychology; psychologists used empirical methods with other psychologists to formulate it. That is, the basis of the original code was a survey conducted to discover psychologists' opinions about situations believed to be ethical in nature, about behaviors in which psychologists should and should not engage, and about principles psychologists should uphold. And Nagy asserts that in updating the 1992 APA code, "an empirical basis...was the foundation of the code" (Nagy 1994: 505). Such traditional accounts have failed, however, to explain why the opinions of the psychologists from whom the code has been derived should be given any special epistemic weight.

Others argue that, in addressing questions of theoretical ethics, psychotherapists should rely upon professional philosophers to provide the intellectual justification for the ethical issues involved in psychotherapy. And, indeed, ethics, as a branch of philosophy (e.g. Pojman 1995a, 1995b), is devoted precisely to such theoretical issues.

To address this contentious issue, bioethicists have begun to rely upon *both* medicine/biology *and* the more traditional ethical disciplines. As Callahan notes, "with time these two sources become mixed, and it seems clear that both can make valuable contributions." Accordingly, in bioethics, physicians learn from philosophers and theologians. And philosophers and theologians "draw strongly upon the history and practices of the life sciences to grasp the aims and developments of these fields" (Callahan 1995: 251, 250). If psychotherapists want to draw upon the experiences of bioethicists, we need to develop a theoretical ethics pertaining to psychotherapy that possesses a deep appreciation for theoretical ethics *and* the aims and nature of psychotherapy (that is, an ethics that grows, in some sense, out of the practices and theories of psychotherapy). Accordingly, it may be optimal for philosophers, psychotherapists, and others to collaborate in constructing an adequate theoretical ethics for psychotherapy.

Clinical ethics

In contrast to theoretical ethics, clinical ethics have to do with the practical ethical decisions a clinician makes, "with the ethics of clinical practice and with ethical problems that arise in the care of patients" (Fletcher and Brody 1995: 399). According to Callahan, clinical ethics "typically focuses on the individual case, seeking to determine what is to be done here and now with a patient" (Callahan 1995: 250). As such, clinical ethics is one form of applied ethics, which is often contrasted with theoretical ethics (Pojman 1995b; Veatch 1989a). However, as we shall see, it is problematic to distinguish too sharply between applied and theoretical ethics.

Psychotherapists face two broad classes of clinical ethical issues: those related to the processes of therapy and those related to the goals of therapy (these issues will be addressed more systematically in Chapters 8 and 9 respectively). A clinical ethical analysis of Mike's psychotherapy would include questions like the following:

How should Mike's therapist interact with him?

What therapist qualities ideally characterize the therapeutic relationship?

How should a therapist

- treat Mike's depression?
- handle Mike's lying to his wife?
- address Mike's failure to be tested for HIV or to request that his sexual partners be tested?

Would it have been better (more good) for Mike's therapist to have evaluated his substance abuse?

What goals should be established (would be best, or "most good") for Mike's therapy?

What kind of person should Mike become (e.g. mentally healthy, self-aware, more honest, etc.)?

How does a clinician address possible conflicts in goals?

- the conflict between Mike's goal of reduced depression and a therapist's goal of Mike developing healthier intimate relationships – characterized by Mike's monogamy, his honesty with his wife, or both?
- the conflict between the goal shared by Mike and his therapist – minimizing Mike's depression – and a third-party payer's goal – minimizing costs?

Should a therapist *always* defer to a client's stated goals for therapy or defer to a third-party payer's goals? If not, under which circumstances should a therapist not accept a client's or third-party payer's goals?

What responsibility, if any, does a therapist have to weigh the beneficial effects for the client of minimizing the client's ethical sensitivities (no more "shoulds") against the effect of such an action on society? That is, is it the *therapist's* responsibility to weigh individual-client mental health (one form of good) against societal well-being (another form of good)? If not, whose responsibility (if anyone's) is it?

In addressing such questions, applied ethicists distinguish between "principles-oriented" or "top-down" approaches to ethical decision-making and "case-oriented" or "bottom-up" approaches (Callahan 1995; Fraser 1989). In the former approach, principles derived from philosophical analysis (e.g. autonomy and beneficence) are applied to concrete cases to provide answers to clinical ethical issues. One could argue, for instance, that a proper application of the principle of promise-keeping would have led Mike's therapist to refrain from violating Mike's confidentiality on the golf course.

By way of contrast, clinicians employing bottom-up approaches would immerse themselves in the particularities of Mike's case. They would find the brief rendering of the case given here superficial and inadequate, lacking essential nuance, detail, context, narrative, and history. The *context* of a clinical ethical decision is considered critical (Jonsen *et al.* 1992).

One example of a bottom-up approach is a new form of casuistry, a "method of analyzing and resolving instances of moral perplexity by interpreting general moral rules in light of particular circumstances" (Jonsen 1995: 344). Advocates do not reject ethical principles, but thoughtfully consider the appropriateness of those principles in a given clinical instance. As Jonsen puts it, "principles are seen to be relevant to cases in varying degrees: In some cases, principles will rule unequivocally; in others, exceptions and qualifiers will be appropriate" (ibid.: 349).

A second type of bottom-up approach, proposed by feminist ethicists, also stresses the importance of context (e.g. Sherwin 1992). In contrast to the rationalistic, top-down approaches sometimes considered characteristically male, feminist ethicists place "a far heavier emphasis on the context of moral decisions, on the human relationships of those caught in the web of moral problems, and on the importance of feeling and emotion in the making of moral decisions" (Callahan 1995: 253).

It may be inappropriate to draw too stark a distinction between case- and principle-oriented approaches. Edel points out that "the great moral philosophers...explicitly connected their theory to...practical problems of their time" (Edel 1986: 317). And so their approaches involved both principles *and* cases, and employed both top-down *and* bottom-up thinking. And Callahan (1995), Veatch (1989a), Clouser (1989), and others remind us that no sharp distinction can be drawn between ethical theory (or theoretical ethics) and applied or clinical ethics. One dialectical alternative is known as "wide reflective inquiry" (Brody 1989; Callahan 1995; Daniels 1979; Rawls 1980). According to Callahan, this approach "espouses a constant movement back and forth between principles and human experience, letting each correct and tutor the other" (Callahan 1995: 252). Such an approach is very similar to how many therapists approach theories of psychotherapy: their theories are influenced by their clinical practice, and their clinical practice by their theories, with both practice and theory being revised continually by exposure to one another.

Virtue ethics

Psychotherapists and others who employ virtue ethics stress the stable ethical characteristics of persons rather than the ethical principles people employ, the way they resolve ethical dilemmas, or the behaviors they exhibit. For example, Doherty (1995) argued that therapists should be caring, a virtue Mike lacked but which Doherty, feminists (e.g. Noddings 1984), and others have emphasized. And Mike's therapist failed to exhibit what Dyer called the "central virtues of the medical profession" (Dyer 1988: 108): trustworthiness and respect for confidentiality.

Meara, Schmidt, and Day addressed the relevance of virtue ethics for psychologists and other therapists. They provided this definition: "The concept of a virtue or trait of character denotes a quality or qualities of a person that have merit or worth in some context, and these qualities are often related to matters of right conduct (i.e. morality)" (Meara *et al*. 1996: 24).[3] They think virtue ethics complement more traditional principle ethics and need to be integrated with them. They also assert, however, that virtue ethics make a distinctive and important contribution to ethics.

Several features of an approach to ethics that emphasizes virtue can be identified. The person is the focus of attention, not abstract rules, type of ethical reasoning, response to ethical dilemmas, or moral behaviors. We need to ask "Who shall I be?" not "What shall I do?" (Jordan and Meara 1990: 107). Virtue ethics provide a pervasively psychological approach to ethics. And so Drane held that character, a term related to virtue, refers to "personality structure, with special emphasis on its ethical components" (Drane 1994: 291). "Virtue" incorporates the behaviors, ways of thinking, judgments, perception of ethically relevant features of situations, relationships, emotions, and motivation of people (Punzo 1996; Meara *et al*. 1996). Virtue ethics is also more wide-ranging and inclusive than approaches employing principles alone. As Brody put it, virtue ethics is "a broader perspective that embraces the whole of a life and not simply the one decision that is at hand"

(Brody 1994: 211). Finally, many virtue ethicists emphasize the role of a community in shaping virtues (MacIntyre 1984; Meara *et al.* 1996). Others who emphasize virtues are, however, more self-focused, concerned about the desirable characteristics of individual persons and give little attention to community (see Meilaender 1984).

From the perspective of virtue ethics, therapists can, and perhaps should, exhibit particular virtues. Meara *et al.* (1996), for instance, suggested that therapists should exhibit prudence, integrity, respectfulness, and benevolence. And, as we shall see in Chapter 9, therapists may establish goals for clients, like "becoming mentally healthy", that are perhaps best understood as virtues. And virtues can be used as criteria for evaluating therapy outcomes.

Social ethics

In contrast to the clinical ethicist's focus on the micro-picture of the clinical encounter and the self-focused virtue ethicist's focus on the character of the individual person, those who pursue questions of social ethics focus on macro issues. Social ethics can be defined as "the normative study of *communal* conduct" (Facione *et al.* 1991: 9, emphasis added), in contrast to personal ethics, which is concerned with value judgments about *individual* conduct.

Accordingly, social ethics has to do with the ethical dimensions of personal partnerships (e.g. marriage), families (variously defined), various social structures, communities, and society as a whole. Among the issues addressed are justice (especially distributive justice), the proper relationship between individuals and larger social entities, social policies, the "good society," and the general welfare. When addressing psychotherapy, social ethics can involve ethical analyses of society's impact on psychotherapy and of psychotherapy's impact on society.

That social ethics is not foreign to psychology may be seen in the statements of purpose of groups such as the American Psychological Association (APA) and the American Psychological Society (APS). They exist, in part, for the purpose of "promoting human welfare" (APA 1994: 1) and "the improvement of human welfare" (APS 1988: 1). And ethical analyses of psychotherapy that address its social impact (e.g. Rieff 1959) now have a long history.

Although philosophers do not always distinguish social ethics from ethics in general, I think it important to do so here for several reasons: to highlight the ethical aspects of regulatory and policy decisions (especially those made by third parties) which are playing an increasingly large role in the lives of psychotherapists; to address the relationship between society and both professionalism and professional ethics; to counteract a common image of ethics as the solitary individual wrestling with a very personal ethical decision; and to highlight the social ethical dimensions of psychotherapy at a time in history when many think it too individualistic.[4]

Callahan discusses a key dimension of social ethics – regulatory and policy ethics. This aims "to fashion legal or clinical rules and procedures designed to apply to types of cases or general practices." For instance, one goal in bioethics is to develop "legal and policy solutions to pressing societal problems that are ethically defensible and clinically sensible and feasible" (Callahan 1995: 250, 251). Success in doing so can be seen in the guidelines developed to regulate the ethics of human experimentation (Department of Health and Human Services 1991; Sieber 1992). However, recent US efforts to forge a policy consensus about health-care reform illustrate the many difficulties of this type of ethical task and the political entanglements social ethics often entails. Indeed, that debate vividly illustrates what Elshtain argues is universally true, that "ethical dilemmas are inescapably political and political questions are unavoidably ethical" (Elshtain 1995: 757). More controversial are reported plans by third-party payers to provide reimbursement only for empirically validated or supported treatments (see the efforts to specify such treatments in the US – Kendall and Chambless 1998; Nathan and Gorman 1998; Sanderson and Woody 1995; Task Force on Promotion and Dissemination of Psychological Procedures 1995; for European efforts, see Grawe *et al.* 1996; Roth and Fonagy 1996).

The close ties between professionalism and society are another reason why social ethics is important. Many have argued that the very notion of a professional is inextricably societal and political. Professions exist "in order to play certain social roles and to further certain social purposes" (Bassford 1990: 130), purposes which contribute to the general welfare. When professionals obtain licensure, they engage in political tasks: persuading legislators to grant therapists a special status and (perhaps of more importance) convincing society that psychotherapists possess distinctive expertise that can benefit all. As Michels notes:

> in a sense, a profession can be seen as a group of people to whom society has delegated power and authority based on the assumption that they have certain knowledge and skills that are not generally available and that are required for decisions in a certain area.
>
> (Michels 1991: 70)

Kultgen (1988) carefully examines the structure of professions in society. He considers both the benefits to society of professionalism and the problems it produces. By doing so, he engages in social ethical analysis.

In addition, Ozar asserts that professional ethics has a societal dimension. Professional ethics arises, not simply from within the profession, but from an ethical discussion between professionals and society members. The professional obligations delineated in codes of professional ethics are "obligations whose content has been worked out and is continually being affirmed or adjusted through an ongoing dialogue between the expert group and the larger community" (Ozar 1995: 2106). And so, any comprehensive ethical analysis of psychotherapy, if conducted by *professionals*, requires social ethics.

Social ethics thus poses questions that broaden the ethical discussion about psychotherapy. For example, is it right for third-party payers (like Mike's HMO) to set limits on payments for psychotherapy sessions? What are the benefits (and costs) to society of unlimited access to psychotherapy? Which forms of psychotherapy are most beneficial to society? Is present access to mental health care just? Does everyone have a right to receive psychotherapy? To best advance the common good, what policies should govern third-party payers? Is it good for psychotherapists to free clients from a sense of moral obligation (from "shoulds")? What would be the impact on families (however defined), on local communities, and on society as a whole if everyone were so freed? And, more broadly, what should be the role of psychotherapy in society?

When considering social ethical dimensions of psychotherapy, it is evident that all five dimensions of ethics are intertwined (cf. Callahan 1995). Formulating codes of professional ethics involves professionals negotiating with other members of society, and so involves questions of social ethics. Questions about the intellectual warrant for social ethics require theoretical ethics. Many clinical ethicists stress the importance of context in addressing clinical issues, contexts which social ethics address. Most virtue ethicists stress that virtues arise in a social or community context and contribute to the well-being of a society. Finally, social ethics is closely tied to cultural ethics.

Cultural ethics

The major difference between cultural ethics and social ethics is that the former focuses on the critical analysis of culture and the particularities of various societies. Societies (or cultures) are analyzed and contrasted to understand the ethical perspectives of other cultures and to learn more about one's own. Cultural ethics, according to Callahan (1995), thus involves relating ethics to broader historical, ideological, and cultural factors. Such cultural analysis is an essential component of attempts to understand psychotherapy as a universal, cross-cultural process of human change. To the extent psychotherapy involves values or ethical dimensions, the *different* answers various cultures give to ethical questions need to be examined.

Cushman (1993, 1995), Hare-Mustin (1994), and others have offered cogent cultural analyses to illumine the moral discourse and the values implicit in psychotherapy. Hare-Mustin, for instance, demonstrates how "there is a predetermined content in the conversation of therapy: that provided by the dominant discourses of the language community and culture." Through an analysis of such discourses,[5] we can learn about "both prevailing ideologies and marginalized discourses." She points out, for instance, that "men's sexual urges are assumed to be natural and compelling;

thus, the male is expected to be pushy and aggressive in seeking to satisfy them" (Hare-Mustin 1994: 19, 23, 24). By examining such dominant (and thus often unobserved and hidden) discourses in a culture, we can see ethical dimensions of therapy that would otherwise remain occluded. Through an examination of interactions, for example, between Mike and his therapist (or between the therapist and his male buddies on the golf course), discourse analysis holds promise for illuminating implicit ethical assumptions present in a particular culture.

In contrast to US individualism and emphasis on autonomy, African peoples, in their ethics, emphasize tribal community, family belonging, and reciprocity (Paris 1995). This echoes Asian Indians' rejection of the primacy of autonomy as an ideal for human beings (Varma 1988) mentioned in the first chapter. Such cross-cultural ethical reflection can help us to understand our own ethical positions, and is crucial when therapists work with clients whose cultural values they do not share.

In summary, "ethics" is a rich, multi-faceted term, involving multiple overlapping dimensions: professional ethics, theoretical ethics, clinical ethics, virtue ethics, social ethics, and cultural ethics. A full-fledged ethical analysis of psychotherapy will thus perforce be wide-ranging.

The science–ethics relationship

Because psychology is a science and psychotherapy is often considered an applied science, any examination of the meaning of ethics requires consideration of the relationship between science and ethics. Ethics and science were once sharply distinguished. As discussed in the first chapter, positivists claimed that we can draw meaningful conclusions only from scientific thinking and logic; most ethical reflection was accordingly viewed as meaningless (Callahan 1995; Slote 1995). Because this view was widely held, Callahan observed that "matters of ethics and values had been all but banished from serious intellectual discussion" (Callahan 1995: 249). And so, ethical positivists would think it meaningless (because not empirically demonstrable) to assert that it was *unethical* for Mike's therapist to violate Mike's confidentiality (although we could empirically establish that many people would judge it harshly or report having "negative" emotions about it, and that a given percentage of the population would disapprove of it), that Mike *should* not lie to his wife, or that it was *wrong* for poor inner city residents to be treated unjustly.

As positivism has lost its hold in the philosophy of science and other disciplines (Edel 1986; Koch and Leary 1992; Robinson 1985; Suppe 1977), bioethicists, psychotherapists, and other scholars are again giving serious consideration to ethics (including formulating ethical principles to guide behavior), without the sharp distinctions drawn by the positivists. Such efforts often cross the steep disciplinary walls erected by the positivists; philosophers and scientists are again learning from each another.

In fact, as traditionally conceived, ethics includes an empirical component. This component "describes actual beliefs and customs" (Pojman 1995b: 2) and seeks to "describe or explain the phenomena of morality or to work out a theory of human nature which bears on ethical questions" (Frankena 1973: 4). And clinical ethicists are "actively engaged in accumulating and developing as rich a set of facts as possible as well as interpreting them" (Fletcher and Brody 1995: 400), a position similar to that espoused by K. S. Kitchener (1984) for counseling psychologists. The descriptive methodologies of the natural sciences and other disciplines can clearly make substantial contributions to such efforts (cf. Tugendat 1990; Waterman 1988). As Frankena noted, "Moral philosophers cannot insist too much on the importance of factual knowledge and conceptual clarity for the solution of moral and social problems" (Frankena 1973: 13).

Although such descriptive inquiry is frequently distinguished from theoretical ethical thinking, the two are interrelated, since theoretical ethics tells us what "counts" as an ethical or moral phenomenon (Brody 1989) and descriptive assertions (especially about human beings) are required in any ethical theory.

A misconception about the relationship between science and ethics must be avoided, however. Empirical generalizations do not lead directly and conclusively to ethical conclusions. Because of the lingering effects of the positivistic philosophy of ethics, it remains commonplace to assume that what is "ethical" or "moral" is merely a matter of consensus or cultural influence. Ethics and morality, on this account, are reduced to custom (which can be investigated scientifically), to ways in which societies perpetuate themselves. Ethics thus does not pertain at all to what is actually right or good. Ethicists, however, commonly distinguish ethics from custom, consensus, and etiquette (Pojman 1995b; Veatch 1989b): ethics is characterized by the defensible reasons offered to support the ethical conclusions drawn.

"Ethics" and related terms

"Ethics" is distinguished from "morality" by some, but the terms are used synonymously by others. No standard distinction between the terms exists (Annas 1991; Ladd 1978; Margolis 1966). I will primarily use the term "ethics" rather than "morality" because the latter often carries negative connotations, perhaps because of its association with the negatively-tinged "moralizing" (Cushman 1995: 280; Fairbairn and Fairbairn 1987: 9) and "moralistic." Moralistic is often used to refer to a narrow, conventional, simplistic, judgmental, or rigid imposition of ethical principles on others. I will use it to refer to that negative use to which some people put ethical principles in their relationships with others.

To complicate matters further, however, both "ethical" and "moral" are used in more than one sense. Of the first sense, Frankena notes, "the terms 'moral' and 'ethical' are often used as equivalent to 'right' or 'good' and as opposed to 'immoral' and 'unethical'" (Frankena 1973: 5). For example, "It is ethical to charge a fee for therapy as long as the fee is reasonable and clients are informed about financial arrangements ahead of time," but "It is unethical to violate confidentiality." However, "moral" and "ethical" can also be used in a more general sense to refer to particular types of problems or judgments. Here, the terms refer to that which pertains to morality or ethics, and have as their opposite "nonethical." For example, "confidentiality is an ethical issue" but "whether to live in Minneapolis or Allentown is a nonethical issue."

Another important distinction can be drawn between moral and nonmoral evaluative considerations, with ethics taken as a broad, over-arching discipline that embraces both (Annas 1991). Violating Mike's confidentiality, and Mike's lying to his wife would both be considered moral issues, for instance, but the preference Mike's therapist exhibits for chartreuse cars, and Mike's love of country and western music would be considered nonmoral (representing their aesthetic values). Although no consensus exists about how to properly sunder moral and nonmoral, Annas describes four traditional distinguishing marks:

(a) a distinction of kind between moral and nonmoral reasons, (b) a strict demand of responsibility ("ought" implies "can"), (c) the promi-nence of duty or obligation as the basic moral notion, and (d) an essential concern for the noninstrumental good of others.

(Annas 1991: 330)

To these Pojman adds the following marks of what is moral: universaliz-ability ("moral principles must apply to all who are in the relevantly similar situation" – 1995b: 7) and overridingness (moral considerations "trump" those that are nonmoral). And Frankena holds that moral values must "embody some kind of social concern or consideration" (1976: 126).

The moral–nonmoral distinction is crucial to an ethical analysis of psychotherapy, in part because it has been used to distance science and psychotherapy from ethical analysis. In response to the claim that science is value-laden, some have acknowledged that science properly involves values (e.g. Laudan 1984; Longino 1990; Popper 1976), but only nonmoral, scien-tific values. As I am using "ethics," however, the analysis of such nonmoral values is part of the task of ethics.

Psychopathology can also be viewed in terms of the moral–nonmoral distinction. Mike's depression would generally be evaluated in nonmoral terms: he would not (or should not) be considered morally blameworthy (responsible) for being depressed (especially if the depression stemmed from biochemical abnormalities, from childhood maltreatment, or from a noxious, controlling, punishing work environment over which he had little control and to which he had learned to respond as though he were helpless). By way of contrast, many would argue that he was morally blameworthy (responsible) for his affairs and for his lies, as his therapist was morally blameworthy (responsible) for violating Mike's confidentiality. Ethics, as I am defining it, applies to both the moral and the nonmoral aspects of psychopathology.

The moral–nonmoral distinction has also been applied to psychotherapy, with Hartmann (1960) first espousing the influential view (see Strupp 1980) that psychotherapy, properly conducted, affects "health values" (a type of nonmoral values) but not "moral values." Although I have argued for a similar distinction (Tjeltveit 1986), I now see some forms of it as problematic, and the relationship between "moral" and "nonmoral" in analyzing the ethical dimensions of psychotherapy will need further exploration in due course, especially in our considerations of ethical theory in Chapter 4 and of the goals of therapy in Chapter 9. Again, however, as I use the term, ethics encompasses both moral and nonmoral evaluative considerations.

My use of "ethics" must also be distinguished from two frequent misunderstandings of ethics (misunderstandings perhaps partly responsible for the common lack of interest in ethical analysis among psychotherapists): limiting ethics to "moral dilemmas" and missing the subtle *ethical* implications contained within much psychological language.

"Ethics" is often used to refer exclusively to especially difficult or subtle issues, like "the ethics of gene splicing." Such thorny issues sometimes arise in therapy, for instance, in situations involving conflicting values. However, "ethical," as used here, is a much broader and more fundamental term. It includes such issues as whether it is better to be guided by general ethical principles (such as autonomy), by the functional impact of one's actions on the well-being of society, or by the traits (qualities of character, or virtues) therapist and client optimally exhibit. Those more general ethical issues are regularly faced by clients and therapists. Indeed, they undergird therapy and shape its discourse.

Another reason why the ethical dimensions of psychotherapy may be discussed so rarely (and often go unrecognized entirely) is that many of the evaluative words used by therapists mask those dimensions. For instance, "healthy," "well-adjusted," "appropriate," "mature," and "rational" are terms not only descriptive, but evaluative (primarily involving *non*moral evaluations). Such words describe characteristics that are valued, that are considered good or ideal in a person. They thus provide answers to questions posed for millennia by moral philosophers.

Finally, the relationship of ethics and "values" requires brief mention: "values" are connected to the concerns of ethics (as discussed in this chapter) for some people, but not for others. For instance, when Rokeach (1973) argued that the definition of values should not include the words "should" or "ought," words that virtually define "moral" for many, he clearly distanced himself from ethics in his empirical investigations of values. For some philosophers, by way of contrast, values are central to ethics, with ethics embracing both moral values and nonmoral values. For still others, investigating "values" permits one to address ethical issues while being scientifically reputable, and without the interminable wrangling about ethical dilemmas associated with philosophy. "Values" is thus a term that bridges the science–philosophy divide.

At one point in history, before psychologists began empirical investigations of values, "values" was a term associated with one side of that divide, the philosophical side. Scientists were concerned with facts, and philosophers with values. To claim to derive values from facts was seen as fallacious. More recently, however, the strict fact–value distinction has been attacked on many fronts.[6]

Taking full advantage of the rich literature on values in psychotherapy requires teasing out the multiple meanings of values and exploring further the fact–value distinction. It is to that task that Chapter 5 and a portion of Chapter 6 will be devoted. Doing so will permit us to obtain maximum benefit both from the empirical research on the role of values in therapy and from the theoretical reflection contained in that literature. It will first be necessary, however, to unpack what I mean by claiming that psychotherapists regularly and pervasively address issues that are ethical, that therapists function as "ethicists."

3

Psychotherapists as ethicists
Engaging in difficult, essential tasks

Mike's therapist, like most therapists, probably does not consider himself an ethicist. Furthermore, Mike, like most clients, probably does not think of his therapist as an ethicist. Indeed, he might not have gone to a therapist if he thought therapists functioned as ethicists.

People disagree about the meaning of "ethicist." It is both contrasted and equated with such terms as moral philosopher, value theorist, and moralist. All of those terms refer to someone who addresses moral or ethical issues or values, but they often carry significantly different connotations about *how* ethical issues and values are approached. When I contend that therapists function as ethicists, I am therefore drawing upon a particular understanding of the meaning of ethicist, an understanding I set forth in this chapter.

In what follows, I will define ethicist, address the relationship between that definition and "ethical expertise," discuss how being professionals influences (or should influence) the ways in which therapists function as ethicists, delineate some functions performed by ethicists, and describe the variety of ways in which psychotherapists function as ethicists.

Definition

By ethicist, I mean a person who reflects on, has convictions about, and/or attempts to influence others about ethical questions and issues. That some people perform such ethical tasks problematically is disputed by few; whether some people perform ethical tasks especially well is more controversial.

I will use "moralist" or "moralizer" to refer to those who attempt to impose values on others, who are concerned with regulating the moral lives of others, or who simply tell other people what to do. This is often done in an excessively narrow, conventional, and authoritarian way. The moralist or moralizer is thus moralistic and engages in moralizing with others. This distinction between ethicist and moralizer is not, of course, an absolute one. Ethicists fall on a continuum, varying in the specificity and rigidity of their ethical stances and the extent to which they uphold the freedom of others to make ethical decisions. Accordingly, ethicists, including psychotherapists, exhibit varying degrees of moralism.

If moralizers exemplify a problematic approach to ethics, perhaps others address ethical issues especially well. That is, some persons may possess ethical expertise. If that is true, understanding ethical expertise can provide us with important insights about how psychotherapists can perform ethical tasks well. But some people deny the existence of ethical expertise.

Can ethicists possess ethical expertise?

Professionals are expected to be competent in what they do. Indeed, professional codes of ethics mandate that professionals limit their practices to their areas of competence. But what does it mean to possess competence or expertise in the arena of ethics? And do psychotherapists possess such expertise?

Veatch has suggested that physicians, by virtue of their expertise in the medical realm, are often considered to possess expertise in the realm of medical ethics – by "generalization of expertise" (Veatch 1973: 29). Likewise, some think that psychotherapists, by virtue of their expertise with mental health problems, have expertise with related ethical issues, by generalization of expertise. Can that claim be justified?

Some assert that – given the "subjectivity" or "relativity" of ethics – the very idea of ethical "expertise" is meaningless. Indeed, Caplan (1989) points out that there are good reasons for being skeptical about claims to ethical expertise. And some conceptions of ethical expertise – that the moral judgments of certain ethicists are infallible or that some ethicists never make mistakes in matters moral – seem extremely difficult to justify.

More defensible definitions of ethical expertise exist, however. To address whether it is legitimate to talk about ethical expertise or competence, however, we need to be clear about the meaning of that phrase. Three meanings of "ethical expertise" may be distinguished:

1   Ethical expertise arises when society *considers* certain persons to have expertise or treats them as though they do.
2   Ethical expertise is a function of advanced education, requiring a Ph.D. or extensive advanced course work in ethics, moral philosophy, or value theory.
3   Expertise exists when ethicists either make correct ethical judgments or make coherent, rational arguments for ethical positions.

According to the first usage, experts have expertise because society, or some segment of society, says they do, or treats them as though they do. And so Rieff (1959), for instance, analyzed how society has been influenced by psychoanalysis because psychoanalysts (following Freud, "the moralist") have come to be regarded (in a process Rieff (1966) calls "the triumph of the therapeutic") as expert at tasks that are moral in nature. Because of the respect accorded therapists in society, they *function* as experts. What is critical, in this usage of "expertise," is not the grounds that are used to determine whether someone has expertise, for instance, ethical correctness, sound argument, or advanced training. What is critical is that at least certain segments of society interact with some persons *as though* they have expertise.

Although it is important to recognize that at least certain segments of society believe or act as if such "experts" exist (and so the first usage of "expertise" is valid), that fact does not settle the question of whether advanced training should be a prerequisite for the honorific title "expert," or whether such persons should be considered ethicists, possess better values, or reason better about ethical issues. Society may well grant its imprimatur on some persons for inadequate, poorly thought out, or incorrect reasons.

And so we need to consider whether we are *justified* in considering some persons to have especially worthy answers to ethical questions. An answer to this question can clarify whether the meaning of "ethicist" can involve ethical expertise.

Which persons warrant the honorific title "ethicist"?

In keeping with the first understanding of "ethical expertise," some would define "ethicist" as follows: anyone to whose answers to ethical issues society (or some segment of society) gives particular heed. But by this definition, Adolf Hitler and Jim Jones would be considered to have ethical expertise, and to be ethicists, because they held particular moral views to which others gave particular heed. However, most who would grant Hitler and Jones the status of "ethicist" would consider them bad (or even evil) ethicists. If we aspire to a definition of "ethicist" with positive connotations, we need a richer meaning of "ethical expertise." Doing so requires the development of *reasons* for attributing expertise to certain persons.

Some argue that "ethicist" should be restricted to persons with formal philosophical training in ethics, moral philosophy, or value theory. Addressing ethical issues is their central professional objective and expertise. Macklin, for instance, points to particular reasoning skills at which philosophers excel, including "conceptual analysis, illustrating subtle distinctions between facts and values, clearing up ambiguities in key terms, and pointing out flaws in reasoning" (Macklin 1989: 119).

On that understanding of ethical expertise, society could only appropriately give the honorific title "Psychotherapist as ethicist" to those rare individuals with advanced training both in philosophy and in one of the psychotherapeutic disciplines.

Limiting "ethicist" to those with advanced training in ethics is consistent with reserving the term "psychologist" to those with advanced training in psychology or "medical doctor" to those with advanced training in medicine. This approach rests upon the assumption that the divisions between disciplines and professions correspond to discrete functions, so that lay people (those without specialized, advanced training) in no way function as physicians, psychologists, or professional ethicists.

However, the divisions between professional roles set out in the academy or by governmental licensing boards may not always function as they are supposed to. "Lay" people in fact attempt to address physical health problems – sometimes disastrously and sometimes well. Likewise, the professional bioethics consultant on a neonatal intensive care unit functions in part as a psychologist of sorts (assessing family functioning and intervening to decrease distress) when interacting with family members about dilemmas such as terminating life support, dilemmas that are at once medical, familial, emotional, and ethical. Hence, lay people do, in some genuine sense, "practice medicine." And ethicists "practice psychology." *De facto* functions may thus not be coterminous with *de jure* professional distinctions.

Furthermore, professional training does not prevent errors in one's area of expertise. The training that Mike's therapist received did not insure his competence: he failed to detect and treat Mike's alcohol abuse, and committed an infraction of professional ethical standards by violating Mike's confidentiality. Although he possessed the requisite formal training and was undeniably a therapist in the eyes of a state licensing body, in light of those lapses, few would argue that he possessed exceptional expertise as a therapist. Or even that he was a good therapist. Likewise, someone may have professional training in ethics yet draw faulty logical conclusions or endorse ethically problematic views. By way of contrast, some people who lack formal training in ethics may reason very well about ethical issues (Meehl 1981) or otherwise address ethical questions well.

And so if we strive to define an ideal ethicist, we need a substantive concept of ethical expertise. Caplan argues for such a concept, one not limited to those with advanced philosophical training:

> Expertise in ethics appears to consist in knowing moral traditions and theories. It also involves knowing how to apply those theories and traditions in ways that fruitfully contribute to the understanding of moral problems. But, most importantly, ethical expertise involves the ability to identify and recognize moral issues and problems, a skill that may be enhanced by training in ethics, but one that is not by any means restricted to those who have this training or that is beyond the intellectual capacities of those who do not have this training.
>
> (Caplan 1989: 85)

If one were to hire an ethicist, one would undoubtedly seek someone with such expertise. And if therapists function as ethicists, and ethicists have the potential to develop such ethical expertise, then it is incumbent upon therapists to insure that they possess or develop that competence.

Professional philosophy may play a role in the development of such expertise, in the development of the ideal ethicist, but formal training in philosophy is not essential for such expertise (Baylis 1989; Caplan 1989). Accordingly, I will draw upon the thinking of philosophers, but without presuming that their answers to the ethical issues that *psychotherapists* address are necessarily the best answers.

Advanced training in philosophy may not be the only kind of advanced training that helps to address the specialized ethical issues involved in psychotherapy, however. Advanced training in psychotherapy may also be beneficial. While acknowledging that facts derived from scientific investigations do not give mental health professionals ethical expertise, Michels argues that scientific knowledge:

> may make possible the life experiences which can lead to a refinement of ethical sensitivities. For example, the physician has no special claim to skill in deciding who shall live or who shall die because of his knowledge of anatomy or physiology. However, his knowledge of these fields may have led him to an unusual amount of experience in caring for dying people and may have allowed him that special privilege and responsibility of making scientific or technical decisions which lead to life and death results. Experiences such as these can lead to ethical expertise.
>
> (Michels 1991: 70)

This suggests (again in parallel with recent developments in bioethics) that psychotherapists may best develop ethical expertise, and become optimally effective psychotherapist-ethicists, if we mount interdisciplinary efforts (Callahan 1995) related to the ethical dimensions of psychotherapy.

Let me recap my argument thus far. In order to explore most fully the functioning of all who address ethical issues, I will use "ethicist" in a broad sense to refer to both professional/academic ethical experts and lay persons who address ethical issues. I will reserve the terms "moral philosopher," "value theorist," and "philosophical ethicist" for professional or academic ethicists.

I assume that all psychotherapists are ethicists, but not all are "good" ethicists; that is, not all reason well, or provide optimal answers to ethical questions. Therapists can benefit from dialogue with professional philosophers, and their ethical expertise is likely to increase as a result. But the philosophical ethicists with whom they discuss those issues need dialogue as well – with psychotherapists – so they can fully understand the ethical dimensions of psychotherapy.

Psychotherapists functioning as ethicists employ the full range (all six dimensions) of ethics discussed in Chapter 2. Psychotherapists functioning as ethicists engage primarily in clinical ethics, but doing so optimally requires theoretical ethics as well, and hence may benefit from the expertise of professional philosophers. And good therapists can be thought to possess certain professional virtues. In addition, the fact that psychotherapy occurs within a broader social and cultural context means that psychotherapists address issues of social and cultural ethics. Finally, professional ethics sets limits on *how* psychotherapists function as ethicists.

Professional ethics and limits on the nature of therapeutic interactions

Codes of professional ethics limit the freedom of therapists to influence client values, and thus affect all of the various roles in which a psychotherapist functions as an ethicist. Psychotherapists who interact with clients moralistically, condemning those who disagree with them, are behaving in violation of codes of professional ethics. The underlying ethical principle is that psychotherapists should have a special kind of relationship with their clients, one characterized by disinterest and beneficence. "Disinterest" (in this sense of the word) does not mean a lack of interest in the client, but being primarily concerned with the client's (not the therapist's) needs. Therapists who act in a professionally responsible manner will strive to be objective rather than biased. Further, they will be primarily concerned with client well-being rather than their own interests. And they will grant to clients a substantial measure of freedom to choose the values they wish, rather than imposing their values on clients. That is, professional therapists will exhibit beneficence.

The ethical principles of the American Psychological Association, for instance, state that "psychologists seek to contribute to the welfare of those with whom they interact professionally" (APA 1992: 1600). Similarly, A. L. Caplan notes that:

> the threat of abuse or error is so great that the social role assigned to moral experts or those with moral expertise must be confined to the tasks of exhortation and giving advice. Society should not create an elite of moral experts who have the authority to impose their judgments on others.
>
> (Caplan 1989: 74)

Hence, the psychotherapist's influence is limited in some ways by virtue of being a professional, limited in ways discussed in greater detail later in the book. For example, as an ethicist, the therapist will respect the autonomy of others, will address the ethical aspects of a situation primarily by raising questions and presenting options and, if an attempt is made to influence clients, will do so with reasoned argument and in a way which clearly upholds the client's right to dissent. The concept of the professional thus carries within it standards that guide (and limit) professionals as they work with clients.

The roles of the ethicist

In asserting that ethicists reflect on, have convictions about, and/or attempt to influence others about the ethical aspects of practical situations, I am suggesting that ethicists perform multiple roles. When psychotherapists function as ethicists, they may be engaging in one or more of those roles. These variegated functions require further explication.

Reflecting about ethical issues

Psychotherapists and others reflect on ethical issues in a variety of ways. The ideal: psychotherapists think *well* about ethical issues, think clearly, analytically, consistently, and coherently. Therapists will avoid, for instance, the fourteen cognitive errors (e.g. inconsistency) that Meehl (1981) noted may be present in a person's ethical convictions. When an ethical question arises, the facts and context of the situation need to taken into consideration. And A. L. Caplan's (1989) concept of ethical expertise applies: thinking well about ethical issues will be aided by an acquaintance with the history of other attempts to address the questions with which the ethicist is wrestling. For a therapist functioning as an ethicist, that may mean careful reflection on what other therapists have argued are worthwhile ("good") goals in therapy, on what moral philosophers across the millennia have had to say about ethical matters, or, best, on what both sets of traditions can contribute.

Ethicists exhibiting excellence in reflection on ethical issues, according to Ruddick and Finn, provide "a wider range of principles and categories and a sharper eye for self-serving presuppositions and implicit contradictions," and the ability to provide a "clear description of moral aspects and reasons" (Ruddick and Finn 1985: 42, 45).

Accordingly, a therapist reflecting on Mike's situation may focus solely on the means necessary to reduce his depression (that is, to bring about the nonmoral good of decreased depression). Or, in a more detailed, more adequate ethical analysis, the nonmoral good of Mike's decreased depression may be balanced against moral concerns about his lying and infidelity. If Mike's therapist were to engage in careful moral reflection about his own behavior, he might balance the nonmoral good of *bonhomie* with his friends on the golf course against several other ethical issues: violating the promise he made to Mike to preserve confidentiality, violating his own profession's code of ethics, violating the law governing client privilege, and the potential

harm (negative, "non-good" consequences) of violating Mike's confidentiality (e.g. if Mike's moralistic boss fires him after learning of his affairs).
Such ethical reflection may clarify a therapist's course of action.

Holding ethical convictions

Ethicists holding particular ethical convictions may believe, for instance,
that it is *good* to express one's feelings, to be assertive, honest, rational, or
creative, to remain faithful to one's spouse so long as that commitment is
freely chosen and meets one's needs in the moment, and so forth. They may
believe that it is *right* to tell lies in certain circumstances, to put one's own
needs ahead of those of others if health is thereby achieved, to have one's
sexual needs met even if that involves violating societal strictures, or to do
anything so long as one has *chosen* to do so *authentically* and no one else is
harmed. Or they may believe that it is *virtuous* to be honest, to treat others
justly, or to be healthy.

Sometimes ethical convictions are limited (minimalist) and sometimes
very extensive (maximalist). Meehl, for instance, describes himself as a
"moral minimalist" (1989: 370), that is, employing a limited set of ethical
principles (cf. Callahan 1981 for a critique of moral minimalism).

Convictions may be present at the level of particular values, for example,
"It is good to be assertive." They may also be present at the level of ethical
theory (discussed in Chapter 4), for instance, the belief that it is meaningless
to talk about ethical obligation, or that there are objective moral standards
to which intuition has access. In evaluating the appropriateness of an act,
one ethicist may focus on its consequences; a second may hold that certain
acts are right or wrong regardless of their consequences (e.g. "incest is wrong
whether or not damage to a child can be discovered.").

The ethical principles that appear to have guided Mike's therapist were
the centrality of the nonmoral good of reduced depression and the importance of honoring clients' therapy goals. He either did not regard Mike's
infidelity and lying to be ethically problematic, or his convictions about the
proper role of the therapist (what a good therapist does, or what a therapist
should do) led him to believe that those issues were beyond the purview of
therapy, of brief therapy, or of therapy in which Mike did not label those
issues as problematic.

Influencing others

Therapists functioning as ethicists may also strive to influence others. Or
they may influence others although not intending to do so. Again, the scope
and manner of this influence vary extensively.

In their relationships with clients, many psychotherapists strive to minimize their influence on client values. That is, they put aside or "bracket"

their ethical convictions (save those intrinsic to therapy itself), often striving to work within the client's own moral framework (as a way of exhibiting beneficence). But when working with clients whose moral convictions are extensive and life-pervasive, some therapists may be tempted to influence such clients to "loosen up." In that kind of subtractive ethical influence, therapists strive to reduce client adherence to particular ethical views. By way of contrast, therapists engaging in additive ethical influence strive to get clients to adopt a particular ethical view (e.g. to adopt the view, "it is good to seek pleasure for oneself"). Those who are ethical agnostics (unsure about their ethical convictions) may either accept clients' ethical convictions or strive to influence clients to decrease their allegiance to both strongly held positive ethical views ("I should strive to eliminate poverty and injustice") and strongly held negative views ("I should not have lustful thoughts about my married co-worker"). Wallace sees a danger in absolute perspectives of any stripe. And so he sees an "ever-present need to rein the human quest for certainty, lest it lead to 'positive' or 'negative' absolutisms, to dogmatism or skepticism respectively" (Wallace 1991: 75). Albert Ellis's vehement rejection of all "shoulds," an absolutism ironically cloaked in rhetoric abjuring all absolutism (in favor of the ideology he labels "rationality"), vividly illustrates the latter.

Therapists may influence client ethical views and behavior in several distinguishable ways: ethicists may function as teachers, consultants, coaches, advocates, role models, and midwives.

An ethicist may teach others about ethics. This may mean teaching people how to think well about ethical issues, teaching the full range of what others believe to be the correct answers, teaching what the ethicist believes to be the right answers, or some combination of those roles. Some teachers simply proclaim the "right" answers and expect students to parrot those convictions. However, a person would generally be considered a *good* teacher only if he or she, while teaching the content of various traditions and taking occasional stands, sees as primary the obligation to help students arrive at their own ethical conclusions, well-reasoned and in dialogue with ethical traditions, that is, to teach students to reflect well ethically.[1] As Agich puts it:

> Knowledge of ethical concepts, principles, and theories certainly serves to organize one's observations and judgments, but the primary goal is not to teach those concepts and principles in some theoretically sophisticated way; rather, the goal is to develop skills of judgment such as identifying the relevant ethical aspects of the case and the ethically acceptable options.
>
> (Agich 1990: 390)

The ethicist may also strive to influence others in the role of consultant.

Consultants, who presumably possess some relevant expertise, provide an independent evaluation of a situation. They generally make recommendations that the consultee has the right to accept or reject. Sometimes those recommendations are made directly, but consultants may also frame situations so that the consultee will likely choose what the consultant thinks best without the consultant being overt about his or her convictions. Finally, the consultant may, in light of the consultee's goals, simply set out a spectrum of workable options and leave the final decision to the consultee.

In the bioethics literature, discussions of ethics consultants primarily refer to philosophers consulting with physicians about the ethical decisions physicians must make (Agich 1990; Fletcher and Brody 1995). But the psychotherapist can also serve as an ethics consultant, consulting with clients about the ethical dimensions of their lives, including balancing the nonmoral goods of optimal psychological well-being with other ethical principles. Although therapists may not see themselves as playing the role of ethical consultant, clients seeking help for complex life problems often look to their therapists for answers to problems that intermingle mental health[2] and ethical issues.

Suppose Mike had said to his therapist: "I just don't know what to do. Some of the time I love my wife, and feel like I should be faithful to her. But I get so mad at her, and these other women are so beautiful, and it's so exciting to be with them. But then I feel bad, deceiving my wife. I feel guilty about that, and then I get depressed. I just don't know what I should do. What do you think?" In that situation, Mike has given his therapist permission to serve as an ethical consultant, a role that must be balanced with other roles (which may also involve ethical issues to some extent).

Psychotherapists may also function as coaches of the ethical dimensions of clients' lives. The therapist/coach equips the client/athlete with the skills necessary to reach an agreed-upon goal. Beginning with the client's existing skills, therapists give practical guidance and direction so the client can function at the highest level possible. Mike's therapist, for instance, coached Mike on how to decrease his depression (a nonmoral good) by challenging his depressogenic habit of using "should statements." He employed subtractive ethical influence to reduce the salience of Mike's moral compunctions against cheating on his wife and lying.

Ethicists may also advocate certain ethical positions, setting forth reasons in support of those views, asking questions likely to lead others to adopt those positions, or otherwise persuading others to adopt their ethical perspectives. Doherty illustrated advocacy in his work with a client whose wife had ended their marriage. The client was contemplating leaving the region, which would have effectively ended his relationship with his two young children. In the context of a strong therapeutic alliance, Doherty decided to "challenge him in explicitly moral terms....I gently but forcefully told him that I was concerned that his children would be damaged if he abandoned them" (Doherty 1995: 22). The therapist explains the reasons for his ethical views (thereby engaging in theoretical ethics) as follows:

> I consider commitment the moral linchpin of family relationships. It is more than a private, idiosyncratic value that I may or may not choose to promote in therapy. To maintain professional integrity, I believe I must bring this moral value to bear in the therapy I provide and in my teaching and supervision.
>
> (Doherty 1995: 24–5)

Likewise, Cushman argues that "because of the intersecting traditions of my life, I value certain moral concepts, and I want my work as a psychotherapist to reflect those concepts" (Cushman 1995: 289). He lists several: mutual respect, cooperation, caring, enjoying and cherishing life, and honoring cultural differences. For Cushman, moral influence is central to the therapeutic endeavor:

> It is the job of the psychotherapist to demonstrate the existence of a world constituted by different rules and to encourage patients to be aware of available moral traditions that oppose the moral frame by which they presently shape their lives.
>
> (Cushman 1995: 295)

A subtler form of influence is the psychotherapist's function as role model. A client may surmise the therapist's ethical convictions or observe the therapist's behavior (with some distortion likely whenever clients surmise and observe) and strive to emulate the therapist's ethical convictions or behavior.

Finally, the ethicist may seek to influence others in the ethical sphere as a midwife influences others, by assisting in what is believed to be a natural process, a process through which something within an individual emerges. A client's own values will emerge in the context of the proper therapeutic relationship, advocates of this position believe. And we can be confident that these values will be "natural" and, hence, "good."

Individual differences

Psychotherapists differ widely in how they function as ethicists. The ethical aspects of Mike's treatment, for instance, would have been addressed differently by other therapists. And Mike's therapist might function differently with other clients. Furthermore, therapeutic relationships can be analyzed from a variety of ethical perspectives. The existence of those differences is one reason the topic of this book is so challenging. In this section, I want to delineate briefly some of those individual differences. Because many correspond to the various dimensions of ethics and the various roles of ethicists, this will serve to summarize Chapters 2 and 3.

To varying degrees, psychotherapists address issues that fall within the purview of professional ethics, theoretical ethics, clinical ethics, virtue ethics, social ethics, and cultural ethics. The predominant focus of most therapists is clinical ethics, with professional ethics also shaping their practices. Issues of social ethics have come to the fore in recent years as therapists have become concerned about managed care organizations interjecting themselves into what used to be the privacy of the therapeutic relationship. And the internationalization of psychology and growing concern about effective treatment of ethnic minorities have raised questions of cultural ethics.

The three roles of the ethicist discussed in this section are also emphasized by therapists in disparate ways. Therapists vary in the extent to which they reflect on ethical issues, have ethical convictions, and influence client values. They also differ in the ways in which they engage in those tasks.

In reflecting on ethical issues, therapists can be unconscious or otherwise unaware of their function as ethicist and their ethical convictions, or they can reflect on them consciously. They can adopt uncritically what parents, religious bodies or traditions, culture, professors and supervisors, or professional colleagues assert about ethical issues, they can rebel against those ethical sources, or they can rationally reflect on what they believe. And such rational reflection can occur either in isolation from, or in dialogue with, a particular ethical community and/or the history of ethical deliberation.

We can also contrast the ethical convictions of psychotherapists on the dimension of ethical minimalism versus maximalism. Some have extensive sets of ethical commitments; others have few or no ethical convictions.

With regard to influencing clients, therapists vary in the extent of their efforts to influence client values: Some adhere to the traditional view and strive to affect client values minimally; others more readily introduce ethical concerns. Cushman (1995) and Doherty (1995) may represent a trend toward more conscious ethical influence, though they are far from advocating the view that moral influence should be a *central* goal of therapy. In terms of how such influence is attempted, therapists can function in ways similar to teachers, consultants, coaches, advocates, role models, and midwives.

Some therapists address ethical issues in the same way across all therapeutic relationships; others continuously *tailor* their handling of ethical issues to particular clients' needs, circumstances, dynamics, and behaviors. To examine only one therapeutic relationship involving a therapist of the latter type would produce a misleading understanding of that person's functioning as an ethicist.

Finally, therapists differ in the expertise they possess regarding ethical issues, along all three dimensions of expertise I have discussed. Society assumes psychotherapists have ethical expertise to varying degrees, paying more heed to therapists when they speak to some issues than when they speak to others.

If ethical expertise is understood in terms of advanced education in ethics, moral philosophy, or value theory, few therapists have ethical expertise. Although a few have studied ethics formally or read in the area of moral philosophy, most have likely not been formally exposed to the discipline of ethics.

The quality of the reasoning therapists employ in their reflections on ethical issues also varies. And so, regarding this and the following dimension of individual difference, some would want us to speak of psychotherapists who function as *good* ethicists. That is, some are willing to evaluate the *quality* of a psychotherapist's functioning as an ethicist.

From the perspective of some ethical communities or psychotherapeutic perspectives, judgments about the quality of a therapist's ethical reasoning would be based on the content of their ethical thinking, on the particular answers they give to ethical questions. Some humanistic psychologists, for instance, stress self-actualization as the highest good for human beings or the central human virtue. By way of contrast, as noted earlier, African peoples tend to stress tribal community, family belonging, and reciprocity (Paris 1995).

And so various psychotherapists, in functioning as ethicists, call upon different ethical traditions and give different answers to ethical questions. That is, their values, concepts of virtue, and ethical theories differ. Values will be discussed in Chapter 5 and virtues in Chapters 8 and 9. It is to a discussion of ethical theory that I now turn.

Part II

Intellectual tools for examining values and ethical theory in therapy

Assumptions and criteria for analysis and decision-making

4

The spectrum of ethical theories in psychotherapy

When a psychotherapy client asserts that he cannot possibly disagree with his boss because that would be "disrespectful," or when a therapist argues that rape is wrong, we can analyze those assertions in terms of theoretical ethics. In doing so, we explore various aspects of the intellectual grounding for ethical assertions, actions, or character.

In this chapter, I will address several dimensions of ethical theory (also known as theoretical ethics, philosophical ethics, or moral philosophy): is it meaningful to use such terms as "respect" and "wrong"? is it rational to do so? if we decide that meaningful assertions about goodness, rightness, and virtue are possible, on what basis can we make such ethical assertions? what reasons or principles do we use, should we use, when we make ethical decisions? how do we know what is good, right, or virtuous? for instance, how do we know that it is good to respect others or wrong to rape? and, finally, in what relationship do issues about goodness, rightness, and virtue stand to religion?

I address these questions despite the fact many therapists think them unanswerable. And some think discussion of them is guaranteed to promote dissension and to divert energy from the more important activities of research and practice. I address ethical theory in this chapter for three major reasons: so therapists can be better therapists, so therapists can be better ethicists, and so all of therapy's stakeholders can better work together to understand therapy, improve it, and establish its optimal role in a society.

As the case below should make clear, optimal assessment and treatment of clients requires, in at least some circumstances, an understanding of the *reasons* they hold particular values. If we do not know, for instance, that an ethnic minority member's sense of obligation to family is rooted in a particular understanding of reality and truth, we may not be able to understand or work with that individual optimally.

A familiarity with ethical theory can also help psychotherapists become better ethicists (and thereby better therapists). In terms of the definition of ethicist I introduced in Chapter 3, knowing ethical theory can help therapists reflect well on ethical theory (reflecting on clients' ethical theories, the therapists' own ethical theories, and ethical theories that underlie therapy theories, practices, and social arrangements), develop and articulate more sophisticated and adequate convictions about ethical theory, and optimally influence clients with regard to ethical theory.

Reflecting well about ethical theory means developing a greater depth of understanding of the ethical dimensions of psychotherapy. A sole focus on specific values (e.g. "Racism is wrong") or virtues (e.g. "honesty") is sometimes not enough. We often need to know *why* clients or therapists hold particular values, the arguments they provide (explicitly or implicitly), the reasons for holding ethical beliefs. Ethical theory addresses that more fundamental level of analysis.

Of greatest importance is the fact that an understanding of ethical theory can help therapists better understand clients. If we understand the reasons a client holds a particular value, we can provide therapy within the client's ethical framework or, with due caution, work with the client to change a problematic ethical theory. But because clients hold a wide variety of ethical theories, working within the framework of their ethical theories requires knowing about the broad spectrum of possible ethical theories.

In contemporary culture, therapy as a social practice entails particular answers, or particular sets of answers, to the questions of theoretical ethics. Familiarity with ethical theory in general permits more rigorous thinking about those questions and the answers ethicists (from the pre-Socratics to the various postmodernists) have proposed. That permits us to develop a better understanding of the ethical character of psychotherapy in general.

Finally, therapists, like other people, function on the basis of (implicit or explicit) answers to the questions of theoretical ethics. Psychotherapy is not simply value-laden; it is also laden with ethical theory. Psychotherapists' ethical theories may simply reflect uncritically what was taught them by parents or supervisors. But I assume it is better that therapists function with examined ethical theories rather than unexamined.

Indeed, a central theme in the professional literature concerning therapy's value-ladenness is the need for therapists to be aware of their own values (e.g. Adleman 1990; Corey *et al.* 1993; Lakin 1988). But I can be aware of the particular values I hold without being aware of the reasoning that lies behind them, or of alternative ways of thinking about ethical issues. Knowledge of ethical theory can increase self-awareness about that underlying level of ethical theory. That self-awareness makes it more likely that I will deal respectfully and efficaciously with clients whose answers to the fundamental questions of ethical theory are different from my own.

Being able to reflect well about ethical theory can also help us better understand ethical dilemmas that arise within therapy clients, within therapeutic relationships, within the psychotherapy professions, and within a society (especially concerning the role of therapy in the society). The role of therapy in society, to be addressed in Chapter 10, is in a state of transition in the US, as managed care stakeholders come into conflict with therapists and clients who sometimes employ different ethical theories.

Ethical theory can also help therapists develop and articulate more sophisticated, more adequate ethical convictions. Kitchener (1980a) and Bergin (1980a) assert that individual therapists need to justify the particular values they hold, to explain *why* they believe what they believe. That task involves ethical theory. Furthermore, therapists and others need to develop better ethical theories (Prilleltensky 1997), for instance, theories that avoid narrowness and take into account the wisdom contained in alternative ethical positions.

In addition, knowledge of ethical theory should permit therapists to become better ethicists by making it easier for them to influence clients in the most ethical manner. This means in part that therapists avoid influencing the ethical convictions of clients in ways that are untoward (Tjeltveit 1986). If therapists convert clients to their values, and there is evidence that they sometimes do (Beutler and Bergan 1991), it may also be the case that, as Bandura put it, "clients have been...converted to the belief system, vernacular, and interpretations of reality favored by their respective psychotherapists" (Bandura 1969: 81–2). In most instances, I think it inappropriate, indeed unethical, for therapists to convert clients to therapists' own ethical theories. Therapist influence on fundamental client beliefs is far more likely to be appropriate, however, if therapists are aware of their clients' ethical theories and their own.

Finally, improved ethical theory should permit psychotherapists to articulate more effectively what the role of psychotherapy in a society should be. Because psychotherapists receive reimbursement and other forms of public support, public accountability to therapy stakeholders is essential. Justifying the trust the public places in therapists (and justifying the reimbursement therapists receive) requires effectively articulating why psychotherapy is good and right, and what its proper limits should be. Ethical theory can help us to do so.

In this chapter, then, I will explore some aspects of ethical theory pertinent to psychotherapy. In doing so, I do not purport to add a new element to therapy, but rather to shed light on aspects of therapy hitherto obscured.

This is, of course, an exceedingly complex task, for at least two reasons: philosophers are deeply divided on how best to think about ethical theory (see Stout 1988); and the ethical convictions, virtues, and behaviors of clients and therapists inevitably consist of some combination of psychological factors and considered beliefs. As Margolin notes, a therapist facing an apparent ethical conflict regarding roles in a marriage must sort out "whether the conflict regarding roles reflects vastly divergent ideological positions or whether the ideological differences are accentuated by relationship issues" (Margolin 1982: 798). A comprehensive understanding of the ethical character of psychotherapy would thus require a consideration both of ethical theory and of the sort of sophisticated transdisciplinary moral psychology now rapidly being developed (e.g. Deigh 1992; Flanagan 1991; Flanagan and Rorty 1990; M. Johnson 1993; Kendler 1992; L. May *et al.* 1996; Platts 1991; Thomas 1989; Wren 1990).

This chapter is more limited in scope: I will provide a brief review of ethical theory, presenting some major questions which ethical theory addresses, and some approaches to answering those questions, those I think most relevant to therapy.

To ground this discussion of ethical theories, consider the following:

> Sandra picks nervously at her sleeve. "He got really mad at me last night," she says. "I told him I had to go see my Dad. And then he just blew up. I remember the exact words José used. I keep going over them in my head: 'What do you mean, you "should" go see your father? What about *my* needs? I'm the man of this house. You married *me*, not your father. And we agreed that *I* am the head of this household.'"
>
> Sandra sighs deeply and continues, "I get so torn up about it. I mean, I want a good marriage, but I really do need to go see my father. He's not doing very well, and just my being there really cheers him up. I feel so badly when I don't go visit him, so incredibly guilty. It's my obligation as a daughter. And I simply can't have his next-door neighbor think I'm neglecting him – that would just be awful! I know I should be a good daughter. But when I try to be a good daughter, José tells me I'm being a bad wife. And I *want* to be a good wife. I guess I could have stayed home. We're renovating our kitchen. We both really want it looking nice. But I would have felt too guilty if I'd stayed home."
>
> Her therapist, Tania, responds warmly, congruently, and empathically, "So you would have felt too guilty..." An intern in the second month in this placement, Tania conceptualizes Sandra's problem to be low self-esteem. If Sandra could get in touch with her own feelings and feel better about herself, she would begin to improve, no longer living by the conditions of worth that make her feel so "awful." She needs to become a fully functioning person, casting off externally derived shoulds, and all external authorities. Tania recalls reading with enthusiasm from Rogers' *On Becoming a Person*, "Neither the Bible nor the prophets – neither Freud nor research – neither the revelations of God nor man – can take precedence over my own direct experience" (Rogers 1961: 24). And so Tania helps Sandra get in touch with her feelings.
>
> Tania discusses Sandra with her supervisor, Dr Schwartz. She reviews the case: Sandra's presenting complaint was the sudden onset of a significant fear of public speaking. Because she works in a public relations firm, the fear was causing significant occupational impairment. The phobia began when Sandra was told to provide "less than full disclosure" to the press about a client corporation's pollution of a local stream. Early

therapy sessions focused on her work-related fears. But those faded from view as Tania responded to Sandra's marital conflicts and guilt.

Dr Schwartz, who describes himself as a feminist Rational-Emotive therapist, focuses on how Sandra could begin to address the power issues and the sex-role issues in Sandra's marital discord and to challenge Sandra's irrational thinking (like her numerous "should" statements). He asks what cognitions lie behind Sandra's beliefs about a woman's role in marriage. Tania begins, "Well, she talked about this sermon she heard that really struck home."

"Ah, religion!" interrupts Dr Schwartz. "I remember well something brilliant Albert Ellis wrote a few years ago: 'The fairly obvious fact' Ellis said, is 'that what we usually call neurosis, nervous breakdown, mental illness, or some other term denoting serious emotional malfunctioning is really a subtle designation for religiosity'" (Ellis 1978: 10).

Tania, for whom spirituality is important, but who is uncomfortable both with her supervisor's clear rejection of religion and with the enthusiasm of Sandra's black Pentecostal Christian tradition, is unsure how to respond. She recalls, however, that Sandra has stressed that "Honor your father and mother" was the Scriptural passage behind her sense of obligation to her father. And Sandra had mentioned with enthusiasm the strong, independent women in her church. Plus the clear message from the pulpit (delivered by preachers of both genders) that males and females are equally responsible to "strive for holiness" and that "the Word of the Lord comes to *all* who are ready to hear it."

Tania also knows that the marital tension stems in part from José's rejection of all religion and spirituality, including the Catholic religion of his youth. She knows he has formulated his beliefs about the submission of women from his own scattered readings in conservative political philosophy and sociobiology. "It's a fact of nature," he has told Sandra, "that the male partner is the superior of the female. Just look at the animal kingdom."

Supervision following the sixth therapy session is interrupted by a telephone call. The case representative from Sandra's managed care provider has finally returned Dr Schwartz's call, six days after Sandra and Tania had received a letter stating that only two more sessions had been authorized for Sandra, for a total of eight sessions. Using the well-honed confrontive skills he developed in his RET training, Dr Schwartz launches an attack on the irrationality of the session limit. He argues for the rights of clients to receive health care (including mental health care), Tania's assessment and therapy skills, and, most importantly, the benefits of therapy for Sandra.

When Dr Schwartz pauses to catch his breath, the representative jumps into the conversation and wearily reads from a script, "Consistent with its belief in scientifically based clinical care, and with its contract with your client's self-insured employer, Health Options Systems Services has established a panel of leading clinical psychological science experts. They have reviewed available research evidence and determined appropriate treatments and session limits for various diagnostic groupings. We reimburse only therapy that treats serious psychological problems (not elective therapy for personal growth) and only empirically supported treatments. The panel's guidelines indicate that clients with Specific Phobias need only eight sessions of cognitive-behavioral therapy. And Sandra will soon reach that limit. Now, on the forms you submitted you diagnosed Sandra as having a Specific Phobia. That's correct, isn't it, Dr Schwartz?"

"What health options does Sandra have, then?" asks Dr Schwartz, with uncharacteristic meekness.

Sandra, Tania, and Dr Schwartz decide to pursue Sandra's only available option: appeal the eight-session reimbursement limit to the Health Options Oversight Panel (HOOP). They fill out the six-page HOOP form and submit it. They assert that the elimination of Sandra's irrational thinking and its replacement with more rational thinking should be the goal of therapy, a task "elegant" Rational-Emotive Therapy (RET) (Ellis and Bernard 1985) should be able to accomplish by the end of Tania's internship year, within fifty sessions. When asked to explain why this goal should be pursued, they write, "Rationality. Sandra's right to mental health care and her right to choose her own treatment and treatment goals should be preserved. Furthermore, extended therapy would substantially benefit her mental health and, possibly, her physical health, as ample research has indicated."

After three weeks, HOOP responds to the appeal with a succinct, "Appeal denied."

Sandra takes the rejection in her stride, stating, "Well, I'll be okay. I haven't been very nervous at work lately anyway. I'll just pray more. And bring all this up in my Bible study. And don't you worry about that ninth session. You couldn't have known they wouldn't pay. I'm an honest person and I believe in paying my bills."

Tania seriously considers a career change.

And Dr Schwartz has an interesting conversation with his stockbroker about his retirement stock portfolio. "I've got a great tip for you, Dr Schwartz," she says. "Buy stock in Health Options. Their earnings are way up. What's more, they just landed new contracts with two Fortune 500 corporations! Let me tell you, Dr Schwartz, I think the future of that stock is very bright!"

A variety of theoretical ethical issues may be seen in this case. Part of the complexity of this case, and of understanding those issues, stems from the fact that the interests and ethical convictions of numerous parties are at stake. To address the ethical nature of this therapeutic relationship, we need to consider not only the values and ethical theories of Sandra and Tania, but also those of others with an interest in this therapeutic relationship. Those stakeholders include: Sandra's husband, José; Sandra's father; Sandra's employer (because its productivity may be enhanced by employees who are "well-adjusted" or mentally healthy; however, because the company is self-insured, large therapy expenses would hurt the company and its employees); the client corporation for whom Sandra speaks (if she remains in therapy and becomes more self-confident and assertive, she may decide to reveal to the public the corporation's illegal dumping of toxic wastes); Dr Schwartz; Tania's training program (which, due to its training philosophy, wants its students to have long-term clients); the internship site; Health Options Systems Services (HOSS); the HOSS panel of clinical psychological science experts; and the HOSS stockholders. Each party has a stake in how therapy is conducted; each has ethical convictions relevant to Sandra's therapy; varying approaches to Sandra's therapy will have differing consequences for each. The psychotherapy office has become (has always been?) very crowded indeed.

Is it meaningful to talk about goodness, virtue, and moral obligation?

Can we legitimately assert that a particular behavior is right, a particular end or goal for therapy good, or a particular characteristic of a person virtuous? Is it valid to claim that Sandra's desire to look after her father is right? that her becoming more rational would be a good therapy outcome? that Tania's warmth and compassion are virtuous?

Some ethical theorists think it legitimate to answer those questions; others think not.

In their ethical theory, logical positivists asserted that it is cognitively meaningless to answer ethical questions. They claimed we can make only two kinds of meaningful assertions: analytic (e.g. those of logic and mathematics) and empirical (originally defined narrowly as assertions verified by observation) (Toulmin and Leary 1992). Ethics, metaphysics, and theology were accordingly dismissed as cognitively meaningless (O'Donohue 1989; Pojman 1995b; H. Putnam 1993). Emotivism, notes Koch, "was the more or less official view of logical positivism" (Koch 1969: 140). Emotivists hold that ethical assertions are, in fact, nothing but expressions of emotion. And so A. J. Ayer "held that the moral judgment that murder is wrong reduces to the emotional expression 'Murder – Boo!'" (Pojman 1995b: 270). Ayer would thus assert that "It is good that Sandra cares for her father" really means "Hurrah for Sandra!" and nothing more.

Because logical positivism has influenced psychology so profoundly and pervasively (Leahey 1997), some psychotherapists assume the truth of its ethical theory. But others think it both justifiable and meaningful to make ethical assertions. And so some who accept logical positivism as a philosophy of science but reject it as an ethical theory, along with some who take seriously the intellectual challenges to logical positivism that have led most philosophers to reject it (Suppe 1977), think it both justifiable and meaningful to make ethical assertions like, "It is good for Sandra to be free of crippling fears" or "Corporations ought not to dump toxic wastes illegally in order to maximize profits."

In contrast to logical positivism, relativism permits us to make some meaningful ethical claims, albeit claims that are quite limited in scope. Although different types of relativism have been distinguished (Wong 1991), Pojman defines relativism as the view "that there are no universally valid moral principles, but rather that all moral principles are valid relative to culture or individual choice" (Pojman 1995b: 26). That is, the truth of a moral claim is relative to a particular culture or person. A relativist might thus assert that the moral assertion, "It is good for persons to be autonomous," is true in Western cultures, but not in other cultures. Or might state, "Because of the values my wife and I share, it would be wrong for me to impose my values on her. But it would be right for José to impose his values on his wife because doing so is consistent with the moral view he and Sandra have chosen. Feminist ethics are true for me, but not for José and Sandra."

The polar opposite of relativism, ethical absolutism, holds that "there is only one correct answer to every moral problem." Regardless of person or culture, "absolute principles...provide an answer for every possible situation in life" (Pojman 1995b: 268). "Authoritarianism" and "dogmatism" are terms often used to characterize this view.

Relativism has produced devoted champions and equally devoted foes, with advocates often producing vivid examples that support their positions. Relativists point to particularly egregious examples of cultural hegemony, like missionaries who declared immoral the nakedness of natives. And so they would point to the absurdity of Sandra's claim she is *obligated* to prevent her father's neighbors from thinking she is neglecting her father (absurd unless she chose that obligation or it was a cultural belief). Absolutists, on the other hand, might point to the Holocaust, asserting that – whatever Nazi Germany or any other culture might hold – the annihilation of millions of Jews was *wrong*. According to absolutists, the failure of relativists to acknowledge the immorality of genocide and other moral absolutes (like the necessity of honoring one's parents) has led, and will lead, to horrendous consequences. To avoid that dire fate, we need to adopt absolutism.

Some psychotherapists succumb to the temptation to engage in such either–or thinking about the meaningfulness of moral discourse, reducing the ethical alternatives to either relativism or absolutism. For example,

Richardson made the following observation about two psychologists who write about morality:

> Gergen and Shotter seem to engage in an extended form of what Foucault called "Enlightenment blackmail," insisting that we either must endorse their counter-Enlightenment constructionism and what Gergen calls the "morality of relativism," or stand convicted of an Enlightenment absolutism that tends to breed domination and intolerance.
>
> (Richardson 1995: 317–18)

But Richardson immediately adds, "There just may be a middle ground." And, indeed, many who have wrestled with the ethical dimensions of psychotherapy – psychologists, other psychotherapists, philosophers, and others – hold some kind of middle ground.

It is far easier, however, to say that one holds a position "in the middle" than to clearly describe that middle ground, to specify which particular region within that middle ground is best, or to explain why we believe that position is best. Indeed, I think the precise nature of the optimal middle ground between relativism and absolutism is one of the most crucial, and interesting, issues faced by those striving to understand the ethical character of psychotherapy.

Psychotherapists have adopted a variety of approaches to that "middle ground." Some advocate an extensive set of ethical convictions; others argue for a more limited set. Discriminations between issues considered ethical and non-ethical are made in different ways. Consider, for instance, Sandra's desire (a) to be a good wife (to be virtuous) and (b) to have a beautiful kitchen. Some would consider neither to be an ethical issue because no obligations or rights are involved; others would consider both to be ethical issues, because both involve some sort of ideals; still others would consider her desire to be virtuous "ethical," but not her aesthetic desire to have a beautiful kitchen.

When making ethical judgments, some advocates of a middle ground focus on abstract universal principles and give little weight to the context, culture, and personal convictions of participants; others take those contextual factors very seriously. (This they see as the grain of truth in relativism: making wise ethical decisions about moral matters requires close attention to relevant contextual factors, that is, requires making judgments "relative" to context and culture.) The latter group would consider Sandra's religion and ethnicity, and the culture and contexts of the other stakeholders in her therapy, to be very important in an ethical analysis of her therapy, although they would not assume that those contextual factors fully determine the ethical conclusions that should be drawn.

Finally, many who hold a "middle ground" ethical position argue for an attitude on the part of the psychotherapist that is "ironic and self-critical" (L. A. Sass 1988: 263) and humble. Rejecting relativism, Richardson and Woolfolk note, "we can make valid interpretations and come to valid substantive ethical insights, even if they are never final or certain" (Richardson and Woolfolk 1994: 222). And, rejecting absolutism, Prilleltensky argues that there is "a big difference between searching for the best moral option under a particular set of circumstances and the pursuit of a dogmatic set of rules" (Prilleltensky 1997: 518).

Some postmodernists occupy a middle ground between relativism and absolutism (e.g. Bauman 1993, 1995). Other postmodernists are ethical skeptics or relativists. As Prilleltensky (1997) and Rosenau (1992) note, two orientations, the skeptical and the affirmative, characterize postmodernism's rejection of modernism's hopes for reason and the self (whether the self is viewed as the detached, objective observer or the self-aware, subjective experiencer – Taylor 1989). The skeptical postmodern orientation (ironically) resembles the ethical theory of logical positivists in its refusal to take any moral stands. By way of contrast, affirmative postmodernists use the methods of deconstruction, but do so to further moral aims. Their approach, Rosenau notes, is "nondogmatic, tentative, and nonideological." But, she continues, "many affirmatives argue that certain value choices are superior to others" (Rosenau 1992: 16).

Unfortunately, no single term satisfactorily captures the full range of views held by those in this "middle ground." This dispute about terminology reflects deep underlying philosophical differences. For example, to describe the "middle ground," Pojman uses the label "ethical objectivism," which he defines as "the view that moral principles have objective validity whether or not people recognize them as such" (Pojman 1995b: 272). But some who reject both relativism and absolutism argue for *subjectively* valid ethical principles. Carl Rogers (1961), for instance, stated that:

> the good life, from the point of view of my experience, is the process of movement in a direction which the human organism selects when it is inwardly free to move in any direction, and the general qualities of this selected direction appear to have a certain universality.
>
> (Rogers 1961: 187)

Still others (e.g. Richardson and Woolfolk 1994; L. Sass 1988) are drawing upon, and developing, very sophisticated hermeneutic approaches that avoid what they consider to be a problematic subject–object (or subjective–objective) dichotomy.

I will use the imperfect term "moral realism" (Brink 1989; R.W. Miller 1991; Shweder 1990) to refer to the middle ground between relativism and absolutism. By that term, I mean positions which hold that ethical convictions can refer to something real, to something that is not artificial, not imaginary, not *fully* constructed by participants in moral discourse, which hold that "moral facts and true moral propositions" (Brink 1989: 14) exist. I deliberately don't specify what "real" means, as I intend "moral realism" to be a rubric embracing a variety of metaphysical, epistemological, and axiological convictions that share in common only a rejection of skepticism, relativism, and absolutism. But all moral realists would hold, for instance, that the wrongness of rape is a real, or genuine, wrongness, whatever any particular individual may choose to believe, or any culture holds.

I will touch below upon the nature of some of those underlying disputes about the nature of the "middle ground" of ethical realism, because those disputes stem from differing answers to questions about the basis of goodness and moral obligation, about ethical principles, and about ethical knowledge. I should note, however, that those holding the logical positivist ethical theory may find the following sections to be of little personal benefit, because they believe there is no cognitively meaningful answer to ethical questions. Since the discussion of ethical principles and knowledge in later sections in this chapter assumes that some behaviors are right or good and some persons virtuous, emotivists and relativists would find the remainder of this chapter of interest only as a way to increase their awareness of other ethical positions, lest a failure to do so should result in imposing their ethical theory on clients or failing to work within the framework of a client's ethical theory.

The basis of goodness and moral obligation

How can we justify a claim that it would be *good* for Sandra to be free from anxiety and depression? that it is *wrong* for the company Sandra represents to illegally dump toxic wastes? that Tania and Dr Schwartz were *right* to appeal HOSS's refusal to pay for more than eight sessions of Sandra's therapy? that it was *virtuous* for Tania to be warm, empathic, and congruent?

Answers to those ethical questions cannot be justified in the manner scientific assertions are justified (see Chapter 6). So how *can* they be justified? On what basis can we make ethical assertions?

Before we examine four general types of justifications for ethical assertions, two basic distinctions must be made – between aretaic and deontic ethics (or between an ethics of character and an ethics of duty) and between moral and nonmoral judgments (discussed briefly in Chapter 2). These distinctions are important in part because they clarify the breadth of the ethical issues for which justification is necessary.

An aretaic judgment (from the Greek *arête*, meaning excellence or virtue), or an ethics of character, has to do with ethical judgments about "persons, motives, intentions, traits of character, and the like, and we say of them that they are morally good, bad, virtuous, vicious, responsible, blameworthy, saintly, despicable, and so on" (Frankena 1973: 9). For example, a person characterized by the good end of honesty (a person whose character is honest) would be considered worthy of praise. Therapists making aretaic judgments may assert that a person is "healthy," "rational," or "a good therapist."

A rough parallel can be drawn between aretaic assertions about virtues and the idea of a trait in psychology: both refer to relatively enduring or consistent characteristics of persons. What distinguishes a moral trait, or "virtue," from a general trait is that a *normative* judgment is made about that consistency: it is regarded as praiseworthy or blameworthy, good or bad.

By way of contrast, a deontic judgment (from the Greek *deon*, which means duty), or an ethics of duty, has to do with a person's actions, not with his or her character or traits. According to Frankena, when we make a deontic judgment, "we say that a certain action or kind of action is morally right, wrong, obligatory, a duty, or ought or ought not to be done" (Frankena 1973: 9). For instance, we may assert that it would be wrong for Tania and Dr Schwartz to defraud Health Options or wrong for José to demand that Sandra be submissive. Or we may argue that it is right for Tania to maintain confidentiality in therapy.

Frankena distinguishes between aretaic and deontic judgments, but suggests they are actually "complementary aspects of the same morality" (Frankena 1973: 65; see Meara *et al.* 1996). So, if Tania asserts that Sandra has become healthy or rational (that is, possesses the virtues of health or rationality), her aretaic judgment implies deontic judgments about particular acts: Sandra's behaviors are, in the main, healthy or rational. The reverse is also true: evaluating specific behaviors sometimes implies an overall evaluation of the person. If Sandra's behaviors were consistently judged to be healthy or mature, we might consider her a healthy or rational person.

Although the primary reason for introducing the aretaic–deontic distinction in this context is to make clear the breadth of ethical concepts for which justification is needed, the distinction has practical advantages: careful thinking about virtue and obligation can help clients make such judgments more appropriately ("appropriately," of course, entails an ethical judgment about what is appropriate). Therapists can support deontic assertions – for example, "Clients such as Sandra *should* honor their financial obligations to therapists when having the financial resources to do so (and perhaps even when not)" – but can challenge clients' overly-quick jumps to aretaic judgments (e.g. "I'm such an awful person!" "Why?" "Because I shouldn't have spent $100 gambling in Atlantic City. I should have paid my bill to you instead"). In addition, judgments about a client's character can sometimes not only be warranted, but important to therapy. A recidivist incest offender may need to have some sense of himself or herself as flawed, blameworthy, or in need of help – so he or she will not claim that a particular incestuous act was "just a slip. Yes, I did something wrong. But I'm okay now." For such a person to refrain from *any* self-evaluation would be problematic, as would making either an entirely positive or an entirely negative self-evaluation.

A second distinction – between moral and nonmoral judgments – is also important. As discussed in Chapter 2, moral refers here to a particular kind of judgment, whose opposite is nonmoral rather than immoral. According to Frankena, whose views on this point are not universally accepted, *moral* judgments have to do with:

> rules, principles, or ideals…that pronounce actions and agents to be right, wrong, good, bad, etc., simply because of the effect they have on the feelings, interests, ideals, etc. of *other* persons or centers of sentient experience, actual or hypothetical….On this conception, a morality must embody some kind of social concern or consideration.
>
> (Frankena 1976: 125–6)

To use an example unrelated to therapy, in playing baseball, one could assert that when there are two outs, loaded bases, and a full count, a base runner *ought* to run on any pitch. However, we would not label as immoral a player's failure to run. Stupid, perhaps, but not immoral. This is because whether or not to run is a nonmoral issue. On the other hand, if a base runner failed to run because he or she had accepted a bribe to throw the game, we might properly term that act immoral – because cheating is a moral issue.

Sandra's psychotherapy raises several moral issues. Is it wrong for corporations to illegally dump toxic wastes? Are third-party payers obligated to pay for therapy whenever doing so would benefit clients? Do people have a right to therapy? Was it right to file an appeal of HOSS's decision to pay for more than eight sessions of therapy? Was it wrong for HOOP to deny the appeal? Nonmoral normative issues are present as well. Is it good that Sandra has a beautiful kitchen? Would her reduced depression and anxiety be a good outcome? Is Tania's goal that Sandra develop greater emotional self-awareness a good therapeutic goal? Is Dr Schwartz's goal that Sandra adopt an elegant RET philosophy a better ("more good") therapeutic goal?

I think the justification of nonmoral values is particularly important, because I believe that mental health values, which when broadly defined are the most important values involved in psychotherapy, are generally *non*moral values, though usually intermingled with moral issues to some extent. Justifying nonmoral values involves asking questions like these: on what basis does Dr Schwartz claim that rationality is the best possible way for Sandra to function? do Rogerians claim that the fully functioning person is to be preferred to a person whose life is directed by externally imposed conditions of worth? do we claim that mental health is to be preferred to mental illness?

In clinical practice, however, the neat moral–nonmoral distinction often breaks down. Therapists cannot always address nonmoral values without also addressing moral values, as when moral and nonmoral values conflict. For example, one source of Sandra's tension is balancing her perceived nonmoral aspiration to have a beautiful kitchen with her perceived moral obligation to her father. And a therapist who tries to avoid moral issues by focusing solely on the nonmoral goal of Sandra's happiness would be privileging nonmoral considerations over moral. Sandra's dilemma has arisen in part because she is trying to balance her happiness against what she sees as an obligation, an ideal, or both, to be a good wife *and* a good daughter. Therapists who believe that Sandra's happiness is *all* that matters have adopted an ethical theory in conflict with Sandra's more complex theory, which combines an allegiance to nonmoral values (like happiness) with an allegiance to moral values. Furthermore, because those therapists would be trying to replace her moral values with nonmoral values, they would have entered the moral realm.

And so whatever ethical stance one takes concerning Sandra's situation, both moral and nonmoral issues become involved. And so moral and nonmoral ethical assertions alike need justification. A broad array of justifications for ethical assertions has been proposed. It is to a consideration of four types of justification that I now turn.

Social contract

Some argue that moral standards are based on agreements about how societies are to function. For instance, Tania should maintain confidentiality concerning Sandra's therapy because society has agreed therapists will do so. What is critical is that consensus has been reached, not the specifics of the consensus. Ethical judgments are justified by reference to such agreements. So, for instance, if the legitimacy, indeed, the goodness, of psychotherapists is challenged, therapists need only point to legislation establishing licensure.

Critics of this position would argue that the mere presence of an agreement does not provide a convincing basis for ethical assertions: people have entered into less than optimal, indeed, bad, wrong, and even evil, agreements. Mere consensus is not enough; convincing *reasons* for it must be set forth.

But even if unsatisfactory as a full-fledged justification for ethical assertions, a social contract can serve the very important function of articulating agreement among those with deep ethical differences. One need not have consensus on the level of ethical theory to agree, for instance, that the licensure of mental health professionals benefits society. Likewise, there can be – and, indeed, I think there is – a social contract among therapists and society that a certain core of consensual values will be present in therapy and that ideas falling outside of that consensus will not ordinarily be part of therapy. Although a social contract approach to justifying ethical convictions does not address the deepest level of justification, as I will argue in Chapter 10, the idea of social contract relevant to psychotherapy is vitally important. It can be an important part of a social philosophy regarding psychotherapy, and can contribute to public policy pertaining to psychotherapy.

Tradition

Some claim that morality is fundamentally about tradition or custom. Anthropologist Ruth Benedict, for example, believed that morality "is a convenient term for socially approved habits" and "the good" is "that which society has approved" (Benedict 1934: 73). What has always been believed to be good, right, and virtuous is the basis for making ethical judgments. In that formulation, of course, an appeal to tradition is relativistic because ethics becomes relative to the culture to which a tradition belongs. In part because of opposition to that relativism, most moral philosophers (e.g. Frankena 1973) join with many psychotherapists in rejecting tradition as a basis for making ethical assertions. It is, of course, possible to *consult* and *draw upon* a tradition without blindly accepting it. We can, for instance, read critically from the Freudian, Rogerian, or Skinnerian traditions as part of an attempt to determine an optimal ethical course in therapy.

In an important sense, tradition (or communities of discourse) forms the basis of *all* ethical thinking. MacIntyre (1966, 1984), for example, argues that tradition shapes what and how we perceive morally, how we define moral terms, how we talk about ethical issues, and how we resolve ethical dilemmas. Furthermore, Taylor (1989) argues that the modern identity rests upon a variety of ethical traditions about "the good," in relationship to which we define ourselves. Whenever we speak about the self, then, we draw upon these multi-layered ethical traditions about the self. And Kirschner (1996) documents how psychoanalysis, although intending to be anti-religious and scientific, in fact drew upon themes from the religious and Romantic traditions in its morally-loaded account of the goals of human life.

These commentators thus argue that we are profoundly shaped by the communities and traditions of which we are a part, that we are inescapably shaped in complex, multi-faceted ways of which we are but part aware – because it is hard for us to see (and understand) a tradition when that tradition shapes how we see (and understand) ourselves and the world. And yet we ignore culture and tradition at our peril. And so we need to examine tradition critically, employing some sort of criteria in doing so. But the fact we base our ethical views in part on tradition is unavoidable. And too often neglected.

Definism

Definists argue that ethical judgments are "rooted in the nature of things" (Frankena 1973: 99), that is, are rooted in a particular definition of "the nature of things." What *ought* to be and what is *good* are based on what *is*.

The challenge facing advocates of this view is to establish and properly define "the nature of things."

A variety of definitions of "the nature of things" has been employed in justifications of ethical assertions. In this section, I will discuss in turn "nature," other metaphysical understandings of reality, and the self as bases for ethics.

According to ethical naturalists, nature itself is the basis for ethics. Employing a wide range of understandings of "nature," they would all argue that Sandra's desire to care for her father arises, in some way, from nature.

Campbell's (1975) evolutionary ethics, which employs a strictly materialistic metaphysical understanding of nature, emphasized survival as the good toward which evolution aims. In explaining Sandra's desire to care for her father, naturalistic ethicists might argue that her desire to care stems from the survival value to the species associated with such care. Skinner also held such a naturalistic view (Vogeltanz and Plaud 1992), as do Schwartz and Bilsky in their research efforts to establish the "universal psychological structure of human values" (Schwartz and Bilsky 1990: 878). And Wallach and Wallach (1990) argued for another form of naturalistic ethics, asserting that human motivation provides a basis for an ethics concerned for the common good.

In the example given above, José held a variation of this view in asserting that the animal kingdom ("nature") teaches us that "the man" should dominate "the woman." Although most psychotherapists would reject José's views, his vulgar ethical naturalism should be carefully distinguished from more sophisticated versions of naturalistic ethics (e.g. Brink 1989; Flanagan 1996; Rottschaefer and Martinsen 1990; Ruse 1986; Wright 1994).

Although appealing to many, naturalistic ethics has been subject to ample criticism as well (e.g. Gewirth 1986; P. E. Johnson 1995; Kitcher 1985), including criticism from scientists who reject the claim that naturalistic ethics is "the" scientific approach to ethics, and from feminists concerned that the deeply conservative conclusions drawn by some naturalistic ethicists enshrine in "nature" social arrangements that are deeply damaging to women and that are, in substantial measure, cultural, not biological. In her discussion of the reasons for the development of feminist bioethics, for instance, Sherwin noted that "many moral theorists believed that subordination was the natural condition of women" (Sherwin 1992: 43–4).

Humanistic psychologists hold another form of naturalistic ethics, with nature as the basis of human goodness (DeCarvalho 1989, 1991). Rogers, for instance, claimed that "both personal and social values emerge as natural, and experienced, when the individual is close to his [or her] own organismic valuing process." If we are in touch with the (natural) organismic valuing process, it "will prove to be an organized, adaptive, and social approach to the perplexing value issues which face all of us," and will make for the "survival and evolution of [the human] species" (Rogers 1964: 167, 160). Browning points to the implicit ethical theory upon which humanistic psychologists rely: harmony will result when each person strives to fulfill his or her own potential. Drawing upon a Romantic view of "the nature of things," some humanistic psychologists believe that individual desires and feelings, when not corrupted by society, will harmoniously blend with those of others so everyone's needs will be met. Rogers' basic assumptions about "nature," the assumptions giving rise to his ethical assertions about "fully functioning persons," are thus quite different from those held by other naturalistic ethicists.

Another form of "naturalistic ethics," one that draws upon still another understanding of "nature," can be found in some forms of Roman Catholic ethics, especially those derived from Aquinas (Edel 1991). To oversimplify, some Catholic moral theologians assert that the nature of human sexuality, properly understood, has to do with procreation in the context of heterosexual marriage. Sexual relations that are not between husband and wife for the express purpose of procreation are accordingly viewed as unnatural, and hence immoral. Birth control, homosexuality, masturbation, and abortion are all viewed as wrong, in part because they are unnatural. That concept of nature thus produces an ethical stance substantially different from that resulting from materialistic understandings of nature. Indeed, Flanagan's (1996) metaphysical position explicitly rules out any "transcendent" considerations in his naturalism, whereas the Catholic position assumes that God is inextricably linked to nature, as its creator and sustainer. Hence, simply invoking "Nature" does not resolve ethical questions. People also need to explicate and justify their understanding of nature.

Other attempts to ground ethics "in the nature of things" rest on other metaphysical foundations. Plato and Aristotle, for instance, intertwined metaphysics, epistemology, and ethics in ways foreign to much modern (and postmodern) thinking. And some religious thinkers rely upon metaphysical assertions, such as the existence of God, to ground ethics. Marty (1983), for instance, argues that human health and well-being are gifts from God (while also arguing that reason and careful empirical investigations offer important clues to help answer ethical questions). Those holding other religious traditions have different assumptions about "the nature of things." I spent one New Year's Day, for instance, with a Japanese woman who prayed to a rock god. She believed that that god (the rock) was the basis for her duty to pray to it. When I, an insensitive 21-year-old, asked her if she *really* believed that rock was a god, she slowly responded, "I am Japanese." In retrospect, my judgment at the time should have been seasoned with the kind of caution I earlier urged for critics of José's vulgar evolutionary ethics. Psychotherapists likewise need to distinguish between simplistic (and sometimes irresponsible) forms of a position and sophisticated and responsible forms of that same position. With regard to theological bases for ethics, for example, some philosophers (e.g. Adams 1987; Quinn 1978) have recently developed philosophical bases for Christian ethics that address many of the previous criticisms of such positions.

Finally, some argue that ethical assertions find their basis in the self. Those who hold this view differ significantly, however, because they hold different beliefs about the self (see Taylor 1989). Existentialists argue that individual choice makes a particular act or decision right or wrong, good or bad. The fact that a person makes an authentic choice is crucial, not any intrinsic characteristics of the act or decision itself. As Guignon notes, Medard Boss believed that, "once genuine freedom is achieved, 'mankind's ethics becomes self-evident' and we will be able to 'define man's basic morality'" (Guignon 1993: 222). So, we *choose* goodness, we *choose* health. Goodness and health cannot be "done" to us, chosen for us, or given to us. They do not exist prior to our choices, like something awaiting discovery. They come into existence as we choose them, and not before. Goodness and rightness, accordingly, are radically individual and unique. Heidegger and others have also stressed – in ways that differ from existentialists – that human beings are "self-constituting" (Guignon 1993: 223).

The self is central to ethical judgment in a second way in Aristotelian ethics (MacIntyre 1984; Sherman 1989). Virtuous persons can see what is good and bad, right or wrong, in ways those who are not virtuous cannot. Ethical judgments are based on, or grow out of, a person's virtue or character. In addition, Aristotle had clear beliefs about the nature of the human beings, the selves, whose virtue or character permitted clear ethical vision. For Aristotle, rationality was the highest end for a human being, so the rational person was happiest, and most moral. Again, metaphysical assertions about human nature underlie definist ethical positions that find a basis for ethics in the self.

Some who focus on the self contend that goodness and virtue arise out of selves who actualize their potentials. Maslow's self-actualized persons were described by him as "strongly ethical" and capable of "greater love" (Maslow 1956: 183, 182). His claim was that within each individual lie dormant characteristics (some moral, some nonmoral, and some not ethical at all) awaiting expression. This claim entails metaphysical assumptions, as ideas about self-actualization rest on the metaphysical belief (or "romantic faith" – Guignon 1993: 222) that individual potentials will harmoniously blend so the needs of all people will be met.

And so a wide variety of perspectives is held by definists, though all base their ethical convictions on "the nature of things." In addition to the metaphysical task of clarifying and justifying their position on the "nature of things," definists must also address the so-called is–ought, or fact–value, problem. As noted earlier, it was long widely held that we cannot draw ethical ("value" or "ought") conclusions from descriptive ("fact" or "is") premises. Engelhardt and Wildes argue that "human nature is a biological fact, which must be placed within a moral vision in order to derive moral consequences from it" (Engelhardt and Wildes 1994: 142). "The nature of reality" must thus be understood in moral terms. Similarly, Holmes (1984) notes that one cannot move from the premise of a particular "is" to an "ought" without the "ought" already being contained in the "is" of the premise.

Non-naturalism or intuitionism

Some argue that the questions, "How we are to justify ethical beliefs?" and "What *reasons* should we give?" are poorly formulated. Ethical judgments are *self*-justifying, not being the type of judgment that we can justify through reason or nature. Someone may claim to know that this is the case by claiming that ethical judgments are intuitively obvious, or clearly and distinctly true (Frankena 1973). We need go no further than our sense of what is moral. Sandra's sense of obligation to her father can be understood to be intuitively obvious. She needs to balance her conflicting, intuitively justifiable moral leanings. Meehl adopts a sophisticated version of this position, arguing that we adjust our ethical ideas in response to persons he labels ERDERVE-qualified, that is, those who have "Extended Rational Discussion [based on] Extensive Real [and] Vicarious Experience" (Meehl 1981: 7). The most serious challenge which advocates of this position must address is the lack of agreement about the intuitions on which ethics is supposed to be based.

Virtues and principles

What principles should we use to decide what is good, right, or virtuous? What principles would it be best for Sandra to use when she makes ethical decisions? What principles should Tania use? What kind of person should Tania be? If the therapeutic relationship is optimal, what kind of person will Sandra be when therapy is at an end?

These are questions addressed by the area of ethical theory known as normative ethics (Frankena 1973). Less abstract than the two areas of theoretical ethics just discussed and often more immediately helpful in addressing a concrete ethical question, two general approaches have traditionally been used: teleological (or consequentialist) and deontological (Pojman 1995b). They focus, respectively, on the consequences of actions (e.g. "Will this behavior bring about the good end of better mental health for Sandra?") and on basic ethical obligations (e.g. "Will this action respect Sandra's autonomy?").

Virtues

Although teleological and deontological approaches have dominated discussions of ethics in the twentiethth century, in the last two decades virtue ethicists have strongly challenged their dominance. Virtue ethicists ask questions like these: what kind of person is Sandra? what is her character? what personal characteristics or virtues ought to present in the professional psychotherapist qua professional? what character ideals would it be best for Sandra and Tania to develop?

Meara, Schmidt, and Day (1996) distinguish between "principle ethics" and virtue ethics, although regarding them as complementary. To praise Tania for being a *just* woman (for exhibiting that virtue), for example, is complementary to asserting that she should *act justly* (in accord with the deontological principle of justice) with her clients.

However, virtue ethics emphasizes dimensions of ethics that principle ethics does not. Virtue ethics addresses the emotions and motivations of ethical agents, moral perception (the ability to see what is ethically relevant in a particular situation), practical ethical reasoning ability (prudence), and the personal characteristics of the self, including "the whole of a [person's] life" (Brody 1994: 211; see Punzo 1996). When Dr Schwartz says that Tania is "a good therapist," for instance, he is evaluating her as a person, making a judgment about her motivation, integrity, ability to see what is in clients' best interests, and consistent willingness to benefit clients. By way of contrast, principle ethics is more cognitively oriented and abstract (e.g. addressing which principles we ought to employ in making ethical decisions) and more focused on specific ethical decisions and behaviors.

Psychotherapists have recently argued that "good psychotherapists" exhibit particular virtues. Doherty (1995) emphasizes three: caring, courage, and prudence. Meara, Schmidt, and Day (1996) point to four: prudence, integrity, respectfulness, and benevolence. And K. S. Kitchener (1996b) argued that therapists should take seriously the feminist virtues of caring (Noddings 1984) and trustworthiness (Baier 1993).

Teleological or consequentialist theories

These approaches assert that we can best answer ethical questions by focusing on the *telos* ("end") of an act, that is, on its consequences. The basic ethical principle is maximizing positive consequences. More specifically, according to Frankena, "teleological theory says that the basic or ultimate criterion or standard of what is morally right, wrong, obligatory, etc., is the nonmoral value that is brought into being" (Frankena 1973: 14). Different teleological theories focus on different consequences, that is, on different ends or nonmoral goods (e.g. personal happiness, a healthy family system, or the improvement of human welfare in general). Should Sandra (and Tania) strive above all to maximize the nonmoral good of freedom from psychological distress? the nonmoral good of a satisfying marriage?

Traditional answers to those questions (which face everyone, including the advocates of virtue ethics) include egoism (focusing on the best interests of the self), altruism (focusing on the good of others), and utilitarianism (focusing on maximizing the general good).

Egoism, not to be confused with egotism, holds that, in making ethical decisions, one should consider what will further one's own well-being. Sandra needs to look out for herself, concerning herself with others only to the extent that doing so will benefit herself.

Psychotherapists (Wallach and Wallach 1983) and psychologists (Schwartz 1986) generally embrace egoism. Schwartz argues that this is because they erroneously assume science requires it. Many psychologists may believe that the *only* reason human beings perform actions traditionally labeled "moral" is to receive some personal benefit, whether decreased superego-generated anxiety in Freudian accounts, or receiving reinforcement and avoiding punishment in behavioral accounts. Because human beings inevitably act to further their own well-being (psychological egoism), egoistic principles must therefore be used to address ethical questions (ethical egoism). But Schwartz points out that this jump from psychological egoism to ethical egoism is a *non sequitur*. That human beings are customarily concerned about themselves does not mean we *should* always try to maximize our own interests. Batson (1990) has recently challenged psychological egoism on empirical grounds, arguing that, in at least some instances, persons are motivated altruistically, that is, are motivated to benefit others. Furthermore, Wallach and Wallach (1983) have documented the harmful consequences of egoism and outlined the advantages of alternatives to it.

I suspect that another reason egoism continues to be widely held is its frequent pairing in a false dichotomy with altruism. Motivation is viewed as being either egoistic or altruistic. Altruists, in one construal of the term, hold that our decisions about what is good, right, and virtuous should always be based on what will most benefit others, whatever the cost to the actor. Because therapists are acutely aware of the harmful impact of such "altruistic" motivation (e.g. the stress produced in Sandra by her desire to give sacrificially to both father and husband) and because therapists see that clients who claim to be altruistic are often, in fact, motivated egoistically, therapists affirm ethical egoism.

To reduce ethical options to just the altruist and the egoist is problematic, however. As anyone balancing commitments to self, relationships, children, and career knows, most people balance concern for the best interests of others with a concern for oneself. And this was, in fact, Sandra's situation. To reduce her choices to being selfish or altruistic (being solely concerned about others) is to misunderstand the nature of her dilemma.

Rejecting both egoism and the false egoism–altruism dichotomy, Doherty (1995) and others have recently argued that psychotherapists' overemphasis on the well-being of the individual needs to be replaced with a balanced concern for the client(s), the well-being of family members (especially children), and the well-being of the community.

By way of contrast, advocates of *utilitarianism* argue that, to make ethical decisions, we need to determine what produces the most goodness (or what produces the most utility, or usefulness, in reaching that goodness). Frankena briefly summarizes this position: "the right is to promote the general good" (Frankena 1973: 34). Utilitarian elements are often included in the statements of purpose of professional associations. The American Psychological Association, for instance, states in its bylaws that one of its purposes is "to advance psychology...as a means of promoting human welfare" (APA 1994: 1).

That statement alone, and utilitarian positions in general, offer Sandra and Tania little concrete aid when they confront ethical issues in therapy, however. The position must be fleshed out with much more specific principles, principles delineating which actions will contribute to that general good and which principles we should employ in thinking about ethical issues in therapy. We need more specific guides to action, what K. S. Kitchener (1984) called rules, when we confront specific ethical situations.

And, indeed, some psychologists have adopted more carefully worked out utilitarian positions. The goal of Wallach and Wallach's (1990) ethical approach, for instance, is to contribute to the common good. And when Skinner, sociobiologists, and Cattell (Gorsuch 1984) emphasize the good of the survival of the species, they are employing utilitarian ethical theories.

Different consequentialist ethical positions thus emphasize the need to consider the consequences of actions in Sandra's life and therapy, but disagree about the consequences considered most important.

Deontological theories

If teleological theories emphasize the consequences of actions in determining what is good, right, and virtuous, deontological theorists stress one or more principles that address whether an act is right. As Pojman points out, "for the deontologist, there is something right about truth-telling, even when it may cause pain or harm, and there is something wrong about lying, even when it may produce good consequences" (Pojman 1995b: 270). And so, if discriminating against Sandra, and other minorities or women, best contributes to some general good, a utilitarian would declare that discrimination right. A deontological theorist, however, might use the principle of justice to reject discrimination – whatever its consequences – because that action is unjust.

Deontologists can employ one or more principles. Achieving positive consequences can be *one* principle a deontologist uses in deciding what is good, right, and virtuous. However, deontologists hold that, in at least some situations (and for some deontologists, in all situations), another principle or principles are needed: principles or rules, such as those involving equality, freedom, harm-avoidance, justice, or promise-keeping, should be used to decide what is right.

Biomedical ethicists generally employ deontological principles to address ethical issues, perhaps the most influential formulation being that of Beauchamp and Childress (1994; see Gillon 1994). Beauchamp and Childress argue for four basic ethical principles: respect for autonomy, nonmaleficence (avoiding harm), beneficence, and justice. Those principles have been praised, vilified, and used extensively in bioethics education, as well as being employed to understand professional ethical issues in psychotherapy. To those four, K. S. Kitchener (1984) added a fifth principle, "fidelity," and Meara, Schmidt, and Day (1996) a sixth, "veracity." Applied to concrete situations, these principles are believed to help therapists to understand their duties to clients and to conduct psychotherapy in an optimally ethical manner. And, as Bersoff (1996) notes, such principles are essential when psychologists (however virtuous) address ethical dilemmas, especially those arising in novel or conflictual situations.

Indeed, the greatest ethical dilemmas for clients and therapists occur when ethical principles are in conflict. Sandra's dilemma had to do with balancing the principle of her own welfare, on the one hand, with her perceived obligations to her husband and father, or her desire for a good marriage and a good relationship with her father, on the other hand. Part of the reason for Dr Schwartz's uncharacteristic silence in response to the Health Options' case manager was the conflict between his commitment to veracity (he believed Specific Phobia was the best diagnosis for Sandra) and his commitments to beneficence (he and Tania were obligated to act in Sandra's best interests), to justice (he believed it wrong to deny benefits to a client so clearly in need of therapy), to respect for autonomy (Sandra's choice to continue therapy should be honored), and to fidelity (Tania should maintain a therapeutic relationship with Sandra until therapy reaches its "natural" end). In addition, the Health Options' case manager faced an ethical dilemma: Sandra's well-being versus the limited benefits provided by her employer, as clearly spelled out in the explicit agreement into which Sandra (through her employment agreement), the clinic at which she was being seen, and Health Options had entered.

Dilemmas often arise because different stakeholders in therapy use different principles: Dr Schwartz believed that psychotherapy should be reimbursed until clients have adopted the "elegant RET" philosophical position. Health Options' administrators thought it would be wrong (because a violation of the agreement between it and Sandra's employer and because extensive therapy is harmful to the best interests of US business in a competitive global environment) to pay for fifty sessions of therapy when Sandra's only diagnosable problem, her fear of public speaking, could be eliminated in eight. Still others would argue that it would be wrong to "cure" Sandra in such a way that, after she returned to work, she lied to the public without anxiety about her client corporation's illegal pollution. It would be wrong, they would argue, to focus so exclusively on Sandra's well-being that society as a whole was harmed.

Some resolve such conflicts rigidly; others do so more flexibly. Some use only one principle; others (e.g. Frankena 1973) produce mixed models that combine deontological principles (like justice) with a consideration of the general good. It may well be that therapists use ethical principles like they use theories of psychotherapy: many are sloppy eclectics (using whatever approach seems applicable, with no concern for consistency across time or situation), some are nuanced eclectics (intuitively applying different approaches depending on the circumstances, without being able to easily articulate their reasons for doing so), and a few are systematic eclectics (able to state clearly which approach they use in which situation – and why).

In conclusion, clients and psychotherapists continually decide the best course of action to take. This often involves decisions about what is good, right, and virtuous, decisions based, in part, upon virtue, upon teleological or deontological principles, or upon some combination of those approaches. When a client employs a different ethical theory than that used by his or her therapist, it is generally incumbent upon the therapist to work, to the extent possible, within the client's ethical framework.

Ethical knowledge

A very difficult question of ethical theory remains: just how do we *know* what is good, right, or virtuous? How can Sandra know that "it's not right for me to neglect my father when he is in need and I can help him"? How can Tania know that Sandra should guide her life by her feelings instead of by "externally derived shoulds"? On what epistemological basis can Dr Schwartz claim that clients will function optimally if adopting the ethical philosophy of elegant RET?

Different people propose very different answers to these questions (Sinnott-Armstrong and Timmons 1996). Unless working with a homogeneous population, therapists are likely to encounter clients who use different approaches to ethical knowledge. In this section, I will discuss eight approaches, several of which contain very dissimilar subtypes, and most of which can be combined in some fashion.

Knowledge through tradition

Some turn to the answers provided by tradition, whether religious, secular, professional, or some combination thereof. If I want to know what ought to be done, I learn the answers traditionally given. Although psychologists join with philosophers in roundly rejecting the idea that people should uncritically accept tradition, tradition may well be the most significant source of ideas about what is good, right, and virtuous for most people. And, as noted earlier, we tend to be shaped far more than we are aware by the ethical traditions in which we are immersed. Tradition thus shapes the "knowledge" obtained by advocates of each of the following positions.

Knowledge through reason alone

The Ancient Greek philosophers challenged a reliance on tradition, arguing instead that reason should be used to obtain ethical knowledge. In the Enlightenment, reason regained ascendancy, and efforts to obtain knowledge through reason alone continue (e.g. Donagan 1977; Gert 1975, 1988; Toulmin 1950). But others, most notably Nietzsche and some of his postmodern intellectual heirs, have reacted strongly against reason. MacIntyre, who labels efforts to found ethics on reason or other "certain" foundations as "the Enlightenment project", asserts that:

> Nietzsche jeers at the notion of basing morality on inner moral sentiments, on conscience, on the one hand, or on the Kantian categorical imperative, on universalizability, on the other. In five swift, witty and cogent paragraphs he disposes of both what I have called the Enlightenment project to discover rational foundations for an objective morality and of the confidence of the everyday moral agent in post-Enlightenment culture that his moral practice and utterance are in good order.
>
> (MacIntyre 1984: 113)

Three responses to Nietzsche's challenge are common: affirmative postmodernists claim that modest ethical knowledge, although difficult to obtain, is possible; skeptical postmodernists reject the possibility of moral knowledge; and others (who may reject the implicitly ethical categories "premodern, modern, and postmodern") continue to assert that ethical knowledge is, in some fashion, obtainable through reason.

Knowledge through the scientific method

Scientifically-oriented psychotherapists tend to be suspicious of those who rely on reason alone, seeing that as mere "armchair philosophizing." They turn instead to science to provide knowledge. Although many who are devoted to science (especially when they understand science through the lens of logical positivism) argue that *ethical* knowledge is an impossibility, others look to science as a source of ethical knowledge. Accordingly, to answer the ethical question "what kinds of therapy, and how much therapy, *should* Health Options reimburse?", Health Options established a panel of scientists. They relied upon scientifically derived data to determine the types of acceptable therapy (those empirically supported) and the limits for such therapy (the number of sessions clients with a particular problem typically take to respond to treatment). They thus argue that science can tell us which forms of therapy work and that knowledge can answer the ethical question of the proper level of reimbursement for therapy.

That simple use of science to make ethical decisions needs to be distinguished from more sophisticated efforts to use science in decisions about practice (see Hayes *et al.* 1995; Kendall and Chambless 1998; Nathan and Gorman 1998; Roth and Fonagy 1996; and the discussion in Chapter 6). Kendler, for instance, argues that, while "psychology is unable to validate moral principles because of the logical impossibility of inferring ethical imperatives from empirical data" (Kendler 1993: 1046), it can contribute to policy decisions by making evident the consequences of alternative proposals.

Another attempt to provide ethical knowledge based on science has been mounted by sociobiologists and others whose conception of science is closely tied to materialistic metaphysics and a particular understanding of evolution. They argue that we can know what should be done by carefully thinking about evolution, the aim of which is (the nonmoral good of) survival. The ethical theory which results is a defensible form of utilitarianism, in which the well-being of society and the earth (controversially equated with the survival of the human species) is the criterion used to determine what should be done. Clearly, however, ethical conclusions reached in this way are not determined by science alone, but by an understanding of evolution in combination with a particular metaphysical commitment and an ethical allegiance to species survival as the highest good. Science as empirical endeavor is thus joined with an extensive set of philosophical commitments. As such, sociobiologists are better characterized as striving to obtain ethical knowledge through an implicit combination of reason, nature, and ethical conviction.

Knowledge through an explicit combination of reason and nature

Some classical approaches to ethical knowledge explicitly combine assumptions about human nature (as understood from a particular philosophical perspective) and reason. To varying degrees, these positions are open to revision based on experience with actual, not hypothesized, nature (although a theory-free grasp of "actual" nature is difficult or impossible to achieve).

Aristotle's ethical theory holds that human beings achieve happiness and goodness by behaving in harmony with their essential nature, which is rationality, the end or *telos* to which human beings, by nature, should move. Nature and reason are thus essential both to human beings and to ethics. Aristotle adds, however, that the person with moral vision, who can know what is good, right, and virtuous, and behaves accordingly, is the virtuous person. So, to *know* what is good, one must *be* good. And virtue is shaped by habits conducive to goodness.

In addition, some religious ethical positions, based on "natural law," hold that by examining nature, including human nature, we can know what human beings, as created by God, should do.

Knowledge through extra-rational personal qualities

Tania's implicitly encouraging to Sandra to "get in touch with her feelings" is but one example of a heterogeneous spectrum of approaches to ethical knowledge that have this in common: extra-rational (meaning beyond or outside of reason, not necessarily irrational or anti-rational) aspects of a person can produce trustworthy knowledge about what is good, right, or virtuous. An early example may be found in Pascal's assertion that, "the heart has its reasons, which reason does not know" (1958: 78).

Romanticism, with its roots in a response to the Enlightenment, stressed culture and instinct (with a meaning different from that of contemporary biology) as critical sources of knowledge and identity. Those in this tradition hold radically different positions. On the one hand, some humanistic psychologists (see L. A. Sass 1988) make eloquent appeals stressing the goodness of human nature, the trustworthiness of feelings, and the positive benefits to individuals and society of trusting the "organismic valuing process" (Rogers 1964). On the other hand are those who stress the feelings associated with one's racial group (instinct and culture) found in "the Nazi cry to think with the blood" (MacIntyre 1966: 75).

Other Western ethicists have also stressed ways of knowing what is good, right, and virtuous that do not use, or emphasize, reason. Some, for example, David Hume, emphasized "moral sense," a "faculty" involving emotions or sentiments by which we know what is right and wrong (Kurtines *et al.* 1990). Scottish Common Sense Realists stressed "conscience" as a way to make ethical distinctions (Sprague 1967). And intuitionists have stressed that we know intuitively what is good, right, and virtuous. Since these positions have significantly influenced Western culture, clients often hold them.

Finally, existentialists argue that only those moral decisions that are freely chosen, or authentic, can be called moral. Accordingly, one knows what is right only through a process of authentic choice.

Knowledge through divine revelation

This general approach to ethical knowledge can take several forms. Sandra's belief in her obligation to care for her father came in part from her black Pentecostal tradition, which holds that God's will, as revealed through Scripture and the inspiration of the Holy Spirit, produces knowledge about what is good, right, and virtuous. William James (1978) noted that adherents of a variety of religions report experiencing mystical states that include a noetic component. Others claim different forms of direct, unmediated knowledge of God's will.

Many Jews, Christians, and Muslims view sacred scripture as a compendium of (or otherwise revealing) the divine will. This can take primitive forms, like a person closing his or her eyes, opening up a Bible, and randomly putting his or her finger down to discern "God's will." But there have also long been thinkers who have combined reason with Scripture. For instance, Moses Maimonides, a medieval Jew, combined Aristotelianism with Jewish Scripture and tradition in formulating an ethical position (Maimonides 1975a, 1975b). And, in a position now being revived (e.g. MacIntyre 1988, 1990), Thomas Aquinas combined Aristotelianism with Christianity in his "Great Synthesis," producing seven virtues – courage, justice, practical wisdom, temperance, faith, hope, and love – the last three requiring revelation to be known. And very sophisticated intellectual accounts of ethical knowledge that rely, in substantial measure, on Scripture continue to be espoused (e.g. Adams 1987; Hays 1996; Mouw 1990; Quinn 1978).

Knowledge arising out of relationships

Some argue that knowledge about what is good, right, and virtuous arises only within the contexts of relationships, relationships producing forms of knowledge otherwise unobtainable. MacIntyre (1984) argues that human beings achieve such knowledge by being rooted in particular communities. What is distinctive about recent history is not that we lack such communities but that our present community asserts, contrary to fact, that individuals cut off from community can obtain ethical knowledge.

In addition, feminist ethicists have emphasized the importance of relationships. Noddings (1984), for instance, sees in relationships a source of knowledge about caring, about how we should live. Other feminists (e.g. Friedman 1991; Hoagland 1991), however, criticize those who see traditional relationship patterns as a source of moral knowledge when those patterns harm women.

Some religious ethicists have also argued that ethical action, and consequently knowledge, arises out of a relationship with God (Long 1967). Faith involves personal transformation, which leads to changed behavior, like that following a person falling in love.

Knowledge through hermeneutics

Finally, Guignon (1993), MacIntyre (1984), Richardson and Woolfolk (1994), L. A. Sass (1988), Taylor (1989), Vitz (1990), and others have argued that ethical knowledge is rooted in the interpretation of narratives, stories, and other forms of discourse. We make sense of our existence, we know what is good, right, and virtuous, by the understanding we develop through hearing, telling, and interpreting stories. As Guignon notes, the stories or narratives we construct "have a 'moral' to the extent that their resolution implies the achievement of some goods taken as normative by our historical culture" (Guignon 1993: 236). We learn to become therapists (learn what ought to occur in therapy) by hearing stories about therapy conducted by master therapists, by a careful review in supervision of what actually happens (told in narrative form) in particular therapy sessions, and by listening to clients who rely heavily upon stories to tell about themselves and their problems. Psychotherapy, on this account, is an attempt to recraft the stories of clients who have gone astray: clients (rather than events or other people) begin to author their stories. Clients move in the direction of a final chapter of their own choosing, that is, toward a better, more good, or more right concluding chapter. Stories are thus held to be a vitally important way in which therapy participants obtain ethical knowledge.

Those who stress the importance of narratives also stress the inescapability of the hermeneutic task of *interpreting* those stories. They would argue that to obtain ethical knowledge relevant to Sandra's therapy, we must interpret the story of Sandra's life as a whole, including the role of therapy within that emerging story. Telling Sandra's story includes an account of her striving to be honest at work, getting anxious when told to lie, striving to be a good wife, good daughter, and good homemaker, and becoming depressed by her failure to fulfill all of those roles satisfactorily. The end of her story is unresolved, but "the end" of her story will most likely be "happy" if it "makes sense" in terms of the story that began long before she entered therapy and if she is an active participant in its "writing."

To conclude, people employ a wide variety of approaches to obtain ethical knowledge. A few clients and therapists may articulate such epistemological positions explicitly. But it is more likely that they "operate with a partially articulated and somewhat incoherent set of vague general principles…and unexamined ethical intuitions" (Meehl 1981: 6). And, of course, many employ mixed ethical models, relying upon more than one source of knowledge about ethics.

Ethical theory in relationship to religion

In a previous age, many people simply assumed that religion was the appropriate basis for ethics. By way of contrast, some now think it inconceivable that an adequate ethical theory could be based on religion, spirituality, or both. These polarities are also present in clients and therapists: some cannot imagine approaching questions of good and bad, right and wrong, virtue and vice, from any but a spiritual or religious perspective. But others assume that to turn to religion or spirituality in the realm of ethics is to choose superstition, falsehood, and irrationality. Sandra exemplifies the first approach; Dr Schwartz the second. And Tania occupies an uneasy position between them.

In this section, I will address the following question: is it sometimes necessary – if we want to understand the ethical theory employed by clients and therapists – to include a consideration of religion and spirituality?

One could conclude, after reading some psychotherapy literature, that religion is extinct. But empirical research indicates that a consistent 95 per cent of Americans believe in God, with 88 percent reporting that they pray (Hoge 1996). However, the role of religion has changed for many people. As Hoge notes, "religion is as alive as ever, but it is diversifying" (Hoge 1996: 38). Accordingly, psychologists of religion argue that we best understand religiousness from a multi-dimensional perspective (Hoge 1996; Hood *et al*. 1996; Wulff 1996). Two important ways in which religion is diversifying, notes Hoge, are a waning of denominational loyalty and the increasing privatization of religion, a change perhaps reflected by the fact that many prefer to think of themselves as "spiritual" but not "religious." But if spirituality is a private matter, therapy is supposed to be a place to talk about "private" issues, and so should address spirituality when relevant to a client's therapeutic progress.

The fact that many people consider themselves religious or spiritual may, however, be irrelevant to the concerns of this chapter, because religion and spirituality may be unrelated to ethical theory. This would certainly be the case if Dr Schwartz were conducting therapy with a client whose views on religion mirrored his own: religion plays no role in their lives. But religion was vitally important for Sandra, as is the case with many African–Americans (Boyd-Franklin 1989). And religion was clearly linked to her ethical theory. Rejecting relativism, she believed that God is in some way the basis for what is good, right, and virtuous. She believed she should exhibit virtues consistent with being a good wife and daughter, and that she had certain (deontological) obligations to her husband and father. She had knowledge of those obligations because they had been revealed through Scripture, the direct inspiration of the Holy Spirit, and the words of the male and female preachers, inspired by the Holy Spirit, whom she heard at her church.

By way of contrast, spirituality played a minimal role in Tania's ethical theory. She had embarked on a very private spiritual journey whose primary ethical implication was her desire to respect and learn from others.

Although 95 percent of Americans believe in God, only 47 percent "consider faith to be relevant to the way they live their lives" (Shafranske and Malony 1996: 565). To understand in depth the ethical theories of that 47 percent, however, it may be necessary to consider religiousness. As Shafranske and Malony note, "in keeping with their belief and value commitments, religions provide prescriptions for living" (ibid.: 570). In addition to the specific ethical content found in those prescriptions, a religion may – from some perspectives – provide a basis for goodness, moral obligation, and virtue, and provide an approach to moral knowledge.

We can therefore conclude that, since some therapists and many clients base their values, and their ethical theory, in some substantial measure on their religious or spiritual convictions, no account of values and ethics in therapy that claims to be adequate and comprehensive can ignore religion and spirituality. We sometimes need to address religion and spirituality; sometimes we do not.

To understand well the relationship of ethical theory and spirituality/religion, careful assessment of religion and spirituality is necessary (E. W. Kelly 1995b; Lovinger 1996; Richards and Bergin 1997). Particular religious traditions approach ethical questions in a variety of ways. Indeed, there is rarely unanimity *within* the major world religions. Long (1967, 1982), for instance, has set forth a classic taxonomy of how Christians have addressed ethical issues. Some focus on reason as the sole or primary source of ethical standards. Others focus on ethical prescriptions deriving from God, as revealed through Scripture, the community of the faithful, or both. Still others believe that virtue and good or right behavior arise out of a relationship with God that transforms people.

Jewish ethicists are also divided about whether to rely on reason or on authoritative tradition. Kellner (1978) and Jacobs (1978), for instance, note that some Jewish writers have focused on reason as a source of Jewish approaches to what is good, right, and virtuous, but others have focused upon divine commandments, as revealed in sacred writings. Also controversial is the existence of a Jewish ethics independent of the *Halakha*, or Law (Lichtenstein 1978). Different Jewish groups give different answers. To the extent a particular client says "For me, there is no ethics independent of the *Halakha*," of course, a therapist's failure to understand the *Halakha* and its associated ethical theory will mean he or she will fail to understand how the client approaches questions of mental health and morality.

Other religious traditions may also influence an individual's approach to addressing ethical issues in psychotherapy (E. W. Kelly 1995b). Amore (1973), for instance, discusses how Theravada Buddhism involves moving toward a Path or goal, which includes morality.

Conclusion

Therapists and clients alike answer the questions of ethical theory in a wide variety of ways. The questions posed in ethical theory are definitely daunting – yet an awareness of our own implicit and explicit answers to them is vital. Effective therapy for Sandra, and for other clients, requires no less.

5

Unpacking diverse understandings of "values"

"Values" is a remarkably elastic term, put to use by psychotherapists, psychologists, sociologists, philosophers, and the general public in a wide assortment of ways. Many also use the term to talk about and understand the ethical dimensions of psychotherapy. For example, upon hearing about Sandra's therapy (the example discussed in Chapter 4), a therapist may remark:

> Well, I don't believe therapy is value-free. Values are clearly involved in Sandra's therapy with Tania. And so Tania will need to be aware of her own values so she doesn't impose them on Sandra. But that's all that's needed. There's no need for philosophical ruminations about "ethical theory" and the like.

I take issue with those sentiments on several grounds. The literature addressing values and the role of values in therapy offers far more practical and theoretical benefit to therapists than that. And it is never possible to sunder "values" entirely from ethical theory. Indeed, on some accounts of "values," ethical theory and values are inextricably bound. Finally, focusing solely on "values" to understand the ethical character of psychotherapy is problematic because the term is used in so many different ways. Encouraging therapists to be "aware of values" is not helpful unless we clearly define "values." We need to move beyond recognizing that "Therapy is not value-free" to a well-developed understanding of the *ways* in which it is value-laden. That requires conceptual clarity.

For all those reasons, I am convinced that understanding the ethical character of therapy will benefit from a clarification of the many meanings of "values."

In the face of the variety of definitions of values, we can adopt several approaches. Unfortunately, two of the most common – denial of that variety and "my definition is best, so I can ignore the others" – are decidedly *un*helpful. A better approach exists and should be adopted. Accordingly, in this chapter, in addition to attempting to clarify the multiple meanings of values, I will argue for a particular approach to the problem of multiple understandings of "values."

In the final section of the chapter, I will draw upon that discussion of "values" in a brief review of psychological research on the role of values in therapy. I will focus on findings pertinent to understanding the ethical dimensions of therapy, findings that are not always intuitively obvious.

Multiple (theory-laden) meanings of "values"

In 1914, Ralph Barton Perry pointed to a problem which those who seek to understand "values" still face:

> One can not collect values as one can collect butterflies, and go off into one's laboratory with the assurance that one holds in one's net the whole and no more than the whole of that which one seeks. There is no perforation about the edges of values to mark the line at which they may be detached.
>
> (Perry 1914: 141)

Because of the shapelessness of "values," Maslow suggested that the term can be thought of "as a big container holding all sorts of miscellaneous and vague things" (Maslow 1963a: 120). Consequently, "values" is used in so many different ways that, if not careful, we can end up being more confused than clear.

Suppose, for example, that a group of people discusses "Sandra's *value* of 'a good marriage.'" One person might understand that to mean her feelings about marriage, another her thoughts about it, another her behavior, and a fourth all three (with none addressing what is actually good, right, or virtuous). And others may think that that value (if authentic) reflects her own choice, or is an outgrowth of who she, at the deepest level, really is as a person. Still others may think "value" reflects attempts by the Fundamentalist Christian preachers of her childhood to impose upon Sandra their patriarchal religious ideology. "Her value is a product," others might assert, "of her particular cultural and historical background." Finally, some may use it as an ethical term, in accord with some of the philosophical approaches discussed in Chapter 4.

A taxonomy of definitions of "values"

Those assumptions about the meaning of Sandra's "values" illustrate some important differences among types of definitions of values. Those differences can be summarized in the following taxonomy:

- values as psychological

- values as ethical
- values as a means by which the powerful impose their will on the weak
- values as choices
- values as authentic expressions of an individual's nature
- values as cultural and historical.

A word of qualification is in order: many definitions combine one or more of those emphases. Also, I will not address distinctions between definitions of "values" that would be important for other purposes. Much is to be gained by using those "richer" definitions and distinctions; I focus here on key distinctions that shed light on how the term "values" is used to understand the ethical dimensions of therapy. To make the taxonomy more useful, I will address each of those six types of definition in turn.

Psychological definitions of "values" emphasize a variety of psychological concepts: cognitions, affect, behaviors, motivation, social influence, attitudes, traits, and so forth. Skinner, for example, asserted that "to make a value judgment by calling something good or bad is to classify it in terms of its reinforcing effects" (Skinner 1971: 105). Sandra's valuing a good marriage would thus mean "behaviors associated with marriage are positively reinforcing to her."

Other psychologists emphasize different psychological concepts. When psychoanalysts "study values," Michels (1987) notes, "they mean that they trace their developmental roots, hidden meanings, and psychic significance" (Michels 1987: 42). The psychoanalyst's interest in Sandra's "value" regarding marriage would accordingly be directed toward its childhood origins and unconscious meanings. Others emphasize emotions when discussing values. Fishbein and Ajzen (1975), for instance, treated "evaluation" and "affect" as synonyms. Rokeach (1973) focused on values as a particular type of belief. And still others (e.g. Rest 1984), in attempting to provide a full account for morality, address cognition, affect, *and* behavior.

According to psychological definitions, then, values are what people value, judge to have value, think to be good, or desire (Frankena 1967: 230). Frankena additionally notes, however, that others employ a second type of definition of values:

> what *has* value or *is* valuable, or good, as opposed to what is *regarded* as good or valuable. Then "values" means "things that have value," "things that are good," or "goods" and, for some users, also things that are right, obligatory, beautiful, or even true.

I refer to this as an ethical definition of values.

Kitchener described the contrast between psychological and ethical in this way: "There is an important distinction between what one's client actually desires and what is desirable or ought to be desired by one's client" (R. F.

Kitchener 1980b: 15). In making similar distinctions, Peperzak (1986) contrasted factual and normative meanings of values, and J. P. Johnson (1967) the descriptive and the normative sides of value questions. I use the labels "psychological" and "ethical" because in the former type of definition, "value" pertains to some psychological process, to valuing. Psychologists, including those who conduct empirical research on "values," generally employ some type of psychological definition. I label the second type of definition of values "ethical" because such definitions address "an arena traditional to philosophical ethics" (Rescher 1969: 55).

Some who employ psychological definitions of values aspire to exclude the ethical from their definitions. Skinner, for example, clearly differentiated his psychological understanding of "values" from the kind of classical understandings of ethics I discussed in Chapter 4:

> The behaviors classified as good or bad and right or wrong are not due to goodness or badness, or a good or bad character, or a knowledge of right and wrong; they are due to contingencies involving a great variety of reinforcers, including the generalized verbal reinforcers of "Good!" "Bad!" "Right!" and "Wrong!"
>
> (Skinner 1971: 113)

And Rokeach (1973) argued that definitions of values "should avoid" words like "ought" and "should", words many regard as quintessentially ethical. Indeed, in the context of delineating the requirements for a scientifically fruitful conception of human values, Rokeach made the rather remarkable assertion that such a conception "should represent...a *value-free* approach to the study of human values" (Rokeach 1973: 3, emphasis added).

In contrast to those whose psychological definitions of "values" eschew (or claim to eschew) the ethical altogether, most users of ethical definitions of "values" acknowledge the psychological dimensions of the term but focus on the ethical. They thus employ mixed ethical-psychological definitions of "values."

Some psychologists also employ ethical definitions of values. The preamble of the Ethics Code of APA, for example, states: "This Ethics Code provides a common set of *values* upon which psychologists build their professional and scientific work" (APA 1992: 1599, emphasis added). "Values" clearly refers, not just to the products of psychological processes of valuing, but to the goodness and rightness of those values. Compare also psychologist Isaac Prilleltensky's definition of values: "I define moral values as benefits that human beings provide to other individuals and communities. Thus, I treat values as entities, ideas, or predispositions to action that have the potential to promote the good life and the good society" (Prilleltensky 1997: 520).

By way of contrast, some assert that, even if there is "a good life," human beings cannot know what it is. "Values" are accordingly viewed with considerable suspicion: they are understood to be a means by which the powerful impose their will on the weak. Some postmodernists would thus assume that Sandra's "value," a good marriage, is *really* about attempts by the Fundamentalist Christian preachers of her childhood to impose upon Sandra their patriarchal religious ideology. Such postmodernists would "deconstruct" her value claims, understand them in terms of power, and be suspicious of any ethical claims made on behalf of that or any other "value."

Accordingly, some advocates of this third type of definition, like some who use ethical definitions, take a clear stand on the issues of ethical theory discussed in Chapter 4. Other users of this definition, like Kristiansen and Zanna (1994) in their aptly titled article, "The rhetorical use of values to justify social and intergroup attitudes," assume that stated values *can* be used as rationalization, to justify discrimination, or for defensive purposes. They do not, however, assume that values are "nothing but" efforts by the powerful to impose their will on others.

A fourth set of users of the term understands "values" in terms of freedom. If Sandra's value is genuine, she must have chosen to adopt it, although she could have done otherwise. A person is never coerced into holding a true value, not coerced by others and not coerced from within by psychological forces – whether by biological determinants, by reinforcement history, or by unconscious determinants. Dickson (1994), for instance, adopted a Sartrean perspective and argued that freedom is "the source of all value" (Dickson 1994: 15). Advocates of this definition reject the claims of psychological researchers who assert that values are the products of psychological processes that can (in principle) be described in scientific laws. They hold that values are chosen, not determined. On this understanding of values, then, human decisions "create" values (MacIntyre 1984; Perry 1914).

Still others assert that values, true values, are authentic expressions of an individual's nature. Self-actualized persons, asserted Carl Rogers, learn to "live by values which they discover within" (Rogers 1961: 175). Similarly, Nerlich (1989) argues that values can be correct if they emerge authentically from a person's nature. Although often associated with definitions emphasizing freedom, this type of definition is different: Maslow, for instance, flatly rejected the Sartrean position that we possess unbounded freedom to choose our own values. He asserted that "human nature carries within itself the answer to the questions: How can I be good; how can I be happy; how can I be fruitful?" (Maslow 1987: 60). Maslow might have suggested, for example, that if it was not in Sandra's nature to value authentically a good marriage, no amount of choosing could make it authentic for her.[1]

Although phrased in individualistic terms (and often understood as focusing solely on the uniqueness of the individual's valuing), Rogers and Maslow claimed a universality for the values healthy individuals discover within themselves. Rogers, for instance, asserted that, "in persons who are moving toward greater openness to their experiencing, there is an organismic commonality of value directions" (Rogers 1964: 165). The universality of values exists because human beings share a common nature, an "organismic" nature.

Definitions of values that focus on universal values that arise from individuals getting in touch with their authentic nature bridge the psychological–ethical divide I discussed above. They are clearly psychological in their focus on the subjective psychological processes of valuing; they also make universal ethical claims about values, albeit focusing primarily on nonmoral ethical assertions,[2] especially the good life.

I discuss this as a distinct form of definition because humanistic psychologists regularly distinguish their position from all others. In addition, the psychological emphases in this type of definition are quite different from those of researchers studying values within the traditional empirical paradigm.

Finally, still others employ a sixth type of definition, emphasizing values as cultural and historical. As Barry Schwartz notes, "values are often contextually determined, sociohistorical phenomena that can be created or destroyed by the very beings whose behavior is guided by them" (Schwartz 1990: 7). Sandra's valuing "a good marriage" could thus be seen as arising out of a particular cultural context: the world of the twentieth-century black Pentecostal Church in the midst of an ethnically diverse US culture that is profoundly shaped by television.

In contrast to ethical, empirical, and humanistic attempts to draw universal conclusions about values, cultural definitions emphasize that values are distinctive to the particular cultures and periods of time that produced them. Values are thus historically and culturally contingent. Support for this view can be found in the findings of Shalom Schwartz's (1994) extensive cross-cultural research program, which has identified cultural differences among value types.

"Values" thus refers, in Frankena's words, to "what is valued, judged to have value, thought to be good, or desired" (Frankena 1967: 230). But in contrast to psychological definitions (in which individuals "value," "judge," and so forth), when cultural-historical definitions of "values" are employed, cultures in particular historical periods "value," "judge," and so forth.

Individual and cultural values are not, however, easily distinguished, and "the line between these is elusive" (Kluckhohn 1951: 400). The individualistic training most psychotherapists receive, however, makes it more difficult for them to see how culture and history shape values than how individuals shape values. Indeed, we may be shaped by culture and history much more than we are aware. Part of the challenge of getting at such values is that they tend to be invisible to the participants in a given culture and period of time: we may at times be "too close" to such values to see them clearly. "Some of the deepest and most pervasive of personal and cultural values," Kluckhohn observes, "are only partially or occasionally verbalized" (ibid.: 397). When we change cultural settings, or when clients bring other cultures to us, however, we often see clearly how much culture and history shape our values.

Some view values exclusively in cultural terms; others add a cultural and historical dimension to different types of definitions, for example, to psychological or ethical definitions. Accordingly, the cultural and historical dimension of "values" can be examined whatever definition of values one employs. Because I think that dimension to be very important, in Chapters 6 and 7 I will consider some ways in which history and culture have both shaped and obscured the ethical dimensions of psychotherapy. And I will consider the history of "values" in the next section.

The origins of diversity: a brief history of the manifold meanings of "values"

It was not until 1895 that "values," in its contemporary psychological-philosophical range of meanings, first entered the English-language professional academic literature (Werkmeister 1973). And the German-language origins of those meanings were but slightly earlier. I want to review briefly the fascinating history of those meanings for two reasons: to clarify the first five types of definitions discussed above, and to make clear how some of those differences originated in attempts to answer certain challenging issues in ethical theory. Those issues (which we still face today) include the basis of goodness and moral obligation, the nature of human beings, and ethical knowledge, including the relationship of science and ethics.

Darwin provoked the crisis that gave rise to the use of "values" in its present psychological-philosophical range of meanings. Before Darwin, many concerned with the intellectual basis for ethics (including religious, non-religious, and anti-religious advocates of Enlightenment ideals and opponents of those ideals) based ethics on the distinctiveness of human beings. Kant, for example, accepted scientific efforts to understand nature (e.g. in the realm of physics – J. P. Johnson 1967), but did not apply the causal approaches used in such scientific explanations to key aspects of human beings, whom he saw as unique. He tried to recover the integrity of morality from certain Enlightenment efforts he thought did not do justice to morality, focusing on aspects of motivation he thought central to it. Of relevance to "values," moral motivation meant being free and "a radical break from nature" (Taylor 1989: 382). Taylor notes as especially important that "Kant explicitly insists that morality can't be founded in nature or in anything outside the rational human will" (ibid.: 364).

In his theory of evolution, Darwin challenged the claims by Kant and others that human beings are distinct. In Taylor's words, "natural science" was introduced "into the very depths of [the] inner nature" of persons (Taylor 1989: 416). Persons, once considered beyond the ken of science, were no longer.

Nineteenth-century continental ethicists thus faced a major dilemma, which Schacht described in these terms:

> Their fundamental task was to find some new way of understanding the nature and place of morality in human life, given that it can no longer be supposed either to consist of some set of divine commandments or to have a strictly rational basis and derivation. They further sought to discover some other basis and warrant for morality.
>
> (Schacht 1991: 516)

Two responses to that dilemma – by the German value theorists and by Nietzsche – are vitally important in the development of different meanings of "values." I discuss them because, as Kockelmans notes, "Through the work of [the German value theorist] Lotze and Nietzsche, the notion of value became an essential element of many philosophical theories, particularly in the domain of ethics" (Kockelmans 1991: 524). And from philosophy, "values" entered psychology.

The German value theorists sought to combine the evaluative problems in economics, aesthetics, ethics, and religion into one central problem, that of Value. Their goal was to understand the nature of Value in general so solutions to the evaluative (values) problems in those fields could be discovered (Rescher 1969; Schacht 1991; Werkmeister 1970). To accomplish that task, they borrowed a term, "values," previously used primarily in mathematics (Kockelmans 1991), economics (Kockelmans 1991; Pepper 1950; Werkmeister 1970), and aesthetics (Kockelmans 1991).

Of central importance for my purposes, the German-speaking value theorists used "values" in a way that affirmed both science and traditional ethical convictions, and also took into account Darwin's challenge to traditional accounts of morality.

The value theorists were, however, by no means unified in their answers to the common problems they addressed. The doctrine of Lotze "set up a dualism of two realms, that of *fact* (or being) and that of *value*" (Rescher 1969: 50), with both included in his concept of "validity." His followers, who evinced a clear commitment to philosophical Idealism, sharply distinguished between scientific methodologies and methodologies employed in the humanities (Edel 1991; Tillich 1959).

By way of contrast, the value theorists associated with Brentano affirmed the relevance of empirical methods for understanding values. And they de-emphasized the dualism associated with Lotze's school (Rescher 1969). J. P. Johnson notes that those in Brentano's school rejected "any purely speculative or metaphysical resolution of the value question [and] demanded that the question be brought to the forum of empirical science, in particular the science of psychology" (J. P. Johnson 1967: 67). Psychology was important because these value theorists focused on the psychological processes giving rise to values: human responses (e.g. love, hate, desire, and emotions) to life experiences produce knowledge of values. (Value theorists debated about which psychological processes were most important to valuing.) These value theorists thus made two central assertions: we can pursue empirical, psychological analyses of values because human beings value (J. P. Johnson 1967; McAlister 1982). And we can make ethical claims; we can "elucidate objectively apprehensible intrinsic values" (Schroeder 1991: 529).

In other words, these German value theorists adopted a *psychological* approach to values which was broadly empirical *and* which they believed eventuated in *correct ethical* judgments. Their concept of values grew out of their commitment both to science and to ethical realism. Their ambitious, very difficult intellectual endeavor thus attempted to bridge is and ought, fact and value, description and evaluation. The tension, the "opposition of the descriptive and normative ways in value philosophy" (J. P. Johnson 1967: 70), still exists in contemporary value theory. And in the term "values."

In terms of the taxonomy of definitions of "values" I set forth earlier in this chapter, the value theorists' definition of "values" wove together psychological and ethical elements. Subsequently, of course, those threads frequently unraveled. But both those employing psychological approaches to "values" and those emphasizing ethical approaches can find in the value theorists their intellectual forebears.

In contrast to the German value theorists, Nietzsche sharply attacked both Darwin (Werkmeister 1970) and traditional morality (MacIntyre 1984). The term he shared with the value theorists, "values," played a central role both in his critique of existing morality and in the constructive alternative he proposed (Alderman 1991; Frondizi 1963). But that critique and proposal introduced new definitions of "values," definitions different from those of the value theorists.

Nietzsche rejected both religion and Enlightenment moral philosophy, arguing that they are profoundly inadequate bases for morality. He saw clearly, Johnson (1967) asserts, that:

> [existing] value ideas and judgments merely describe the conditions of their emergence and development in consciousness and function as instruments in the service of natural life and existence. They do not sustain any objective import bearing upon a metaphysical order of value and man's relation to that order.
>
> (J. P. Johnson 1967: 64)

But Nietzsche also asserted that if we adopt a scientific approach (like that of Darwin) to understand human beings, including human values, we face a major problem: "Now that the lowly origin of these values becomes known, the whole universe seems to have been transvalued and to have lost its significance" (Nietzsche 1909: 10). Consequently, "man has lost an infinite amount of *dignity*" (ibid.: 19). That, cried Nietzsche, was intolerable (Werkmeister 1970).

Nietzsche's "diagnosis" led him to a clear understanding of the philosopher's task. As Detmer interprets Nietzsche's views: "We cannot live *without* values, but we cannot live *with* the values *of the present*. Thus, we must destroy these values of the present and create new and better values for the future" (Detmer 1989: 277).

Nietzsche's use of "values" thus exhibits both a critical side ("destroy") and a constructive side ("create"). Because some people influenced by him emphasize the critical side and others emphasize the constructive, more than one definition of "values" can be traced to Nietzsche.

Nietzsche strove "to unmask false candidates for the role of the new morality" (MacIntyre 1966: 223). As critic, he vigorously attacked Christianity, the emancipation of women, democracy, socialism, Platonism, utilitarianism, traditional value standards, hedonism, and human equality (Berkowitz 1995; Werkmeister 1970). Taylor argues that it was of particular importance that Nietzsche, "taking a fateful turn against the Enlightenment, declared benevolence the ultimate obstacle to self-affirmation" (Taylor 1989: 343).

Nietzsche was a very effective critic. Indeed, MacIntyre (1984) has argued that Nietzsche definitively demolished the Enlightenment project of finding a modern, objective justification for morality:

> It was Nietzsche's historic achievement to understand more clearly than any other philosopher...not only that what purported to be appeals to objectivity were in fact expressions of subjective will, but also the nature of the problems this posed for moral philosophy.
>
> (MacIntyre 1984: 113)

Skeptical postmodernists have interpreted Nietzsche's critical side to mean that societal efforts to justify morality are, in fact, nothing but one party attempting to gain power over another. Taylor notes, for example, that the neo-Nietzscheans Foucault and Derrida focus exclusively on Nietzsche's critical side, especially "on Nietzsche's sense of the arbitrariness of interpretation, on interpretation as an imposition of power" (Taylor 1989: 488). Neo-Nietzscheans thus "deconstruct" ethical assertions, doing so in accord with their definition of "values": "a means by which the powerful impose their will on the weak," the third type of definition of "values" discussed above.

But to focus exclusively on Nietzsche's critical side is to ignore the constructive proposals he made (Berkowitz 1995). Stemming from his radical diagnosis of the human dilemma, Nietzsche's "cure," MacIntyre notes, was for individuals "to transcend the limitations of all hitherto existing systems of morality, and by a 'transvaluation of values,' to prophetically introduce a new way of life" (MacIntyre 1966: 223).

But there are at least two interpretations of what such a "transvaluation" or "revaluation" of values entails. One interpretation emphasizes the unconstrained autonomy of the individual to choose values; the second emphasizes creativity, stemming from an individual's nature, as the basis for transvalued values.

On the first understanding of Nietzsche, values are chosen. Values are not "discovered" because, as Kaufmann put it, "there is no meaning in life except the meaning man gives his life" (Kaufmann 1967: 512). If marriage was truly a value for Sandra, for example, it was only because she *chose* to value it, not because it possesses any inherent worth or goodness. Morality, for Nietzsche, is what the will of the autonomous individual heroically creates (MacIntyre 1984). Nietzsche thus understood "values" to be the free, unique, and unanalyzable creations of the individual, the heroic expressions of the human will. About those "values," neither metaphysics nor moral tradition, neither Christianity nor science, has anything to say.

The second interpretation of Nietzsche's constructive ethical proposals is subtly, yet significantly, different. The emphasis is not on the will of the autonomous individual creating new values, but on the creativity of the individual (Schacht 1991), with creativity arising from the individual's nature, not simply from his or her choices. Nietzsche thus proposed a "naturalization" of morality (Schacht), with a person's nature seen as the genesis of values. This naturalization can be seen in Nietzsche's concept, "will to power," which produces values and which Nietzsche saw as an "altogether natural inclination to exert fully one's own force or strength toward some goal" (Alderman 1991: 903).

In setting forth this vision of the best possible life for persons, creativity arising from individuals' natures, Nietzsche is proposing a normative ethics (Alderman 1991; Berkowitz 1995). On this reading of Nietzsche, both the skeptical deconstructionists who focus only on his critique of existing ethical positions, and the existentialists who think Nietzsche focused solely on individuals' choices (an interpretation in which no general conclusions about the good life can be drawn, because all persons must choose their own), overlook Nietzsche's constructive ethical vision.

In developing his normative ethics, Nietzsche drew upon older ethical traditions and developed a theory about the best life for individuals (Berkowitz 1995). In proposing these transvalued or revalued "values," Nietzsche thus appears to be using an ethical definition of the term.

But Nietzsche's is a limited and idiosyncratic theory of ethics and, hence, understanding of "values." Morality and values stem from the nature of creative human beings, and so are, in a sense, objective. But that nature is contingent. That is, the nature from which values arise is dependent on the circumstances of the individual person. As Schacht points out, Nietzsche's naturalization of morality:

> acquires an objective basis in reality, even if a contingent one, since these are matters reflecting characteristics human beings actually possess as the living creatures they are. But morality thus "naturalized" is pluralistic as well as contingent, since human beings differ significantly in their constitutions, in their ability and potential, and in what their optimal flourishing and development require.
>
> (Schacht 1991: 521)

The limited and pluralistic nature of Nietzsche's ethical perspective means his normative theory and understanding of "values" differ from those of humanistic psychologists. As discussed earlier in this chapter, Rogers and Maslow made universal claims about their vision of the good life. Perhaps in part because he was less influenced by relevant strains within Romanticism, Nietzsche did not.

Nietzsche's ethics and definition of values also contrast sharply with other naturalistic approaches to ethics and values. His emphasis on autonomy and the individual's will to power and his understanding of "nature" (including its contingent and pluralistic character) make his (idiographic) naturalistic approach to values very different from the (nomothetic) naturalistic approaches (e.g. Schwartz and Bilsky 1990) of psychological scientists who use empirical methods to uncover universal laws or structures pertaining to values. Furthermore, Nietzsche's naturalistic ethics is different from that of ethical naturalists who see evolution as the sole basis for ethics. The ethical ideals they put forth (e.g. survival and adaptation) are decidedly *not* a part of Nietzsche's richer, more strenuous vision of the good life, a vision that includes spontaneity, reinterpretation, and creativity (Werkmeister 1970).

By now the reader must wonder, "How is it that Nietzsche can be interpreted in so many ways: as a critic of traditional values, as an enthusiastic advocate of the freedom of the autonomous individual to choose entirely new values, and as a champion of values arising from the nature of individuals?" Berkowitz's observation illuminates: "Nietzsche rejects the very idea of natural or rationally intelligible ends, yet he also affirms them and cannot do without them; this pervasive tension both binds his thought together and tears it apart" (Berkowitz 1995: 4). Depending on which strand of Nietzsche one focuses upon, then, his ethical stance and definition of values will appear to vary.

These tensions in Nietzsche's thought have left us a rich legacy of definitions of "values" that originated in his writings. From Nietzsche's critical side comes a definition of "values" as masked attempts by one party to gain hegemony over others, as a means by which the powerful impose their will on the weak. And, depending on how the "transvalued" values of his constructive side are interpreted, "values" can mean either the choices of an autonomous, meaning-creating individual, or the creative act of a person attuned to his or her individual nature. Nietzsche emphasized all three in his provocative philosophy. But all three types of definition have clearly influenced some psychologists (and clients) in their uses of "values"; all three types differ significantly both from the definitions of those who measure "values" with psychometrically adequate psychological tests and from the definitions of many of those who engage in philosophically sophisticated theoretical ethics regarding values.

It would appear that others have pried apart what Nietzsche tried (with but limited success) to hold together in his philosophy. In this regard, he is like the other source of our current range of psychological-philosophical uses of "values," the German value theorists. Both introduced "values" and gave the term new sets of meanings as part of complex, ambitious efforts to solve some fundamental problems of ethical theory, psychology, and philosophy. Those who use "values" in one of the senses they did may well be adopting, in part, the ethical theory for which that definition of "values" was first developed.

Although Americans did not find the intellectual problems Darwinism posed for ethics as compelling as did the German value theorists and Nietzsche, the new uses of "values" caught on. Munsterberg, a German value theorist in the school of Lotze, brought the term to the US from Germany (Perry 1954; Rescher 1969; Tillich 1959) after his arrival at Harvard in 1892 as successor to William James. Although his was a decidedly idealistic and dualistic understanding of values, American psychologists and philosophers soon began to employ the term in some of its other uses.

The American use of the European heritage of value theory was selective. Psychologists focused on the valuing process, on values defined psychologically. And empirical methods seemed well suited to understand those "values." And so, by 1913, Henderson discussed a "Scale of Values," which included a distinction between "moral, intellectual, social, economic, taste, and health values" (Brown 1914: 59). But what became the Allport–Vernon–Lindzey Study of Values gave the empirical measurement of values its greatest impetus. Allport (1967), who was clearly concerned with both psychological and ethical issues, based his test on six dimensions of values set forth by Spranger, with whom he had studied in Europe. Those who take the self-administered test, long one of the major psychometric instruments measuring values (Braithwaite and Scott 1991), indicate their relative preference for items. This permits the classification of people in terms of Spranger's six types of "values" or "interests": theoretical, economic, aesthetic, social, political, and religious (Vernon and Allport 1931). Despite

Allport's interest in ethics, the test does not ask what respondents *should* be interested in or prefer, but only what they *do* prefer. The test thus employs a strictly psychological definition of "values," and fails to tap into the ethical dimension of "values." In addition, the test does not address "the ordering of the six categories of value in respect to their ethical worth" (Vernon and Allport 1931: 232), an explicitly ethical task that Spranger (1928) tackled.

In the early part of the twentieth-century, then, American social scientists substantially deviated from the attempts of the early value theorists to ground ethics (along with aesthetics, economics, and religion) in values, and to address the objectivity of the valuing process which produces such values. The Americans also deviated from the concerns that led Nietzsche to use "values" in a new set of ways. Psychologists no longer addressed ethical issues – what is good, right, virtuous, and valuable – when the word "values" was used. It was, of course, often possible to address those issues *and* to measure values as psychologists did. But that rarely occurs, and the uses of the term are now very fuzzy indeed.

Reviews of the psychological literature on values (Braithwaite and Scott 1991; Levitin 1973; Tisdale 1961; Wilson and Nye 1966) reveal that a wide variety of psychological approaches have been adopted, with different investigators focusing on different psychological processes or different aspects of behavior. Braithwaite and Scott noted that few of the tests of values they reviewed "either provide justification for focusing on particular facets of the value domain or involve systematic sampling of items to represent these facts" (Braithwaite and Scott 1991: 664). Psychological approaches to values thus range from approaches closely related to economic approaches (e.g. Fischhoff 1991; Kahneman and Tversky 1984) to approaches emphasizing the role of culture and individuals in creating and destroying values (e.g. B. Schwartz 1990).

Although many of the psychologists who adopted empirical approaches hoped thereby to sidestep the philosophical issues that spawned the new uses of "values," Edel points out that the concept did not become clarified through those approaches: "What happened was simply that the different interpretations that had characterized the general theory of value in philosophy now reappeared in the usage of the social scientists" (Edel 1988: 27). Ethical theory and associated philosophical issues thus remained in the picture, albeit beneath the surface of psychologists' empirical work on values.

Humanistic psychologists developed, or rather, revivified and gave some new twists to, a set of definitions of "values" with deep roots in Western philosophy, especially in Nietzsche and Romantic thought (Browning 1987; Taylor 1989; Wallach and Wallach 1983). They focused on a person's freedom to choose values and on values as the products of one's true self or inner nature, on values as the products of Maslow's self-actualizing tendency or of Rogers' organismic valuing process. Because of the presumed origin of such values – the experiencing of the individual subject – empirical tests of such "values" were rare. Indeed, adoption of this understanding of "values" may be why noted therapy researcher Hans Strupp lamented, "We don't know how to research the problem" of values in therapy (Strupp 1980: 397).

In summary, several themes have emerged in this brief review of the use of "values" in the US:

1   A move toward a descriptive, empirical, psychological approach to values in academic psychology and a concomitant, inconsistent move away from the classical concerns of ethics and from ethical definitions of "values." Psychologists thus tend to use psychological definitions.
2   Definitions of values proliferated: as psychologists have studied various behaviors and psychological processes, each purportedly "getting at" what values are "really" all about, new definitions have appeared.
3   The explicit, extensive philosophical reflections of the German value theorists and Nietzsche receded into the background, giving way to implicit ethical theories and the more limited (and often implicit) meta-physical commitments (and the occasional denials of any metaphysical commitments) characteristic of the American pragmatic and empirical traditions.
4   Humanistic and existential psychologists retrieved elements of Nietzschean and Romantic thought in developing concepts of "values" focusing on individual choice and on the origin of values within the subjective experiencing of persons.

Two final developments round out the history of the taxonomy of values: postmodernists retrieved the critical side of Nietzsche and exhibited suspicion of any ethical use of "values." And cultural anthropologists, cross-cultural psychologists, and greater sensitivity to ethnic and other minorities have produced greater attention to values as cultural and historical phenomena.

Because of these developments, "values" is used in a wide variety of ways. And so when a client or researcher uses the term, an essential first step is to clarify the particular definition of "value" intended.

Values in context

To understand Sandra's value, "a good marriage," or to understand the value of any client, it often helps to know more than the definition of "value": we need to know the context of that value. And that is true however "value" is defined, and whether one employs traditional empirical methodologies or a hermeneutic approach (Walsh 1995). In a discussion of professional ethics, Meara, Schmidt, and Day stress context in even stronger terms: "Espousing values without awareness of context is usually unproductive and unethical" (1996: 32).

Several dimensions of a value's context may be relevant: the context of other values, the context of the concrete situation in which the value is expressed, the clinical context, the cultural context, the context of ethical theory, and so forth. The context that helps us best understand a particular value will vary, of course, with *why* we want to understand it.

Situating a particular value in the context of a person's other values is often very beneficial. For instance, it is more helpful to know "Sandra values marriage more than she values autonomy" than to know only that she "values marriage." Recognizing this, researchers have been concerned in tests of values with the relationships among values (e.g. Rokeach 1973; S. H. Schwartz 1992). And Prilleltensky (1997) argues that a balance among the values endorsed by psychologists is critical. A commitment to autonomy, for example, is ideally concomitant with a commitment to social justice.

It has been suggested that "the concrete context of value application" may also deserve attention (Schwartz and Bilsky 1990: 889) . Sandra may endorse "independence" on a test of values, but in the concrete settings of work and home she may exhibit dependence. Indeed, in their review of tests of values, Braithwaite and Scott (1991) noted that values (defined psychologically) are likely to influence the behavior of *some* individuals in *some* situations, but not of other individuals or in other situations. Accordingly, they urged researchers to explore "the circumstances in which values are useful in explaining human behavior" (Braithwaite and Scott 1991: 746). And by 1996, Seligman and Katz reported several studies converging on a single finding: individuals may construct different value systems in different situations rather than applying one abstract value system to all situations. That is, as the context changes, individuals' value systems may change.

The context of the clinical setting may be particularly important. In a review of the role of values in therapy, Consoli and Beutler (1996) urged researchers to examine value issues that arise in actual therapy cases (e.g. value issues related to divorce). The therapist's background may be an especially important element in the clinical context. If Sandra's therapist has worked exclusively with battered women for twenty years, had negative experiences as a child with religion and marriage, views blacks and women as helpless victims of an oppressive, Euro-centric patriarchy, and has little experience of a healthy marriage, the role in therapy of Sandra's value, "a good marriage," would likely be quite different than if her therapist had parents who had had a good marriage, is herself in a healthy marriage, sees black women as unusually strong and capable, and has deep spiritual roots. Because those two therapists would be likely to understand Sandra's commitment to a good marriage in very different ways, the role of Sandra's values in their therapy with her is likely to be very different. But the client's background is also an important element of the clinical context. If a client has a history of enmeshed relationships, the value of independence may be a very important goal in therapy. But if the client is unable to form lasting intimate relationships, the importance of the value of independence may need to diminish in the client's life, and that of intimate relationships and sustained love increase. The role in therapy of the value of independence will thus vary as the clinical context varies.

In addition, the cultural context of a particular value, although often difficult to detect, can be very important. Cultural anthropologists and others have documented differences among the values held by those in different cultures (again, no matter how values are defined) and in the meaning ascribed to particular values. For example, Schwartz and Bilsky, using empirical measures of values, have found "numerous possible differences in the meaning of specific values as a function of cultural context, though perhaps fewer than one might expect" (Schwartz and Bilsky 1990: 889).

Still other dimensions of a value's context might be considered important: understanding a value in the context of a person's overall psychological functioning (McClure and Tyler 1967; Strupp 1980), in the context of the person's community, in the context of the person's biological nature ("embodied ethics"), and in the context of the natural environment (the concern of environmental ethics).

Finally, an individual's values can be understood within the context of a particular ethical theory. In contrast to some modern ethical theories that see values as belonging within the minds of individuals, Taylor notes that other ethical theories hold that:

> ideas and valuations are...located in the world, and not just in the subjects....True knowledge, true valuation is not exclusively located in the subject. In a sense, one might say that their paradigm location is in reality; correct human knowledge and valuation comes from our connecting ourselves rightly to the significance things already have ontically.
>
> (Taylor 1989: 186)

On that account, then, values ought not be sundered from the context of broader ethical considerations.

But making that assertion brings back the problem of the plethora of definitions of values, a problem to which I now return.

The problem of multiple definitions of values: a proposed working solution

In attempting to make sense of diverse understandings of "values," I face an interesting dilemma: *all* the definitions discussed seem legitimate, at least in some circumstances. Sandra's values, for example, clearly involve psycho-logical processes. And so, psychological definitions and psychological research methodologies (whether quantitative or qualitative) seem valid. Furthermore, most would agree that Sandra's value, "Rape is wrong," refers to something that really is wrong: rape. And so ethical definitions seem valid, although the nature and scope of that validity is widely disputed. Furthermore, it is quite possible that some people in Sandra's life have used "values" to impose their will on her. And most therapists would argue for the importance of "choice" in Sandra's adoption of values and endorse her selection of values that are consistent with "who she really is" (i.e. with her nature). And, finally, many would acknowledge a cultural and historical component to her values.

Given that variety of apparently valid uses of "values," how do we use the term "values" to understand the ethical dimensions of psychotherapy? I want to mention several problematic approaches to the problem of definition before turning to one I think more promising.

Denying that the term is used in very different ways will not solve the problem. Nor will failing to be clear about one's definition. Using the term in inconsistent ways is particularly problematic, especially using "values" psychologically but drawing from it conclusions that are ethical. For example, "My empirical study of values suggests we *should....*" As I will discuss in the final section of this chapter and in Chapter 6, employing empirical methods and psychological definitions of values can make impor-tant contributions to our understanding of the ethical dimensions of psychotherapy. But doing so requires using "values" in a consistent way and exhibiting due regard to the complexities of the science–ethics relationship.

Handy (1969, 1970) and P. Rosenthal (1984) suggested that, given its many uses, "values" should be avoided altogether. But since clients and researchers are likely to continue to use it in a variety of ways, that "solu-tion" seems unrealistic. And avoiding "values" will not solve the psychological and philosophical problems addressed under the heading of "values."

Others faced with the variety of definitions stipulate one definition as best (Gaus 1990) and may use that definition exclusively, rejecting all others. A pragmatic reason for not adopting that approach is that other people – clients, therapists, researchers, and so forth – will likely continue to use "values" as diversely as ever. Whatever the virtues of any particular defi-nition, I am not sanguine it would escape the fate of the best efforts of many others: the definition is politely acknowledged, then ignored or added to the growing list of extant definitions. But I am not in favor of the "single defi-nition" solution for another reason: I don't think there is one "correct" definition of the term. As discussed above, more than one definition possesses some validity.

But accepting all definitions can create its own set of problems. Since those definitions entail decidedly different intellectual claims concerning "values," accepting all definitions can mean accepting contradictory claims. But there is another way to look at the validity of those definitions: *definitions of "values" are valid, not in general, but to address a particular question, to solve problems in a given arena, or for some other specific purpose.* Although each definition is valid in *some* way, none is valid for *all* purposes. And so we accept different definitions, but accept each only in part.

If different definitions of values are valid for different purposes, no definition is useful for all purposes. E. M. Albert's solution is thus not helpful. Defined as "a general label for a heterogeneous class of normative factors" (Albert 1956: 221), her "values" are so abstract they are not helpful for many particular purposes. Simply listing different definitions of values is also unhelpful, unless the purpose for which each is helpful is specified.

The problems with those "solutions" point us in the direction of a better approach to the problem of diverse definitions of "values": *matching a definition of "values" with a particular purpose.* If a client uses values in a particular way or set of ways, for example, the therapist should work within that usage of "value," at least at the outset. And a researcher should employ a definition of value that is consistent with the purpose of his or her inquiry and that is clear. Clarity is important because when a definition is unclear, the term may be interpreted by people in *each* of the ways discussed in this chapter. I think it is also important to take seriously the valid points made by advocates of various uses of values, even if one does not employ their definitions. One need not become a critical postmodernist, for example, to recognize that the powerful can use the term "values" to impose their will on the weak.

Accordingly, I think it can be legitimate to employ a single definition of "values," but only if one is clear about the definition being used and if other meanings of "values" are taken into account, perhaps by using other terms for those meanings. For example, the empirical researcher who employs a psychological definition of values could address ethical or power issues using terms other than "values," such as terms like "ethical" and "power."

More than one definition can also be used. In any given instance, we should use the definition that is most apt. For example, Rescher pointed out that *some* valuings are simply a matter of taste (and thus strictly psychological) and *other* valuings pertain to what is, in reality, good. An "adequate theory of value," he asserts, "has to be prepared to take both types of valuings into account" (Rescher 1969: 56). "Values" would thus be used in a psychological sense in the first situation, but in an ethical sense in the second.

Selecting the definition of "values" that best matches the purpose of this book – understanding the ethical character of therapy – is no easy task. Because so many of its uses are non-ethical and because the variety of definitions is often confusing, I have considered minimizing use of the term and using words other than "values" to address ethical issues. Alternatively, I have considered stipulating an ethical use of the term in this book. But for three reasons, I think it better to use the term in all its uses, albeit doing so carefully.

First, as noted above, people will continue to use and interpret "values" in its full range of meanings whatever strategy I employ. And so it is better to explicitly use "values" in its various meanings and be clear about my uses of the term in particular situations.

Second, the varying definitions of "values" reflect, and may in part stem from, unresolved issues in the field of ethics in the West. As Edel (1988) noted, social scientists picked up uses of the term that originated in the philosophical debates of value theory and ethics. Using the term in ways that make clear its varied meanings makes its linkages to those philosophical issues more clear.

Finally, different uses of "values" contribute to our understanding of the ethical dimensions of psychotherapy in different ways. Definitions of values that are *non*-ethical can help us learn about the *ethical* dimensions of psychotherapy. Understanding "values" as a means by which the powerful impose their will on the weak, for example, can shed light on therapists imposing their values on clients, an issue that is clearly ethical in nature. And, as the following section should make clear, strictly psychological definitions of values can, when used in empirical investigations, produce valuable insights into the ethical character of therapy.

The ethical relevance of psychological research on values in psychotherapy

D. Rosenthal (1955) pioneered empirical research on the role of values in therapy. Although employing psychological definitions of values, this research is relevant to understanding the ethical character of therapy. Rosenthal found that client values (moral values relevant to psychological conflicts that are commonly present in therapy) moved in the direction of therapist values in successful therapy. No such movement was found in unsuccessful therapy or with nonmoral values.

Subsequent research (Beutler *et al.* 1994; Consoli and Beutler 1996; T. A. Kelly 1990; Tjeltveit 1986) has confirmed yet also qualified that finding. It appears that clients sometimes but not always adopt therapist values, with the extent of the influence depending on the type of values measured, the similarity of therapist and client values at the beginning of therapy, and other factors. This finding, that psychotherapy is not value-free, raises professional ethical questions about the appropriateness of therapists converting clients to their own values (Tjeltveit 1986) and gives credence to neo-Nietzscheans' suspicions about the role of "values" in the coercive influence of the powerful on the weak. Furthermore, if clients do adopt therapist values, therapists need to think clearly about which values it is *best* (ideal) for clients to adopt. Or, perhaps, which values they *should* adopt.

The empirical finding that therapists sometimes influence client values (defined psychologically) thus raises issues of values (defined ethically) that get to the heart of the ethical dimension of psychotherapy.

A related research question addresses the relationship between therapy outcome and values, including the relationship between therapy outcome and (1) the initial similarity of therapist values and client values, (2) particular therapist values, (3) therapist influence on client values, and (4) client perception of therapist influence on their values. Again, empirical findings have been mixed. Therapy outcome is apparently associated with a complex pattern of initial similarity and dissimilarity of values. And findings vary with different measurements of values and with other factors not yet isolated (Beutler and Bergan 1991; Beutler *et al.* 1994; Consoli and Beutler 1996; Kelly and Strupp 1992). The promise, however, is to match therapist and client values to improve therapy outcome.

Although that line of research may appear to be purely empirical, it also raises important ethical questions. Although rarely thought of in these terms, "positive therapy outcome," the good end toward which therapy aims, is an *ethical* concept. That is, it is a nonmoral good, or a "value," defined ethically. To the extent values (defined psychologically) enter the therapeutic relationship in ways that produce successful therapy, then, that nonmoral end, that good outcome, is of great ethical interest because it pertains to human flourishing, to the good life for human beings.

Beutler, Machado, and Neufeldt also noted that researchers have examined the relationship between the values of therapists and clients. Some substantial differences were uncovered. They noted that, "These differences, coupled with the potential power that therapists have over clients, underline the need to evaluate the roles of therapist values on therapy outcome" (Beutler, Machado, and Neufeldt 1994: 240). The ethical dimension of that "evaluation" would be of great interest to those concerned about the ethical character of therapy.

Empirical researchers have also examined therapist values, especially mental health values. Jensen and Bergin (1988) and E. W. Kelly (1995a) found considerable agreement among therapists concerning values (defined psychologically) that pertain to mental health and therapy, but some differences were found in the areas of sex, religion, and materialistic self-advancement. While those findings do not resolve the ethical question of which values *should* pertain to mental health and therapy (therapists could be mistaken), areas of both value consensus and value divergence among therapists warrant close attention. Areas of divergence may be of particular ethical interest, since they may stem from differences among therapists at the level of underlying ethical theory.

The focus on mental health values by Consoli (1996), Consoli and Beutler

(1996), Jensen and Bergin (1988) and E. W. Kelly (1995a) illustrates the recent research emphasis on specific values or particular types of values. Mental health values have been emphasized for two reasons: therapy more appropriately influences them alone (and not moral or other types of values) (Hartmann 1960; Strupp 1980) and mental health values may more likely be influenced in therapy than other types of values. But distinguishing them conceptually from moral or religious values has proved difficult. And there is some empirical evidence that certain types of mental health values vary with certain measures of religiousness in samples of therapists (Jensen and Bergin 1988) and non-therapists (Tjeltveit *et al.* 1996). This suggests that differences in values, even mental health values, may stem from underlying convictions at a fundamental intellectual level, the level of ethical theory.

Conclusion

Saying that "a good marriage" is one of Sandra's "values" can be interpreted in a wide variety of ways. It is essential that those seeking to understand the ethical dimensions of therapy select a definition carefully, in accord with their purposes, and be clear about how they are using it. And when we understand the various ways in which others use the term, we can derive greater benefit from the empirical research and other literature on the role of values in therapy.

But whether we use ethical or non-ethical definitions of "values" to better understand the ethical character of therapy, the task is very difficult. Some of this difficulty stems, I think, from differences in ethical theory that underlie various uses of values. And some of the difficulty stems from the intellectual and social contexts in which such ethical inquiry (and all clinical practice) inescapably takes place, contexts that have shaped (and shape) how we think ethically. It is to those contexts that I now turn.

Part III

Ethical dimensions of the contexts of psychotherapy

6

The intellectual contexts of psychotherapy
Ethics and science

When we think about psychotherapy, we often begin with a fifty-minute hour. A client and therapist sit down. Taking a deep breath, the client commences: "Mom and Dad called last night...."

From the typical ways of thinking about such sessions – in supervisory sessions, case conferences, and quiet, self-reflective moments – rich and vital understandings of therapy develop. In Chapters 6 and 7 I pursue a different approach: exploring psychotherapy's sociohistorical contexts to see how those contexts have both shaped and obscured the ethical character of therapy. Orlinsky (1989), MacIntyre (1984), feminist bioethicists (e.g. Sherwin 1992), and others have stressed the importance of such contexts in general; Cushman (1992, 1995), Fancher (1995), Hale (1971, 1995), Kirschner (1996, 1997), Pilgrim and Treacher (1992), and L. A. Sass (1988) have emphasized the importance of such contexts for understanding psychotherapy in particular.

I will describe how four different contexts have formed, and form, the ethical dimensions of psychotherapy. These contexts often influence therapy in ways that are "so pervasive as to be nearly invisible" (L. A. Sass 1988: 248). I will also try to make more visible what is "nearly invisible" by suggesting new ways to understand those contexts. For example, psychology's positivistic heritage leads some to assume that ethical reflection is meaningless. And so, desiring to be scientific, many therapists do not engage in ethical reflection. But alternative understandings of science, ethics, and their relationship permit the pursuit of *both* science *and* ethics in exploring the ethical character of therapy.

I will begin with two of psychotherapy's intellectual contexts – ethics and science – before turning in Chapter 7 to two of its social contexts – clinical practice and business. Exploring each context should help us to gain insight into the ethical aspects of psychotherapy and understand why it is so difficult for therapists to see, acknowledge, and think about those aspects. In this chapter, I will first address how key Western values (defined ethically) make substantive ethical reflection about values difficult, then I will address psychotherapy's scientific context.

The ethical critique of ethics

Observing that ethical standards cause problems for people, some philosophers, psychotherapy theorists, and psychotherapists have vigorously challenged those standards. These critiques of ethics are deeply ironic, however, because they often, and perhaps always, draw upon *ethical* sources. They are, in other words, ethical critiques of ethics.

In one type of ethical affirmation, some ways of living are seen as good, or higher, more good, or better than others. In his brilliant monograph on the making of the modern identity, Taylor describes how "basic goods" for which human beings strive, goods like freedom and altruism, move and motivate human beings. He then documents the history of how these "basic goods" have driven many of their adherents to repudiate "all such goods" in the West. And so, continues Taylor, "they are caught in a strange pragmatic contradiction, whereby the very goods which move them push them to deny or denature all such goods" (Taylor 1989: 88). And that denial of any goodness profoundly challenges any ethical claim that some ways of living are better ("more good"; higher) than others.

The Protestant Reformation, argues Taylor, provided a major impetus to that challenge. Responding to a hierarchical social milieu in which the "higher calling" of being a priest, monk, or nun was viewed as qualitatively superior to ("more good" than) other ways of living, the renegade priest Martin Luther proclaimed the goodness of such "common" life activities as love and work. He demonstrated this behaviorally by marrying Katherine von Bora, a nun. Through the Reformation, the lives of ordinary people were affirmed and seen as worthy of equal respect with those having allegedly higher religious callings.

Another important root of the ethical critique of ethics was the intellectual and political climate in Germany in the nineteenth century, the climate in which Freud came to intellectual maturity. Moral philosophers of that era, notes MacIntyre (1966), came to "see the moral as something they are bound to condemn" (MacIntyre 1966: 220).

Nietzsche launched what was probably the most vigorous philosophical attack on ethical pretensions. Proudly proclaiming himself "an immoralist," Nietzsche ridiculed ethical perspectives claimed to be superior or higher than others. This Nietzschean "leveling" of ethical positions, of positions that claimed to occupy higher moral ground than others, is deeply ironic, however: Nietzsche's challenge was based on convictions of his own that were deeply ethical (Schacht 1991): he valued especially the creative freedom of the individual to produce transvalued values. This tension in Nietzsche is neatly captured in the subtitle of Berkowitz's 1995 work *Nietzsche: The Ethics of an Immoralist*. Nietzsche's attack on morality, reflected in his claim to be an immoralist, was joined with his ethical vision, which served as a basis both for his critique of ethics and for his constructive ethical position.

Nietzschean leveling has been extended to a variety of hierarchical order-ings. The civil rights, feminist, and gay rights movements have challenged the supposedly "higher" nature of Caucasian heterosexual males. As noted above, neo-Nietzschean skeptical postmodernists have pushed the critical side of Nietzsche even further, seeing all ethical claims to be "imposed order" (Taylor 1989: 102). As a result of this ongoing attack on ethical claims, Joe Klein, in a piece of contemporary cultural analysis, noted that "it became illiberal...even to make moral judgments" (Klein 1992: 19).

The practice of psychotherapy contrasts sharply with such strong attacks on ethics; psychotherapists accept some claims to goodness and reject the opinion that no particular human goal or quality is higher than any other. They do so because intrinsic to psychotherapy is the conviction that some ways of living are better than others, are "higher" or "more good." A person goes to therapy because they want a *better* way of living; the therapist helps the client reach that (good) goal. Psychotherapy thus assumes that all ways of living are not equal: mental health is better than mental illness, no symp-toms is better than many, adaptive behavior better than maladaptive, insight than ignorance, authenticity than inauthenticity, self-actualization better than phoniness, mediocrity, and suffering.

Cognizant of the problems of attacking *all* ethical principles, some have launched a moderated attack on ethics. In contrast to an ethical position that denies *any* good and rejects *all* claims that certain goals are better than others, this alternative ethical position affirms individual autonomy, which is seen as the sole human good. Autonomy thus understood is the good, suggests Taylor (1989), that provides the concealed motivation of the neo-Nietzscheans. From this basis, all other ethical claims are attacked, in part because making ethical distinctions has led throughout history to decreases in freedom. Because the "values" of the powerful or the majority have too often been imposed on the powerless or the minority, some passionately propose that, with the one exception of freedom, we avoid entirely making ethical distinctions, avoid discussing what is good, ultimately good, right, and virtuous, lest freedom again be curtailed. The one remaining good: to preserve freedom (or, using trendier terms, to "liberate" people or be "eman-cipatory").

Freedom as the sole good, and the individualism to which it is often tied, has been subject to severe critique from other ethical perspectives (e.g. Bellah *et al.* 1985; Guignon 1993; Sampson 1993; Wallach and Wallach 1983). Critics have challenged the vagueness of "freedom," the failure of users to specify what people are supposed to be free *for*, advocates' unac-knowledged, *de facto* reliance upon richer ethical traditions (Taylor 1989), and the failure to balance freedom with other ethical ideals, such as commit-ment, justice, truthfulness, and community (Doherty 1995; see Prilleltensky 1997).

Balancing ideals related to therapy will be discussed further in Chapter 9.

My central point here is that philosophers have critiqued all ethical reflection, often doing so on the basis of covert ethical stances. These ethical critiques of ethics warrant careful attention: some ethical positions are indeed problematic. But the duplicity of the claim to be ethically neutral, to be without ethical sources, deserves challenge. A more accurate picture of the current reality is this: the critiques of ethics are not value-free; rather, different ethical positions are competing with one another to determine which is best.

Psychotherapy theorists have created their own variants of the ethical critique of ethics. They describe how making ethical distinctions and judgments leads to emotional disturbance, or is evidence of a lack of mental health. Freud, for example, functioned at times as an unabashed moral critic. Wallace points out that Freud was "positively acerbic toward the 'golden rule'", for example, claiming it "was not only psychologically unworkable and maladaptive for the individual, but that it cheapened the love for family and friends" (Wallace 1986: 99, 100). Indeed, "as early as 1900 Freud was using psychogenetics as an instrument to demolish man's moral pretensions" (ibid.: 90). But Freud's was a balanced ethical critique, for he realized the importance to civilization of moral rules and self-restraint (Wallace 1986; Wallach and Wallach 1983) and saw the suspension of moral rules in psychoanalysis as a temporary expedient to help clients develop insight and make positive changes. Neo-Freudians such as Wilhelm Reich (Wallace 1986), Erich Fromm, and Karen Horney (Wallach and Wallach 1983), however, viewed moral injunctions in more consistently negative terms. Horney's (1950) memorable phrase, "the tyranny of shoulds," for instance, emphasizes the inexorably maladaptive consequences of ethical principles in the life of the neurotic, admitting no positive role for them.

For Carl Rogers, ethical standards become "conditions of worth" that prevent persons from functioning fully. And so he asserted that healthy clients move "away from 'oughts'" (Rogers 1961: 168), basing that claim, of course, on his ideas about "the good life."

And Ellis regularly addresses ethics in negative terms such as "absolutistic, dogmatic shoulds, oughts, and musts" (Ellis 1987a: 121). High moral standards are irrational and cause emotional disturbance. Ellis critiques all strong ethical convictions. He lumps together silly "shoulds" (e.g. "I should be able to make my partner deliriously happy at all times") and more substantive shoulds (e.g. the repeated incest offender's, "I should not rape my 6-year-old niece"). He then critiques all strongly held "shoulds" as absolutistic and irrational. The source of his critique: his deeply held ethical convictions about the best ("most rational") way for human beings to live. Similarly, Burns lists "SHOULD STATEMENTS" as a type of cognitive distortion (Burns 1980: 40). In the hands of clients, of course, such attacks on "shoulds" are often translated into the self-contradictory, "Oh, that's right. I shouldn't use 'shoulds.'"

Because of this therapeutic/ethical critique of ethics, Doherty concluded that, when "egocentric therapeutic morality" is at work, "every expression of obligation is unhealthy until proven otherwise" (Doherty 1995: 29). And Bellah, Madsen, Sullivan, Swidler, and Tipton note that "the therapeutic view...not only refuses to take a moral stand, it actively distrusts 'morality' " (Bellah *et al*. 1985: 129).

But it is far easier to identify this therapeutic animus against morality than to recognize its ethical origin. One source: the aspiration of most therapists to be value-free. As Beutler notes:

> Our mentors have implied, if not overtly said, that if it only were possible surgically to remove the therapist's values, he or she would be a more effective clinician. In the greatest of therapeutic paradoxes, a valueless clinician is valued.
>
> (Beutler 1989: 4)

Therapists who make ethical assertions while aspiring to such value-freedom must therefore hide their ethical stances. And, when critiquing the ethical positions of others, they must disguise the ethical bases of those critiques. At times this deception is intentional; more often, I suspect, therapists' ethical stances become hidden even to themselves.

Many therapists who have never read the philosophers just discussed, or who do not share all the views of those therapy theoreticians, share their deep suspicion of ethics. They have no special need for the observations of those philosophers and theorists: the victims of overly harsh and rigid moral standards come daily to therapy, seeking assistance for problems often made worse, at least in part, by their own moral standards. Clients' deontic words, "obligation," "ought," and "duty," produce human pain, and so therapists sometimes flinch at the thought of using them. The human cost seems too high. An elegant solution to eliminating a client's pain appears evident: eliminate the "shoulds" that cause the pain.

But it is not just the deontic moral "shoulds" that seem troublesome. *Any* ideal, any notion of human flourishing, any concept of virtue can produce pain in clients. For if a focus on obligation can produce guilt, a focus on flaws of character or virtue can produce shame (Fossum and Mason 1986; G. Kaufman 1992, 1996). Both duty and virtue, both deontic and aretaic judgments, thus seem objectionable: they harm people.

This ethical critique of ethics stems from a fundamental moral conviction, "we should avoid harm," and its corollary, "all that causes harm is to be eschewed." Although some therapists acknowledge that ethics is in some sense valid, and that harm stems from *misuses* or psychopathological *distortions* of ethics, many see ethics itself as the cause of client problems. The practical effect of the belief that ethics harms people is that ethical convictions – of clients and therapists – are pushed underground.

The ethical convictions underlying the belief that it is good to minimize harm are complex, however, because one person's harm is another's benefit. Some see increased assertiveness, for example, as boon, but others as bane. Likewise with loss of religious faith. This is because an understanding of what is harmful rests on some broad ethical vision of what is good and right: harm is what deprives a person of what is good or right. In the absence of consensus about what is good and right, there will not be agreement about what is harmful.

Taylor (1989) suggests that four fundamental moral ideas are central to the modern identity: reducing suffering, freedom, equality, and universal justice. The first three have been used – by philosophers, psychotherapy theorists, and therapists – to critique particular ethical positions and some problematic ways people use ethics. Those ideas have therefore contributed to a decline in explicit ethical reflection in the West, though they have not led to the absence of ideas about what is good, right, or virtuous, of ideas that guide behavior and shape character, of ideas used to critique ethics.

The problems identified by the ethical critique of ethics are real: ethics has been used to harm people and to deprive them of freedom and equality. Some conclude that ethics should therefore be rejected. But an alternative is readily available: uses of ethics that do not harm people or deprive them of freedom and equality. Critiques of ethics can be very valuable. But they will become more valuable when the ethical convictions used to critique ethics and inform psychotherapy, convictions now largely implicit, become explicit.

The scientific context

"Psychotherapy should be based on science." That pivotal assumption (along with other aspects of the scientific context of psychotherapy) shapes the ethical dimensions of psychotherapy, yet also obscures them.

Psychologists (Freedheim 1992; Routh 1994), psychiatrists (cf. Karasu 1980), and other mental health professionals (Talley et al. 1994) have long aspired to base the practice of psychotherapy on science (e.g. Gesell et al. 1919). Indeed, McFall asserted that "there is only one legitimate form of clinical psychology: grounded in science, practiced by scientists, and held accountable to the rigorous standards of scientific evidence" (McFall 1991: 79; see Sechrest 1992; Hayes et al. 1995; Meehl 1997).

Such strong assertions about the proper relationship between science and practice generate spirited attack and passionate defense (see Kazdin 1996). But I want to focus here, not on that broader debate, but on the relevance of science, and the scientific context, for the *ethical* dimensions of therapy.

"Science answers scientific questions, but not those that are *ethical*," some assert, "because science is an objective, 'value-free,' ethically neutral endeavor." Others claim that science *does* contribute to ethics by uncovering ethically relevant facts. I address that dispute in this section, considering whether, or in what ways, science, and certain ways of thinking about science, contribute to the ethical dimensions of therapy.

But a second issue must also be addressed. Because I believe that science, appropriately conducted and understood, does contribute in very important ways to the ethical dimensions of therapy (and to our understanding of them), I will turn in the last part of the chapter to this question: to understand well the ethical dimensions of psychotherapy, should we rely upon science alone, or upon science *in conjunction with* ethics?

Science's contribution to the ethical dimensions of psychotherapy

I want to begin by reviewing briefly some history that bears directly on the relevance of science for the ethical dimensions of therapy. But first, a caveat: as Kendler noted, "the relationship between psychology and ethics depends on the societal meaning that is assigned to each term" (Kendler 1993: 1046). And so all arguments, including mine, depend on the meanings given to those terms. People holding understandings of science and ethics different from those outlined in earlier chapters will no doubt understand their relationship differently (cf. Kitcher 1985; Midgley 1978; Singer 1981; Wright 1994).

Those who first taught psychology courses in the US would have thought it very odd to question the contribution of psychology, understood as science, to ethics. Odd for two reasons: psychology was not then a science (in the contemporary sense of the word), and psychology was part of ethics.

Mental philosophy, moral philosophy, and moral science were the branches of knowledge to which psychology first belonged (Evans 1984; Leahey 1997). As such, psychology courses were first offered in the US, most likely in 1840 at Marshall College (later Franklin and Marshall College) (Evans 1984), long before the "New Psychology" of Wundt, James, and Hall (see Fay 1939; G. S. Hall 1894).

"Old Psychology" was introduced into the college curriculum in the 1800s because American colleges sought to shape the character and ethical ideals of their students. And the discipline of psychology "aimed to inculcate moral virtues" (Sexton 1978: 3). In the typical pattern, a college's curriculum culminated in a wide-ranging course in moral and mental philosophy taught to seniors, usually by the college president, who was generally a clergyman (Bryson 1932; G. S. Hall 1894; Ross 1979; Schmidt 1930). The substantial psychological content in these courses was integral to their ethical intent. In his 1870 *Lectures on Moral Science*, the president of Williams College, Mark Hopkins, succinctly articulated the importance of psychology:

What man ought to do will depend on what he is, and the circumstances in which he is placed. Mental science, or psychology, will therefore, be conditioned [that is, be foundational] for moral science....The province of psychology will...be to show what the faculties are; that of moral philosophy to show how they are to be used for the attainment of their end.

(cited in Evans 1984: 43)

And so, Leahey notes, for the Old Psychologists, "psychology was the gateway to moral knowledge and the mainspring of moral action" (Leahey 1987b: 12).

But with the transition from Old Psychology to New Psychology, psychologists sought disciplinary independence, rejected philosophical methods (and sometimes all of philosophy), and strove to be objective scientists. And so psychology and ethics divorced.

New Psychologists wanted, for a variety of reasons (O'Donnell 1985; Ross 1979), to establish psychology as an independent discipline (Bellah *et al.* 1983) and, especially, as a scientific discipline. Leahey (1987b) notes that whereas Old Psychology saw itself as subordinate to ethics, "deserving study not as an end in itself but as a means to the greater end of morality," New Psychology "wanted to establish its science as a valuable end in itself" (Leahey 1987b: 12). Many psychologists assumed this independence required severing their ties with philosophy (Camfield 1973).

Indeed, "anti-philosophical rhetoric," Toulmin and Leary note, "came to typify behavioral psychology in the United States" (Toulmin and Leary 1992: 600). And so Sexton observes, "terms like philosopher and philosophy became terms of opprobrium" (Sexton 1978: 6). And this anti-philosophical tenor was not limited to academic psychology. Lightner Witmer, the founder of clinical psychology, claimed his approach "was a protest against philosophical speculations" (Reisman 1976: 48).

But declaring independence from its philosophical parent was not the only reason psychologists moved away from addressing ethical issues. The growing specialization characteristic of the late nineteenth century (Higham 1979) also played a role. Any attempts to address ethical issues (such as those involved in psychotherapy) would, psychologists feared, dilute and confuse the identity of the nascent discipline.

The scientific aspiration to achieve objectivity and ethical neutrality, to become "value-free" (Leary 1980; Robinson 1981), was another reason psychologists stopped addressing ethical issues. That is, they assumed that, when investigating a topic, including an ethical topic, a psychologist *qua* scientist ought to remain neutral (Ross 1979). Consequently, New Psychologists "proudly cast off moral, especially religious, values in the name of science" (Leahey 1987a: 361). Again, academicians were joined by clinicians who aspired to ethical neutrality. Freud, for example, "took pains to keep clinical apart from moral evaluation" (Hartmann 1960: 17).

Psychologists' embrace of logical positivism further distanced them from overt, conscious ethical reflection: ethical assertions were now either regarded as meaningless or redefined. Consider this excerpt from a poem:

> A thought
> Is surely neither bad nor wrong
>
> Or right or good?
> No, no.
> Define
> and thus expunge
> The *ought*,
> The *should*!
> ...
> Truth's to be sought
> In *Does* and *Doesn't*.

(Skinner 1972: 348–9)

Lest there be any doubt about its meaning, B. F. Skinner exegeted his poem: "But what about the possibility that [a thought] might be right or good? No, logical positivism will take care of that. By defining our values we expunge them."

Although the logical positivist philosophy of science has fallen out of favor, many still assume the truth of its *ethical* claim: ethical assertions are cognitively meaningless. Other scholars, indifferent to that philosophical debate, focus on producing scientific knowledge. They seek facts, not values (defined ethically), from science. As Karasu noted:

> Science and ethics have been viewed as two distinct and separate entities, almost antithetical: science as descriptive, ethics as prescriptive; science as resting on validation, ethics as relying on judgment; and science as concerned solely with "what is," ethics as addressing "what ought to be."

(Karasu 1980: 1502)

And so the resistance to ethical reflection among scientifically oriented practitioners is powerfully overdetermined: psychology's desire to be an independent discipline, scientists rejecting the philosophical methods employed in ethics, the logical positivist doctrine that ethical assertions are meaningless, the desire to be objective, and a sole focus on scientific knowledge (interpreted as ethically neutral) all keep psychotherapists from overtly and consciously addressing ethical issues.

But this avoidance of explicitly ethical reflection is deeply problematic, because practitioners cannot avoid addressing ethical issues in psychotherapy. One solution to this problem is to turn to science for answers to ethical questions. And, indeed, despite the many reasons for avoiding ethical reflection and sharply distinguishing science and ethics, some nevertheless maintain that scientific findings can contribute to ethics. That is, some philosophers and some psychologists insist that:

> Although psychology is appropriately distinguished from ethics, psychotherapy's scientific context can shed light on the *ethical* dimensions of therapy. Old Psychologists were partly right: an adequate ethics requires an adequate knowledge of human beings. Since psychology's scientific methods produce such knowledge, science contributes to ethics.

Suppose that we are asked to evaluate the ethical dimensions of Dr Johnson's newly invented "Neo-Cognitive Therapy." Ethical questions we might address include: is it a "good" treatment? Is there anything "wrong" with it? Which ethical characteristics ("virtues") does it tend to produce in clients?

Science will be relevant to those ethical questions to the extent it produces facts pertinent to an ethical evaluation of "Neo-Cognitive Therapy." As Frankena asserts, "moral philosophers cannot insist too much on the importance of factual knowledge...for the solution of moral and social problems" (Frankena 1973: 13). If a carefully designed empirical study determines, for instance, that Neo-Cognitive Therapy does not reduce psychological symptoms or otherwise help clients reach the goals Dr Johnson claims for it, it is not a "good" therapy. If it consistently harms clients, it is wrong for therapists to use it with clients. And a client choosing between that and alternative therapies would find quite relevant facts about the effectiveness (and thus "goodness") of those treatments (Roth and Fonagy 1996; Nathan and Gorman 1998). And so, "description can inform prescription" (Faust and Meehl 1992: 203).

Waterman (1988) argues that scientists can contribute to ethical reflection in two ways. First, science can help evaluate claims about human nature that are relevant to ethics. For instance, Waterman adduces empirical evidence that supports the assumptions Rawls (1971) made about human nature in his theory of justice. B. Schwartz (1990) warns, however, that a scientific study of "human nature" (e.g. of human values) may, in fact, be the study of human behavior *in a given sociohistorical context*, but nothing more. And so we must exercise caution when tempted to draw universally applicable ethical conclusions from a "human nature" so transitory and culturally specific.

Second, Waterman asserts that scientists can evaluate the empirical claims contained in teleological (or consequentialist) normative theories. As discussed in Chapter 4, those theories maintain that we can best answer ethical questions by focusing on the *telos* ("end") of an act, that is, on its consequences. For instance, "It is unethical for therapists to engage in sexual relations with their clients because doing so consistently produces negative consequences: psychologically damaged clients." Science is relevant to such theories because empirical investigations promise to tell us whether purported consequences actually follow from such acts. If they do, such acts are unethical.

On the basis of such a teleological ethical theory, Imber, Glanz, Elkin, Sotsky, Boyer, and Leber (1986) asserted that "significant positive ethical values" (defined ethically) "derive from" the findings of the US National Institute of Mental Health collaborative study of treatments for depression. Likewise, Beutler and Harwood's claim that "empirical research *should* form the basis for selecting and implementing treatment" (Beutler and Harwood 1995: 89, emphasis added) rests upon a consequentialist ethical theory and scientific findings to draw its ethical conclusions. If measurable positive outcome is the end to which psychotherapy aims, we should be able, in principle, to determine empirically which form of therapy is best, or "most good." And so, other things being equal, we can determine which form of therapy we should pursue.

And so, despite a scientific context that has contributed to psychotherapists' overdetermined avoidance of ethical issues and desire to distinguish sharply between science and ethics, scientific findings are relevant to *some* ethical questions, for the reasons just discussed: the consequences of an action are often ethically relevant. And science provides us with knowledge about consequences, knowledge about which we can be reasonably confident. Science thus contributes to ethics.

Understanding psychotherapy's ethical dimensions: "science alone" or "science and ethics"

Because science can help us to address ethical issues, it is possible to make the further claim that we can, or even ought to, rely on science *alone* to address ethical questions. In this section, I want to examine that claim, along with the claims of those who acknowledge science's contributions to addressing such ethical questions but argue that we also need to use other methods, methods from ethics.

Suppose we are confronted with an ethical issue such as which therapy goal is best ("most good") for a given client, which virtues a good therapist possesses, or what obligations therapists owe their clients. Some say science alone will provide whatever meaningful answers we can obtain. Others eagerly draw upon relevant empirical findings, but also take full advantage of relevant ideas, methods, and principles from professional ethics, philosophical ethics, clinical ethics, virtue ethics, social ethics, and cultural ethics, including approaches (discussed in Chapter 4) that obtain ethical knowledge through tradition, through reason, through an explicit combination of reason and nature, through such extra-rational personal qualities as intuition or choice, through divine revelation, through relationships (including communities), or through the interpretation of narratives (e.g. in hermeneutic approaches). That is, they argue that we best answer ethical questions with a combination of science and ethics. And they thus argue that psychotherapy (as an inescapably ethical activity) should be based, not only on science, but also on ethics.

The scientific context of psychotherapy thus gives rise to an important dispute: how to best address ethical issues in psychotherapy. How we resolve that dispute has important implications for how we understand therapy, how we educate therapists, and how we think about the ideal role of therapy in society.

Science alone

Psychotherapists who strive to rely on science alone to address ethical issues can do so in several distinguishable ways. All are variants of "scientism," defined by Taylor as "the belief that the methods and procedures of natural science...suffice to establish all the truths we need to believe" (Taylor 1989: 404). Two varieties can be distinguished: philosophical scientism (the philosophy that scientific methods are the best or only way to obtain all varieties of truth, save those of logic and mathematics) and *de facto* scientism (referring to those who are, in fact, guided only by science, although they do not espouse philosophical scientism).

A bold doctrine, philosophical scientism at times extends the proper realm of science from its customary objects of inquiry (e.g. physical, biological, social, and psychological topics) to the realm of ethics (thus answering the questions posed by the German value theorists). Psychotherapists aspiring to be scientific have been among the devotees of this doctrine. As Doherty noted, "A cornerstone of all the mainstream models of psychotherapy since Freud has been the substitution of scientific and clinical ideas for moral ideas" (Doherty 1995: 9). Advocates claim the methods of science can be applied fruitfully to all topics. Indeed, McFall (1991) claimed it is possible for psychological scientists to use the same "objective" evaluations they use to determine what is "good science" to judge clinical activities.

Proponents provide a variety of arguments to justify expanding the range of science to include ethical issues. Some claim to derive ethical assertions (understood in a traditional way) from science alone; others redefine what has traditionally been labeled ethical (scientific methods are then used to investigate the redefined "ethical" phenomenon); still others (perhaps most) do both.

The attempt to build ethics on a scientific foundation is not new. J. B. Watson (1924), "considered behaviorism a foundation for all future experimental ethics" (Dukes 1955: 24). And Clark Hull argued that questions of moral behavior (Ash 1992) and value (Hull 1944) could be addressed through empirical methods. Cattell ambitiously titled his 1972 book *A New Morality From Science*. And Nagy claimed an "empirical basis" as "the foundation" of the revision of the American Psychological Association's code of ethics (Nagy 1994: 505). As is typical, no other basis for the code was mentioned.

Another important strand of philosophical scientism is associated with the ethical theory held by logical positivists (cf. Proctor 1991). As discussed above, logical positivists held that traditional ethical assertions are not cognitively meaningful because they are not based on science. The philosophical scientism associated (but not identical) with logical positivism redefines "ethical" issues before asserting that science alone provides us with knowledge of them. If, for instance, ethical assertions refer, not to what is good or right, but solely to *feelings* about goodness and rightness, those feelings can be investigated empirically in the way all other emotions are investigated.

In contrast to "expansionists" (Graham 1981) who espouse philosophical scientism and advocate expanding the role of science to embrace ethics, those who exhibit *de facto* scientism aspire to restrict the range of science or make modest claims for science. Nevertheless, since they restrict their attention to scientific findings, they end up being influenced only by science when they address ethical issues.

Those exemplifying *de facto* scientism can be divided into two groups: ethical agnostics and the single-mindedly scientific. Ethical agnostics believe that a scientist *qua* scientist ought not, in principle, to address ethical issues. As Parloff noted:

> many, following the precedent of Freud, disclaim interest in influencing the values of patients, on the basis that as scientists they are concerned with reality and facts and do not presume to be in a position to provide the patient with a philosophy of life.
>
> (Parloff 1967: 14)

Believing ethical issues to be beyond the scope of their discipline, they remain undecided. Believing in a strict separation between science and ethics, they may set aside or "bracket" all ethical issues (Drane 1982, 1991; Dukes 1955).

Another source of ethical agnosticism is applying the intellectual habits learned as scientists to ethical matters. Barlow, for instance, asserts that "one of the principal virtues of a good scientist is skepticism" (Barlow 1996: 236). When skepticism is applied to ethical matters (where considerably less certainty is possible than in the realm of traditional scientific topics), ethical skepticism may be the result. Similarly, when the principle of parsimony is applied to a situation in which ethical issues are intermingled with scientific issues (as they often are, for example in the ethical dimensions in psychotherapy), explanations tend to be restricted to the scientific dimension of the problem. To keep matters simple, the investigator may ignore, or remain agnostic about, the problem's ethical dimension.

Those who are single-mindedly scientific, in contrast both to those advocating philosophical scientism and to ethical agnostics, have no interest in broader theoretical issues. They devote their lives to reading, designing, conducting, and writing-up experiments. Their theorizing extends at most to scientific micro-theories. They have neither time nor desire, neither the training nor the inclination, to engage in ethical reflection. They know or like science best, or science is all they know.

But when faced with ethical issues, both ethical agnostics and the single-mindedly scientific appear to draw solely upon what they know – science – to address those ethical issues. Although their philosophical convictions do not mandate that science *should* play such a role, science alone informs their ethical convictions. The result: *de facto* scientism.

The major claim of scientism relevant to this discussion – that we can rely on science alone to address ethical issues – rests, at least in its strongest philosophical form, on the following:

> The methods and assumptions of science must be sharply distinguished from those of ethics. Strictly objective and driven entirely by data, scientists properly employing the scientific method can be ethically neutral and value-free. Therefore, they need not draw upon the discipline of ethics in any way to answer the ethical questions ethics traditionally addressed.

Those convictions are important because if ethics is intermingled in some way with science, any conclusions supposedly drawn from science alone derive, in fact, from both science and ethics, not from science alone.[1]

Three types of challenge face the claim that we need science alone to answer ethical questions: (1) certain values (defined ethically) are intrinsic to the scientific endeavor; (2) certain ethical convictions (not intrinsic to science) do, in fact, enter into psychological research, whatever the researchers' aspirations to ethical neutrality; and (3) science, although essential to ethical endeavors, cannot fully address ethical issues. I will address each challenge in turn.

I should first note, however, that even if the first two challenges are accepted, modified forms of the "Science only" claim can be espoused: (a) "We can rely on science alone (science being ethically neutral *in the main*, with the exception of those few and inconsequential values that are intrinsic to science) to address ethical issues"; and (b) "Ethical convictions not intrinsic to science can be present in the early stages of a research program, but will eventually be weeded out as hypotheses are subjected to empirical test."

Values intrinsic to science

Philosophers of science, ethicists, and theoretical psychologists (Graham 1981; Haan *et al.* 1983; Laudan 1984; Longino 1990; Proctor 1991; Riley 1974; Stevenson and Byerly 1995; Thackray and Mendelsohn 1974; Waterman 1988) no longer find plausible the claim that science (even when properly conducted) can be, or should be, entirely free of values (defined ethically). Certain values (ethical assertions of a particular type) appear to be intrinsic to the scientific endeavor.

Controversy has developed, however, over the specific values science supposedly requires and the extent to which they permeate it. Howard (1985) argued that science requires "epistemic values." In describing the standards scientists use, he set forth the following values associated with science: predictive accuracy, internal coherence, consistency with other theories, unifying power, fertility, and simplicity. (I refer to these as ethical values because, for instance, it is considered *good* for a scientist to predict accurately. Most of the values considered intrinsic to science are nonmoral ethical values, with the exception of honesty: Scientists who lie about their results are considered immoral or unethical.) Cournand (1977) points to the scientific values of honesty, objectivity, tolerance, doubt of certitude, and unselfish engagement. Hofstadter and Metzger (1955) list tolerance, honesty, publicity, testifiability, individuality, and cooperativeness. In Rokeach's (1979) empirical investigation of values associated with science (employing five methods), the highest rankings were given to the terminal values of wisdom, freedom, self-respect, and a sense of accomplishment, and to these instrumental values: intellectual, capable, honest, and responsible. And Popper (1962/1976) adds to truth, "our decisive scientific value," the values of relevance, interest, significance, fruitfulness, explanatory power, simplicity, and precision.

Popper distinguishes between *"purely* scientific values" (similar to Howard's 1985 "epistemic" and Laudan's 1984 "cognitive" values) and *"extra*-scientific values," such as human welfare (Popper 1976: 97). He stresses that scientists ought not to confuse the two.

But Toulmin (1975) argues that *two* ethical stances have historically characterized scientists: the Newtonian and the Baconian, reflecting the emphases of Newton and Bacon. The first stance sees the purpose of science to be strictly intellectual, to obtain truth about nature; the second sees the purpose of science to be human welfare (cf. Hofstadter and Metzger 1955).

He suggests that with colleagues, scientists stress the Newtonian, but with funding agencies the Baconian.

Popper argues for the Newtonian morality of science, relegating the Baconian to the status of "extra-scientific." Although the existence of the American Psychological Society (APS) stems from a desire to strengthen scientific psychology (their emphasis is clearly on Newtonian morality), the wording of its statement of purpose, "to promote, protect, and advance the interests of scientifically-oriented psychology in research, application, and *the improvement of human welfare*" (APS 1988: 1, emphasis added), makes it evident that a Baconian element is present in the scientific morality of the APS as well. This is also true of the American Psychological Association (APA). Its statement of purpose includes both the Newtonian goal of advancing psychology "as a science" and the Baconian goal of "promoting human welfare" (APA 1994: 1).

Rejecting both Baconian and Newtonian moralities, Skolimowski (1975) argues for a third morality of science: the Copernican. Copernicus wanted an intellectual understanding that would include the physical, the moral, and the aesthetic orders. In calling for "a broader conception of science which will be based on a broader conception of knowledge or on the unification of the cognitive with the normative," Skolimowski (1975: 134) joins others (e.g. Braybrooke 1987; Haan *et al.* 1983; Keat 1981; E. V. Sullivan 1984) who address the need for a new philosophy of the social sciences that will tie ethical considerations more closely and explicitly to the social sciences.

A consensus that science is value-laden thus coexists with deep disagreement about which values (defined ethically) are intrinsic to science. Kendler's (1993) observation, that any account of the relationship between psychology and ethics will depend on how each term is defined, is clearly relevant here. But the disagreement is more fundamental than definitional disagreement. Deep differences about the nature of science and about ethics are manifest.

What is evident is that science and ethics are deeply intertwined. And that separating them crisply is neither possible nor desirable.

The presence in the heart of science of essential ethical principles requires intellectual justification. Reasons must be provided for claims that these values are good, that one is most important, and that they merit our allegiance. That is a task for which ethics is well suited, but science not. Indeed, noted philosopher of science Larry Laudan argued that we need a systematic way to evaluate ethically the goals of scientific inquiry, an "axiology of inquiry" because "methodology gets nowhere without axiology" (Laudan 1987: 29).

To summarize, when science produces ethical knowledge, ethical assumptions essential to science play a role in producing that ethical knowledge. Science and ethics thus both play a role. The scientific context thus shapes the ethical character of psychotherapy and our understanding of it through a combination of the scientific method, data, *and* ethical convictions intrinsic to science. A value-laden science contributes values (defined ethically) to therapists. But "the fact," as Laudan observed, "that the axiology of inquiry is a grossly underdeveloped part of epistemology and philosophy of science" (Laudan 1987: 29) points to one way in which the scientific context, by neglecting the ethical component of science, has obscured the ethical character of science, and, by extension, of psychotherapy.

Advocates of scientism have, as noted above, a ready response to this first challenge to the claim that science alone can produce ethical knowledge: science is inconsequentially value-laden. We can rely on science alone (science being ethically neutral in the main, with the exception of those few values that are intrinsic to science) to address ethical issues. We can focus on Popper's (1962/1976) scientific values, and strive to expunge from science all extra-scientific values.

This proposal faces at least two problems. First, as noted, deep divisions about which values warrant the honorific label "scientific" exist. Indeed, Popper considered "extra-scientific" certain values which several of the authors cited regard to be essential to science. Second, as Popper observed, "it is practically impossible to achieve the elimination of extra-scientific values from scientific activity" (Popper 1976: 97). This is particularly likely when scientists investigate morality (Kurtines *et al.* 1990). Waterman concurs, warning that "when psychologists design studies of morality, they are very likely guided by their own moral preferences" (Waterman 1988: 296).

By way of contrast, Kendler (1992) argues that impartial research can be conducted on sensitive topics. And Rokeach (1973) claimed to be able to conduct value-free research on values.

One way to address the role of extra-scientific values (however defined) in science is to review briefly investigations of their role in scientific research. It is to that task, addressing the second challenge to the claim that ethical conclusions can be based solely on science, that I now turn.

Extra-scientific values

To discover the influence on science of "extra-scientific" ethical convictions, some scholars have examined researchers' autobiographies. Leary did so, discovering a clear "heritage of moral concern" in both pre-Wundtian scholars and modern psychologists (Leary 1980: 283). Although the value-free ideal kept the moral concerns of the latter from appearing in their published psychological writings, Leary found that many prominent psychologists "are still extremely concerned about changing the human world for the better" (ibid.: 300). For instance, the personal memoirs of central figures in animal-learning theory (Edward C. Tolman, Clark Hull, and B. F. Skinner) make clear their concern to benefit others. Kendler (1989) points to Kurt Lewin, for whom Nazism and his failure to rescue his mother from a Nazi concentration camp led to a concern for applied ethics through his program of action research.

Morawski (1982) did another type of uncovering. Examining the Utopian visions in the writings of early psychologists G. Stanley Hall, William McDougall, Hugo Munsterberg, and John B. Watson, she found "programs for societal improvement" both in their Utopian and their professional writings (Morawski 1982: 1082). Skinner contributed his own Utopian vision in *Walden Two* (1948), articulating an underlying ethical theory involving the ultimate good of survival (Leahey 1987b) or an ethic of justice (D. S. Browning 1987).

Steininger (1979) and Leahey (1987b) also documented how psychologists, striving to be value-free, have in fact made ethical assertions and relied on operative ethical theories. McLure and Tyler (1967) discussed how researchers investigating values draw upon their own values in doing so. Hence, although they have done so in different ways (Leary 1980), many psychologists have pursued ethical aims, extra-scientific ethical aims, in their research.

But perhaps the most important moral convictions surreptitiously wedded to science are those linked to scientism, the view that science alone provides the truths we need (with the exception of those derived from mathematics and logic). In his careful historical review of the making of the modern identity, Taylor notes that there were *not* "conclusive reasons" for adopting the belief that natural science provides us with all the knowledge we need. Adopting the creed of scientism was, instead, "a leap of faith" powered by "a moral vision": "one *ought* not to believe what one has insufficient evidence for" (Taylor 1989: 404). I doubt that any ethical convictions in the scientific context of psychotherapy have been of greater importance for our understanding (or lack thereof) of the ethical dimensions of psychotherapy.

But devotees of scientism, under conviction that science alone provides us with knowledge about ethical matters, have a ready response to the presence of extra-scientific values in science: ethical convictions not intrinsic to science can be present in the early stages of a research program, but will eventually be weeded out as hypotheses are subjected to empirical test. Sometimes relying upon the positivist distinction (Leary 1980) between the context of discovery (where extra-scientific convictions are valid) and the context of justification (where they are not), they often hold that extra-scientific values "are gradually sifted out" (Kurtines *et al*. 1990: 283) as researchers pursue values that are intrinsic to science.

Some of the concerns of advocates of scientism are legitimate, albeit not limited to those holding their ethical views. Mixing ethical or political convictions with science can be dangerous (Proctor 1991), with the former Soviet Union's insistence upon Lamarckian biology being perhaps the most vivid example. Furthermore, I agree that ethical assumptions present in the early stages of a research program (in its context of discovery) should change over the course of an investigation if clear and convincing evidence is discovered that conflicts with them. For example, a researcher convinced abortion is wrong for one reason – its harmful consequences to women (the "post-abortion syndrome") – appropriately drops that ethical conviction if the existence of such a syndrome cannot be established empirically. Or the reverse. Finally, I think science is an uncommonly good way to answer a number of important questions, and so I share (in moderate form) the views of those who want to rely upon it whenever it is applicable.

But ethics can aid even those scientists who operate with traditional understandings of science by helping to identify implicit ethical convictions in scientific inquiries.

The authors cited above, however, claim that completely eradicating extra-scientific values from science is impossible. Continuing to insist that ethical convictions be severed from "good" scientific work may serve, not to eliminate such ethical convictions, but to make them invisible to scientists and those who consume research. Accordingly, scientists should make their extra-scientific values explicit, in accord with science's values of openness and accountability to peers.

In any case, to the extent that ethical convictions are present in the practice of science, whether values intrinsic to science or extra-scientific values, science itself may benefit from a careful ethical analysis of the role of such ethical convictions in science. That is, Laudan's (1987) call for an "axiology of inquiry" applies not only to values intrinsic to science but also to extra-scientific values, whether those extra-scientific values reflect researchers' personal convictions or ethical assumptions contained within psychological theories.

Advocates of scientism may find Laudan's proposal unconvincing because it conflicts with their moral convictions that one ought not believe in anything, including axiology, for which there is no solid scientific evidence. Their claim, of course, is decidedly paradoxical: their ethical convictions ban ethical convictions. But because I believe it valid to hold ethical convictions, I think advocates of scientism can enter the ethical debate about the relationship of science and ethics. Indeed, they must. Because their ethical convictions have powerfully shaped, and obscured, the ethical character of therapy: obscured it because, if therapy is to be based on science alone and the scientist ought not to turn to ethics to address ethical questions, values intrinsic to science are given no voice, indeed, they are banished.

The ethical claims of scientism therefore warrant careful ethical scrutiny. But to do so is a task that is ethical, not scientific.

In conclusion, in my review of the scientific context of therapy, I have challenged a strict fact–value, science–ethics distinction in two ways: I first argued that science produces facts that are relevant to values (defined ethically); I then argued that ethical convictions, and the discipline of ethics, can contribute to, indeed are intrinsic to, science. And that extra-scientific values are often present in science, and need careful ethical scrutiny.

To the extent scientific research is based not simply on empirical data, but on data *and* the ethical beliefs of scientists, the practice of psychotherapy (and our understanding of its ethical dimensions) will be based on both science and ethics. Kurtines, Alvarez, and Azmitia (1990) argue that we need to acknowledge that values are involved in science and devote our energy to determining *how* they influence science. They thus offer one reason we should turn to both science and ethics to address ethical questions. I will now address others as I consider the third challenge to scientism.

Science and ethics

Let me begin by reviewing my argument. The claim that the descriptive enterprise of science can, by itself, provide knowledge about ethical issues without drawing in any way on the methods and concepts of ethics has faced two challenges: intrinsic to science are values (defined ethically) and scientists often draw upon extra-scientific values in their research. Regarding the first challenge, I have argued that ethics is, in some regards, essential to science, so science is in every instance intertwined with ethics. Regarding the second challenge, ethics can be helpful to scientists in teasing out implicit ethical assumptions even if scientists are capable of achieving value-freedom. (Indeed, they may *need* to draw upon ethics to identify implicit ethical assumptions before eliminating them.) But in the more likely instance that extra-scientific ethical assumptions are inextricably bound to the scientific effort, scientists always draw upon some ethical concepts and methods, and would benefit from doing so more openly, carefully, and systematically, taking advantage of the concepts, methods, and history of ethical reflection found in ethics.

But there is a third reason science alone cannot adequately understand psychotherapy's ethical dimensions: science cannot answer certain ethical questions that ethics can answer.

Let me set forth what I think science (as traditionally understood) can and cannot say about ethical matters. Science can describe but not prescribe, can tell us what *is* but not what *ought* to be. Science can provide facts – facts, for instance, about the consequences of an action and the most effective way to reach a goal. But science cannot tell us at the most fundamental level what is good, right, or virtuous. And science cannot adjudicate conflicts between ethical principles (Sadler and Hulgus 1992). Science cannot address ethical questions, Meehl asserted, because "the value neutrality of a descriptive science obviously gives it *no* competence to pass an 'empirical' judgment on the statement of a normative discipline such as ethics, law or political theory." But he added, "I have yet to find a social scientist who makes this remark and is internally consistent on this issue" (Meehl 1970: 3).

The reasons for that inconsistency, discussed above, are manifold. But I would propose one additional reason: many therapists believe scientific knowledge does sometimes determine what is good or right. They assert, for example, that scientific evidence documenting the efficacy of therapy establishes that therapy is good, or that the empirical evidence that child abuse harms children makes it clear that parents should not abuse their children. As I argued above, science does make valuable contributions to ethical deliberation. But science alone does not permit us to draw such ethical conclusions, whether we employ a teleological (consequentialist) normative ethical theory or a deontological normative ethical theory (see the discussion in Chapter 4).

Waterman explains why we cannot draw ethical conclusions from science alone when using a teleological normative ethical theory:

> When philosophical teleologists claim that a behavior has moral value because of its consequences, they are making two assertions: (a) The behavior has certain specificable [sic] consequences, and (b) those consequences are to be valued....The latter assertion is not empirical, however....The adequacy of any statement that some types of consequences constitute a better criteria of moral value than do other types of outcomes can be judged only in philosophical terms.
>
> (Waterman 1988: 292)

And so Waterman cautions that we cannot use "empirical evidence as the ultimate criteria for deciding claims about what constitutes morality."

Waterman's qualification that empirical evidence cannot be the "ultimate" criterion for deciding ethical claims is very important, as is the qualification in my claim that science cannot tell us *at the most fundamental level* what is good, right, or virtuous. Suppose we seek an effective method for reducing depression. Reviewing the research literature, we may be tempted to conclude that scientific evidence documenting the efficacy of therapy establishes that therapy is good. Scientific research thus appears to tell us that cognitive therapy is "good." But it can, in fact, only tell us cognitive therapy is instrumentally good, not ultimately good, that cognitive therapy is good as a *means* to reach the more fundamental good of reduced depression. We can only draw the conclusion that cognitive therapy is good by combining scientific findings *and* this more fundamental ethical judgment: it is good to reduce depression. Of course, on some accounts, reducing depression is good because reducing depression aids the survival of the species. But in that case, human survival is the ultimate criterion (most fundamental good) used in the ethical argument. As such, it must be justified, because from the *fact* of human survival we cannot conclude that the end of human survival is *good or right*. And so Strupp correctly concludes that "the value of psychotherapy" cannot "be conclusively derived from research" (Strupp 1986: 129).

Teleological theories are especially important in evaluating the ethical character of therapy, because therapy is often justified in terms of the end, or goal, of improved psychological functioning or decreased psychological problems. It is in these covert assumptions about the goodness of therapy goals that much of the ethical character of therapy lies (see the discussion in Chapter 9). But, reinforcing my point, Perrez argued that "the positive foundation of the goals [of therapy] cannot be adequately achieved scientifically" (Perrez 1989a: 170).

And so, not science alone but science in combination with ethics permits us to conclude that psychotherapy is good. We can validly draw that conclusion from scientific findings that therapy reduces psychological problems *and* the ethical claims that (1) we decide the goodness of an activity by evaluating whether it brings about some fundamentally good end and (2) reducing psychological problems (the goal of therapy) is fundamentally good.

If we cannot derive ethical conclusions from science when we employ teleological ethical theories, neither can we derive ethical conclusions from scientific findings when we employ deontological theories. The *obligation* to be honest, for instance, is not, and cannot be, a strictly scientific finding.

And so, when striving to understand the ethical dimensions of therapy, we should rely on both science and ethics. And when practicing psychotherapy, which always includes those ethical dimensions, we should draw upon both science and ethics.

Several advantages accrue to those who draw upon both science and ethics. Doing so permits us to critically evaluate values intrinsic to science as part of an axiology of inquiry. It permits us to detect extra-scientific values in scientific research (our own and those of others), to try to eliminate or minimize those values, or (perhaps) to choose those values more wisely. Finally, therapists who base their practice, not only on science, but also on science and ethics, can better address the ethical dimensions of psychotherapy.

Drawing upon both science and ethics is not new. Prominent psychologists, such as Wundt and James, have long been committed both to experimentation and to philosophical reflection. Indeed, William James remained concerned "simultaneously with normative ethics and a scientific psychology" (Rambo 1980: 50), as have Martin (1995), Perrez (1989a, 1989b), and M. B. Smith (1961). Sadler and Hulgus have recently articulated a particularly helpful model of clinical problem-solving, a complement to the biopsychosocial model, that sets forth "three core aspects of the clinical encounter: problems of knowledge, ethics, and pragmatics" (Sadler and Hulgus 1992: 1315). In their model, the clinician ideally draws upon the sciences in making clinical decisions, but also draws upon other disciplines, including ethics.

Unfortunately, some will no doubt interpret their model, and my argument, as attacks on science. But Sadler and Hulgus's model is not an attack on science; nor is my argument. Nothing whatsoever prevents scientists from conducting the highest quality scientific research yet also drawing upon the discipline of ethics to address ethical questions. Nothing whatsoever prevents psychotherapists from drawing upon relevant scientific findings to guide their practice yet also drawing upon the discipline of ethics to address ethical questions.

I suspect that some will misinterpret my argument because the ethical claims of scientism are often confused with science itself. I reject scientism, but I do not reject science. Again, one can conduct science and champion relevant scientific findings without also claiming that science alone provides us with valid claims to knowledge.

I do, however, hold a position similar to, but subtly and significantly different from, one often held by advocates of scientism. I am convinced that practice should be based on *relevant* scientific findings, *when available*. Where science has a clear word to offer the psychotherapist, the therapist ought to listen. And so, because I hold that ethical position, I agree with Meehl's ethical assertion that those who deny the need for quantitative research are "unethical" (Meehl 1997: 91).

I differ, however, from the advocates of scientism because I believe that, when faced with a question for which relevant scientific knowledge is not available, therapists need not rely upon scientific findings. Indeed, since we cannot in principle obtain answers to some ethical questions from science, and since ethical issues are always a part of psychotherapy, it would be absurd to expect therapists to base their practice solely upon science.

"Psychotherapy should be based on science" was the claim with which I began this section. And I heartily concur (on ethical grounds) that psychotherapy should be based on *relevant* scientific findings. But psychotherapy should also be based on ethics. And until psychotherapists do so more explicitly and with greater sophistication, psychotherapy will never reach its fullest potential.

Psychotherapists wanting a high degree of intellectual certainty will be disappointed by my proposal. They recognize correctly that, absent dogmatism, ethical reflection simply cannot promise such certainty. But in contrast to those who use the scientific method to address all questions, to obtain certainty, William James, according to Perry, argued:

> in effect, that if a fact or a problem does not fit a technique, so much the worse for the technique. If a problem cannot be solved by rigorous mathematical or experimental procedure, then it must be solved as well as possible. *That* problem is not solved by substituting another problem

that *can* be dealt with rigorously. Indeed, it is quite possible that in the theoretical, as in the practical field, the important problems are those which cannot be solved rigorously – problems such as...value.

(Perry 1943: 124)

I encourage the adoption of James's approach. When we address the ethical character of psychotherapy, we do well to address it "as well as possible." And that means, I am convinced, drawing heavily, wisely, and well upon both science and ethics.

Conclusion

The scientific context of psychotherapy has both shaped and obscured psychotherapy's ethical dimensions in a variety of ways. Unfortunately, dominant understandings of science have overdetermined psychotherapists' avoidance of ethical discourse. The desire to be objective and value-free, the failure to recognize values intrinsic to science and the role of extra-scientific values in science, accepting the false dichotomy of science *or* ethics, the ethical doctrine of scientism (that human beings *ought* to be guided in all matters, including ethical, by science alone), and the failure to recognize that scientism is an ethical position and ought not be equated with science itself have all occluded our awareness of the ethical dimensions of psychotherapy and prevented us from thinking about them well.

On the other hand, values intrinsic to science (e.g. openness, collegiality, and honesty) may be applicable to therapy. More importantly, science provides helpful facts about consequences (e.g. the consequences of dysfunctional beliefs or of particular forms of therapy) that are often quite relevant to therapy and its ethical dimensions. Consequently, science unequivocally makes important contributions to the ethical character of therapy. And should do so.

But an optimal understanding of the ethical endeavor of psychotherapy, and the psychotherapist as ethicist, requires that therapy be based not only on science, but on science *and* ethics.

7

The social contexts of psychotherapy
Clinical practice and business

Almost all psychotherapy takes place, neither in the ivory tower of the ethi-cist nor in the laboratory of the researcher, but in the concrete social contexts of clinical practitioners whose livelihood is psychotherapy. We need to understand those social contexts because, as Sarason notes, "the substance of psychology cannot be independent of the social order" (Sarason 1981: 827). Because psychotherapy's social contexts both shape and obscure its ethical character, I will address them by focusing on clinical practice and business.

The context of clinical practice

The arena of human suffering and disordered lives, the clinical context in which therapy occurs, is both ancient and contemporary. Human need preceded the development of modern psychotherapy, as did efforts to produce human change (Gamwell and Tomes 1995; Grob 1994). And there are decided continuities between psychotherapy, ancient healing rituals, and other attempts to change people (Frank and Frank 1991).

Psychotherapists now perform tasks, including ethical tasks, historically accomplished by others. Indeed, Freud asserted that "our predecessors in psychoanalysis" were "the Catholic fathers" (Freud and Pfister 1963: 21). Therapists also inherited ideas, roles, and values from other professionals, including other religious leaders, educators, nurses, and physicians (E. Caplan 1998; Frank and Frank 1991; Hale 1971; Holifield 1983; Levine and Levine 1970).

Psychotherapy's medical heritage

I want to focus on only one of those professions, medicine, because it has affected, affects, and has the potential to affect the ethical character of therapy in a variety of especially significant ways. Bioethics, medicine's increasingly sophisticated ethical tradition, offers significant conceptual resources to those addressing the ethical dimensions of therapy. But for psychologists, psychotherapy's medical context has too often obscured the

ethical dimensions of psychotherapy because psychologists resist acknowledging the important ways in which medicine (and medical ethics) has
influenced therapy – and so they do not draw upon bioethics as explicitly
and fully as they could. Finally, critics charge that the medical context has
influenced the ethical character of therapy in at least two deeply problematic
ways: individualism and inappropriate uses of the medical model that reduce
those biopsychosocial problems that have an ethical dimension to problems
considered merely medical.

To address the ethical dimensions of psychotherapy's medical heritage, I
will first address medical ethics, then turn to the medical-ethical concept of
"mental health." Finally, I will consider many psychologists' curious resistance to draw overtly upon bioethics.

Bioethics: resource and source of problems

Medical codes of ethics – including and preceding the famous Hippocratic
Oath (Amundsen 1995) – have long codified the behavior expected of physicians. Recent medical advances, increasing litigation, and renewed
philosophical reflection have given rise to the field of bioethics (Beauchamp
and Childress 1994; Engelhardt 1996; Gillon 1994; Reich 1995a). As they
seek to understand and address the ethical dimensions of psychotherapy,
psychotherapists of all professions can fruitfully draw upon the ethical
concepts, arguments, and discussions generated by bioethicists, upon the
recent emphasis on the virtues that professionals should exemplify, and upon
the development of clinical ethical decision-making strategies.

I want to mention briefly two relevant concepts (there are more) from
medical ethics: the idea of the professional and a focus on the individual
client. All psychotherapists inherit both; both concepts are, in part, ethical;
both have deeply shaped psychotherapy.

As legatees of the social ethical idea of the professional, psychotherapists
are obligated, as professionals, to strive to benefit clients and fulfill other
duties (Haas and Malouf 1995). For example, society can count on professionals, when "professional" is understood substantively, to make the public
welfare a primary concern (Watson 1954). This means, argues Orlinsky, that
there is a distinctive quality to the relationship between therapist and client,
a decidedly ethical quality:

> The innermost core of the *therapeutic contract* is a conception of the ideal
> helping relationship, which often has an "ultimate" or "sacred" quality.
> This inner ethical core also influences the *therapeutic bond* by setting a
> model for it.
>
> (Orlinsky 1989: 435)

The ethical character of a "profession," I am convinced, is central to what it means to be a psychotherapist. But the meaning of "professional" is eroding on two fronts: some people, corporations, and government entities reduce the professional psychotherapist to mere "provider," jettison the ethical core of what it means to be a professional, and regard therapists as nothing more than providers of certain services, like any other providers of any other goods or services. And some psychotherapists think the therapy relationship is entirely private, denying they are accountable to anyone but their clients and tending to assert their rights but not their obligations. Because this degradation of the meaning of professional is so important, I will return to it in Chapter 11.

A positive thrust of medical ethics, concern for the well-being of the individual patient, has a troublesome side as well, one that becomes especially problematic in psychotherapy. The Hippocratic Oath, notes Veatch, holds that "the physician's obligation is to benefit the patient according to the physician's judgment" (Veatch 1989b: 46). Unfortunately, in its modern form this principle "leads the physician to focus on the patient as an isolated individual" and the profession of medicine to become "ultra-individualistic" (ibid.: 48). That may be valid when a malady is, in fact, wholly within an individual's body (as is true with some medical problems). But it becomes a problem when practitioners of medicine (Veatch 1978) or psychotherapy (Doherty 1995) ignore the well-being of a community or of society as a whole, fail to balance concern for self and others, or exhibit no concern for the natural environment.

And so Sarason argued that one of the roots of clinical psychology's deeply flawed "a-social" nature was that "it became part of a medically dominated mental health movement that was…blind to the nature of the social order" (Sarason 1981: 833). As a result of that alignment with medicine, and for other reasons, the psychotherapist became, in Cushman's words, "the doctor of the interior" (Cushman 1992: 22). To be sure, some approaches to medicine (e.g. public health) avoid individualism. And psychotherapists need not draw upon the individualistic strain in the medical heritage. But that strain exists and has affected psychotherapy, often in ways invisible to those who participate in it. And so it requires conscious attention.

A mixed medical/psychological/ethical concept: "mental health"

The clinical context has changed. Problems once addressed in ethical terms are now considered matters of "mental health," to be addressed by "mental health" professionals.

But it is a mistake to distinguish too sharply between ethics and mental health, or to address all ethical problems under the rubric of mental health. The relationship between health and ethics is complex. And distinctions between the two, and concepts combining health and ethics, have a long heritage. The powerful images of health and illness were long ago extended metaphorically beyond the realm of physical illness. Socrates thought of himself as a "physician" or "healer" of souls (McNeil 1951; Meilaender 1984), as did Plato and Aristotle (Taylor 1989), plus some early Christian thinkers. And the twelfth-century Muslim mystic and reformer, Al-Ghazzali, discussed diseases "of the heart" for which the sole remedy is medicine derived from religious law (McNeil 1951: 63).

Cross-fertilization of concepts occurred in other ways as well: ethical convictions influenced medical convictions. Masturbation was held by generally accepted medical opinion to be a "dangerous disease entity," a disease associated with serious physical and emotional problems (Engelhardt 1974: 234). And physician Samuel Cartwright, in a "Report on the Diseases and Physical Peculiarities of the Negro Race" (1851), delineated differences between African-Americans and Caucasians. These differences were physical ("in the membranes, the muscles, and tendons and in all the fluids and secretions" – Cartwright 1981: 305), behavioral (among the diseases discussed: "Drapetomania, or the disease causing slaves to run away," and "DYSAESTHESIA AETHIOPIS…A DISEASE PECULIAR TO NEGROES – CALLED BY OVERSEERS, 'RASCALITY'" – ibid.: 320), and ontological ("the great primary truth, that the negro is a slave by nature, and can never be happy, industrious, moral or religious, in any other condition" – ibid.: 311).

Although future generations may be as profoundly revolted by our ideas about disease as most of us are by Dr Cartwright's, there is now widespread consensus that most disorders we now label physical illnesses are appropriately labeled diseases. This does not mean, however, that we no longer make ethical judgments when diagnosing illnesses. When we label a problem a disease, we usually make ethical *and* medical judgments. For instance, we make the nonmoral ethical judgment that it is good to be free from cancer, and bad to have it. The widespread societal consensus about such judgments may often, however, make their ethical character invisible to us.

We also make nonmoral judgments about mental disorders. The Fourth Edition of the *Diagnostic and Statistical Manual of Mental Disorders* (DSM-IV; American Psychiatric Association 1994), for instance, repeatedly uses the value-laden criteria of "marked distress" and "impairment" in social, occupational, or other important areas of functioning to differentiate between disorders and problems that are not disorders. The DSM-IV drafters clearly think it is not good for people to experience psychosocial impairment and subjective distress. And even critics of the DSM-IV agree that schizophrenia bears at least a close resemblance to physical illness. And that it is a bad problem to have. Although we would not make moral judgments about schizophrenia (e.g. "people should not become schizophrenic"), we do make *non*moral ethical judgments (e.g. "it is not good that my sister developed schizophrenia"). *Moral* ethical questions tend to arise, not in the decision about whether a disorder exists, but in what to do about it (e.g. "society ought to provide treatment for schizophrenics, whatever the cost"; "we should help homeless schizophrenics by taking them all off the streets and putting them in hospitals"; or "the rights of all people, especially those labeled 'mentally ill,' should be preserved").

More controversial are other extensions of the medical model, or the concept of "health," to psychological problems. Kovel documents the ways in which the mental hygiene movement produced a change in how human problems were viewed: people were no longer considered "bad," but "sick" (Kovel 1980: 82). And Freud powerfully expanded the concepts of illness and medical treatments to include psychological problems and treatments. He drew out analogies between physical disorders and psychological problems and developed corresponding treatments.

Szasz (e.g. 1974) and others vigorously criticize the claim that psychological problems are mental illnesses. Their concern is that – whatever the commonalities – there are significant *dis*analogies between physical illnesses and psychological problems. Commingling medical terminology with psychological problems results, they claim, in decreased responsibility, egregious violations of autonomy, and other problems.

Often overlooked in debates about the medical model is the fact that the concept of mental health – whether viewed in strictly medical terms, in strictly psychological terms, or in terms of a biopsychosocial model – contains an inextricably *ethical* component. For example, Margolis noted that Freud produced a "mixed model that shows clear affinities with the models that obtain in physical medicine and at the same time with the models of happiness and well-being that obtain in the ethical realm" (Margolis 1966: 81–2). And so Freud's genital ideal served as a goal, an ethical ideal, toward which a person undergoing psychoanalysis would move. Improved self-esteem, self-actualization, and personal growth later became common (value-laden) therapy goals.

"Mental health" and "mental illness," in the case of Freud and others, are thus value-laden terms (Caplan *et al.* 1981; Engelhardt and Spicker 1978). The extent to which they are value-laden hinges, in part, on how health and illness are defined. We can view mental health either as the absence of disease or as a positive state of well-being. Although, as we have seen, values inform ideas about the former, there is greater consensus about illness (and thus health understood as freedom from illness) than there is consensus about health as a positive state of well-being. Part of the reason for this is that concepts of health understood as positive well-being are generally more value-laden than concepts stressing freedom from illness. And the concept of *mental* health is the most value-laden of all.

But I think the failure of Jahoda (1958) and others to identify a consensus among mental health professionals about the meaning of positive mental health stems both from fundamental differences among mental health professionals about the ethical ideals which underlie various concepts of mental health or ideal human functioning, and from their failure to discuss those ethical ideals.

When psychological problems are viewed in either strictly medical or strictly psychological terms, however, the underlying ethical differences are unlikely to be resolved: participants do not observe, no less discuss, the ethical and other dimensions of psychological problems. As Schofield (1964/1986) observes, psychiatrists have frequently failed "to appreciate that the human suffers some pains not because he is sick but because he is human" (Schofield 1986: 146).

One reason for the poverty of ethical articulation that afflicts therapists is that they are, in Jahoda's words, "all trained to exclude values from our thinking; and the way we try to exclude them is not to talk about them" (cited in Schofield 1986: 15).

From Jahoda's diagnosis, one part of the treatment becomes evident: we need to think and talk more about the *ethical* component of psychological problems and therapy goals, however the broader debate about medical and psychological aspects of human problems and change processes is resolved. I will return to that task when discussing therapy goals in Chapter 9.

Psychology's curious estrangement from bioethics

Behind the puzzling resistance of US psychologists to draw overtly on medical ethics lies the profession's significant historical debt to medicine, a debt of which many clinical psychologists are unaware or which may would prefer to downplay. Although modern psychotherapy also drew upon university counseling centers and community/child guidance clinics (VandenBos *et al.* 1992), Strupp notes that "members of my generation who first became acquainted with psychotherapy around 1950 have no difficulty perceiving its deep roots in medicine" (Strupp 1986: 120). Indeed, E. L. Kelly noted that "the term *clinical* [in 'clinical psychology'] is borrowed from its medical usage" (Kelly 1947: 75).

But the medical influence on clinical psychology was by no means limited to the adjective "clinical." Before the Second World War, US psychologists who conducted therapy in medical settings did so under medical supervision (D. L. Moore 1992). The war brought major changes for psychologists because the needs of military personnel far outstripped the number of available psychiatrists. So psychologists began conducting psychotherapy, but almost always under medical supervision (Abt 1992; J. G. Miller 1946). After the war, the Veterans Administration sparked a massive increase in the training of psychologists, who learned to become psychotherapists under medical supervision (J. G. Miller 1946; D. L. Moore 1992). Cummings recalled that he and other psychologists who began private practices in those post-war years "bootlegged their psychotherapy training and supervision off campus from congenial psychiatrists" (Cummings 1992: 845).

And when psychologists in the American Psychological Association began developing its own ethics code in the post-war period, Meehl and McClosky (1947) pointed to the ethics codes of other professions, including medicine. Until the APA developed its own code, "psychologists had been largely bound by existing codes of other professions, most notably medicine" (Wolman 1965, cited in Steere 1984: 20).

Psychologists did not want to remain in a perpetually inferior status to psychiatrists. For that and other reasons, they sought professional autonomy. But some psychiatrists had long been wary of psychologists functioning autonomously as psychotherapists. Indeed, a "suspicious" New York Psychiatric Society appointed a committee 1916 by "to inquire into the activities of psychologists" (T. V. Moore 1944: 472). The committee concluded that "the sick, whether in body or mind, should be cared for only by those with medical training," unless under "direct supervision" by a physician (ibid.). Deep disputes between psychologists and psychiatrists continued in the 1920s (Burnham 1974; Goode 1960; Seashore 1942). In 1937, Woodworth documented professional "jealousies" with psychiatrists. Menninger (1943) referred to psychologists who practiced therapy as "zealots." Opposition continued into the 1950s (Cummings 1992) and later. Indeed, psychoanalytic institutes banned psychologists despite Freud's support of "lay" analysts (Abt 1992; Maher 1991), relenting only under court pressure to do so (*Practitioner Focus* 1989). Clinical psychologists and psychiatrists fought similar battles in the United Kingdom (Pilgrim and Treacher 1992).

Psychologists faced a daunting task: to obtain psychiatry's prestige, respect, financial rewards (Sarason 1981), status as independent professionals (which was seen to require an independent code of ethics), and societal sanction to do psychotherapy, while at the same time distinguishing themselves from psychiatrists.

And so when they developed a code of ethics (Hobbs 1948), justified it, and revised it, psychologists focused almost exclusively on its empirical basis (McGovern *et al.* 1991; Nagy 1994; Sexton 1965). By doing so, psychologists refused to depend on medicine (from which they were trying to free themselves), distinguished themselves from psychiatrists, built upon a distinctive strength of psychology (expertise in research), developed a code targeted to problems for which the Hippocratic tradition was not well suited (Raimy 1950), and forged their own identity as an independent profession. Although they acknowledged drawing ideas from social workers and psychiatrists, psychologists stressed the untested nature of those ideas. Psychological research would test them, making them scientific (Sexton 1965).

Like its earlier separation from its philosophical parent, psychology's separation from its medical parent may have helped it become an independent profession. But the manner in which it did so has made it difficult for psychologists to see the rich ethical heritage of medicine and to take full advantage of bioethics as they addressed the ethical character of psychotherapy.

Although bioethics should not be the sole source of the ethical standards of the psychotherapist, I think it a very positive development that some psychologists are now drawing more richly on bioethics (e.g. the journal *Ethics and Behavior*, and K. S. Kitchener's 1984 adaptation of Beauchamp and Childress's approach to medical ethics). Indeed, medical ethics has likely shaped the ethical perspectives of psychologists more than most would acknowledge. And bioethics offers resources far more substantial than most are aware. And so therapists would benefit from being aware of that influence and drawing *selectively* upon the expertise of bioethicists in addressing the thorny issues of the ethical dimensions of psychotherapy.

In conclusion, psychology has experienced an unfortunate double estrangement from its moral sources, first from philosophy and then from bioethics. (And a triple estrangement if we count its estrangement from the spiritual and religious ethical sources of many of its practitioners and clients.) If Taylor (1989, 1992) is correct (and I think he is) that ethical sources move and motivate all people, and that we benefit from being consciously aware of them and explicitly drawing upon them, then psychotherapists would do well to identify, articulate, and build upon their moral sources, including those found within psychotherapy's medical heritage.

Clinical reality

One final aspect of the clinical context deserves mention. Fine philosophical distinctions and carefully delineated, bioethically informed concepts of mental health fit the classroom well, but not the pragmatic realities of actual therapy sessions. Therapists rarely have the luxury of extensive in-session reflection, and surely not of seeing a particular moment of therapy in terms of the history of Western (or, better, global) ethical reflection. The client speaks; the therapist must respond. Time is not available to answer adequately all the ethical questions that arise in therapy – if, that is, answering adequately means thoroughly researched, academically reputable answers. Uncertainty is the lot of the therapist. As Wallace notes, "while both clinicians and researchers trade in uncertainty and ambiguity, the former must decide and act, often in the face of insufficient information and inadequate theories" (Wallace 1991: 90).

How, then, does a therapist respond? With the words of one's best supervisor gently echoing in one's brain, with theoretical concepts, with research findings, with reason, with one's gut, within the context of one's own psychological framework. But also, one would hope, by reading and reflecting – outside of therapy sessions – about ethics and therapy, so the "spontaneous" responses in therapy sessions are shaped by careful ethical reflection.

Addressing the pragmatic and ethical issues that face the clinician (Sadler and Hulgus 1992) without fully satisfactory answers is probably intrinsic to the endeavor. However, *never* engaging in thoughtful reflection – about the goals of therapy, about the psychotherapist's role as ethicist, and about the ethical character of psychotherapy – is not.

The context of business

Paralyzed by anxiety about speaking in public but holding a job that requires her to speak in public, Sandra seeks therapy. She knows she can do so because her job has "good benefits." Drawing on the understanding of therapy she gained from traditional psychotherapy textbooks, Tania, her therapist, establishes ground rules and goals for Sandra's therapy: Tania will provide a warm, empathic, and congruent relationship to facilitate Sandra becoming fully functioning; Sandra will set and reach her own goals as part of her "journey of personal growth." Tania does not think about the economic side of Sandra's therapy because she is not interested in business, the financial side of professional practice was not covered in graduate school, and when she began her internship she was told, "The Business Office will take care of that. Just concentrate on becoming a good therapist." Her supervisor, who came to professional maturity when insurance companies routinely reimbursed therapists, assumes Sandra's therapy will be fully covered. And so Dr Schwartz focuses on Tania's need to rid her client of her maladaptive philosophy of life (that is, of beliefs not in accord with the doctrines of Rational-Emotive Therapy).

The managed care company Sandra chose to provide her medical benefits will reimburse those therapists (and only those therapists) who agree to reach the quality and cost-effectiveness goals established by Sandra's employer. To operationalize "quality and cost-effectiveness," Health Options has established a panel of scientists, which determined that therapists can effectively treat in eight sessions those, like Sandra, with Specific Phobias. In the absence of any clinical reason to vary from that guideline, Health Options denies payment after Sandra's eighth session with Tania. Sandra, no longer fearful of speaking in public and unable to pay $85 a session on her own, terminates.

Psychotherapy is, among other things, a business relationship. Involving economic transactions between therapists, clients, and others (Orlinsky 1989), therapy is a form of employment for therapists and an expense for clients, businesses, and governments. As Rosenberg notes, a profession is "a marketplace phenomenon – or, relatedly…an object of government policy"

(Rosenberg 1979: 443). Understanding the psychotherapy profession therefore requires addressing its economic context. That context can shape the
ethical character of therapy in a variety of ways, but it can also obscure it.
For example, thinking of Sandra's therapy solely as one of her employer's
business expenses obscures many of its ethical dimensions. But if the therapy
goals put forth by Tania and Dr Schwartz are *good* goals, or Sandra has the
right to be reimbursed for an unlimited number of therapy sessions, financial
considerations affected the ethical dimensions of Sandra's therapy: her rights
have been violated and she does not reach the good ends articulated for her
by her therapist and therapist's supervisor.

In the rapidly changing health care climate in the US (Austad 1996;
Moffic 1997; Trabin and Freeman 1995), the UK (Knapp 1995; E. Smith
1997; A. Williams 1994), and other countries (Desjarlais *et al.* 1995; H. M.
Sass and R. U. Massey 1988), complex economic forces are affecting therapy,
at times helping clients reach therapeutic goals, at times preventing them
from doing so, and consistently shaping the ways in which people receive
therapy. Consequently, "psychotherapists can no longer practice as if
psychotherapy were independent of its economic environment" (Austad and
Berman 1991a: 3).

"The rape of psychotherapy" is how Ron Fox (1995: 147), former president of the American Psychological Association, described managed care's
effect on therapy in the US. Karon called these new forms of health care "a
growing crisis and national nightmare" (Karon 1995: 5). And Blanck and
DeLeon (1996) report that some consider managed care immoral – because
it is depriving clients of their rights and making them powerless.

Powerful ethical convictions underlie those attacks on managed care and
make clear the close ties between economic and ethical considerations. Fox
contended that "the care of the sick, the damaged, and the infirm cannot be
done in a vacuum absent of values and moral responsibility." And, using
explicitly moral language, he asserted that "the wrongs that are being done
in the name of saving money are simply unconscionable" (R. E. Fox 1995:
147).

I will focus in this section on but a few key aspects of the complex business context of therapy, those relevant to understanding ethical dimensions
of therapy. The business context of therapy is related to therapy's ethical
dimensions in several ways. (1) *Economic considerations affect therapy* – money
can either facilitate therapy and help clients reach good ends, or prevent that
from happening. But (2) *limited financial resources* have meant that third-
party payers (governments, employers, insurance companies, and managed
care entities) are less and less willing to pay for therapy, or are willing to pay
for it only in circumscribed circumstances. And so, critics charge, third-
party payers violate clients' right to receive health care and prevent clients
from receiving therapy of sufficient length to maximize their well-being.
Third parties can thus keep clients from reaching good therapy goals. But

the third parties deny those charges, arguing that they have eliminated unnecessary and wasteful therapy, like long-term therapy for Sandra to reach goals established by her therapist and her therapist's supervisor, but *not* by Sandra, for whom eight sessions of managed care therapy alleviated her presenting problem, anxiety about speaking in public. They also challenge the claim that people have an unconditional, unqualified right to be reimbursed for an unlimited number of therapy sessions. (3) When addressing therapy, some business entities *consider economic considerations alone* (or are believed to do so). If psychotherapy is viewed *only* as a business, decision-makers try to eliminate all ethical considerations: decisions about therapy are based solely on its economic costs and benefits. (Ethical decisions are not eliminated, of course, but made in particular ways, and implicitly.) (4) By way of contrast to such economic reductionism, many therapists and managed behavioral health care companies (see Trabin and Freeman 1995) argue that therapists, society, and clients need to *balance economic with other considerations*. That is, psychotherapy's stakeholders can consider a society's limited financial resources and also address quality of care and professional ethical considerations.[1]

Economic considerations and the ethical dimensions of psychotherapy

If money is available to pay for therapy, clients can enter therapy and potentially reach the goals (good or bad) set for them; if money is not available, they cannot.

In general, those whose economic well-being is affected by therapy want a say about its goals and the way it is conducted. Those who pay for therapy or receive income from it – clients, therapists, and third-party payers – are all interested in its goals (including goals considered good, right, or virtuous) and about its process (how therapy is conducted, its ethical character, and the number, frequency, and cost of sessions). Clients generally want high-quality therapy at a reasonably low cost (preferably covered by a third-party payer). Therapists vary in their economic goals: some want only to earn enough to survive financially, and some enough to thrive. Third-party payers want to be cost-effective (spend as little as necessary) as clients reach therapy goals.

Striving to maximize one's own financial well-being (whether motivated by greed or by a desire for a fair financial arrangement) can affect therapy. Indeed, health economists have proposed "target income theory," based on what McGuire characterizes as "the derogatory view that physicians prescribe treatments not according to clinical norms but according to the economic norm that they should make a certain amount of money" (McGuire 1992: 10). Therapists reject that theory, denying that it explains the behavior of *most* therapists. They point instead to the greed of third-party payers, emphasizing compelling stories like that reported by Fox: "The chief executive officer of a major managed care firm received salary, bonus, and stock options last year of $9.8 million, plus dividends on his stock shares of $11.4 million!" (R. E. Fox 1995: 150).

In fact, economic incentives can influence the actions of clients, therapists, *and* third-party payers. Profit motivates *all* parties when free market systems of health care operate (Salmon 1990). Such systems, note Austad and Berman, are "subject to greed and misuse" (Austad and Berman 1991c: viii). As A. Williams (1994) observes, when health care professionals work with clients until they are as healthy as possible, care can be limitless. When therapists provide interminable therapy, have full caseloads, and receive standard fees, they do very well indeed. On the other hand, some managed care arrangements provide both therapists and managed care entities with strong financial incentives to *under*treat clients (Trabin and Freeman 1995). Greed can thus influence the behavior of all therapy stakeholders.

Although corporations have financial incentives to undertreat their employees, they have countervailing financial incentives to treat them well. Corporations face the expense of therapy, but can benefit financially from employees who receive it. Both mental illness and psychotherapy have economic consequences (McGuire 1992). Untreated mental illness and substance abuse among a corporation's employees can harm a company economically. And providing psychotherapy can produce positive economic consequences for corporations. Positive medical consequences can also result from psychotherapy. And since corporations pay for medical treatment, the cost of providing psychotherapy is offset by lower expenses for those medical problems (Finney *et al.* 1991; McGuire 1992; VandenBos and DeLeon 1988). Furthermore, some businesses provide therapy for employees assuming it will result in better attendance records and safer, more productive employees (Trabin and Freeman 1995). Freed from emotional burdens, they can function on the job more effectively.

Fewer medical problems and higher productivity are good ends (understood ethically) of therapy that benefit employers economically. Because economic and ethical considerations converge, enlightened self-interest motivates employers to provide employees with basic coverage for mental health services.

Excessive economic self-interest (greed) among psychotherapists has traditionally been kept in check, therapists argue, by professional standards and codes of ethics (along with other factors). Since they are supposed to further client well-being, professionals are not supposed to provide unnecessary therapy, even if extra therapy is profitable. But this assumes therapists are ethically motivated to benefit clients. Without the "moral leverage" of ethical ideals, Doherty argues, "therapists who advocate maintaining generous mental health insurance benefits sound suspiciously like military defense contractors arguing that reduced military spending will threaten national security" (Doherty 1995: 3).

But the poverty of ethical articulation affecting most therapists makes it difficult for them to provide convincing *ethical* arguments for the claim that professionals are primarily concerned with the best interests of clients. And the present system has spawned enough abuses that even strong opponents of managed care (e.g. R. E. Fox 1995) acknowledge the need for health care reform. But the current crisis in mental health reimbursement has another, more fundamental source: differing ethical visions of psychotherapy goals and processes. The modest ethical vision of corporations and managed care entities often conflicts with the more extensive ethical visions of therapists and clients.

Ethical ideas about psychotherapy – about good therapy goals and the kinds of therapy that should be reimbursed – thus affect ideas about the level of financial reimbursement for therapy. And the level of reimbursement sometimes determines which therapy goals can and cannot be reached.

Some insist that clients ought to determine therapy goals. Or that goals ought to be determined by therapist and client with no interference from "outside" parties. And indeed, as traditionally conceived, therapy involved therapist and client alone, unbesmirched by crass economic considerations. If clients and therapists were the only stakeholders in therapy, they could, in free countries, pursue therapy in whatever way they pleased. However, with the exception of therapy involving wealthy clients able to afford therapy and therapists able to charge clients low or no fees, most therapy is paid for, in part or in full, by some third party. And so other stakeholders are often concerned about therapy relationships. And the economic and other factors introduced by such third-party payers are now significantly shaping therapy's ethical character.

But this third-party involvement, and its consequences for the ethical character of therapy, is not new. Business became involved in counseling in the US at a relatively early stage in its development. Corporation-sponsored therapy aimed at the goal of adjustment (Baritz 1960). Assuming the happy worker was a productive worker, one unlikely to join a union, Western Electric began to provide counseling to employees in 1936, conceiving of it as "a method of helping people think in such a way that they would be happier with their jobs" (Baritz 1960: 104).

More widespread corporate involvement in psychotherapy did not develop until the 1960s and 1970s when health insurance programs began covering psychotherapy (VandenBos et al. 1992). The therapeutic contract thus involved therapist, client, and third-party payer, a tripartite arrangement much more complicated, difficult to understand, and impersonal than that negotiated by therapist and client alone. But VandenBos, Cummings, and DeLeon pointed out that "economic factors, such as government support and insurance reimbursement, have played a major role in making psychotherapy a viable social enterprise and profession" (VandenBos *et al.* 1992: 97). Reimbursement meant more people *could* receive therapy. And they did. The number of mental health professionals grew accordingly, with the number in the US increasing from 23,000 in 1947 to 121,000 in 1977 (Kiesler and Morton 1988) and the number of US psychologists jumping over 300 percent from 1974 to 1992 (Frank and VandenBos 1994).

Many factors led to widespread health insurance (Starr 1982), including the high cost of treatment, laws mandating mental health coverage, and ideas about a right to health care. Unions and others negotiated for health insurance as an employee benefit, and then for mental health coverage, because reimbursed treatment for physical and mental health problems was seen to be good. Insurance companies placed some limits on coverage, including lifetime maximum benefits, deductibles to be met before reimbursement would begin, requiring clients to cover part of the cost, and, most significantly, limiting coverage to diagnosable mental disorders (Starr 1982; Trabin and Freeman 1995). The last was important because third parties began dictating which therapy goals would result in reimbursement: once a client no longer suffered from a diagnosable mental disorder, reimbursement purportedly stopped.

But traditional indemnity insurance plans, at first the most common type of insurance, required little interaction between third-party payer and professional (Starr 1982) and, from the perspective of the therapist, little interference. Insurance companies trusted therapists to diagnose accurately. And many therapists saw few clients who would not "fit" into some diagnostic category.

But in response to increasing health care costs, federal legislation, and other factors (Trabin and Freeman 1995; VandenBos *et al.* 1992), new forms of third-party payment for mental health problems developed rapidly in the 1970s and 1980s. The "quiet" third party in psychotherapy began to speak more loudly and "interfere" in therapy in unprecedented ways. Third-party payers began to manage care previously managed by therapists, and to pay for therapy in some circumstances but not others. And self-insured employers questioned funding long-term therapy aimed at clients' personal growth (Trabin and Freeman 1995).

Therapists responded angrily to the new limits placed on them. They raised a wide range of complaints, especially about denial of payment for treatment, and denial of payment for treatment deemed too long (R. E. Fox 1995; I. J. Miller 1996; Seligman 1996). The "corporatization" of health care (R. E. Fox 1995; Salmon 1990) was decried, because the new health care corporations were allegedly concerned about profits, not patients (Eisenberg 1986), and failed to exhibit compassion or a commitment to equity, quality, or any social obligation to the poor. Seligman raised other concerns about Managed Care Organizations (MCOs):

(a) MCOs endanger three basic patient rights: choice of provider, facility, and modality; personal privacy; and decision-making ability.
(b) MCOs make clinicians directly economically dependent on insurers, and thus frequently create a conflict between the well-being of the patient and the operating profits of the MCO company or insurer.
(c) MCOs "deprofessionalize" care by hiring the "cheapest" person willing to do the work....
(d) Treatment decisions based on the judgment of the consumer and clinician should be primary. They should not be subordinated to the judgment of insurers, case mangers [sic], or employers.

(Seligman 1996: 5)

Seligman thus raises profound ethical questions about managed care.

Trabin and Freeman (1995) acknowledge that managers in some forms of managed care, especially during periods of rapid growth, have exhibited poor clinical judgment, inappropriately denied treatment, and harmed clients. However, they stress the diversity of managed care providers (see Austad 1996), noting that most problems occurred with those that limited mental health expenditures to 3 percent of total health expenditures. Entities spending 7 percent provided quality care and were still cost-effective, spending less than the average of 10 percent devoted nationally to mental health care. However, Trabin and Freeman voiced concern about survey findings suggesting that those who purchase health services are perceived to be more concerned about cost and less about quality of care. Since most of psychotherapy's ethical dimensions have to do with matters of quality, the direction that evolving systems of health care take in the future will have profound effects on the ethical dimensions of psychotherapy.

Careful analyses of the financial incentives in various approaches to therapy reimbursement and the trend of greater accountability will likely be of particular importance in determining *how* economic factors shape psychotherapy in the future. That is important because the ethical character of therapy will be determined in part by financial incentives and in part by the ways in which third-party payers, therapists, and clients are accountable to one another.

The economic incentives found in traditional forms of insurance pull therapists in the direction of *over*treating clients (Trabin and Freeman 1995). One reason is the unique nature of traditional indemnity health insurance (Starr 1982): within limits, the more therapists bill insurance companies, the more therapists get paid. So, therapists have a financial incentive to find "disorder," to provide extensive treatment, and to charge increasingly steep fees. Health care is thus disconnected from the market forces that exist in other businesses. Although health insurance for mental health problems is ostensibly limited to demonstrable mental disorders, reimbursement is sometimes sought for therapy with people whose problems do not meet strict diagnostic criteria. It is extended to the "worried well," to persons suffering from ordinary unhappiness (Schofield 1986). Indeed, Regier, Narrow, Rae, Manderscheid, Locke, and Goodwin (1993) estimated that, of the 23.1 million Americans seeking treatment each year in the *de facto* mental and addictive disorders service system, 10.4 million did not meet the diagnostic criteria for any current mental disorder. Of that 10.4 million, 34.1 percent had past, but not present, diagnoses. That leaves 6.8 million Americans with no (past or present) diagnosable mental disorder receiving mental health/substance abuse services.

By way of contrast, the economic incentives in some forms of managed care pull companies and therapists in the direction of *under*treating clients (Austad and Berman 1991b). Research in the field of economics and mental health has made it clear that the specific features of a payment system substantially influence access to therapy, the quality of the care provided, and its costs (McGuire 1992). This is especially true in the arena of mental health, where demand for services varies with the availability of reimbursement more than the demand for physical health services varies. Consequently, US mental health costs grew at an even faster rate than other health care costs (Broskowski 1991). Although much of this increase has been attributed to the expenses of inpatient treatment (I. J. Miller 1996), ambulatory mental health organization expenditures in the US grew from $388 million in 1969 to $5.3 billion in 1988, with expenditures in per capita constant dollars going from $1.94 to $4.96 (Redick *et al.* 1992). That is, when controlled for inflation, the costs of ambulatory mental health services increased 156 percent.

To control costs, some managed mental health care entities mandate greater therapist accountability. Third-party payers expect the psychotherapy professions to provide empirical evidence for the effectiveness of psychotherapy and individual providers to document the progress clients make and follow practice guidelines (R. E. Fox 1995). But Fox, while acknowledging the need for therapists to be more accountable, argued that managed care companies need to be more accountable as well. For example, he noted they require therapists to maintain liability insurance but some have attempted, unless legally prohibited from doing so, to "avoid responsibility for the adverse effects of their decisions on patients" (ibid.: 150). Similarly, I. J. Miller (1996) argued that managed care entities should provide consumers with accurate information about cost and quality so they can make wise, informed decisions about their health care. And, in fact, Trabin and Freeman report that some purchasers of health care services are beginning to require managed care entities to be more accountable, for example, by developing "outcomes management programs" and providing "data from them periodically in order to demonstrate clinical effectiveness and value" (Trabin and Freeman 1995: 20). As Austad notes, "all managed care is not the same" (Austad 1996: 6). Greater accountability will permit all therapy stakeholders to make more informed evaluations of specific managed care entities. One way in which managed care organizations are being made more accountable is by providing potential clients (consumers) and other interested parties with evaluations of each managed care organization that offers services to a given population (Knutson *et al.* 1996). In Indiana, for instance, service providers are rated annually on a "Provider Profile Report Card" which "describes the relative performances of each of the service providers" (Newman *et al.* 1997: 1).

This call for accountability could produce an important dialogue about the ethical dimensions of psychotherapy because all parties are expected to be forthcoming about the value-laden issues of therapy goals, therapy effectiveness, and the quality of services provided.

Unfortunately, however, this demand for accountability can disrupt the clinical relationship and pose serious threats to confidentiality (R. E. Fox 1995). If decisions about therapy goals and length of sessions are made by those third parties alone, both client and therapist are disempowered and their freedom is abridged. And very private information may need to be sent to third parties. Client confidentiality may be compromised.

Differing financial incentives and demands for accountability shape (and will shape) the ethical character of therapy because clients, therapists, and third-party payers have very different perspectives on psychotherapy. Behind those differences and behind economic decisions lie ethical differences among psychotherapy's stakeholders. They hold different visions about which therapy outcomes and which therapy processes are good, right, or virtuous and so make different choices. Corporations sometimes appear to make decisions about therapy solely on cost considerations. If a corporation's business advisor were told, "Tell this corporation how to make more money," the answer with regard to psychotherapy might be "Therapy that is as short as possible, inexpensive, efficient, and not wasteful, and that avoids hospitalizations and lawsuits, decreases expenses, maximizes productivity and profits, and reduces expenditures for medical treatments." The *de facto* ethical ideals in the corporation's economic interests are evident in that list. By way of contrast, if a therapist's business advisor were told, "Tell me how to make more money," the reply might be "Therapy that is long, expensive, fully or mostly reimbursed, and accessible to everyone in a society. Therapy in which therapist and client alone set goals. And therapy that involves little or no paperwork and produces satisfied clients who refer new clients to you." The *de facto* ethical ideals in the therapist's economic interests are evident in that list as well.

The business context of therapy affects its ethical character in another way, by way of the societal structures through which therapy is provided. Those structures reflect ethical ideals. As H. Sass points out, "the structures that exist to provide health care in different national settings" reflect "moral presuppositions and underlying ethical considerations" (H. M. Sass 1988: xiii). Those structures, Sass argues, warrant careful analysis. In analyzing the changes in US health care, Salmon (1990) complained that ethical ideals present in more traditional forms of health care, for example, free or low cost hospital care for the poor, have disappeared in newer forms of health care. (Nothing, save financial well-being, prevents therapists in private practice from offering free or low-cost therapy, however.) And many therapists are convinced the primary commitment of managed care entities is cost effectiveness, not quality of care.

Limited financial resources

Many Americans believe they spend too much on health care for what they receive (M. A. Hall 1997). That is, many believe that too large a percentage of the US Gross National Product is devoted to health care. That fact must be faced. It represents both a crisis of social ethics (raising profound questions of distributive justice, since many Americans lack health insurance), and an economic problem of the first magnitude for those ultimately paying for psychotherapy, which includes taxpayers. As Austad and Berman put it, "costs have increased so dramatically that employers, insurers, and individual consumers are no longer willing to pay unlimited amounts for health care without close scrutiny and accountability" (Austad and Berman 1991a: 3).

The US devotes 14 percent of its Gross National Product (GNP) to health care (M. A. Hall 1997), 40 percent more than any other developed country (R. G. Frank 1993). Davis (1989) notes that US expenditures are in contrast to the 6 to 9 percent of GNP spent by most European countries and Japan. And Davis adds that, although health spending as a percentage of national productivity stabilized in those countries during the 1980s, the percentage continued to grow in the US. Sensenig, Heffler, and Donham (1997) reported that in the mid-1990s, US health care expenses (as a percentage of GNP) finally began to stabilize, due to managed care. As noted above, the percentage of health care expenditures devoted to mental health had been growing even faster than the overall growth of health care expenditures (Broskowski 1991). Costs escalated as benefits expanded.

Limited resources for psychotherapy is a global problem (Desjarlais *et al.* 1995; Knapp 1995). As Williams notes, all societies work within budget constraints and restrict "good" health care: "No society can afford to offer all its members all the health care that might possibly do them some good. Each society has therefore to establish priorities" (A. Williams 1994: 829). The great difficulty of doing so, an ethical difficulty, is that "expanding one good thing will always be at the expense of other good things" (ibid.: 830). Any country could greatly expand the availability of psychotherapy, maximizing the good that therapy produces. Doing so might, however, mean losing some of its productivity and global competitiveness. Therapists would do well in that scenario, but not workers who lose jobs to foreign competition because high health care costs forced their employers out of business.

Employing economic considerations alone

In the face of those economic pressures and the perceived need to reduce health care costs, one set of "solutions" presents itself: take into account only economic considerations, permit them to trump all others, or make them primary. Although many therapists feel this valorizing of economic considerations, this economic reductionism, characterizes all or most managed care entities, I am disinclined to think it true of all. I do not raise the issue of economic reductionism, however, to make an empirical claim about managed care. I do so to clarify the ethical implications of viewing psychotherapy in exclusively economic terms. Unless educated in the virtues of taking a broader perspective on psychotherapy, the business school graduates increasingly in charge of health care reimbursement will view psychotherapy in primarily financial terms. Those, like me, who think it important that psychotherapy stakeholders consider economic *and* ethical issues in making decisions about therapy reimbursement need to know the logic likely to be used by those thinking exclusively in economic terms in order to respond to them effectively.

Two features of an exclusively business perspective are especially relevant to the ethical character of therapy: the common (but fortunately not universal) lack in business of an ethical analysis of the ends or goals of psychotherapy, and reducing therapists to commodities, treating them like any other business product.

In MacIntyre's (1984) analysis of contemporary culture, the figure of the manager is central. The manager works in an organization, for example, a corporation or government bureaucracy, that exists to further certain ends. The task of managers is to "direct and redirect their organizations' available resources, both human and non-human, as effectively as possible toward those ends" (MacIntyre 1984: 25). Those ends are *given* to the manager; it is not his or her task to think about them because, as MacIntyre notes, "questions of ends are questions of values, and on values reason is silent" (ibid.: 266). It is, however, the task of the manager to be effective in achieving assigned ends. And about effectiveness, rational judgments can be made.

If the primary end of the corporation is profit, the manager assigned the task of determining mental health benefits will seek to maximize corporate profits when determining mental health benefits. The manager may thus reduce or subordinate the goals of therapy – autonomy, freedom from mental illness, mental health, self-actualization, insight, healthier primary relationships, and so forth – to economic considerations, to numbers on an accountant's spreadsheet. The intrinsic goodness of those ends, or any sort of qualified right of individuals to receive treatment to achieve them, will be lost from view. Lost, that is, unless therapists and others articulate clearly psychotherapy's pervasively ethical character.

A second problem produced by an exclusively business approach to psychotherapy is viewing the therapist as a commodity, exchangeable with any other therapist. "Commodifying" the therapeutic relationship, making therapists commodities or providers of a commodity named therapy, making therapy "just a business relationship," permits a therapeutic relationship to be terminated as any other business relationship is terminated. And, in fact, some managed care entities have informed clients/employees by mail that their long-standing therapeutic relationships would, after a date in the near future, no longer be reimbursed, adding that the client/employee could contact a substitute therapist who would meet any mental health needs the managed care entity chose to authorize. This ignores the empirical evidence about the importance of the therapeutic alliance (Horvath and Greenberg 1994; Orlinsky *et al.* 1994). Furthermore, treating clients and therapists as means to an end, and not as ends in themselves, violates Kant's basic ethical principle that people should always be respected as worthy in and of themselves, as ends, and never merely as means to some end.

Let me provide a second example of the clash of business and therapeutic cultures, of the failure of an exclusively business perspective to take seriously professional standards and ethics, the importance of therapeutic relationships, and client well-being. This example is from my own experience. I was socialized in a therapeutic culture that placed primary emphasis on client well-being and took the client–therapist relationship very seriously. For example, long-term and vulnerable clients were prepared to cope with their therapist's vacations well ahead of the therapist's departure. After completing my internship, I joined a clinic that, through a complex process, became part of a corporation that attempted to expand to provide behavioral health services across the nation. The attempt to expand failed, leading to layoffs and the Chapter-11 bankruptcy of the parent company of the clinic at which I worked. But clinical services continued and optimism was expressed about the long-term viability of the local clinic. But one morning, the day after I returned from vacation, I received a phone call informing me that the clinic had filed for a Chapter-7 bankruptcy and would close at 5 p.m. that day. I was unable to reach the client I had scheduled at 6 that evening, but was told she would be notified of the clinic's closing and told how to contact me so we could continue therapy. The client was not notified, nor was I notified she was not contacted. And so she showed up for her appointment to find the door locked, the clinic shuttered. Although this client was unperturbed and a colleague loaned me his office until I could make more permanent arrangements, it became evident to me that an exclusively economic and legal approach to the business of psychotherapy led to a decided callousness to client well-being and to the importance of "intangibles" like the therapeutic alliance. That is, a strictly "business" approach to therapy can lead to serious ethical problems.

To be sure, economic evaluations of mental health delivery can be conducted, indeed, should be conducted, with greater sensitivity to the persons involved and to therapeutic alliances. In this regard, Knapp (1995) provides a helpful alternative, outlining four principles – economy, efficiency, effectiveness, and equity – that economic evaluations of therapy can employ so the evaluations are not narrowly economic, but include ethical components as well.

But therapists' failure to be explicit about therapy's ethical dimensions, of the goodness of therapy ends and the irreducibly important (and ethically vital) therapeutic alliance, will lead to a problematic reduction of psychotherapy to nothing but an economic problem. Unless, that is, therapists and others make a clear and convincing case for the importance of ethical considerations in therapy. As Doherty notes, "therapists' failure to attend to the broader moral and community dimension has left psychotherapy vulnerable to being managed as just one more commodity in the health care marketplace" (Doherty 1995: 8).

Balancing economic with other considerations

The obvious solution to the problems of thinking about therapy in solely economic terms is for psychotherapy stakeholders to use non-economic considerations as well, especially those that are scientific and ethical. Although McGuire (1992) notes that introducing professional norms into economic evaluations of health care systems makes them more complex, he thinks that doing so makes the evaluations more adequate. Yates (1995) articulates the need for scientist-manager-practitioners with expertise in both science and business. He also describes models for research and practice that take into account both science and business. Fox noted that "the laws of the marketplace are ill-suited" for the work of caring for others, but acknowledged the legitimate needs of purchasers of mental health services. Their business needs can be met, he argued, "without destroying the integrity of the psychotherapeutic contract" (R. E. Fox 1995: 147, 149). Likewise, Knapp noted that economics "cannot replace the judgments of decision-makers, but it ought to be able to supplement and inform them" (Knapp 1995: 23).

Knapp and others have articulated criteria that psychotherapy stakeholders can use, in conjunction with cost-effectiveness, to improve the systems through which psychotherapy is provided. Knapp suggested economy, efficiency, effectiveness, and equity. Trabin and Freeman (1995) argued for improving value and quality along with cost-effectiveness. And, as noted above, Fox (1995) stressed the importance of the integrity of the therapeutic contract. Finally, Abe-Kim and Takeuchi (1996) suggested cultural competence, a component of the quality of services provided, as a criterion by which managed care should be evaluated.

To determine whether a particular system of managed care has met those criteria, we need to draw upon economics, science, *and* ethics. Ethical analysis comes into play, for example, when we define what "quality" means in psychotherapy or consider the goodness of the goals we use to determine whether therapy is "effective." Ethical analyses are also relevant when evaluating the quality of the relationship between therapist and client, the ethical character of that relationship. Finally, addressing equity, the fair distribution of therapeutic services, requires social ethical reflection, reflection that considers not just the therapist and client, but the needs of a society as a whole.

And so therapists, if taking into account scientific, business, and ethical concerns, must expand the traditional identity of therapists as professionals concerned exclusively with their clients. As Knapp (1995) and Austad (1996) note, therapists have duties to patients *and* to the public.

In summary, by pointing beyond the therapy dyad to the broader social context, the business context of therapy shapes our understanding of its ethical character. It does so in other ways as well, like providing the resources to reach therapy goals which we believe to be good. But business considerations also block clients from reaching their goals. And employing economic considerations alone can block from our view the ethical character of therapy. In the current economic climate, the ethical character of the therapy relationship and of therapy goals is especially likely to be lost in debates over cost-effectiveness. And so it is especially important that therapists clearly articulate the ethical basis of therapeutic relationships and therapy goals, the ethical character of therapy process and outcome. It is to those topics I will turn in Chapters 8 and 9.

Conclusion

Any psychotherapy session represents the culmination of a long and variegated series of interlocking sociohistorical developments. I have argued that the ethical, scientific, clinical, and business contexts of therapy have shaped, and continue to shape, the ethical dimensions of psychotherapy. At times, those contexts have also obscured, and obscure, those dimensions. Because those contexts influence therapists, clients, and third-party payers in rich, subtle, and powerful ways, they shape the ethical character of psychotherapy.

Part IV

Change in psychotherapy
Ethical facets

8

Ethical dimensions of the techniques, strategies, and processes of therapy

Which means to therapeutic ends?

To evaluate the ethical character of what occurs during psychotherapy, we need to think carefully about the goodness, rightness, and virtues of the various techniques, strategies, and people in therapeutic relationships. Consider this vignette:

> "My life is messed up. And my sister and my boss both told me I should get some help."
>
> After those opening words, Bob, a 33-year-old foundry worker, describes his situation. His second wife has left him, perhaps permanently. With the help of his extended family, he is taking care of their three children, a 10-year-old girl from his first marriage, a 9-year-old boy from his wife's first marriage (Bob adopted him and considers him his own), and a 3-year-old daughter from their marriage together. Bob's 28-year-old wife left him to live with a 23-year-old she met over the Internet. That relationship, however, appears to working out less well in person than in cyberspace.
>
> After providing those skeletal facts, Bob continues, "And now I'm really confused. Should I forgive her and try to work it out? Or forget about her and get on with my life? I've done it before. I mean, start over. But I had only one kid then, not three. But I could do it.
>
> "So what should I do? That's my question. That's why I'm here. What do you think?"
>
> Dr Peterson asks a variety of assessment questions. He learns that Bob is suffering from mild-to-moderate levels of depression and anxiety. Bob reports functioning well at work and having a good relationship with all three children. But he states he doesn't feel very good about himself as a husband. In the course of the four-year marriage, he has been verbally abusive to his wife, and she to him, although no physical abuse has occurred. Wrathful arguments have broken out in the four months since they separated, with the children at times within earshot. And once a month or so, Bob "copes" by getting drunk. He goes to a neighborhood bar, returning home at closing time and leaving the children in the care of

his oldest daughter. When questioned about the wisdom of this, he reacts defensively. "Look! My daughter is *very* responsible. Plus, the next door neighbor is right there if a problem comes up."

Although tending to externalize blame, Bob has occasional self-reflective moments in which he becomes painfully aware of how far his present life is from his ideals for it (e.g. "I believe in marriage, but I'm a two-time failure as a husband. I mean, how bad can you get? My life wasn't supposed to turn out this way.") A conservative (but not a fundamentalist) Christian, he just began participating with other men in his church in the Promise Keepers men's movement. As a result, he says, he knows he needs to accept more responsibility for his actions. He is warm and affectionate with his children, performs the full range of household responsibilities in the absence of his wife, and espouses a belief in traditional sex roles.

As the initial therapy hour draws to a close, Bob becomes agitated and angrily demands, "We've been talking for an hour now, but you *still* haven't told me what to *do* about my problem. What should I do? Forgive her?"

Dr Peterson reacts strongly and emotionally to what feels to him like an attack. In accord with his analytic training, he notices and processes his reaction: he knows his own affairs played a role in his divorce. "But only in small part," he tells himself. "My wife's unwillingness to forget about those little 'adventures' of mine was the biggest part of the problem." Dr Peterson also wonders whether his class and religious differences with Bob are playing a role in his reaction. But he also thinks about Bob's strong desire to have an authority figure tell him what to do, thinking in terms of transferential issues, unconscious motivation, and the early childhood origins of Bob's problems. And he keeps in mind Freud's doctrine about therapist self-disclosure: "The doctor should be opaque to his patient and, like a mirror, should show them nothing but what is shown to him" (Freud 1958: 118).

And so he simply says, "I don't want to impose my values on you. That wouldn't be fair to you. But I think therapy is a good idea for you. An objective professional can help you sort out your feelings about all this and make a decision. And don't you worry about paying for this. I know how to handle these managed care companies." He chuckles, and says to Bob, "Let me ask you one more question: Have you ever in your life felt, even a little bit, like you'd rather be dead than alive?"

"Well, yes," says Bob, somewhat startled. "But I'd never do anything. Especially not with three kids."

"Good," replies Dr Peterson, saying to himself "Close enough," and checking off "suicidal" on the managed care evaluation form.

He then looks up at Bob and says, "I'll get you all the sessions you want. I can see you again next Wednesday at 4."

To address well the ethical character of the processes of Bob's therapy, of any therapy relationship, or of therapy in general, we need to begin by rejecting a pernicious falsehood: therapists *either* provide "objective, value-free" therapy *or* "impose" their values on clients. Dr Peterson's options are far wider than either being neutral or coercing Bob into adopting his views.

Much of this book has been a sustained argument against the possibility of value-free therapy. It is also not possible, with rare exceptions, for therapists to *impose* their values on clients. Influence, yes; impose, no. In general, therapists simply do not have enough power over clients to impose their views on them. Indeed, if therapists could impose values, they could impose mental health, quickly eliminating the problems clients bring to therapy. Therapy would be universally effective; we would need few therapists.

Between the alternatives of "imposing" values and "value-freedom" is a rich and fascinating middle ground. Murkier, to be sure, than either of those alternatives, but holding the ultimate promise of being both more realistic and more satisfactory. More fine-grained analyses of the ethical dimensions of the therapy process require an exploration of that middle ground, as well as other pertinent issues. Indeed, the processes of Bob's and other clients' therapeutic relationships involve many ethical issues.

Therapy process and ethics

Perez (1989b) suggests that we can evaluate the "ethical acceptability" of therapy methods, plus the "ethical legitimacy of…therapeutic goals" (Perez 1989b: 140). We can thus evaluate the ethical dimensions of both therapy process and therapy outcome, a traditional distinction I am using to divide the material in Chapters 8 and 9.

By process, I mean whatever occurs during psychotherapy. As Orlinsky, Grawe, and Parks (1994) point out, researchers have labeled a variety of therapy techniques, states of relationship, methods, and so forth as "process." These processes can be evaluated (often with very different results) from the perspective of clients, therapists, and outside observers. They can also be evaluated in terms of the types of change clients experience, of specific events in therapy (e.g. the "actions, perceptions, intentions, thoughts, and feelings of the patient and therapist, as well as the relationship between them" – Orlinsky *et al.* 1994: 274), of what causes outcome, and of sequential descriptions of what occurs. And we can employ multiple levels of description. Finally, Frank and Frank (1991) argue that because psychotherapy addresses, and alters, the meanings which clients attribute to life events, those crucial meaning-making and meaning-altering processes warrant the careful attention of anyone striving to understand therapy. All of those dimensions of therapy process can be evaluated ethically.

Psychotherapy process and outcome overlap (Lambert and Hill 1994). For example, some would argue that Bob accepting greater responsibility for his actions is a vitally important means (a process) by which therapeutic goals can be reached. But others would consider his acceptance of greater responsibility a therapeutic goal (an outcome). And others would consider it both process and outcome. Still others, pointing to the variety of ways "process" and "outcome" are used and to some of the problems with the traditional distinction (Shapiro *et al*. 1994; Stiles *et al*. 1994), argue that the distinction is problematic.

I use "process" and "outcome" as terms of art, neither distinguishing them sharply nor intending by their use the assumptions Stiles, Shapiro, and Harper (1994) properly critique. An ethical evaluation of some dimensions of therapy, like "Bob's accepting greater responsibility for his actions," does not depend on "correctly" labeling it process, outcome, both, or neither. A rough distinction can be drawn, however: some ethical issues pertain to the goodness, rightness, or virtue of particular therapy goals or outcomes. They will be discussed in the next chapter. Other ethical issues have to do with what occurs during therapy *regardless of therapy goals*. For example, however we ethically evaluate particular therapy goals, we can consider the rightness of Dr Peterson's violating Bob's confidentiality, the goodness of his treating Bob with respect, or whether Dr Peterson's fairness (his consistently acting justly) is virtuous. Those ethical judgments all pertain to process, and can be made without reference to therapy goals. It is those process-dimensions of therapy, and some that either overlap with outcome or transcend the distinction, that I will address in this chapter.

By an ethical evaluation of psychotherapy processes, I mean thinking about process in terms of what is good, right, and/or virtuous. In this chapter, I will first discuss in general how ethical considerations are relevant to a variety of dimensions of therapy process and to professional standards and ideals. In the second half of the chapter, I will address some specific dimensions of therapy process, like therapist influence on client values.

A variety of ethically relevant dimensions of therapy process can be distinguished. Some pertain to therapy in general, regardless of therapeutic content. For instance, we might assert that it is *good* that Dr Peterson treats Bob with respect, whatever issues he brings to therapy. Other types of ethically relevant therapy process pertain to how therapists and clients address specifically *ethical* issues. For instance, we can ethically evaluate the kind of influence Dr Peterson exerts on Bob's moral convictions. We may think it wrong for Dr Peterson to exert strong pressure on Bob to adopt a "Me-first" philosophy of life and abandon his sense of moral obligation to his three children. Dr Peterson may, however, legitimately explore with Bob whether he wants to hold that sense of obligation more flexibly or balance it with other ideals in a different way. In making the assertion that Dr Peterson's influence on Bob was wrong, we ethically evaluate the manner (process) of Dr Peterson's influence on Bob's ethical convictions.

A full-fledged ethical evaluation of therapy process addresses topics like what it means to be a good therapist (e.g. warmth, timing, empathy, use of effective techniques, and "therapist virtues") and which methods, techniques, and interpersonal qualities are good, right, and/or virtuous (e.g. those that match clients' needs, are effective,[1] are carried out in accord with the theory to which they correspond, respect the client's autonomy, and so forth). And so we can assert that it was good that Dr Peterson listened carefully to Bob and right that he preserved Bob's confidentiality. It was not good that he implicitly promised Bob "objective" therapy and wrong that he planned to lie to (and defraud) Bob's managed care company to insure ample coverage.

Diagnosis can be included as well because, as Fulford suggested, diagnosis "can be thought of essentially as deciding what is wrong with someone" (Fulford 1989: 167). And that, of course, requires a normative sense of some good state from which the person's symptoms deviate, or distinguishing what is wrong with a person (their nonmorally or morally bad state) from what is right with that person.

To clarify further the relevance of ethics to the processes of therapy, I would like to discuss from several perspectives how basic ethical principles and virtues, as discussed in Chapter 4, pertain to therapy processes.

Ethical principles and virtues applied to therapy processes

If, when making an ethical judgment about a particular therapeutic technique or method, someone looks solely at its consequences, ends, or goals, that person is using a teleological or consequentialist theory. Outcome is used to determine whether a particular therapy process is good, right, or virtuous. Those who argue that therapists should exclusively employ techniques that have been empirically supported or validated as effective (effective in reaching some specified good outcome) thus tend to be ethical teleologists.

Others employ principles in making ethical judgments about process (and so use deontological ethical theories). They can consider outcome when thinking about the goodness or rightness of a therapeutic technique, but also use other criteria. Meara, Schmidt, and Day (1996) set forth six basic ethical principles, or criteria, to be used in ethical decision-making:[2] respect for autonomy, nonmaleficence (avoiding harm), beneficence, justice, fidelity, and veracity.

Those six principles can be applied to the processes of any therapeutic relationship, for example, Dr Peterson's therapy with Bob. On one level, Dr Peterson did not show sufficiently high levels of respect for Bob's autonomy because he did not accept Bob's stated goals for therapy and (more significantly) because he did not negotiate with him to develop a richer understanding of how Bob could use therapy (richer than Dr Peterson telling him what to do). On the other hand, Dr Peterson did not reduce Bob's autonomy by telling him what to do. He wanted to improve Bob's ability to make a decision about his marriage by removing psychological impediments that prevented the full expression of his autonomy. And so he exhibited respect for Bob's autonomy.

Dr Peterson did nothing that would obviously harm Bob (nonmalefi-cence) and appeared to be engaged in a process of therapy that could benefit Bob (beneficence). However, their deep, unspoken disagreement about goals (desired outcomes) for therapy – Dr Peterson's insight and autonomy versus Bob's knowing what to do about his marriage and symptom relief – is trou-blesome. Unless that is resolved, Bob is unlikely to continue in therapy, and may either be harmed (by not seeking a therapist in the future because of his negative experience with Dr Peterson) or simply not benefit from his session(s) with Dr Peterson.

Dr Peterson showed a high level of fidelity to Bob.

Thinking about the relationship of Bob and Dr Peterson in terms of justice will not tell us much – if we focus only on the micro-level. But if we expand to the macro-level and think about society as a whole, Dr Peterson's exaggerating Bob's problems to obtain more sessions from his managed care company is clearly wrong (in addition to being illegal). Given a limited pool of money to provide mental health care for a group of people (the present reality for many people covered by some government and managed care plans), Dr Peterson's lying about the seriousness of Bob's problems to obtain more sessions for him may be unjust to other patients whose need for sessions is greater because it may prevent them from receiving needed therapy sessions (Austad 1996).

In submitting a fraudulent assessment of Bob to the managed care company, Dr Peterson is also not being truthful (he is lacking in veracity). Truth-telling, by therapist and by client, is arguably essential to therapy, whether truth is understood in terms of objectivity or plausibility (Frank and Frank 1991), of science or hermeneutics, as historical truth, or as narra-tive truth (Spence 1982). Ideal clients speak truthfully, striving to know the truth about themselves, however uncomfortable that may make them. Ridding ourselves of pleasant self-delusions, courageous self-scrutiny, and an honest view of ourselves were ideals shared by Nietzsche and Freud, ideals that have profoundly influenced how many understand the processes of therapy.

Adherence to important ethical principles should set therapists apart from other people, argues Kitwood. He contends that, "in its uncompro-mising regard for personhood and its resolute pursuit of psychological truth," a therapeutic relationship "has moral qualities that are conspicuously lacking in the everyday world" (Kitwood 1990: 202).

Therapy process can also be understood in terms of the virtues (stable ethical characteristics) possessed by therapists and clients (Graber and

Thomasma 1989). Doherty (1995), for instance, argued that therapists ought to embody three virtues: caring, courage, and prudence.[3]

To apply a virtue ethics perspective to Dr Peterson, we can ask, for instance, whether he lacked courage. We could argue that he lacked that virtue because he failed to tell Bob that his desire for simple answers was unrealistic and because he failed to risk a conversation with Bob about goals that could have resulted either in a more nuanced therapeutic goal *or* in Bob not returning for a second session. Lack of courage may also have been evident in Dr Peterson's failure to communicate honestly with Bob's managed care company about the nature of his problems.

Prudence is, I think, an especially important ethical virtue for the therapist. Doherty defines it as "good judgment or, in the words of *Merriam-Webster*, 'a quality in a person that allows [him or her] to choose a sensible course of action.' Common sense, if you will, backed up by wisdom" (Doherty 1995: 163). This virtue, which I prefer to label "practical wisdom," is seen in people who regularly make wise decisions about difficult matters in complex circumstances. In contrast to Dr Peterson, for instance, a prudent therapist should know that many working class males seeking therapy want symptom relief and practical answers. Helping Bob develop a more nuanced understanding of therapy would therefore likely require building upon those desires.

Meara, Schmidt, and Day link prudence to ethical rules and principles, suggesting that "those who are prudent know what rules or principles might apply and whether they should be applied in a particular instance" (Meara *et al*. 1996: 39). But MacIntyre points out that Aristotle *rarely* referred to rules. Rather, Aristotle held that those who exemplify the virtues exhibit "a capacity to judge and to do the right thing in the right place at the right time in the right way" (MacIntyre 1984: 150). The same difference is present among therapists: some, in asserting that therapists should use only those techniques that have been empirically validated, argue for a rule-based prudential practice of therapy; others argue that the wisdom therapists ideally exhibit cannot be reduced to the application of rules, whether science-based or not.

Therapy processes in ethical perspective

In discussing therapy process and ethics, I began with ethical categories and applied those categories to therapy processes. I now want to do the reverse: to begin with how therapists and therapy researchers discuss process and then ask ethical questions. That is, I will look at therapy processes (e.g. techniques) from an ethical perspective, discerning the ethical convictions (morals) underlying or implied by those processes, because as London suggested, "morals are implied by techniques" (London 1964: 165).

Therapy researchers have identified a wide range of therapy processes

(Elliott 1991; Frank and Frank 1991; Kubacki and Gluck 1993; Mahoney 1991; Orlinsky *et al.* 1994; Prochaska and DiClemente 1994). Although their intent was primarily descriptive, the processes they have isolated have prescriptive dimensions.

To the extent that certain therapy processes produce more positive outcomes (i.e. "good" outcomes) than other therapy processes, we can claim that it is good, and perhaps even right or obligatory, for therapists to employ those processes. The exhaustive review by Orlinsky, Grawe, and Parks (1994) of the relationship between process and outcome variables found that some process variables were, in fact, tied more closely to outcome than others. Process variables robustly linked to outcome included therapeutic bond or alliance, patient cooperativeness, patient expressiveness, and paradoxical intention techniques. From an ethical perspective, the link between paradoxical intention techniques and positive therapy outcome is particularly interesting because therapists using those techniques are, if not overtly dishonest, at least less than fully honest. One ethical principle, truth-telling, is in conflict with another, maximizing client well-being.

Of particular relevance to Dr Peterson's work with Bob, Orlinsky, Grawe, and Parks (1994) found that clarity and consensus about expectations and goals for therapy tend to be important factors in therapy outcome, from the client's perspective and when measured by objective indices, but not from the perspective of therapists. This suggests that Dr Peterson should (is obligated to, if he wishes to maximize the chances Bob will improve) work with Bob to clarify goals and expectations, and develop a consensus.

In contrast to the conclusion drawn by Orlinsky, Grawe, and Parks (1994), Shapiro, Harper, Startup, Reynolds, Bird, and Suokas (1994) and Lambert (1989) found little relationship between process variables (like techniques) and outcome.[4] The Shapiro group conducted a meta-analysis of studies examining the process–outcome relation in thirty-three research publications and found an average effect size that accounted for less than 2 percent of the variance in outcome. Lambert reported that only 1.9 percent of the variance in therapy outcome in four studies could be accounted for by variations in therapeutic technique. He suggested that researchers pay greater attention to differences among therapists, rather than among techniques, because research findings indicate that some therapists are better than others, and we need to understand how and why that is the case. To the extent that outcome is not related to therapy techniques (Beutler 1995, Norcross 1995, and others dispute that conclusion), however, an ethical analysis of therapy process should be concerned primarily with the intrinsic goodness, rightness, or virtue of various therapy processes (process unrelated to outcome), rather than emphasizing the ethical status of techniques based on their relationship to outcome.

One approach to understanding therapy process that has received empirical support is that of Prochaska and DiClemente (1994) and colleagues

(Fava *et al*. 1995; Prochaska *et al*. 1992). They have isolated five general categories of change process, with two subtypes for each based on whether the change process generates change experientially (internally) or environmentally (externally). These change processes are conceptualized at an intermediate level of abstraction, being more abstract than techniques, but less abstract than theoretical frameworks (Prochaska and Norcross 1994).

To illustrate how therapy change processes can be evaluated ethically, I will discuss how five change processes (representing either subtype of all five general categories of change processes) involve issues that can be evaluated ethically.

Education is a change process that can produce a variety of changes in clients. Since education is not value-free, the content and manner of education can be evaluated ethically. Depending on one's ethical perspective, different ethical evaluations would be made if Dr Peterson emphasized educating Bob about the dangers to his health of not expressing his anger directly than if he emphasized the possible harmful effects of divorce on Bob's children. Likewise, ethical evaluations would vary depending on whether Bob was educated about the benefits of long-term therapy or about the benefits of self-help groups. *Corrective Emotional Experiences* are believed to play a role in producing change. Would it be best for Dr Peterson to facilitate experiences in which Bob is likely to feel emancipated from the parental and marital responsibilities with which he is burdened? Or experiences through which he feels empowered to face his existing commitments with new determination? *Self-liberation* increases the autonomy that many in the West think the *summum bonum* (greatest good). Some ethical analyses of this change process are not likely to be controversial, for example, the goodness of freedom from severe mental illness, marked psychological distress, unresolved emotional burdens, or ineffective thinking that prevents Bob from making decisions. More controversial is the question, "Freedom for what?" (Tjeltveit 1989). Would it be ideal for Bob to be free to take better care of himself? free to make a decision about his marriage? free from the parental and marital burdens that cause him emotional distress? A sole focus on freedom thus fails to address the relationship between Bob's freedom and what he sees to be obligations to his children and, to a lesser extent, to his wife. *Counterconditioning*, a change process involving changing responses to stimuli, may be viewed in a positive light if Bob develops new, more adaptive responses to the stimuli of anger and loneliness that are now leading him to drunkenness. But counterconditioning may be viewed negatively if he develops maladaptive responses to the stressful stimuli in his life. Finally, *Reevaluation*, changes in internal consequences, can be viewed in positive ethical light (e.g. if Bob learns to reinforce himself when making good changes and carrying out his responsibilities without undue distress), but in a negative light (e.g. if he learns to manipulate his wife and neglect his children by reinforcing himself only when acting to meet his own needs).

As a general rule, change processes at an intermediate level of abstractness are, by themselves, neither good nor bad, right nor wrong. But when translated into action in a specific context, in a particular therapeutic relationship, their ethical character becomes evident. This underscores a point made by Elliott and Anderson (1994), Hill (1994), Orlinsky, Grawe, and Parks (1994) and by Stiles, Shapiro, and Harper (1994): context matters when we look at therapy process. For example, to ethically evaluate an intervention, we need to know its context because that can significantly affect the intervention's impact on a client. A therapist's pointed confrontation of a client with good ego strength in the context of an established therapeutic relationship may be very effective, but devastating to a fragile client in the early stages of therapy. One intervention; two outcomes, depending on context.

To avoid oversimplifying therapy processes, researchers suggest that more complex models of therapy process be developed (Elliott 1991; Elliott and Anderson 1994; Heatherton and Weinberger 1994; Orlinsky *et al*. 1994; Stiles *et al*. 1994). If ethical evaluations of therapy process are to be done well, they should be no less complex.

Finally, to address the changes in the *meanings* clients and therapists employ to understand therapy and human life, Frank and Frank (1991) and others have suggested that hermeneutic, rather than scientific, methods be used. And Browning (1987), Cushman (1993, 1995), Richardson and Woolfolk (1994), and others have used hermeneutic approaches to ethically evaluate therapy processes.

Ethical underpinnings of professional standards and ethics

We can explore the relationship between therapy process and ethics in another general way: an analysis of the ethical assumptions contained within professional standards and ideals. Professional standards of practice, taught in supervision and course work, imply ideas about what is good, right, and virtuous in therapy. Dr Peterson's decision to obtain further information from Bob rather than immediately answering his question about forgiving his wife is consistent with professional standards, and thus considered good.

Professional codes of ethics set forth both minimal ethical standards concerning the processes of therapy (e.g. no sex with clients) and aspirational standards (what occurs in therapy under ideal circumstances). APA's ethics code, for example, states that psychologists "apply and make public their knowledge of psychology in order to contribute to human welfare" (APA 1992: 1600). Some ethical assumptions emerge only from a careful analysis of ethics codes. "Implicit in the ethical codes," point out Hare-Mustin, Marecek, Kaplan, and Liss-Levinson (1979: 3), "is a model for the client–therapist relationship that fosters the goals of mental health."

But we can also understand the ethical character of therapy process by distinguishing what exceptional therapists do in therapy from what the merely competent do. The aspirational elements of the ethics codes of APA (1992) and other professional associations capture this, in part. The highest levels of ethical excellence, found in outstanding therapists, go well beyond what codes can spell out, however. The ethical question we need to address is this: what therapy processes distinguish average therapists from those who are exceptional? What sets apart the merely competent therapist from the therapist who addresses the ethical dimensions of psychotherapy processes in a way that is outstanding?

Some key, ethically relevant dimensions of therapy process

Because some aspects of therapy process are particularly pertinent to an ethical analysis of psychotherapy, I will focus on them in more depth. I will consider seven conceptually overlapping facets of the process of psychotherapy.

Agreements about particular therapeutic relationships

Bob entered psychotherapy with certain assumptions: Dr Peterson would help him, would tell him what to do about his marriage, and would never tell anyone what he said in the session.

Dr Peterson had a different set of assumptions. The most effective therapeutic approach is generally short-term dynamic therapy. Resolving clients' unconscious conflicts, conflicts that are rooted in their childhoods and responsible for their presenting problems, reduces the problems that lead them to seek treatment and increases their autonomy. (And so Bob would be able to make up his own mind about his marriage.) If Bob's managed care company required information about Bob of the type usually provided to managed care companies, Dr Peterson would provide it. If ever served a valid subpoena by a properly constituted legal authority, he would divulge whatever he was ordered to reveal about Bob. Dr Peterson also assumed that marital affairs are quite common. Furthermore, he considered one of Freud's most profound (yet curiously neglected) observations to be: "The cure for nervous illness arising from marriage would be marital unfaithfulness" (Freud 1959: 195). Dr Peterson's own "infidelity cure" (Wallace 1986: 104) had reinforced that belief, and he congratulated himself on no longer being "tyrannized by shoulds" about it, in contrast to his ex-wife, whose "rigid" moral beliefs and unwillingness to forget about his affairs produced, he believed, the demise of their marriage. In that and similar cases, he assumed, the problem was the partner's overactive superego (seen in "moralistic" beliefs like "thou shalt not commit adultery") rather than the affair itself.

Accordingly, he thought it would be helpful for Bob to see (to be converted to his view) that Bob's own happiness, rather than outdated societal ideals about marital relationships, should be paramount in his decision-making. He assumed Bob would eventually adopt this view, if truly committed to becoming mentally healthy. But since he believed a therapist's values should be "opaque" to the client, Dr Peterson did not divulge those psychological/ethical convictions to Bob.

About more concrete dimensions of the therapeutic contract (e.g. the first session would last fifty minutes), Dr Peterson and Bob agreed.

Neither Bob nor Dr Peterson explicitly thought of therapy as an ethical endeavor, yet both made assumptions pertaining to ethical issues. And therapy clearly addressed ethical issues. Their agreement and expectations about the ethical dimensions of therapy were therefore implicit.

In general, agreements between therapists and clients are ethically relevant for several reasons. Agreements about therapy can either preserve client autonomy (if agreements are mutual) or reduce it (if determined by therapists unilaterally). Agreements about therapy generally assume that the therapist will exhibit fidelity to the client and make the best interests of the client foremost (beneficence). The kinds of relationships therapists and clients establish, sometimes discussed in ethical terms (see discussion below), develop in part because of therapist and client agreements about therapy. Because of this, Ramsey argued against the use of "contract," the traditional term used to describe agreements between therapists and clients. The legal and business connotations of the term do not capture the ethical core of therapy relationships, properly understood, he asserted. And so "'partnership' is a better term...than 'contract.' 'Joint adventurers'...is better still. The concept is one of an ongoing partnership established by an understanding consent, sustained by present continued consent and terminated by voluntary dissent" (Ramsey 1971: 705). But, as discussed in Chapter 7, agreements about therapy are increasingly not agreements between therapist and client alone, but between therapist, client, and third-party payer. And therapists have criticized third-party payers for failing to be clear about their assumptions about "acceptable" therapy goals and for using unduly restrictive criteria for therapy goals. It is also difficult to negotiate an agreement about a particular therapeutic relationship when one can only communicate with one of the parties, the one holding the purse strings, by calling a toll-free number and leaving a voicemail message. Nevertheless, I think it imperative that all stakeholders work together to develop an agreement about a particular therapeutic relationship.

Agreements about therapy are also made about other dimensions of therapy, especially therapy goals. If, as I will argue in Chapter 9, goals are value-laden, the process by which goals are established is a vitally important ethical task. Furthermore, the therapeutic bond (a dimension of therapy process empirically linked to outcome) may stem in part from therapists' and clients' "normative conceptions of how they ought to relate to each other" (Orlinsky *et al.* 1994: 363), that is, to their understanding of the therapeutic contract.

The implicit understanding about therapy in most societies is that it is value-free. And so the implicit agreement between therapist and clients is generally that therapy will be value-free. Because therapy is not, the ethical character of therapy is poorly addressed in those agreements, a serious problem to which I will return in Chapters 10 and 11.

Finally, agreements about therapy have to do with informed consent (Braaten *et al.* 1993; Dyer and Bloch 1987; Faden and Beauchamp 1986; Lidz *et al.* 1984; Tjeltveit 1986). Informed consent is a legal and ethical concept referring to the obligation of professionals to provide clients with information of relevance to them about a professional relationship, such as a treatment's goals, procedures, possible benefits and side effects, and alternatives. Clients then either agree to participate in (consent to) therapy or not. By insuring that clients are knowledgeable about therapy, the process of obtaining informed consent protects their rights and autonomy.

Dr Peterson's failure to inform Bob of the limits of confidentiality meant that Bob did not give truly informed consent to therapy. This could harm Bob. Learning that Dr Peterson has discussed his case with his managed care company or must testify at a custody hearing, for example, could destroy his trust in Dr Peterson.

More generally, therapists like Dr Peterson who imply or state that therapy is value-free ("objective") provide false information about psychotherapy and prevent clients from giving adequately informed consent. In a manner and to an extent appropriate to a particular therapeutic relationship, therapists need to provide clients with information about its ethical dimensions, including possible value conflicts between therapists and clients (Berger 1982). Since this implication of therapy's ethics-laden character has important ramifications for professional ethics, I will discuss it further in Chapter 11.

Some, like Dr Peterson, argue that therapists ought to keep silent about their own values, because explicitness may hurt transference, may make it more likely that clients – eager to please therapists who are seen as powerful authority figures – will "adopt" therapist values, or both. But Frank and Frank (1991) argued that explicit denials that therapists influence client values (like Dr Peterson's claim that therapists are "objective") might magnify the therapist's influence on clients.

By way of contrast, feminist therapists (Feminist Therapy Institute 1990), explicitly religious therapists (e.g. Jensen and Bergin 1988), and others have argued that therapists should be explicit about their ethical convictions. As the Feminist Therapy Institute Code of Ethics states, "feminist therapists recognize that their values influence the therapeutic process and clarify with clients the nature and effect of those values" (Feminist

Therapy Institute 1990: 38). Doing so makes truly informed consent possible. And if clients know their therapist's values, therapists are less likely to have an untoward influence on client values.

Other challenging ethical issues are raised by the informed consent process. The autonomy of some clients is so impaired they are unable to consent to therapy. Ironically, they may need therapy to develop the level of autonomy required to give fully informed consent to therapy, or to engage in a fruitful discussion about the role of values in a therapeutic relationship. As Lowe noted, "often the client is so bewildered and confused that he [or she] can not clearly focus his [or her] values" (Lowe 1976: 220).

Particularly challenging to many therapists and clients is informed consent about ethical issues tied to religious convictions. Lovinger noted that religious clients, fearful of being coerced into altering their religious or ethical beliefs, may want information about their therapist's religious beliefs. But many therapists think those beliefs private, think disclosure of them damages therapeutic relationships, or both. Lovinger's solution:

> to indicate my orientation briefly and state that I have no interest in having other people see it my way. If their religion is important to my patients, then I would certainly be interested in understanding it, as I am interested in anything they would want to tell me.
>
> (Lovinger 1984: 69)

That would no doubt be effective in many cases. But some clients may interpret "I have no interest in having other people see it my way" to mean the therapist is committed to an ethical relativism conflicting with the client's convictions.

Discerning the nature and extent of the information to be provided to particular clients and handling the process of obtaining informed consent are difficult tasks. Suppose Dr Peterson discloses his "sole" value as a therapist: "insuring that my clients are happy." Is he also obligated to spell out its corollary – "and so my concern about your children and marriage is limited to whether or not they contribute to your happiness" – convictions that are at odds with Bob's values? Problems can also arise when therapists provide clients with excessive, irrelevant, or overly complex information. As Handelsman, Kemper, Kesson-Craig, McLain, and Johnsrud (1986) note, even those who use informed consent forms often fail to present information of interest to prospective clients or use language at a reading level higher than that possessed by the average client. And Margolin (1982) points out that providing too much information about therapy may (falsely) persuade a client that the therapist does not really want to work with him or her. Furthermore, short-term therapy provides very little time for detailed discussions about the nature of therapy. A variety of ethical considerations needs to be taken into account (Tjeltveit 1986), with practical wisdom required to handle agreements about therapy optimally.

Preserving and enhancing client autonomy

Therapy processes that deny, restrict, or minimize the autonomy of clients are generally regarded (at least in many Western ethical traditions) as not good or unethical. Good therapy processes, by way of contrast, preserve and enhance client autonomy.

And so behaviorism has been criticized, Macklin notes, because its techniques "may ignore or violate autonomy." In fact, some think autonomy so important that if therapists reduce autonomy, therapeutic effectiveness "is not a morally relevant consideration" (Macklin 1982: 36). From this Kantian perspective, therapy process (preserving autonomy) is the primary ethical consideration; therapy outcome (effectively reaching therapy's good goals or outcomes) becomes relevant only when client autonomy is fully preserved.

Some of the outrage about managed care in the US may arise when those who consider autonomy to be the chief (or only) ethical consideration encounter managed care entities that are perceived to regard effectiveness to be the chief (or only) criterion for making decisions. For the former, the latter's abridgment of client (and therapist) autonomy is unconscionable.

The pernicious falsehood that therapists are either value-free (upholding client autonomy) or impose their values on clients (eliminating client autonomy) stems in part from particular understandings of "autonomy": autonomy, the possession and right of the self-contained individual, is opposed to authority. Ethical convictions (other than autonomy) necessarily stem entirely, it is believed, from authority, which we should profoundly distrust, because it compromises our ethical freedom (Richardson 1989).

Ethical convictions other than freedom also motivate those in the West, however. For example, Macklin notes that "we also think it is a good thing to promote people's well-being and to prevent unnecessary harm from befalling them" (Macklin 1982: 5; see Taylor's 1989 discussion of benevolence). Richardson also documents how therapists who employ a variety of approaches implicitly hold ethical ideals, but explicitly espouse only an uncompromising devotion to autonomy. As a result, he argues, "modern therapeutic wisdom does not represent a clear alternative to traditional belief or rootless modern freedom so much as an enticing but ultimately confused and unsatisfactory blend of the two" (Richardson 1989: 317).

Non-Westerners, as noted earlier, are less likely to valorize autonomy, and more likely to consider it as but one of many ethical ideals. And Westerners are beginning to adopt, or reclaim, positions that affirm autonomy *and* other ethical convictions, but without radically dichotomizing them. For example, Richardson observes that hermeneutic perspectives seek "to recapture something of a premodern sense of belonging and indebtedness to larger realities while preserving undiminished our modern critique of arbitrary authority" (Richardson 1989: 318). And Doherty, who argues for ethical ideals in addition to autonomy, maintains that "the central safeguard for keeping moral consultation from becoming prescriptive and coercive is maintaining respect for the moral agency of the client" (Doherty 1995: 65).

The quality of the therapist–client relationship and therapist treatment of clients

Another ethical element of therapy process is the therapeutic relationship. Psychotherapy, Bickhard asserts:

> is not just an activity to which ethical considerations can be applied, nor just an activity which makes use of moral considerations in selecting its instrumental goals. Psychotherapy is a very special kind of intrinsically ethical relating to another person.
>
> (Bickhard 1989: 163)

Advocates of this and related ethical stances assert that therapy relationships should be non-manipulative; participants ought not to *use* one another to reach some desired end. Relationships between therapists and clients should not be I–It relationships, to use Buber's (1970) term, in which therapists relate to clients as if clients are objects. Rather, relationships between therapists and clients should be I–Thou relationships, characterized by a profound intimacy between persons.

For those and other reasons, how clients are treated is considered by many to be an ethically vital aspect of therapy process. The good therapist treats clients with respect, sensitivity, and genuine caring. Indeed, argues Kitwood, therapeutic relationships have "moral qualities that are conspicuously lacking in the everyday world" (Kitwood 1990: 202).

In apparent contrast, Freud described the therapist as a surgeon "who puts aside all his feelings, even his human sympathy" (Freud 1958: 115). He argued that that "emotional coldness" protects the doctor's own emotional life and helps the client. The ends (outcomes) of client health and therapeutic effectiveness thus justify the means (process) of emotional coldness.

But ethical analyses of therapy diverge at precisely this point. Do ends justify means? Does positive outcome justify any process? Freud appears to have thought so (at least at times). And critics of those who stress outcome studies as the *sole* criterion for determining therapist actions assert they do as well.

Others, however, argue that clients are to be treated as persons of intrinsic worth. Accordingly, we can never justify positive outcomes if achieving them requires us to treat persons as objects or merely as means to an end.

And so therapists should always treat clients as persons, as valuable in and of themselves. Therapeutic processes are thus ethically relevant, whatever their relationship to outcome. (It is, of course, also possible to be concerned about therapeutic effectiveness, as evaluated by empirical research, *and* to treat clients as persons of intrinsic worth.)

Pragmatism, materialism, emotivism, positivism, and a strictly business perspective on therapy have all been criticized for contributing to therapists failing to take seriously the personhood of therapy clients and to therapists treating clients as less than fully human or as means to some end. "Object" relations theory can also be criticized for referring to significant persons in a client's life as "objects" rather than as persons. Positivistic views, argues Bickhard (1989), fail to take seriously humans as ethical beings. And MacIntyre argued that the ethical theory of emotivism (see Chapter 4 above), closely tied historically to positivism, entails "the obliteration of any genuine distinction between manipulative and non-manipulative ends" (MacIntyre 1984: 23). Therapists whose *de facto* ethical theory is emotivism and whose sole concern is positive therapeutic outcome thus have no reason to refrain from manipulating and using others – if doing so helps them reach their goals. Those who reject such a view are drawing upon richer ethical sources, sources asserting that *how* therapists treat clients is important ethically.

Ethical dialogue

"Psychotherapy as moral discourse" or "ethical dialogue" can mean either a description of therapy as an inescapably ethical activity or an ethical ideal about ethical conversations in therapy. (The two connotations are often blurred.) As description, "moral discourse" refers to a wide range of implicit and explicit communications about ethical issues taking place in the structures, concepts, and practices of individual therapists and clients, communities, and cultures (Cushman 1995; Doherty 1995; Nicholas 1994). The ethical ideas embedded in cultures, communities, and professions shape therapy in so many ways – ways often invisible to its participants – that therapists and clients often discuss ethical issues without being aware they are doing so.

Therapists and clients alike function as ethicists in a therapeutic relationship. That is, both reflect on, have convictions about, and/or attempt to influence the other about ethical questions and issues. The result is, or should be, dialogue, a dimension of psychotherapy sometimes overt, but more often understated and implicit. Furthermore, other psychotherapy stakeholders participate in the dialogue about ethical dimensions of therapy as well, especially family members and third-party payers.

When the terms "moral discourse" or "ethical dialogue" are used to refer to ethical ideals, they refer to the *quality* of the discussions between therapist and client about ethical matters. "Dialogue" connotes conversations characterized by these valued ("good") qualities: collaboration (Bergin 1991), negotiation (Aponte 1985), open-mindedness, serious attempts to listen to and understand one another, open-ended exchanges, a willingness to reconsider one's position, give and take, and respect for one another. Ethical issues are explored, Doherty argues:

> in the heart of the therapeutic dialogue, in conversations in which the therapist listens, reflects, acknowledges, questions, probes, and challenges – and in which the client is free to do the same and to develop a more integrated set of moral sensibilities.
>
> (Doherty 1995: 37)

This kind of conversation occurs, if not between equals then between two responsible, competent parties. It will ideally not be implicit or authoritarian. Therapists will not falsely claim neutrality. Tradition and precedent will count less in therapeutic negotiations about values than debate and discussion (Aponte 1985). Finally, in applying Habermas's theory of communicative action to therapy, Kubacki noted that ethical dialogues in therapy are ideally characterized by "the right to dissent or capacity for choice" (Kubacki 1994: 469) and by participants who are motivated to reach consensus or solve problems.

I think ethical dialogue exemplifying those ideals is very important. Indeed, one reason I am writing this book is to foster such ethical dialogue. I do not write as if claiming any final answers. And I am surely neither value-free nor able to impose my values on my readers. I hope, rather, that this book is part of, and will help spawn, an increasingly sophisticated and adequate ethical dialogue about the ethical character of therapy, dialogue among therapists and other therapy stakeholders, and dialogue between therapists and clients.

But Aponte reminds us that, however beneficial dialogue between therapist and client may be, such dialogue is not, finally, between equals. Therapists possess more power than clients, and hence greater moral leverage. He notes that "such leverage places on the therapist the responsibility of certain ethical concerns: what values to communicate and how to exert his [or her] influence" (Aponte 1985: 328). It is to that central but thorny ethical dimension of therapy process that I now turn.

Therapist influence on the ethical dimensions of clients' lives

Therapy may ethically transform Bob. The ways in which Dr Peterson, other therapists, and other aspects of therapy exert ethical influence on clients can be both described and evaluated. In this section, I do both.

Types of influence

A variety of therapy processes can change the ethical dimensions of a client's life. This is partly because so many human characteristics – values, attitudes, cognitions, emotions, behaviors, choices, motivation, identity, locus of control, personality, ethical perceptiveness, learning, social cognition, interpersonal relations, and so forth – are relevant, at least in part, to what is good, right, and/or virtuous. And those characteristics can be understood from the perspective of any of psychology's corresponding subspecialties. And all can be altered in therapy.

The different kinds of relationships that therapists establish with clients can result in different types and degrees of influence on clients. As Weisskopf-Joelson notes:

> therapists range all the way from pure "gardeners" – who view their clients as an appleseed which can grow into the best apple tree through loving care but cannot become a pear tree – to Pygmalions who desire to shape their clients according to an ideal image based on their own value system.
>
> (Weisskopf-Joelson 1980: 462)

Each of the following words (with distinguishable but sometimes overlapping meanings) can characterize influential moments within a therapeutic relationship: educative, advisory, healing, coercive, persuasive, transforming, emancipatory, actualizing, pastoral, priestly, prophetic, exhortative, judging, supportive, authoritative, corrective, and authoritarian. With the exception of the last two, all occupy some portion of the middle ground between relationships that are value-free and relationships in which therapists impose values on clients.

As a result of therapy's influence, client values can be, to use Rescher's (1969) taxonomy, acquired and abandoned, redistributed, emphasized and de-emphasized, rescaled, redeployed, restandardized, retargeted, and upgraded or downgraded. And R. M. Williams (1979) suggested that values can be created, abruptly destroyed, attenuated, extended, elaborated, specified, limited, explicated, made more or less consistent, and experienced more or less intensely. Client behaviors and ethical theories may also be affected in those ways. Other effects on clients have been postulated. Schwehn and Schau (1990) documented, for example, how therapy stabilizes some client values. And B. E. Wolfe (1978) suggested that clients shift their locus of moral authority from sources that are external to those that are internal.

Changes in the ethical dimensions of clients' lives may stem from a variety of processes. Some ethical changes may be side effects of the positive psychological changes clients make. Others may be unintended side effects of the influence processes therapists employ. And still other changes may be the result of intentional efforts by therapists to change some ethical dimension of clients' lives. As Wallerstein notes, some of the pressures therapists exert on clients are "deliberate and avowed, some of them unrecognized and unavowed, some unrecognizable because buried within the framework of the very assumptions upon which the whole endeavour rests" (Wallerstein 1976: 371).

Ethical changes can stem in several ways from the positive psychological changes clients make. Because clients grow, eliminate maladaptive behaviors, employ more adaptive cognitions, develop new identities, have new experiences in therapy (or as a result of therapy), and gain insight, they sometimes reevaluate old ethical positions and behaviors, make new decisions, and move in different life directions. Clients whose lives used to center around psychological problems, either because of the severity of their problems or as a symptom of their problems, find they have new energy to devote to ethical concerns once they make progress in therapy. And finally, of particular importance, clients often develop greater autonomy. As Engelhardt argued, psychotherapy sets "the stage for the possibility of ethical decisions" by freeing clients "from the control of unconscious drives and unacknowledged forces" (Engelhardt 1973: 441). And so clients are free, in new ways, to make ethical decisions and to act ethically.

The persuasive processes of psychotherapy, intended to address issues in clients' lives that are *psychological*, may also affect issues that are *ethical*. For example, Dr Peterson may target Bob's depression by gently challenging his belief that he "should" remain committed to his wife because he promised God, his wife, his family, and his friends that he would do so; Dr Peterson's persuasive abilities may change both Bob's depression *and* his ethical convictions. It is also the case that therapists who create a "safe place" for clients to talk about their psychological problems also create a safe place to make ethical changes. Finally, therapists may use strategies tied to particular theoretical approaches to help clients adopt particular visions of mental health or ideal human functioning, visions inextricably tied to a set of ethical convictions (this will be addressed in Chapter 9). In all those cases, the *ethical* influence is an *un*intended therapy outcome.

Therapists also intentionally employ processes that either address or influence some ethical dimension of a client. These processes may include persuasion (Beutler 1979), social influence, modeling, collaboration in determining goals for therapy (Bergin 1991), education (e.g. about the consequences of various ethical alternatives), pointing out contradictions in an ethical position (Meehl 1981), and converting clients to the ethical stance of therapists (Bandura 1969; Corey *et al.* 1993; Meehl 1959; Strong 1978; Tjeltveit 1986). Distinguishing between processes whose ethical impact is an unintended side effect and those in which the impact is intentional is often difficult, however, because the same processes may be used in both. This may be especially true when moral, religious, and political values are tied to therapists' or clients' ideas about good psychological functioning. If mental health for Dr Peterson means an internal psychological source of ethical authority, but for Bob an external divine source, changes in Bob's ethical theory may come either as an unintended side effect or as a (partly unconscious) desire on Dr Peterson's part that Bob adopt his ethical theory. Finally, as Frank and Frank (1991) point out, therapists who deny they are exerting any ethical influence on clients may, by doing so, actually increase their influence.

I am aware that lists of *possible* influence processes are a poor substitute for a definitive account of the processes that actually influence clients. Unfortunately, we do not know the exact nature of the processes through which therapy influences the ethical dimensions of clients' lives. More extensive context-sensitive research – quantitative, hermeneutic, or both – would no doubt help. But the influencing process may vary from therapy relationship to therapy relationship, and from therapist to therapist. And so the matter is very complex indeed. Progress will come, I suspect, through research efforts on the interface between social psychology and clinical psychology (e.g. Ruble *et al.* 1992; Snyder and Forsyth 1991, and that reported in the *Journal of Social and Clinical Psychology*) and through scholarly and clinical work drawing upon, and integrating, scientific, clinical, and ethical resources.

Inappropriate, appropriate, and ideal influence

The processes through which therapists influence the ethical dimensions of clients' lives can be ethically evaluated: some processes are inappropriate (not good, unethical, wrong, blameworthy); others are appropriate (not wrong) or ideal (good, right, virtuous). In making those assertions, and in this section, I assume (as argued above) that we should do so from a position somewhere within the ample middle ground between relativism and absolutism.

Coercive therapist processes are clearly wrong, save perhaps as a temporary expedient in psychiatric emergencies or cases of child abuse. Also inappropriate are processes that violate the therapeutic agreement, fail to provide clients with adequate information about therapy, and eliminate or reduce client freedom (Tjeltveit 1986). Therapists inappropriately reduce freedom by exerting undue pressures on clients to adopt their moral values, being moralistic or judgmental, or propagandizing (inaccurately presenting ethical options to clients to make them more likely to adopt the views of the therapist; e.g. "If you really want to become healthy, you'll adopt my views on this controversial ethical topic"). For those reasons, the conversion of a client's values and ethical theory to those of his or her therapist is, prima facie, unethical. Therapists should not make clients their ethical clones. However, as we shall see, some forms of therapist influence on the ethical lives of clients, some forms of ethical conversion, may well be appropriate, and even ideal.

Other forms of therapist influence on clients can also be inappropriate. Paternalism, telling clients what to do and taking responsibility for decisions that are properly theirs, is problematic. Kovacs exemplified this attitude in his grandiose claim that therapists should "embrace...our essential role as secular priests" (Kovacs 1987: 16). Judging, condemning, and treating people as objects or mere means to an end are also inappropriate.

Other forms of ethical influence are less than ideal because they lead to negative outcomes. Harmful psychological consequences (increased symptoms) can result from therapy processes that are judgmental, cause shame, or undermine trust in therapy (Nicholas 1994). For example, therapist condemnation, however subtle, of clients who have engaged in unusual sexual practices, or have never engaged in sexual activity at all, can harm clients.

Because of the harmful consequences for clients of negative ethical evaluations, some inexperienced therapists swing to the opposite pole and attempt to make only positive evaluations. Clients are unlikely to be convinced by this, however, especially if carried to an extreme. And providing positive evaluations in all cases is muddleheaded, since therapists would need to praise diametrically opposed actions or thoughts. Sometimes helpful with overcontrolled, hyper-responsible clients, consistently positive feedback is not helpful with undercontrolled, irresponsible clients. And providing it may stunt a client's ethical growth.

Finally, interventions may be inappropriate because they produce negative ethical consequences, as defined by clients or others. If therapist influence reinforces sex role stereotypes, for instance, that intervention is, by feminist ethical standards, inappropriate. The therapeutic ploy of eliminating all client ethical convictions (all "shoulds") may also be deleterious. And Doherty strongly rejects therapeutic interventions that reduce political activism. He laments that:

> although therapists do not tell clients to be politically passive, I see many therapists negatively interpreting their clients' public-service sensibilities and activities. One of Anna's therapists suggested that she was not so much serving other families through her teaching as trying vicariously to heal her own family.
>
> (Doherty 1995: 98)

Therapist interventions may also harm the family and friends of clients, or society as a whole. If Dr Peterson succeeds in convincing Bob to reject his responsibilities as father, for example, his children will be harmed. If Dr Peterson and other therapists consistently defraud third-party payers, society will be harmed. From the perspective of those who think it is not good to harm others, those forms of therapy influence, of therapy process, are – if unaccompanied by countervailing benefits – inappropriate.

By way of contrast, interventions that we evaluate positively will either meet the minimal standards of professional ethics (and so be considered appropriate) or meet aspirational standards (and so be considered ideal). Discussing appropriate or ideal therapist influences on the ethical dimensions of clients' lives is the topic to which I now turn.

Some dimensions of appropriate ethical influence have been discussed previously. Therapists should honor and uphold the therapeutic agreement, fully informing clients about relevant ethical dimensions of therapy and obtaining their full and free consent to therapy. Therapists should preserve and enhance client freedom, eschewing paternalism and enabling them to make decisions that are properly theirs. And clients should be treated with respect, as persons of intrinsic worth.

To evaluate therapists' influence on the ethical dimensions of clients' lives, many therapists use a traditional standard: "Psychotherapists should be neutral." Because "neutrality" bears so many connotations and because I think therapists should aspire to *some* forms of "neutrality," but not others, I want to unpack some of the meanings of "neutrality," discussing it in some detail.

Critics of therapeutic neutrality sometimes characterize "neutrality" in an oversimplified way: "Therapists should hold no views on ethical topics. But if they do, they should never in any way communicate their views to clients." That "neutrality" is scarcely a realistic ideal. But advocates of therapist neutrality hold a variety of more sophisticated, and defensible, understandings of neutrality. Franklin (1990), for instance, distinguishes between five separate meanings of neutrality within the psychoanalytic tradition: behavioral, attitudinal, interpersonal, interactional, and essential. To sort out the meanings of "neutrality" and to understand better appropriate and ideal therapist "neutrality," I will consider his taxonomy in greater depth.

Therapists who aspire to the ideal of behavioral neutrality strive to be ethically anonymous with their clients (Franklin 1990). When therapists do not communicate their ethical views to clients (are ethically anonymous), clients can feel more free to express themselves, need not fear being judged, are less likely to feel pressured to adopt or espouse their therapists' ethical views, and can more easily take full responsibility for developing more mature ethical views, views they have chosen. And therapist and client can focus on therapeutic goals rather than on ethical issues that may be tangential, or irrelevant, to those goals. For those reasons, although complete anonymity is impossible (even Carl Rogers conveyed his ethical views to clients – Truax 1966), "neutrality" understood in that way has some merit, as a general rule of thumb. It is a valid aspirational ideal, a way to overcome some of the problems associated with inappropriate therapist conversion of clients' ethical positions.

But to assert that therapists should *sometimes* strive for ethical anonymity does not mean they should *always* do so.

Therapists exhibiting attitudinal neutrality refrain from judgmentalism (Franklin 1990). Judgmentalism is, of course, an attitude without advocate. No therapist would defend Dr Peterson if he condemned Bob because of his moral views. But rejecting judgmentalism does not require a therapist to be an ethically blank slate. One can hold ethical views (i.e. make ethical judgments) yet not be judgmental. Forcing a choice between attitudinal neutrality and judgmentalism is unfair; better alternatives exist. Advocates of this form of neutrality do, I think, make a legitimate point, however. But it is not that we should be neutral (in the sense of holding or communicating no ethical views); rather, it is that we should be nonjudgmental. To point out a problematic form of therapist influence helps little, however, when we need to determine how therapists *appropriately* influence clients concerning the ethical dimensions of their lives.

Franklin argues that therapists exhibiting the third form of neutrality, interpersonal neutrality, balance their responsiveness to clients. This "enables the patient to explore both old and new ways of relating to others" (Franklin 1990: 196). Interactional neutrality refers to therapists interacting with clients flexibly and with open-mindedness. Franklin thus affirms "balance," "client exploration," "flexibility," and "open-mindedness." All are ethical ideals regarding therapy process. The claim that therapists are neutral thus actually means that therapists adhere to particular ethical ideals for therapy process, rather than being entirely neutral ethically. If therapists are not neutral in the therapy processes they pursue, they may still be neutral about client goals. As we shall see, however, Franklin is hardly neutral about therapy's goal.

Finally, Franklin argues for essential neutrality, by which he means tolerance of ambiguity, "an absence of decided views," "a searching process," and thinking in terms of "provisional hypotheses rather than certainties" (Franklin 1990: 197). The ultimate value of essential neutrality is "furthering the open-ended process of self-inquiry," therapy's goal and Franklin's *summum bonum*.

Franklin's claim that neutrality means an "absence" of views lends support to the claim of R. May (1953) and Christopher (1996) that "neutrality" represents a particular, profoundly problematic ethical viewpoint: relativism. Although that is a plausible interpretation of the views of Franklin and other advocates of neutrality, other interpretations are possible. And, in the case of Franklin, more apt. Franklin does not argue that therapists should have no views, but that they should have no "decided" views. That is, therapists should not hold views so firmly they cannot be reconsidered, or decided in a new way. His ideal therapist operates on the basis of several strongly held ethical ideals or virtues: tolerance of ambiguity, flexibility, tentativeness, and open-endedness.

Franklin argues that those therapist virtues will benefit clients who seek a process of self-inquiry. And they do seem well suited to help overcontrolled, very responsible clients from intact ethical communities (Wallace 1991). But I do not think that those therapist virtues will be most helpful to the undercontrolled, irresponsible client who has no operative ethical community, the client who wants only symptom relief or only to satisfy the authority figure who ordered treatment. For the latter kind of client, "flexibility and open-endedness" regarding ethical convictions are not ideal therapist virtues. They will not permit an optimal therapist response to client ethical convictions like, "I should be able to come to therapy drunk," or "A man should be able to have sex with his woman whenever he wants to. That's *not* rape." Structure, limits, and consequences are needed in such cases, not "neutrality."

I don't think neutrality in and of itself implies relativism for another reason: therapists with full sets of ethical convictions can try to minimize their ethical influence on clients (be "neutral") because they are convinced that doing so is in the best interests of clients. On the other hand, ethical relativists can try to impose relativism on their clients (and so be anything but neutral). The full spectrum of types of influence, ranging from value-freedom or neutrality to imposing one's will on clients, can be exerted on the full range of ethical positions, ranging from relativism to absolutism.

Thinking about ethical influence on therapy clients in terms of a *spectrum* of influence, ranging from no influence to extensive influence, is, I think, more helpful than using a dichotomous "neutral" or "not neutral" (see Doherty 1995). The task therapists face is best understood as determining, not whether to be neutral, but *how much* influence, and *what kind*, to exert on a particular client at a particular time. That will depend on client needs and goals, and requires judgment.

I am also convinced we need to use new terms to discuss the legitimate ethical concerns historically expressed by "neutrality." An alternative: therapists should, as a general rule and unless there are compelling reasons to do otherwise, strive to *minimize* their ethical influence on clients. Aponte espoused such a view: therapists should "attempt to exercise no more influence over clients' values than is required to address clients' problems" (Aponte 1994: 184). This language transcends the false dichotomy of value-freedom or neutrality on the one hand, and imposing one's ethical views on clients, on the other. Yet the essential insight of the traditional view is maintained: clients' best interests are often not served when therapists voice their ethical convictions or otherwise attempt to influence the ethical dimensions of clients' lives. This is, in fact, an old view. Hartmann asserted that the analyst's personal moral valuations are "*best* kept in the background" (Hartmann 1960: 55, emphasis added). His discouraging therapists from expressing their views was a general guideline, not an absolute prohibition. In his view, and mine, therapists properly emphasize what "is required to address clients' problems." And that may or may not require addressing or attempting to influence the ethical dimensions of clients' lives.

Another way in which therapists appropriately address ethical issues is to refrain from making ethical judgments in the early stages of a therapeutic relationship. This captures a valid insight in the idea that therapists should be neutral: not making ethical judgments can be a vitally important *but temporary* expedient early in therapy. More explicitly, ethical discourse generally occurs, if at all, in the later stages of therapy. And so therapists do not stop making ethical judgments, but do suspend them temporarily.

Therapists are advised to avoid making ethical judgments early in therapy so they can provide the conditions necessary for resolving the problems bringing a person to therapy, to produce an ethical moratorium that benefits clients. As espoused by Erikson (1963), a moratorium is a stage between the immature moral views of childhood and the ethical maturity of an adult. To reach ethical maturity, one must pass through that stage. Likewise, therapists may refrain from expressing their ethical views to enable clients to examine their childhood ethical convictions and move to those of adulthood. As Wallace pointed out, dynamic psychiatry's "temporary suspension of standard moral evaluative categories is a means to self-insight, to self-transformative ends" (Wallace 1991: 112). Humanistic psychologies, claims Browning, "may be particularly powerful in providing the psychological space necessary for the arousal of deeper capacities for freedom, initiative, and agency" (Browning 1987: 92).

But not making ethical judgments is temporary and should not be seen as "a recipe for amoral living" (Wallace 1991: 112–13). As Browning notes "the temporary and heuristic suspension of moral judgments should not be confused with the wider elimination of any moral context whatsoever from our acts of care and counseling" (Browning 1982: 11). The nature of that broader ethical context is, of course, disputed.

Clinical judgment is required to decide the appropriateness of overtly addressing ethical issues. As Doherty points out, timing is critical: "Listening, reflecting, and affirming must precede any ethical challenge in psychotherapy; clients must know that we have heard them and care about them" (Doherty 1995: 64). Furthermore, a well-functioning therapeutic relationship must exist. In the early stages of therapy, he argues, some "concealment" of the therapist's views is often therapeutically important. In successful therapy, however, he "almost invariably" engages eventually in "full disclosure" (ibid.: 86).

To summarize, "neutrality" has a wide range of meanings. "Neutrality" cannot legitimately mean, it seems to me, that therapists never hold ethical views, never communicate them to clients in any way, are entirely anonymous ethically, or espouse ethical relativism. But "neutrality" can legitimately mean that therapists should, as a general rule, minimize their ethical influence on clients (especially in the early stages of therapy and when doing so would not harm clients), provide a nonjudgmental environment in which clients feel free to express and explore ethical issues, exhibit flexibility and open-mindedness, tolerate ambiguity, be willing to change their ethical convictions, match their ethical influence strategies (employing the full spectrum of available options) to client needs and goals, and focus on therapeutic goals. Clarity would be served, however, by abandoning "neutrality" in favor of precisely those ethical terms.

Two other alternatives for addressing the ethical dimensions of clients' lives exist: therapists consciously *address* ethical dimensions of clients' lives, or therapists consciously *attempt to influence* them. Although addressing ethical issues may have the effect of influencing them, therapists who simply address the ethical dimension of clients' lives generally attempt to minimize their influence on them and work within the client's ethical framework (Aponte 1994). Furthermore, therapists who consciously try to *change* clients' ethical convictions need to provide greater justification than do those who simply *address* those convictions. And so, while recognizing they are on a continuum and not mutually exclusive, I distinguish between "addressing" and "influencing."

Therapists can address ethical issues in a variety of ways, functioning in the roles of consultant, teacher, and midwife. Meehl (1981) argues that therapists can "correct" clients' ethical views without taking a stance on the content of those views, doing so, for example, by pointing out contradictions within those views. Glasser asserted that Reality Therapists are "not afraid to pose the question, 'Are you doing right or wrong?'" (Glasser 1965: 58). They confront clients with disparities between their beliefs and behavior.

Discussing the consequences of ethical alternatives is another way therapists can help clients to make ethical decisions (Corey *et al*. 1990; Schimmel 1992), one that relies upon a teleological ethical theory and draws upon science. Dr Peterson could thus respond to Bob's question, "Does it really hurt kids when their parents get a divorce?" with relevant scientific findings conveyed in a manner suitably tailored to his needs at that point in therapy. In that and other ways, therapists can help clients to clarify their ethical convictions. Values clarification can be understood in a variety of ways, however. It has been criticized for promising the chimerical but "alluring possibility of moral neutrality" (Meilaender 1984: 79). Although some therapists may think values clarification is morally neutral, others try to clarify values because they are convinced that some clients improve when not confused about values. A belief in the benefit to clients of ethical clarity, one of a therapist's many ethical convictions, may thus motivate therapeutic efforts to clarify clients' values rather than a myth about value clarification's ethical neutrality.

Therapists and clients can also *talk* about ethical issues (Feminist Therapy Institute 1990; Odell and Stewart 1993), doing so in a way that preserves client freedom and is not intended to change clients' ethical views. Dr

Peterson could simply ask Bob about his ethical convictions concerning marriage and forgiveness, and engage him in a conversation about them. When viewed from a hermeneutic point of view, discussions about ethical issues offer "the possibility of a more probing and ultimately challenging dialogue that more directly confronts traditional issues of values" (L. A. Sass 1988: 255).

Acknowledging and affirming clients' ethical assumptions, Doherty (1995) argues, is another way therapists address ethical issues. He does so, for instance, by including questions about clients' community service activities on his intake form. And in the late stages of therapy, he asks clients how they will use what they have learned in therapy on their jobs or in their communities. Doherty set forth a taxonomy of responses therapists can make to clients about ethical issues, from least intense to most intense. Because the most intense involve therapists consciously trying to influence clients, I list here only the five that are least intense, that involve therapists *addressing* ethical issues. Therapists, Doherty (1995: 42–4) asserts, can:

1   Validate the language of moral concern when clients use it spontaneously.
2   Introduce language to make more explicit the moral horizon of the client's concern.
3   Ask questions about clients' perceptions of the consequences of their actions on others, and explore the personal, familial, and cultural sources of these moral sensibilities.
4   Articulate the moral dilemma without giving the therapist's own position.
5   Bring research findings and clinical insight to bear on the consequences of certain actions, particularly for vulnerable individuals.

Clinical judgment is required to determine whether, and when, to use each. For example, in a first session with Bob, a therapist would be wise to go no further than the first level.

Therapists who address ethical issues in therapy function as moral consultants, Doherty maintains. Drawing upon Wolfe (1989: 11), he argues that:

> the therapist's role is to try "to locate a sense of moral obligation in common sense, ordinary emotions, and everyday life...to help individuals discover and apply for themselves the moral rules they already, as social beings, possess."
>
> (Doherty 1995: 19)

Addressing the ethical dimensions of clients' lives without influencing them is very difficult. For instance, Doherty's claim that everyone has a reliable moral sense appears to grow out of his intuitionist ethical theory, a theory not espoused by everyone. Those employing other ethical theories might think Doherty was trying to influence clients to adopt his ethical theory. Similarly, suppose Dr Peterson tries to address ethical issues in Bob's therapy by clarifying his client's values. Bob says, "I really believe marriage is a permanent commitment. But I really need to begin looking out for myself. And this time she's gone too far." If Dr Peterson emphasizes either the pro-commitment side of Bob's ambivalence or the pro-self-interest side, he will likely not only address Bob's ethical muddle, but also influence it.

Consciously addressing ethical issues may thus sometimes influence clients. But the reverse can also occur: consciously attempting to influence clients' ethical convictions may not work; clients might not change their views. Conscious attempts to influence clients can thus become ways in which therapists address ethical issues.

Controversy arises, however, when therapists *consciously influence* the ethical dimensions of clients' lives rather than simply addressing them (Doherty 1995). But advocacy of ethical influence on clients is not new, albeit a muted theme in the history of therapy. Despite the emphasis of his psychoanalytic descendants on neutrality, and the assertions he made that support that emphasis on therapeutic neutrality, Freud argued that "we are often obliged, for therapeutic purposes, to oppose the superego, and we endeavor to lower its demands" (Freud 1961: 143). Although he distinguished between the superego and genuine ethical convictions, Freud no doubt influenced the latter in his conscious efforts to influence the former (and that very distinction can only be made on the basis of some disputed ethical view). Dreikurs was more explicit: "Changing the value system on which patients operate, constitutes an essential part of psychotherapy" (Dreikurs 1967: 103).

The trend to advocate explicit therapist ethical influence on clients is a profoundly important development in a profession historically characterized by devotion to value-freedom and ethical neutrality and by a general neglect of therapy's ethical character. And such explicit ethical influence on clients is likely to increase as the number of managed care therapists, trained to be "directive" (Austad and Berman 1991b: 265), increases.

Although I welcome this trend for several reasons, I welcome it cautiously, embracing it only if therapists exercise influence responsibly and well, giving due attention to protecting client rights and autonomy, insuring that clients are not harmed, and otherwise pursuing such influence appropriately, as discussed in this chapter.

Unfortunately, the range of efforts to influence clients that is considered appropriate is wide. At one extreme is Kovacs' (1987) sublimely confident role as self-appointed priest, and a therapy supervisor quoted by Nicholas. She consulted him about a client who was selling marijuana. His unequivocal response: " 'Simple,' said Bob. 'Tell him it's unethical, and that he can't get better if he does it. Unethical behavior and mental health are contradictory' " (Nicholas 1994: v).

Other therapists exert ethical influence in a more nuanced (and responsible) manner, exhibiting greater awareness of potential problems, showing sensitivity to clients' psychological status, tailoring their influence strategies accordingly, and generally exhibiting wisdom as they address the ethical character of therapy (Cushman 1995; Doherty 1995).

Doherty's (1995) repertoire of influence strategies includes a spectrum of approaches, each respecting client autonomy and matched to the needs of the client and the current state of the therapeutic relationship. He raises ethical issues with clients in the early stages of therapy when appropriate and in ways (discussed above) that make ethical discourse a natural part of the therapeutic relationship. He engages in more active forms of ethical influence only when a well-functioning therapeutic relationship has developed. Even then, "caring and timing" are paramount. He explains that:

> listening, reflecting, and affirming must precede any ethical challenge in psychotherapy; clients must know that we have heard them and care about them. Furthermore, the client must have responded positively to some other clinical challenge in the nonmoral domain, such as a challenge to examine distorted beliefs or unacknowledged feelings, or to try out a new, probably uncomfortable behavior.
>
> (Doherty 1995: 64)

Only then will Doherty make one of his more intense responses to clients:

6   Describe how you generally see the issue and how you tend to weight the moral options, emphasizing that every situation is unique and that the client will, of course, make his or her own decision.
7   Say directly how concerned you are about the moral consequences of the client's actions.
8   Clearly state when you cannot support a client's decision or behavior, explaining your decision on moral grounds and, if necessary, withdrawing from the case.

(Doherty 1995: 44–5)

Preserving the autonomy of the client is vital when therapists consciously attempt to influence the ethical dimensions of clients' lives. Hoffman (1979) emphasized the need for therapists to assure clients that disagreement with their therapist is okay. And that clients have a right to disagree with their therapists. Therapists need to provide such assurance whenever they ethically confront clients. Doherty argues that therapists need to monitor their reactions when clients disagree with their ethical stance. In contrast to moralistic therapists, the morally sensitive therapist "will explore the areas of diverging opinions and then back off" (Doherty 1995: 65). And he offered a helpful guideline: "If a client always ends up agreeing with the therapist, the therapist is probably doing something wrong – being coercive, shaming, or unaware of the client's need to please" (ibid.: 84).

Some therapists argue that therapists should limit their ethical influence on clients to issues *directly related to therapy goals*. Others, including Cushman (1995) and Doherty (1995), argue that a more *general* kind of ethical influence on clients is also legitimate. This valid general ethical influence pertains to universally applicable ethical ideals, to the interests of others as well as the client, and to long-term and not simply short-term consequences of clients' actions. I want to address those two general views.

Some argue that the ethical influence therapists exert should be limited, to mental health values, to ethical convictions directly tied to therapy's psychological goals. Although not in the most recent version, the 1973 ethics code of the American Psychiatric Association codified that view: "The psychiatrist…should not use the unique position of power afforded him by the psychotherapeutic situation to influence the patient in any ways not directly relevant to the treatment goals." Therapist influence should thus be restricted to those problems for which therapists are competent (trained) to treat (i.e. psychological but not ethical problems), and should be consistent with the agreement between therapist and client, which is generally about psychological problems, not broader ethical issues (Tjeltveit 1986). This position requires a sharp distinction between psychological problems and well-being, on the one hand, and ethical issues, on the other. But that distinction, for reasons outlined in the discussion of therapy goals in Chapter 9, is difficult to make.

By way of contrast, Doherty explicitly attempts to promote a more general "ethical self-empowerment," doing so in the careful way described above. Indeed, he even asserts that therapists "have a responsibility to help our clients avoid compromising themselves ethically" (Doherty 1995: 54). He distinguishes between "personal values," like the value of a good education, which are private and idiosyncratic, and "moral convictions," like commitment, "the moral linchpin of family relationships" (ibid.: 24–5). Although he may attempt to influence clients regarding the latter, he will not attempt to influence the former. He also encourages clients to consider the well-being of their family and community as well as their own well-being, an ethical theme Cushman (1995) addresses as well.

Both limited and general ethical influence are often justified in terms of positive outcome: clients will be better off psychologically, ethically, or both. Clients and their families, friends, and communities will benefit. And client moral integrity will be preserved or enhanced (Buhler 1962; Doherty 1995). But to justify process in terms of outcome, we need to address the ethical status of that outcome, a task I will address in Chapter 9.

Unfortunately, one person may think a therapy process ethically appropriate, but a second person may think it inappropriate – because the ethical convictions upon which each bases his or her judgment differs from that of the other. A problem with Doherty's laudable approach is that he appears to be slow at times to recognize that other people sometimes disagree with his ethical views (like his controversial assumptions that everyone has a sense of moral obligation and that moral convictions are clearly distinguishable from personal values). If he empowers clients ethically, with which ethical convictions does he empower them?

Other therapists exhibit that tendency to a greater extent. The American Psychiatric Association Committee on Religion and Psychiatry (1990) criticized a therapist who regarded his client's homosexual orientation to be sinful. That therapist may have tried to ethically influence his client in accord with his own "moral convictions." And Wendorf and Wendorf (1985) criticized Margolin (1982) for imposing her feminist values on clients. Nicholas (1994) approvingly reports a therapist's success in changing a client's definition of what is moral, changing it to her own idiosyncratic ethical views.

And so differing evaluations of the appropriateness of ethical influence on clients often hinge on ethical differences among the evaluators. Some ethical differences are at the level of specific values (defined ethically), but others are at the level of ethical theory. At both levels, most contemporary societies are sometimes deeply divided. Because those profound ethical divisions affect therapy and judgments about it, they represent a deep and challenging problem that therapists and other therapy stakeholders need to address. And to which I will return in Chapter 10.

I now want to turn to the sixth and seventh ethically relevant dimensions of therapist process.

Helping clients

Some argue that appropriate or ideal therapy processes are those that help clients. That leaves unanswered two important questions: what does it mean to help clients? and, what do therapists do when helping a client conflicts with some other ideal for therapists? For instance, a therapist may be able to remove a client's presenting problem (help the client) but only by paternalistically reducing his or her autonomy.

The ideal solution to such ethical dilemmas, of course, is to help clients in a way that benefits them, preserves their rights, and otherwise meets the ethical ideals discussed in this chapter. When such perfection cannot be achieved, clients, therapists, and other stakeholders must exercise prudence when dilemmas arise, determining the best possible balance of those ideals, a balance that is rarely perfect.

Some argue that research will tell us how to help clients. When answers are obtained (and some have been obtained) therapists should then employ methods empirically proven to be effective. As I have argued previously, there is substantial merit in properly qualified forms of this ethical position.

But it leaves unanswered the question I will address in Chapter 9: which therapy outcomes, which therapy goals, are good, right, and/or virtuous?

Choice of therapy goal(s)

One more issue of process needs to be addressed: by what process should therapy goals be determined?

Szasz (1965) asserted that Freud's greatest contribution was creating a new role for the psychiatrist: agent of the client rather than agent of society. Accordingly, clients should choose therapy goals, and therapists are obligated to respect those choices. Rogers strongly encouraged therapists to give "full freedom" to clients, including the freedom to choose any goals, whether "social or antisocial, moral or immoral" (Rogers 1951: 48).

Several difficulties face the idea that clients alone should select therapy goals. As Lowe (1976) notes, some clients are too confused to state their goals. Furthermore, in the current climate, unless clients are sufficiently rich to pay for therapy on their own, third-party payers expect to play a role in determining the goals of a particular therapeutic relationship. And Austad and Berman note that therapists employing brief therapy techniques are required to "take responsibility for the content and *direction* of therapy" (Austad and Berman 1991b: 265, emphasis added).

Therapists may think some client goals inadvisable. For example, most therapists would think it a mistake for Dr Peterson to accede to Bob's request to tell him whether to forgive his wife and stay in his marriage. That would not be in Bob's best interests. Permitting Bob to choose his own therapy goals and helping him would thus be in conflict.

Drawing upon the ethical principles discussed in this chapter sheds light on this problem, however. Dr Peterson should try to maximize Bob's autonomy, treat him with respect, balance his autonomy with Dr Peterson's own ideas about what would be most helpful to Bob, and influence Bob appropriately. A dialogue (Berger 1982; Bergin 1991) between Bob and Dr Peterson, and, as applicable, among Bob, Dr Peterson, and Bob's third-party payer, should develop a clear consensus about therapy goals and expectations. That may also contribute to a successful outcome (Orlinsky *et al*. 1994).

Convictions about therapy goals are again relevant, as therapy stakeholders need to evaluate whether proposed therapy goals are realistic and appropriate (Carroll *et al*. 1985). Or, better yet, ideal. And so the process of negotiating therapy goals hinges in part upon an ethical evaluation of alternative goals, which I will address in Chapter 9.

Having established in exhausting detail that therapy processes can be, and need to be, ethically evaluated, I now turn to the intimately related topic of ethical evaluations of therapy goals and outcome.

9

Ethical dimensions of the goals and outcome of therapy
Therapy as means to which (ethics-laden) ends?

Psychotherapy goals have an ethical character, a *disputed* ethical character. Those goals, and therapy outcomes, can be evaluated ethically by therapy stakeholders, who should develop and articulate more sophisticated and ethically adequate convictions to guide and assess therapy.

To ground this discussion of those controversial assertions, I want to revisit the clinical example used in Chapter 8, examining the goals of three of the stakeholders in Bob's therapy: Bob wants to be less confused, Dr Peterson wants Bob to develop greater insight into the unconscious and childhood roots of his current difficulties, and Bob's third-party payer wants a cost-effective reduction of his psychiatric symptoms. We can ethically evaluate those goals because each stakeholder thinks it would be *good* if, by the end of Bob's therapy, that stakeholder's goal is reached. We can also ask which therapy goal (if any) is ethically superior or best.

Therapy outcomes also have an ethical character. Suppose Bob's therapy has the following outcome: he is less depressed and no longer confused, having decided to divorce his wife. He made that decision after taking seriously his therapist's encouragement to "Take better care of yourself." Dr Peterson employed that intervention to "lower the demands" of Bob's "overactive" superego, to free him so he could develop some insight. As part of "taking better care" of himself, Bob, primary caretaker for all three children during the year-long marital separation, had mounted an aggressive effort to insure that his soon-to-be ex-wife accepted "fair" (50/50) responsibility for taking care of the three-year-old daughter they had together and complete custody of her nine-year-old son (whom Bob had adopted), the product of her first marriage. Therapy did not last long, and so was not expensive, but Bob gained little insight into the deeper roots of his problems. The previously well-adjusted children had, however, developed problems. Two of the three, and especially the son, were acting out and seriously depressed.

The goals set by Bob and his third-party payer were thus reached, but not the goals of Dr Peterson. Furthermore, one outcome, therapy's harmful impact on Bob's children, was a goal set by no one.

If we ethically evaluate the outcome of Bob's therapy, we might conclude that Bob's decreased confusion and depression and therapy's low cost were good outcomes, but Bob's lack of insight was not a good outcome. And the harm to the children was a bad (harmful, negative) outcome. We can also ask whether a better outcome might have occurred, an outcome preserving Bob's gains (and possibly holding therapy costs low) while reducing the harm to his children (and possibly increasing his insight). I relegated the outcomes of low cost and increased insight to parentheses in that last sentence because, in my ethical judgment, they are less important: Bob's well-being and that of his children are more important criteria (principles, ideals, ethical standards) by which to judge the outcome of his therapy. A psychoanalyst or managed care company executive might disagree with my ranking, however. Ethical evaluations of therapy goals and outcomes are disputed.

Some argue that establishing goals and evaluating therapeutic effectiveness are purely technical or scientific matters, and not ethical. I acknowledge the technical and scientific dimensions of those tasks, but argue in this chapter that those tasks also have ethical dimensions. Any judgment of therapy's "effectiveness," for instance, hinges upon some ethical criterion by which effectiveness is judged, upon evaluative (ethical) as well as descriptive considerations. As Orlinsky and Howard point out:

> the judgment of psychotherapeutic outcome is a complex procedure involving two distinct steps often compounded in practice. The *description* of the changes that are probably consequences of participation in psychotherapy is only the first step. Logically, the second step is an *evaluation* of these changes with reference to explicit value standards.
> (Orlinsky and Howard 1978: 320–1)

Addressing the ethical character of goals and outcome, how goals and outcome pertain to what is good, right, and/or virtuous, can mean ethically critiquing the goals and outcome of a particular therapeutic relationship (as I did in a very limited fashion with Bob's therapy) or of some general approach to therapy (e.g. Rogerian). Addressing goals and outcome evaluatively can also mean formulating ideals, or optimal ethical standards or criteria, to be used to establish the best possible therapy goals and the best possible ethical assessment of outcome. Clarifying optimal ethical standards for therapy goals is especially important (if controversial) because – if some therapy goals are better (more good) than others and we know which are best – therapists should pursue those better goals (W. F. May 1984).

Goals and outcome are closely related, although distinguishable. A goal is what one or more stakeholders *want or intend* to happen in therapy; outcomes are what *actually* happens, which may or may not correspond to stakeholders' goals.

In attempting to understand the ethical character of therapy goals and outcome, I adopt a broad approach. I will consider the ethical dimensions of goals and outcomes found in various schools of therapy. But I will not limit the discussion to theories and theoretically-derived concepts because I also want to address dimensions of therapy – seen in particular therapeutic relationships and in therapy in general – not necessarily well captured by advocates of particular positions. For example, those advocates often emphasize, not how their approaches are like those of others, but how they are unlike.

I am also convinced that such ethical evaluations appropriately include careful analyses of therapy narratives. The stories told by therapists, clients, and other therapy stakeholders often pertain to what they perceive to be its good, right, and/or virtuous ends. As Guignon points out, the narratives constructed by therapy participants "have a 'moral' to the extent that their resolution implies the achievement of some goods taken as normative" (Guignon 1993: 236).

Finally, as discussed in the previous chapter, I do not sharply divide process and outcome. And so, for two reasons, I will include in this chapter what some call process. First, what one person calls therapy process (e.g. insight), a *means* to therapy's proper goals, another might call a positive outcome. Second, for some theorists, process and outcome are indistinguishable. Dewey, for instance, asserted that "growth itself is the only moral 'end'" (Dewey 1920: 177). Dewey-inspired therapists thus argue that the goal of good therapy (growth) is indistinguishable from its process (growth). (Not surprisingly, relationships between advocates of this viewpoint and managed care representatives are often rocky.)

Unfortunately, many therapists strenuously resist precisely the kind of ethical reflection on therapy goals and outcome for which I am arguing. This is true, even of therapists otherwise willing to engage in ethical reflection about therapy, true for several reasons discussed earlier. I will mention three.

Many therapists are taught not to make *ethical* evaluations about the ends of therapy, to judge which ends are worth pursuing (Guignon 1993; Richardson and Woolfolk 1994). Indeed, many are "loath" to do so (Parloff 1967: 8), perhaps because they believe such evaluations are beyond their competence or are impossible to do rationally (MacIntyre 1984).

In addition, some ethical assumptions to which therapy goals and outcome are tied are so widely held that their *ethical* character goes unrecognized. For example, Leahey notes that some US psychologists do not notice the ethical character of "individual growth" because it is "so American as to be transparent" (Leahey 1992: 371; see Taylor 1989). Because of a widespread ethical consensus at *some* levels of abstraction, therapists often easily negotiate therapy goals and evaluate outcome. But ethical issues are still present in consensual goals, and deep differences among therapy stakeholders often underlie apparent consensus. Furthermore, therapists can easily formulate goals in ways that command assent among clients but actually mask underlying differences. For example, suppose that when discussing goals with Bob, Dr Peterson had said, "Okay, then, so what we need to do in therapy is get a handle on this stuff you're wrestling with and get you feeling better." Hearing that, Bob may assume he and Dr Peterson shared goals, whereas in fact Dr Peterson's unvoiced goal was to increase Bob's insight, rather than "merely" reducing his confusion and relieving his symptoms. And so superficial agreement about therapy goals may retard deeper ethical reflection about goals and outcome.

Finally, many therapists resist ethical reflection on therapy goals and outcome because they employ an unduly restricted conception of ethics (MacIntyre 1984; Taylor 1989), a conception focused, in Taylor's words, on "what it is right to do rather than on what it is good to be" and on "obligation rather than the nature of the good life" (Taylor 1989: 3). And MacIntyre points to the frequent neglect of virtue and character in discussions of ethics. But questions of goodness and virtue are often more relevant to therapy than questions about right and wrong. We need to ask those broader ethical questions, excluded from narrow conceptions of ethics, to address well the ethical character of therapy goals and outcome.

Despite therapy stakeholders' overdetermined resistance to reflect ethically on therapy goals and outcome, it is, I think, vitally important to do so. Indeed, I think it so important I will repeat from previous chapters several overlapping reasons for therapy stakeholders to do so: to understand therapy's ethical character ("a theory of scientific progress needs an axiology of inquiry, whose function is to certify or de-certify certain proposed aims as legitimate" – Laudan 1987: 29), to uncover and address ethical differences underlying superficial similarities, to become more explicit about implicit ethical assumptions, to help us better evaluate goals and outcome, and to facilitate discourse among all of therapy's stakeholders about appropriate (and ideal) therapy goals and about public philosophies and public policies concerning the optimal role of therapy in a given society (to be discussed in Chapter 10). At its most fundamental level, however, we need to discuss therapy goals and outcome because therapy is supposed to *help* people (beneficence is central to the psychotherapy professions). But we need to be clear about what it *means* to help people. And that requires ethical analysis of therapy goals and outcome, because helping people means helping them change in some positive direction, which direction can be evaluated ethically. Finally, articulating the ethical sources of therapy's goals can enhance therapy's effectiveness. As Taylor notes, ethical articulacy:

> has a moral point, not just in correcting what may be wrong views but also in making the force of an ideal that people are already living by more palpable, more vivid for them; and by making it more vivid, empowering them to live up to it in a fuller and more integral fashion.
>
> (Taylor 1992: 22)

And so the question should be, not whether, but *how* to address the ethical character of therapy goals and outcome. I will first address problematic approaches, then turn to approaches that are more promising.

Unsuitable "solutions"

The easiest way to deal with the ethical character of therapy goals and outcome – and the most irresponsible – is to ignore it. Ethical judgments about outcome are then tacit, and goals covert. And covert goals, argues Karasu, are "ethically the most problematic" (Karasu 1980: 1505).

As discussed in Chapter 4, some assert that there is always one correct answer to ethical questions, including the question of the best therapy goal or outcome. The polar opposite of such absolutism is relativism, the claim we can make *no* universally applicable ethical assertions. But as surely as there is more than one valid goal for therapy, professionals (understood in a substantive sense) can make at least *some* ethical judgments about goals and outcome. We can, for example, rule out therapy goals like guilt-free pedophilia. And so therapists who endorse either absolutism or relativism deny their calling as professionals by fleeing the strenuous complexities of meaningful ethical inquiry.

Extreme skepticism (even if falling short of total relativism) is likewise inadequate. Drawing upon positivist ethical theory and the emotivist ethical theory with which it is often associated, many deny that any ethical assertions can be meaningful. The practical impact of that belief: asking which end or goal is good or right means nothing more than asking someone's preference or emotional reaction. But psychotherapists cannot, as professionals, fully embrace such skepticism because *by the very nature of being professionals* they commit themselves to the well-being of their clients, to benefit clients, to beneficence. And that requires some meaningful idea about what it means to help clients, of the good end toward which clients move in successful therapy. Although some measure of skepticism about ethical claims is important, and the extent of justifiable ethical assertions debatable (see below), being a professional (when the term is used in a substantive sense) requires a commitment to certain ethical ideals. And so, "a professional who holds no moral views" is a troubling contradiction.

Also problematic is vulgar pragmatism, my term for the belief that asking "Does it work?" can tell us which therapy goals to pursue and how to evaluate outcome. If we claim a therapy goal or outcome should be adopted (is good) because it works, we need to know *for what purpose, to what end*, or *for what function* it works. That purpose, end, or function is assumed to be good; therapy is considered good because it helps us to accomplish that good purpose, reach that good end, or restore that good function. But vulgar pragmatism never explicitly specifies those good purposes, ends, or functions, or gives an account of why they are good. And unless they engage in those properly ethical tasks, vulgar pragmatists rely upon covert ethical ideals (unjustified by vulgar pragmatism) in their ethical evaluations of therapy goals and outcome. As Richardson and Fowers point out:

> it is hard to see how we can evaluate different belief systems or ways of life...when whatever we *mean* by pragmatically beneficial or deleterious will be determined by the standards and values of the belief system or way of life we currently inhabit!
>
> (Richardson and Fowers 1994: 5)

Vulgar pragmatism thus obscures the ethical character of therapy goals and outcome.

Vulgar pragmatism needs to be distinguished, however, from philosophical pragmatism, which is one of the approaches that may prove helpful in exploring the fertile middle ground bounded by the inadequate alternatives of vulgar pragmatism, absolutism, relativism, and skepticism. I will turn to that middle ground shortly, but I will first address one final inadequate approach.

Some argue for a simple answer to the question of psychotherapy's goal and optimal outcome: mental health. Partly correct, that simple assertion is inadequate. It is partly correct because therapists should emphasize improved psychological functioning as much as possible (unless having very good reasons not to do so). But it is not the full solution, for several reasons: there is no consensus about the meaning of mental health (understood either as freedom from psychological problems or as ideal psychological functioning) among therapists and among categories of stakeholders (e.g. between therapists and third-party payers). All definitions of mental health presuppose more or less controversial ethical convictions. And the ethical ideals contained in notions of mental health need to be balanced with other ideals, for example, societal well-being.

Fortunately, therapy stakeholders mired in the poverty of ethical articulation that is reflected in, and exacerbated by, those simplistic options, can explore a wide variety of more promising alternatives in the ample middle ground between relativism and absolutism. They can be skeptical of false ethical claims but still make ethical assertions, can be pragmatic but articulate the ends toward which such pragmatism aims, and can strive to help clients reach ideal levels of psychological functioning with full awareness of the complexities attendant upon doing so. It is to the ideals employed in those more fruitful approaches that I now turn.

Multiple ideals: the diversity of valued therapy goals and outcomes

We employ a wide variety of ethical ideals – principles, concepts of goodness, and virtues – to determine therapy goals and evaluate outcome. "Respect for autonomy," for example, is a principle used to claim that therapy should aim at whatever goals clients set for themselves. Every therapist employs – to some extent – that or other ideals.

Some regard such ideals as optional, standards to which therapists and clients may wish to aspire or not. Others assert that some ideals, especially moral ideals (in contrast to nonmoral ideals), are obligatory. W. F. May, for instance, argued that with regard to moral ideals "one lives under the *imperative* to *approximate* the ideal; and this task of approximation is not merely optional" (May 1984: 252). Likewise, Taylor defined a moral ideal as "a picture of what a better or higher mode of life would be, where 'better' and 'higher' are defined not in terms of what we happen to desire or need, but offer a standard of what we ought to desire" (Taylor 1992: 16). Many of the ideals held by clients, therapists, and other therapy stakeholders are nonmoral ideals, however, not carrying that obligatory or "ought" quality. In this chapter, I will address the full range of ideals, moral and nonmoral.

I will begin to address ethical ideals in this section by exploring the perspectives of different therapy stakeholders. I will then consider various types of ideals, differing levels of abstraction, the need to tailor goals (to some extent) to individual clients, contexts, and cultures, and the extent of the ideals employed. I will also document the diversity of ethical ideals underlying therapy goals and evaluations of therapy outcome. In the concluding section, I will discuss how to address these multiple (and at times contradictory) therapy ideals.

Deciding what is good, right, and/or virtuous in therapeutic ends: principles, goodness, and virtues

To ethically evaluate therapy goals or outcome, we can employ ethical principles, some concept of goodness, and/or virtue ethics, the three approaches to deciding what is good, right, and/or virtuous discussed in Chapter 4.

We can use ethical principles, like Meara, Schmidt, and Day's (1996) respect for autonomy, beneficence, fidelity, justice, nonmaleficence, and veracity, to select therapy goals and evaluate outcomes. We can do so in several ways. A principle can serve as a criterion to determine or evaluate desired ends (the goals or outcome of therapy), can serve as the desired end itself, or both. For example, the ideal of "respect for autonomy" could mean that *any* therapy end that respects client autonomy is ethical, that the therapy end that *most* respects client autonomy is ideal or is obligatory, that any therapy end that *fails* to respect client autonomy is ethically undesirable or wrong, or that successful therapy clients ideally exhibit respect for autonomy. The first alternative – that "respect for autonomy" could serve as a criterion to determine or evaluate desired therapy ends – can also be interpreted in different ways: when Bob wants his therapist to tell him what to do, for instance, should Dr Peterson "respect" Bob's autonomy by accepting Bob's choice of therapy goal and tell him what to do? Or would Dr Peterson best respect Bob's autonomy by *not* telling him what to do and engaging him in a course of therapy that enables Bob to become more autonomous? The first would respect Bob's (perhaps autonomous) choice of therapy goal; the second would respect Bob's autonomy by helping him develop greater autonomy.

Although ethical principles can be employed as therapy goals, I have never seen "nonmaleficence," "beneficence," or "fidelity" listed as therapy goals on a treatment plan. "Veracity," "justice,"[1] and "respect for autonomy" (or synonyms) are occasionally listed, however, especially for clients who act out. And I have seen goals like "learn to take better care of oneself," goals that very much resemble ethical egoism (a view that Frankena describes as the belief that "one is always to do what will promote his [or her] own good" – Frankena 1973: 15).

Concepts of goodness are generally much more helpful than principles in determining goals for clients and evaluating therapy outcome. Unfortunately, ethicists and therapists alike have neglected concepts of goodness in the twentieth century, although such concepts play a central role in teleological (consequentialist) ethical theories. When we employ concepts of goodness, we establish therapy goals and evaluate outcome because we believe that a particular outcome is good, better than its alternatives, or the best or ideal psychological end for a client. And so Dr Peterson established the goal of insight because he believes it is good for clients like Bob to develop insight. Bob viewed therapy as a success because at its end he was no longer in a bad (negatively valued) state of confusion and had achieved the good end of clear thinking and greater decisiveness.

Taylor argues that we all have "strongly valued goods" in our lives. We "cannot help," he argues, "having recourse to these strongly valued goods for the purposes of life: deliberating, judging situations, deciding how you feel about people, and the like" (Taylor 1989: 59). And it is primarily (but not exclusively) those goods toward which therapy aims. And we evaluate therapy outcome by whether clients achieve those good ends.

Beliefs about goodness play an integral role in teleological ethical theories because the ethical claims of teleologists are based on whether goodness is produced, on whether some good or bad end (*telos*) results. Accordingly, therapy goals which produce goodness should be chosen, and the best outcomes are those that produce the best ("most good") ends. The nature of the goodness toward which therapy aims is, of course, critical. Therapists rarely employ the overtly ethical language of "good" or "bad." Instead, to denote the goodness to which therapy aims, they use words like "successful," "effective," "symptom reduction," "mental health," "self-actualization," and "insight."

Finally, virtue ethicists evaluate therapy in terms of the ethical character of therapy clients (cf. Meara *et al.* 1996; Toulmin 1978; Weiner 1993). For example, to evaluate Bob's therapy, we can look at the extent to which he becomes mentally healthy, self-aware, more honest, and so forth. That is, the extent to which he becomes psychologically virtuous. In contrast to those who employ principles and judge mental health in terms of actions, those employing virtue ethics make ethical evaluations in terms of whether *individual persons* are mentally healthy (Jahoda 1958).

Although approaches to ethics that employ principles, concepts of goodness, and virtues can be distinguished conceptually, and it is sometimes advantageous to focus on one approach for a particular purpose, at times the three approaches overlap and can be seen as complementary. For example, humanistic therapy can be evaluated in terms of concepts of goodness, virtues, and ethical principles. A humanistic therapist would judge therapy successful if it produces the good end of self-actualization, or if the client possessed the virtue of self-actualization. And Wolfe suggested that "two moral obligations are apparent in humanistic therapy": clients are to "trust in their own experience" and "refrain from responding to externally imposed moral standard or, in the current therapeutic patois, 'one should have no shoulds'" (Wolfe 1978: 47).

The perspectives of clients, therapists, and other therapy stakeholders

Drawing general conclusions about therapy goals and outcome is profoundly difficult because stakeholders use different ethical ideals. Strupp and Hadley (1977) distinguished between the perspectives of society (which employs the standard of an orderly world of conforming individuals), the individual (whose value is happiness and gratification of needs), and mental health professionals (whose standard is "sound personality structure characterized by growth, development, self-actualization, integration, autonomy, environmental mastery, ability to cope with stress, reality orientation, adaptation" (Strupp and Hadley 1977: 190)).

But Stiles (1983) pointed out that the values of individuals *within* each of Strupp and Hadley's three groups sometimes differ. And so their evaluations of the goals and outcome of therapy may as well. Not all clients, for instance, are hedonistic and egocentric. Indeed, some hold sophisticated ideas about mental health and the well-being of society (Lambert 1983). Furthermore, identifiable groups of stakeholders within a society may hold different ethical ideals, and so choose goals and evaluate outcome in different ways. For instance, the ideals held by a Health Maintenance Organization and by a patients' rights organization would likely be quite different. Furthermore, therapists from different schools of therapy choose different treatment goals (Beutler and Bergan 1991), endorse different values (Consoli

1996), and employ different criteria to evaluate therapy's effectiveness (Richardson 1989). Therapists' goals, values, and criteria often arise from differing ethical sources. That, however, raises one of the most important and thorny questions in this book: if the goals of therapy are based on conflicting ethical sources, and therapy's effectiveness is evaluated in ways that vary with evaluators' ethical ideals, is psychotherapy (or in what sense is therapy) a coherent professional practice?

Heterogeneous normality and the prospect of distinguishing "mental health" from other ethical ideals

Mental health,[2] a phrase connoting psychotherapy's goal and optimal outcome, has been distinguished from moral values, virtues, and the entire range of controverted ethical issues discussed in this book. The promise of doing so: we can avoid dissension by selecting ethically uncontested therapy goals and by objectively evaluating therapy outcome. And we can help clients without entering the murky philosophical waters implied by my claim that therapy goals and judgments about outcome entail ethical judgments, that therapists perforce function as ethicists.

Psychotherapists should undoubtedly *emphasize* psychological goals, since we are trained to address psychological issues and most clients assume therapy will focus on them. But I question whether mental health can be severed neatly from other ethical issues, whether we carve nature at its joints by sharply distinguishing mental health from ethics. Addressing that issue well requires a clear and coherent definition of mental health, preferably one commanding general approval. But we do not have such a definition.

One reason for our difficulty in defining mental health, and distinguishing it from ethics, stems from an important fact observed by Stiles, Shapiro, and Elliott: "Psychological normality is heterogeneous" (Stiles *et al.* 1986: 171). That is, people free of psychological problems pursue highly variegated lives, within and across cultures (Marsella and White 1982; Wig 1990). And so the outcomes of psychotherapy, which restores people to normality, are also heterogeneous. Awareness of that fact is, I think, vitally important in understanding the ethical dimensions of therapy goals and outcome.

Distinctions among mental health and other ideals

Distinguishing mental health from other ideals has a long and conceptually rich history.[3] For instance, Hartmann noted that Freud "took pains to keep clinical apart from moral evaluation" (Hartmann 1960: 17). Distinguishing clinical and moral evaluations, or mental health and other ideals, can take two forms: distinguishing mental health from all ethical considerations (claiming judgments about mental health involve no ethical issues) and distinguishing between mental health values and other ethical considerations. Advocates of the latter position acknowledge the value-laden nature of concepts of mental health, but assert that we can, and should, distinguish ethical convictions related to mental health from other ideals. If we do so, some claim, the problems associated with the role of values in therapy will fade to insignificance. As Strupp asserted, "to the extent that the therapist's commitment to essential therapeutic values is realized a number of issues that are frequently discussed in the therapy literature become more or less irrelevant" (Strupp 1980: 400).

I will devote my attention to the latter position because I think all concepts of mental health draw to some extent upon ethical assumptions. As I argued in Chapter 7 and earlier in this chapter, the concept of mental health combines psychological and ethical (and often medical) considerations. It has to do with facts about how human beings function psychologically, but also with ideals about how human beings best function, or should function. And so mental health is a "hybrid" concept, consisting of factual *and* normative assertions (Wakefield 1992b: 374). It is therefore appropriately rooted in both science and ethics. As Jahoda noted, in selecting a definition of mental health, we thus "have to choose what seems best among those definitions intermingling value and fact" (Jahoda 1958: 4). And so in this section I will discuss the legitimacy of drawing sharp distinctions between mental health values (ethical convictions related to mental health) and other ethical convictions. After clarifying some ways in which distinctions have been drawn, I will propose a spectrum of understandings of the psychological-ethical concept of mental health.

Hartmann (1960) gave classic expression to a sharp distinction between mental health values and other ethical convictions. "In his [or her] therapeutic work," he asserted, a therapist:

> will keep other values in abeyance and concentrate on the realization of one category of values only: health values. They are given special consideration in his [or her] work; they are taken for granted; and every therapist will, in his [or her] therapeutic work, consider their realization in his [or her] patients as his [or her] immediate and overriding concern.
> (Hartmann 1960: 55)

Distinguishing mental health values from therapists' more general ethical convictions requires a clear definition of mental health, of the goal toward which therapy aims. Identifying a definition to which all therapy stakeholders give ready assent has, however, proven extraordinarily difficult. Nevertheless, some attempts have been made: Margolis (1966) argued for autonomy, "the capacity of the patient to change his [or her] beliefs and actions freely" (Margolis 1966: 123). And Strupp contended that "a major – perhaps *the* major – tenet of modern psychotherapy" is Freud's conviction about therapy's purpose: "to strengthen the patient's adaptive capacities, to provide whatever assistance may be necessary to enable the patient to lead a more satisfying life as a responsible citizen in our culture" (Strupp 1980: 397). As noted earlier, however, critics of autonomy have pointed to its heavily Western and individualistic character and urged that autonomy be balanced with other ethical ideals. Freud's views have also failed to receive universal acclaim, especially if understood to mean that clients should quietly "adapt" to a pathogenic family or subculture.

Jahoda attempted to identify a consensus about the meaning of positive mental health. She failed. She did, however, identify six categories of concepts used to define mental health, all abstract and all with heterogeneous subtypes. Various theorists, she argued, hold that mental health has to do with a person's attitudes toward self; growth, development, self-actualization; integration; autonomy; perception of reality; and environmental mastery (Jahoda 1958: 23).

Others have identified mental health values associated with particular theoretical persuasions. In his *Operational Values in Psychotherapy*, Glad suggested that patients in successful therapy "integrate themselves in the terms provided by the therapist–leader" (Glad 1959: 302). That is, clients "grow" into the value-laden normality to which their therapist's convictions point. According to Glad:

> Psychoanalysts enhance a genital–parental integration....Client-centered therapists promote emotional understanding, self-acceptance and awareness of others....Interpersonal therapists facilitate skill in social relations, consensual validity and interpersonal security.... Dynamic relationship therapists nurture pride and satisfaction in one's unique autonomy.
>
> (Glad 1959: 302)

Employing empirical methods to investigate mental health values, Jensen and Bergin (1988) found substantial consensus among therapists, as did Haugen, Tyler, and Clark (1991) and Kelly (1995a). Jensen and Bergin found that therapists diverged on values related to sex and religion, however. And Consoli (1996) found that mental health values varied by therapists' theoretical orientation. Tyler and Suan (1990; Suan and Tyler 1990) found that some mental health values varied across racial groups, while Jensen and Bergin (1988), and Tjeltveit, Fiordalisi, and Smith (1996) found that some mental health values varied with some dimensions of respondent religiousness. Finally, Minsel, Becker, and Korchin (1991) found that "culture carriers" gave descriptions of "positive mental health" that varied across cultures and age levels. Some overlap concerning mental health values thus exists among therapy stakeholders, but not complete consensus.

Furthermore, empirical studies, while helpful for other research purposes, contribute but modestly to the task of determining whether mental health values can be sharply distinguished from other ethical considerations. Because those studies of necessity define "values" in *psychological* terms, they can tell us what therapists and other stakeholders believe regarding mental health values, but not what it would be *ideal* for them to believe, or what they should believe.

Smith found little hope that agreement about a conception of mental health could be reached. And so he suggested that we should no longer consider it a theoretical concept, but a label for "a variety of evaluative concerns" (M. B. Smith 1961: 300). He also argued that ethical considerations play a legitimate role in conceptions of mental health. His laudable awareness of the valid role played by ethical convictions in concepts of mental health and of the considerable variety of, and conflicts between, such concepts was, however, followed by a non sequitur: "I question, secondly, whether there is any profit in the argument about which evaluative criteria...are to be included." That kind of skeptical anti-intellectual flight to inarticulacy and covert ethical conceptions of mental health has, regrettably, often been emulated. Few therapists reflect systematically on the ethical character of therapy goals, although a few philosophers (e.g. Engelhardt and Spicker 1978) have done so. Follette, Bach, and Follette (1993) expressed a common attitude. They acknowledged the role played by values in conceptions of health, but concluded that "there is little basis for deciding whose values are the 'right' ones without resorting to dogmatism...if others choose different values about what should constitute psychological health, the therapeutic landscape will be all the richer for it" (Follette *et al.* 1993: 305). Trapped within the hackneyed false dichotomy of absolutistic dogmatism and relativism, they chose the latter. And so failed to explore the rich middle ground between those poles, failed to gather its plentiful harvest.

We will also fail to make optimal progress if we pursue two other approaches to understanding the relationship of mental health and ethics. First, a sole focus on identifying a consensus about mental health will not adequately resolve the *ethical* problems of identifying optimal therapy ideals and distinguishing appropriately between mental health and other ideals. Suppose we identify a consensus. The crowd may be wrong. And, as I noted above, ethicists distinguish ethics from custom and consensus. Consensus is often relevant to, but does not fully determine, ethical judgments. Indeed, in light of the heterogeneity of normality, the diversity of ethical convictions within and between societies, and the logical link between mental health and contested ethical assumptions, we should expect concepts of mental health to *diverge* rather than to converge. The failure of therapy stakeholders to recognize this has prevented the kind of rigorous ethical analyses necessary to adequately understand and address the ethical character of therapy goals and outcome.

Second, therapy stakeholders may inappropriately conflate mental health and ethics, especially when they do not understand the full range of viable ethical alternatives, when they fail to recognize the heterogeneity of normality, and when they equate mental health with their own ethical views. As Roazen notes, therapists can take "rather striking moral positions...via clinical categories without any awareness that the same categories might justify very different moral alternatives" (Roazen 1972: 202). And so therapists can use "mental health" (at times in uncritical ways) to further particular ethical or political causes, to delineate one region within the heterogeneous realm of normality as the sole or best region for those seeking mental health. Doing so is not new (Engelhardt 1978). The concept of self-actualization, for instance, dates back to the ethical writings of Socrates, Plato, and Aristotle (Franck 1977; Norton 1976). And Nussbaum noted that many of the ideas and practices of Hellenistic ethicists anticipated psychoanalysis, with one notable exception: "Psychoanalysis has not always been willing to commit itself to a normative idea of health" (Nussbaum 1994: 26). Ironically, then, some psychoanalysts may have pushed the explicitly ethical from consciousness.

A spectrum of psychological-ethical concepts of mental health

I want to turn now to a constructive proposal for understanding various perspectives on the relationship between concepts of mental health and other ethical ideals: psychological-ethical concepts of mental health range along a spectrum, from mental health as freedom *from* serious psychological problems (mental disorders) to freedom *for* some state of positive mental health. Concepts of positive mental health range from limited ("minimalist") criteria for determining therapy goals or evaluating outcome, to criteria that are extensive ("maximalist"), criteria that fully flesh out the meaning of human flourishing.

Defining mental health as freedom *from* diagnosable mental disorders or other serious psychological problems entails a relatively limited set of ethical assumptions: as a general rule, it is good to be free from the suffering and other problems associated with psychological problems. It is good, for instance, to be free from clinical depression. Harm and dysfunction are always present in mental disorders, asserts Wakefield (1992a, 1992b, 1997), whose conceptual approach explicitly combines scientific and ethical considerations. He maintains that harm is an ethical term pertaining to "harmful consequences for the person," for example, distress and disability; dysfunction is a scientific term that refers to "a condition in which some internal mechanism is not functioning in the way it is naturally designed to function," with "mechanism" denoting physical, behavioral, psychological, motivational, and other features of organisms (Wakefield 1992a: 233).

But harm and suffering are not necessarily bad. Gewirth, for instance,

argues that if Hermann Goering had felt pain (harmful psychological consequences) because of his sadistic behavior toward Holocaust victims,
"obviously we would regard this pain as morally good. Consequently, if the
removal of pain is the aim of psychoanalysis, then this is by no means necessarily a moral aim" (Gewirth 1956: 30). Therefore, although it is generally
good to relieve an individual's distress, in some circumstances it may not be.

Three other ethical complexities are tied to mental health as freedom
from psychological problems. The first can be seen in Wakefield's (1992a)
concept of harmful dysfunction. He asserts that human beings have some
kind of "natural design" in accord with which we function when not disordered (i.e. in accord with which we ideally, or should, function). This
contention rests on scientific findings, philosophical assumptions (historically often tied to particular understandings of science), *and* an *ethical*
assumption, an assumption that, although often linked with science, is
neither a scientific finding nor intrinsic to the scientific method. That
ethical assumption is that it is good to, or we should, function in accord
with the way nature has designed us to function. Although science can
clearly provide us with *some* knowledge about our nature (albeit not at the
level of metaphysics, e.g. whether our nature is nothing but material and
fully amenable to scientific explanation; Christopher 1996; R. B. Miller
1983; Tjeltveit 1989), science cannot tell us that it is *good* that we function
in harmony with our nature, or that we *should*.

Second, freeing someone from a psychological problem (a relatively
uncontroversial therapeutic goal) may produce ethically relevant consequences or conflict with some ethical obligation. Suppose the good end of
reducing Bob's depression can be reached in two ways: quickly reducing it
by dramatically reducing the time he spends with his three children (which
would harm his children and conflict with his obligation to them) or
reducing his depression more slowly by addressing his maladaptive cognitions and expanding his limited repertoire of coping skills (which would
permit him to continue to spend ample time with his children). In that case,
the choice of treatment goal clearly involves, not simply Bob's freedom from
mental illness, but broader ethical issues as well.

Finally, although therapists may wish to limit their influence on therapeutic outcome to eliminating psychological problems, it is hard in practice
to move people *from* those problems without also moving them *to* some new
state, producing an outcome that can be evaluated ethically. Clients working
with therapists who consciously limit their influence to eliminating psychological problems may develop a particular form of positive mental health,
the implicit or explicit vision held by their therapist. Therapy's *de facto*
outcome may thus be a modestly rich set of ethical assumptions about
mental health, about the good life, even when therapists strive only to free
clients from their psychological problems.

Concepts of positive mental health (mental health as freedom *for* some good end) are based on more extensive sets of ethical convictions (Engelhardt 1978) and are even more controversial (Smith 1961). And maximalist (extensive) concepts of mental health are more controversial than minimalist (limited). Although no sharp line can be drawn between minimalist and maximalist concepts, the extremes of the continuum can be differentiated. Parloff, for instance, distinguished between therapists who "are not interested in tampering with the value systems of their patients" and those "willing to accept the responsibility of advocating particular values as being those that foster mental health" (Parloff 1967: 14). In the maximalist category may be found the World Health Organization's definition of health as "a state of complete physical, mental, and social well being and not merely the absence of disease or infirmity" (World Health Organization 1981: 83), Nicholas's (1994) telling her client that he cannot possibly become mentally healthy while selling marijuana, Doherty's (1995) promotion of "ethical empowerment" for clients, and Ellis's aspiration to produce in clients a "profound philosophic change" (Ellis 1987b: 473).

Minimalist convictions, by way of contrast, generally stick closely to clients' stated goals and therapists' training. For instance, if Bob has psychological problems because he does not have the skills to cope with his marital separation, a therapist who establishes "improved coping skills" as a therapy goal would likely receive little criticism. But some therapists would think that to be a paltry, insufficient goal, and others would emphasize other goals. As noted above, however, even minimalist concepts, like Freud's emphasis on adaptive capacities (Strupp 1980), have been criticized. This is partly because modest sets of ethical ideals are often tied to more extensive sets of ethical convictions. For example, Freud can be viewed as espousing the minimalist ideals of adaptation or of "love and work" (Fine 1990). But more extensive ethical commitments were sometimes evident, as in his caustic attack on the moral obligation to love one's neighbor as oneself (Wallace 1986). Accordingly, as is true of concepts of mental health as freedom from psychological problems, minimalist concepts of positive mental health are ethically laden.

Evaluating concepts of mental health and mental health–ethics distinctions

A variety of mental health definitions and distinctions between mental health and other ethical ideals can be defended. Advocates of each face particular conceptual and practical challenges; each working answer to these thorny issues requires ethical justifications and a translation from the realm of the theoretical to that of the practical.

Those arguing for concepts of mental health that involve more extensive ethical commitments have, I believe, a greater responsibility to justify their concepts of mental health than those whose concepts of mental health bear a more modest ethical content. The burden of proof is on therapists holding maximalist views. They need to justify why they should venture beyond their training (unless they have relevant education or experience) and the customary societal agreement regarding therapy. And they face the challenge of addressing deep disagreements about the nature of human well-being and flourishing in many cultures and among ethicists (MacIntyre 1984) without slipping into either relativism or absolutism. Finally, therapists need to be very careful when working with clients who do not share their ethical views, lest therapeutic alliances suffer or clients be influenced inappropriately (Tjeltveit 1986).

Those holding minimalist concepts of mental health, and especially those who define mental health as freedom from psychological disorder, face other problems. They may implicitly introduce richer ethical concepts into their assumptions about therapy goals, and so covertly influence clients. Or, anticipating a theme to be addressed later in the chapter, the overall impact of their "minimalism" may be a problematic individualism and a diminution of clients' relationships with others. In addition, therapists who aspire to limit their interventions to mental health values (conceived in minimalist terms) face the difficult task of differentiating mental health from other ethical ideals. As Odell and Stewart (1993) note, some would think a feminist therapist who endorses non-traditional family roles is advocating *health* values, but others *moral* values.

The greatest virtue of minimalist concepts of mental health is their consistency with the training therapists receive and with implicit societal contracts about the role of therapy. Wallace provides an exemplary account of a modest vision of the role of the professional:

> *Primum non nocere*, the prevention of untimely death where possible, the reduction of gratuitous pain and suffering, the amelioration of disability, the competent and compassionate care of the chronically and terminally ill, and better cognizance of the place and role of the social surroundings in disease and illness are all sufficiently noble aims for a healing profession. The inculcation of happiness, contentment, values, virtue, wisdom, *Weltanschauung*, creativity, and a passionate sense of vocation, on the other hand, are beyond doctors' consignment and competence. With quietly realistic goals we may at most, by helping patients with impediments to fuller exercise of their capacities, enable some, if personal endowment and subsequent fortune permit, to obtain such desirables more than otherwise.
>
> (Wallace 1991: 110)

Mental health as moral or nonmoral, obligatory or ideal

A final issue pertaining to the possibility of distinguishing mental health from other ideals needs to be addressed: whether mental health pertains primarily to nonmoral ideals, or bridges moral and nonmoral ideals. The distinction, a controversial one discussed in Chapters 2 and 4, appears in Hartmann's (1960) classic distinction between moral values and health values. In his schema, health values are *non*moral values. Because one traditional way to distinguish moral from nonmoral is to consider obligation the "basic moral notion" (Annas 1991: 330), the question of whether mental health pertains to moral or nonmoral ideals is often tied to that of whether mental health ideals are considered obligatory or merely aspirational.

Because my definition of ethics includes both moral and nonmoral considerations, and both obligations and aspirational ideals, I frame the issue in this way: does therapy's ethical character have to do with nonmoral and aspirational ideals, with moral and obligatory ideals, or with both? Hartmann's distinction implies that appropriately conducted therapy pertains to nonmoral and aspirational ideals alone. I think therapy has to do with moral and obligatory ideals as well, but is more concerned with nonmoral and aspirational ideals. For example, it would have been good for Bob to develop insight; that was an aspirational ideal. But it was not obligatory for him to do so. We would not say he *should* have done so, or that it was immoral or wrong that he did not.

There may be some situations, however, in which therapy goals involve moral obligations. If, for instance, a father is court-ordered into therapy secondary to neglecting or abusing his children, therapy goals would include stopping the abuse and neglect and his becoming a better father. Those goals are moral and obligatory, not merely aspirational. It would be wrong for him to fail to become a good father if doing so was within his grasp.

In addition, moral and nonmoral considerations sometimes conflict in therapy. In the case study in Chapters 4 and 5, for example, Sandra wanted (established as her therapy goals) to continue to take care of her invalid father (which she believed was her moral obligation) and to be less depressed (a nonmoral good). Sandra's therapist, in establishing goals for her therapy, could focus solely on decreasing her depression. But if doing so conveyed to Sandra that that nonmoral good was of greater importance than the moral good of caring for her father, the impact may be moral, not merely nonmoral. A third alternative would be to help Sandra find a way of living that could preserve her commitment to her father yet be less depressed. But that goal, because including her moral obligation to care for her father, would mix moral and nonmoral considerations.

And so the moral–nonmoral and the obligatory–aspirational distinctions have some merit, but they can be hard to draw, and therapy often involves both. When therapy involves both, mental health can appear to conflict with other ethical ideals. That and other conflicts between ideals will be addressed in the final section of the chapter.

Conclusion

All therapeutic ideals are, in part, ethical. Mental health values can be distinguished from other ethical ideals, but not distinguished sharply. Although mental health and other ideals are defined in many different and often overlapping ways, and are related in a variety of ways, mental health ideals bear at least a family resemblance to one another. Accordingly, I define mental health ideals as a congeries of more or less related ethical ideals that pertain in some way to the elimination of psychological disorder, to optimal psychological functioning, or to both, and that are primarily (but not exclusively) nonmoral.

Distinguishing mental health from other ideals is helpful because psychotherapy professionals should focus their attention on psychological functioning. The use of the phrase "*mental* health" and other terms emphasizing that ideals are *psychological* reinforces that distinction and serves to delimit therapy's scope. The specific ways in which mental health is distinguished from other therapy ideals will depend in part, of course, on the particular concepts of mental health and the other specific ideals being employed.

In this section, I have set forth a spectrum of concepts of mental health, ranging from reducing psychological disorders to extensive sets of ethical ideals. And I argued that a greater burden of proof falls on those whose concepts of mental health include extensive ethical content, are at variance with the cultural contract regarding psychotherapy, or both.

Whatever definition of mental health one employs, however, careful ethical analysis of concepts of mental health is helpful, analysis that eschews relativism and absolutism. This need for ongoing ethical analysis is one reason, however, that a distinction between mental health and other ethical ideals will not function as some of its advocates have desired: it will not free therapists from the responsibility to engage in careful ethical reflection about the goals and outcome of therapy.

Distinguishing mental health from other ideals will also not free therapists from ethical reflection because concepts of mental health are heterogeneous, a reflection of the underlying ethical differences and the heterogeneity of normality that are present in contemporary societies. That reality (and the variety of ideals held by other therapy stakeholders) means we can expect ongoing debate about the ethical character of therapy. We face multiple ideals, a diversity of valued therapy goals and outcomes.

Level of abstraction

Therapy goals vary in level of abstraction. Goals for Bob's therapy, for example, can be stated in increasingly abstract terms, from "able to dispute depressogenic thoughts" to "decreased depression" to "mental health." Those striving to ethically evaluate goals or outcome need to clarify the level of abstraction at which a goal is stated, especially when apparent disagreements exist (e.g. between therapists and clients or between therapists and third-party payers). Agreement is more likely at a middle level of abstraction – between the very specific and the very abstract (Browning and Evison 1991; Neimeyer 1993; Saltzman and Norcross 1990) – and when those discussing therapy goals and outcome do so at the same level of abstraction.

When level of abstraction is ignored, apparent agreements about therapy goals or outcome may mask underlying differences. For example, Lambert noted that those who agree that divorce is a poor outcome may disagree at a deeper level. Freudians may point to the individual's intrapsychic "failure to maintain a satisfying, intimate relationship with a person of the opposite sex (resolving the Oedipal complex)" (Lambert 1983: 25). But others think divorce a poor outcome because it harms family members. Likewise, the goal of autonomy can be affirmed for very different reasons (Taylor 1989) – because persons are "disengaged subjects," are purely rational agents, are Selves whose nature is being actualized, or are created, sinful, and liberated children of God (in Jewish or Christian understandings of human beings). One ethical ideal, autonomy; many underlying understandings of human beings and the good life.

The reverse can occur as well: apparent disagreements can dissolve when two parties begin speaking at the same level of abstraction. If Bob states he wants to be less depressed, and Dr Peterson states he wants Bob to develop greater insight, the apparent disagreement may be resolved by Dr Peterson talking at Bob's level of abstraction and affirming that he, too, wants Bob to be less depressed.

Tailoring goals to the individual, context, and culture

Some therapy stakeholders establish therapy goals and evaluate outcome in terms intended to apply *universally*, to everyone seeking therapy, or at least to everyone meeting certain criteria (e.g. diagnostic). For example, "It would be good if everyone became self-actualized." But others *tailor* goals to particular clients, contexts, and cultures and evaluate the outcome accordingly. Parloff distinguished, for example, between mental health as "the highest level of functioning of which *mankind* is capable" and mental health as "the full utilization of the *individual patient's unique capacities*" (Parloff 1967: 13). Those conflicting approaches stem, in part, I think, from an unresolved conflict about individuality in the West, a conflict traced by Taylor to Descartes and Montaigne. The former sought to draw upon universal criteria and reason; Montaigne aimed instead for "each person's originality" (Taylor 1989: 182). Many, of course, affirm both. An emphasis on universal goals and an emphasis on tailored goals may thus both exist on continua, with varying degrees of support for each. Furthermore, those emphases can be combined in various ways. Beutler and Clarkin (1990), for example, argue that therapists should employ those specific treatments that have been proven effective for a particular problem. They thus argue for goals (understood at a middle level of abstraction) that are universally applicable (as established by research) to decrease the symptoms of individuals with particular problems.

Most therapists tailor goals to the needs of individual clients, thinking it would be good for one client to develop greater assertiveness but good for a second to develop greater sensitivity to the needs of others. Insight may be a goal when a client is psychologically minded; behavior change when clients' actions are producing harm. There is no reason to expect one kind of "improvement," Stiles, Shapiro, and Elliott (1986) suggest, because client needs and aspirations differ. If normality is heterogeneous, goals will be as well: different clients will strive to eliminate their problems and reach different types of normality. Goals are thus improvised for each new client and revised as their situation and desires change. Therapists who claim to tailor goals to the individual may, however, regularly establish the same family of goals, implicitly assuming the goodness, rightness, and/or virtue of those goals applies to all clients.

Therapy's context may also be important in setting goals. Before deciding whether to encourage a woman to assert herself with her husband, for instance, it is important to know if she is living with a batterer and has no alternate living situation. As Hartmann pointed out, adaptation as treatment goal can only be defined "with reference to specific environmental settings" (Hartmann 1939: 318).

Goals may also need to be tailored to cultural context (Marsella and White 1982), at least to some extent. Varma (1988), for instance, suggests that Western forms of therapy be modified for clients in India to de-emphasize autonomy and emphasize interdependence. And Dwairy and Van Sickle (1996) argued that the traditional goals of Western psychotherapy, self-realization and self-integration, be adapted in light of Arabic condemnations of those ideals and Arabic commitment to collective identity.

Tailoring goals to individual, context, and culture can be done either relativistically or non-relativistically. I argue for the latter, asserting that we need not give up the conviction that there are *some* universally applicable ethical truths to alter therapy goals *to some degree* to meet individual needs. Goals can be, should be, tailored to some extent, but broad patterns of ideal human functioning can still be identified. Paying close attention to the level of abstraction is important in this connection; universally applicable ethical truths occur at some levels, with cultural differences occurring at other levels. For example, parental care for children is a cross-cultural ideal that finds expression in different ways across cultures.

Extent of ideals

Therapy stakeholders differ dramatically in the abundance of their ideals about therapy. Some possess few thoughts about therapy goals and outcome. Clients may simply want to feel better, to suffer less. Or they (and other stakeholders) may have extensive sets of ethical convictions, convictions about ethical issues in general, about psychotherapy goals and outcome, or both. Herron, Javier, Primavera, and Schultz (1994) distinguished between three levels of therapy goals: necessity, improvement, and potentiality. Third-party payers are willing to address the first and possibly second levels, but not the third. Those levels correspond roughly to mental health as freedom from psychological disorder, as minimalist positive ideal, and maximalist positive ideal.

Some therapists and clients raise topics in therapy that are broader than mental health. Doherty (1995), for instance, aspires to empower clients ethically. Therapy goals and outcome may thus address a full range of moral, spiritual-religious, and political convictions.

The extent of therapist ideals does not generally become evident in the early stages of therapy, when therapists focus on understanding and accepting clients, and a *de facto* moratorium on addressing ethical issues is commonly in effect. Rather, the full range of a therapist's convictions is more likely to emerge later in therapy, during what Browning called the "stage of reaggregation" (Browning 1987: 92). Late in therapy, clients rethink their understanding about "the good life," their approach to life, their "rules for living," and thus their ethical convictions. An extensive set of therapist ideals may then powerfully influence clients.

But therapists who hold and convey a minimal set of ideals may also significantly influence the ethical convictions of clients. Bob, for example, used Dr Peterson's minimalist "take better care of yourself" as a working ethical rule. Applying that ethical principle, he decided to divorce his wife and significantly reduce his commitment to his children. Even minimal therapist ethical convictions about ideal human functioning can thus profoundly affect clients living by ideals that are more extensive.

Specific ethical ideals

I now want to turn from the very general terms in which I have been discussing ideals to a consideration of the specific ideals that different therapy stakeholders employ when they propose, choose, and evaluate psychotherapy goals and outcomes. In this section I want to highlight some key issues pertaining to therapy ideals, then address the breadth of specific principles, concepts of goodness, and virtues used to formulate therapy goals, evaluate therapy outcome, or both. I will address outcomes intended by stakeholders (e.g. "mental health") and outcomes that are not so intended (e.g. negative effects on clients and family members). I include the latter because unintended consequences are sometimes ethically relevant.

A wide range of therapy ideals has been proposed, at times in the absence of thoughtful engagement with, or even acknowledgment of, alternatives. Some ideals are phrased in positive terms (e.g. "autonomy is a good therapy goal and outcome") and some in negative terms (e.g. "it is not good that therapy produces politically passive citizens"). Those phrased in negative terms draw upon some positive ideal. For example, complaints about therapy producing political passivity draw upon the conviction that active political involvement is good or obligatory.

Some specific ideals apply to all therapy relationships. Others are associated with particular schools of therapy (e.g. a devotee of Skinner would not affirm autonomy as a therapy goal, at least those forms of autonomy rejected by Skinner in *Beyond Freedom and Dignity*). Still other specific ideals apply only in particular therapy relationships. Because various therapy stakeholders make claims about the applicability of specific ideals at each of those levels, I will address all three.

Psychotherapy outcome is traditionally evaluated by comparing a client's functioning at the beginning with the client's functioning at the end of therapy. A good outcome is one in which valued ideals have been reached; a poor outcome is one in which those ideals have not been reached. Such evaluations are important, and should continue.

Two aspects of that traditional approach are notable: *short-term* outcome is generally evaluated (at the time of termination and, occasionally, at a later follow-up, rarely exceeding five years). And only the effects of therapy on the *individual* client are typically considered. One root of that short-term and individualistic emphasis, I suspect, is therapists' commitment to codes of professional ethics, and especially the tradition of the Hippocratic Oath. Its core ethic, Veatch maintains, is that the professional "benefit his [or her] patient" (Veatch 1978: 173). The focus is on the well-being of *the patient*, not the common good. For those concerned about the general welfare, medicine and other professions should be supported *if* that professional concern for individuals benefits society. Documenting the benefits of medicine to society is not difficult. The negative impact of those few rogues who, when restored by the physician to full physical health (normal physical functioning), harm society is more than outweighed by the positive impact of others who, when restored to physical health by physicians, contribute to the well-being of society.

Psychotherapy's positive contributions to society are easily established when therapy's goal is eliminating serious psychological dysfunction. Justifying therapy is more difficult, however, when its goal is some positive psychological ideal. This is true in part because psychological normality is heterogeneous in ways physical normality is not and in part because the definition of positive mental health is disputed. Some therapy outcomes may produce short-term benefit for a client, but long-term harm. And some client changes may benefit the client but harm other people.

To address the full range of consequences of therapy and to counteract what I think are some blind spots of the traditional approach to evaluating therapy outcome, I suggest that proposed ethical ideals for therapy should be subjected to three tests: impact on the individual, impact on others, and long-term impact.[4]

This proposal contrasts with traditional psychotherapy and medical training, which focuses on the individual client. I am proposing instead that ethical evaluations of therapy ideals include an alternation between reflecting on particular persons seeking help and reflecting more broadly. That broad reflection should include these questions: in what kind of society, in what kind of global human community, with what kind of human functioning, would we like to live in ten years? in fifty? In other words, what would be the best outcome for humanity? And in what relationship do therapy goals (and actual outcome) stand to the answers given to those questions?

In light of those questions, the phrases I have been using – "choosing" goals but "evaluating" outcomes – need to be reconsidered. We need, in part, to *choose* desired (good, better, best, ideal, right, virtuous) *outcomes*, then establish the goals that are most likely to produce those outcomes.

I am under no illusion that we will soon develop a cross-cultural consensus about long-term social and individual ideals relevant to therapy. Indeed, given the heterogeneity of normality, ethical differences, and cross-cultural variations, I am confident that such a consensus will not be forthcoming.

Despite that lack of a consensus, I think it important to reflect on the long-term and social effects of therapy, for two reasons: to develop better therapy ideals and to consciously articulate ideals.

Reflection about therapy ideals can produce *some* outcomes that are better than others, and can identify some distinctly undesirable outcomes (e.g. an authoritarian state or a society of individuals concerned only about themselves). Those outcomes would be viewed unfavorably in part because leading to short- or long-term negative outcomes for individuals, families, communities, societies, or the entire human community.

Second, our failure to reflect on the long-term and social effects of therapy will not prevent such effects from occurring; rather, those effects will simply be unplanned, and our goals implicit and covert. Therapy stakeholders can either let those effects occur without reflection, or submit them to critical scrutiny and translate their conclusions into therapy goals. Third-party payers, it should be noted, *do* engage in long-term scrutiny. Using the criterion of expense (with high expense considered bad), they set financial goals relative to therapy (to control therapy's financial outcome). Therapists employ other kinds of socially oriented reasoning to justify therapy to third-party payers (justifying therapy in terms of how it reduces medical expenditures and otherwise contributes to the well-being of society). But given the variety of therapy ideals and the heterogeneity of normality, the key issue for the future will not be therapy versus no therapy, but which *kind* of therapy, for which *purposes*, and toward which *ideal ends*. To address those issues, we will need to consciously articulate therapy ideals.

A hotly contended question prompted my posing the question of the social and long-term effects of therapy: is the social cost of psychotherapy's focus on the well-being of individuals too high? Or, as Bellah, Madsen, Sullivan, Swidler, and Tipton (1991) put the problem, "Are we responsible only for our own good or also for the common good?" (Bellah *et al*. 1991: 81). Individualism has been attacked (e.g. Bellah *et al*. 1985, 1991; Fox-Genovese 1991; Sampson 1988), with calls to move "beyond individualism" (Callahan 1988; Crittenden 1992; Gelpi 1989; Hermans *et al*. 1992; Piore 1995; M. B. Smith 1994) and "beyond self-interest" (Mansbridge 1990), to "reconstruct individualism" (Heller *et al*. 1986), and to understand individualism's historical origins and how deeply it is rooted in Western culture (Stam 1993). But some understandings of individualism and authenticity have also been defended (Taylor 1992; Waterman 1984). The debate is ongoing.

With those considerations highlighted, I want to address ideals pertaining to therapy, considering in turn principles, concepts of goodness, and virtues.

Principles

An ethical principle, for example, an individual's responsibility to others, can serve as a criterion to determine or evaluate desired ends (the goals or outcome of therapy), as the desired end itself, or as both. A successful outcome would thus be a client exhibiting greater responsibility for others, believing he or she should do so, or both. Mahoney, for instance, talked of our "collective responsibilities" (Mahoney 1991: 4), responsibilities tied reciprocally to individual lives. And Doherty speaks of "clients' responsibilities for, and obligations to, their communities" (Doherty 1995: 97; cf. Boszormenyi-Nagy 1987). Doherty also affirms the ethical obligations of commitment, justice, truthfulness, and community, obligations that apply to clients. He asserts that therapists working ethically with clients can (and at times should) address those obligations in therapy.

Ethical principles (obligations) play a different role in therapy when therapists reject clients' principles and/or strive to minimize their adherence to them (e.g. when therapists strive to replace clients' "obligations" with "preferences" and their "shoulds" with "wants"). Freud's hostility to Christians who asserted that people have a moral obligation to love their neighbors (especially when involving self-sacrifice), for instance, no doubt had the effect on some of his clients (and on clients of those who share his ethical views) of reducing their belief in those ethical principles. The reasons Freud opposed that obligation are instructive. Wallace notes two: Freud thought it "psychologically unworkable and maladaptive for the individual," and the injunction "cheapened an individual's love for family and friends" (Wallace 1986: 100). The superego, Freud asserted, must be opposed because "in the severity of its commands and prohibitions it troubles itself too little about the happiness of the ego" (Freud 1961: 90).[5] In the terms I am using, a concept of goodness (the ego's happiness) trumps an ethical principle (loving one's neighbor).

Therapists vary, of course, in their affirmations and rejections of ethical principles – across schools of therapy (with Freudians, for example, generally more willing to "lower the demands of the superego" than adherents of reality therapy – Glasser 1965), across therapists, and across therapeutic relationships with different clients. As an example of the last, some clients may well be so "tyrannized by shoulds" that even therapists with extensive sets of moral beliefs would challenge (try to moderate) those clients' feelings of moral obligation.

Debates also occur between those holding that people (including clients) have obligations to control and inhibit their impulses, and those (therapists and others) who either eliminate the category of obligation entirely or encourage clients to identify and express their impulses and to get their needs met. And, of course, most therapy stakeholders occupy some middle position between those extremes.

Humanistic therapists, in the view of Wolfe (1978), see clients in successful therapy as dropping most ethical principles but adopting two new "moral obligations": "to refrain from responding to externally imposed moral standards" and "to trust in their own experience" (B. E. Wolfe 1978: 47).

The idea that "Clients will increase their commitment to their communities and to justice" is a valid goal for psychotherapy, or is a criterion by which therapy outcome is appropriately evaluated, is foreign to many therapy stakeholders. The role of therapy in reducing adherence to "pathogenic" moral principles is more common. Suppose we evaluate this outcome, "the client's belief in the ethical principles of justice and loving one's neighbor was sharply curtailed," in terms of my three tests. If moral principles (obligations) are entirely pathogenic, the effect of that outcome on individuals in the short- and long-term would be positive. But if societies need their members to look out for one another and be committed to the general welfare, and if justice is important to the proper functioning of a society, therapeutic relationships that undercut clients' moral convictions about justice and neighbor love will be likely to have negative long-term societal effects.

Those who conduct ethical analyses of therapy have sometimes been sharply critical of therapists' *de facto* ideals. The critics' ethical ideals are evident in the terms they use. They may, for example, think it wrong to be "selfish" (defined as "1: concerned excessively or exclusively with oneself: seeking or concentrating on one's own advantage, pleasure, or well-being without regard for others" – *Merriam-Webster's Collegiate Dictionary* 1993: 1060). And so they would criticize therapy outcomes in which people leave therapy more selfish than when they began. Unfortunately, from their perspective, therapy has been characterized as "a process by which nice, normal, neurotic people become more selfish" (B. E. Wolfe 1978: 48).

Concepts of goodness

Therapy ideals are often concepts of goodness rather than ethical principles or virtues. Effective therapy is seen to produce some good end; ineffective or destructive therapy fails to produce a good end or increases some bad (negative, harmful, not good) end. Therapy ideals are rarely discussed in the explicitly ethical language of goodness, however. An exception is Nicholas, who asserted that therapists "must, when possible, consciously work toward fostering goodness" (Nicholas 1994: 224).

Contemporary therapists affirm a variety of goods. The Mental Health Values Questionnaire of Tyler, Clark, Olson, Klapp, and Cheloha (1983), for instance, includes ninety-nine values (Haugen *et al.* 1991). Respondents indicate whether values like "The person is able to forgive other people for their mistakes" (Tyler *et al.* 1983: 23) are indicative of "healthy emotional functioning" (Haugen *et al.* 1991: 25). Jensen and Bergin (1988) included sixty-nine items on their measure of values pertaining to mental health, E. W. Kelly (1995a) included fifty-three, and Consoli (1996) forty-three. In each case, the authors considered other proposed good ends for therapy before arriving at their lists. When consulted, philosophers offer conflicting advice. As Rescher (1969) noted, the Cyrenaics emphasized the good end of pleasure, for Aristotle it was happiness,[6] for Plato, knowledge, the Stoics emphasized virtue, Kant a good will, and the utilitarians concentrated on the general welfare.

As a rule, therapists neglect certain concepts of goodness that have been affirmed throughout history (Gettner 1978; J. D. Frank 1973, cited in Wolfe 1978). Concepts which therapists pass over when setting goals and evaluating therapy outcome include "the redemptive power of suffering, acceptance of one's lot in life, filial piety, adherence to tradition, self-restraint, and moderation" (J. D. Frank 1973, cited in Wolfe 1978: 48), and "advancing knowledge, pursuing honor, or creating something of lasting or absolute value" (Gettner 1978: 1060).

In this section, I will map out concepts of goodness related to therapy goals and outcome. After addressing the goodness of freedom from negatively valued states (e.g. mental health as freedom from disorder), I will discuss concepts of goodness related to the self, to relationships, to balance, and to spirituality.

The good to which therapy aims, many assert, is freedom *from* some negatively valued state. It is good, for instance, to be free from crippling depression, command hallucinations, and panic attacks. Relieving pain and decreasing suffering are widely affirmed as goods among therapists. Most therapy researchers employ such criteria of goodness in measuring decreases in psychopathology or serious symptoms. And when clients' pain and suffering are serious and harm is substantial, even third-party payers and therapists are in accord.

But some forms of pain (e.g. guilt at committing heinous acts) may not be so bad (Gewirth 1956). And J. D. Frank's (1973) mention of "redemptive" suffering points to a long tradition of finding meaning in suffering. Furthermore, many distinguish between mild levels of discomfort (normal unhappiness) and serious suffering (Schofield 1986). Obtaining freedom from the latter is far more important than freedom from the former. Some who fail to distinguish between the two, however, may argue that all discomfort should be eliminated, including the guilt and anxiety that may stem, in part, from holding ethical ideals.

Concepts of goodness pertaining to the self have been the most prominent positive therapy ideals. This has been both celebrated and condemned.

Autonomy is the primary good therapists seek for clients. Although almost all affirm it (Jensen and Bergin 1988), humanistic and psychoanalytic psychologists stress it. Indeed, Szasz (1965), in a somewhat idiosyncratic reading of Freud, argued that "the paramount aim" of psychoanalysis is the "preservation and expansion of the client's autonomy" (Wallace 1986: 7). This has found an especially resonant hearing in the US, because "freedom is perhaps the most resonant, deeply held American value" (Bellah *et al.* 1985: 23).

That it is good for human beings, including clients, to be free from coercion – from without and from within – seems clear, at least in normal circumstances. What is less clear is what human beings are to be free *for*. And, as commentators have noted, the ways in which freedom is commonly understood make it difficult to "address common conceptions of the ends of a good life or ways to coordinate cooperative action with others" (Bellah *et al.* 1985: 24). But consensus about therapy's good ends is precisely what therapy stakeholders need when determining therapy's proper goals, limits, and funding. The language of freedom provides no basis for such discussions. As Guignon noted, unbounded freedom "may be self-defeating. For where all things are equally possible...no choice is superior to any others. Freedom then becomes, in Rieff's [1966: 93] classic line, the 'absurdity of being freed to choose and then having no choice worth making'" (Guignon 1993: 223).

Other good characteristics of the self – attitudes, beliefs, behaviors, and emotions – are claimed by stakeholders as the ends toward which therapy properly aims, or the criterion by which its success or failure is properly judged. Pleasure is the good state some clients assume therapy will produce in them, so they will be consistently happy and at peace. Jahoda (1958) noted that attitudes toward the self, growth, development, self-actualization, and accurate perception of reality have been linked to positive mental health. Others emphasize the content or style of thinking. Ellis and Bernard, for instance, described the good ends toward which Rational–Emotive Therapy aims, the good ends of these "rational attitudes": "self-interest," "social interest," "self-direction," "high frustration tolerance," "flexibility," "acceptance of uncertainty," "commitment to creative pursuits," "scientific thinking," "self-acceptance," "risk-taking," "long-range hedonism," "nonutopianism," and "self-responsibility for our own emotional disturbance" (Ellis and Bernard 1985: 7–9). All, save the second, pertain primarily to the individual.

Good behavioral (rather than emotional, cognitive, or attitudinal) changes in the self are stressed by still other theorists. Assertiveness and social skills are the good ends, for example, toward which behaviorists often want clients to move.

The goodness of the self as a self-contained whole embracing a variety of psychological characteristics is emphasized by still others. Speaking in general terms, Michels identified as one of psychoanalytic theory's values "the significance of the individual as opposed to the collective" (Michels 1987: 42). Empirical researchers have found that psychologists more frequently endorsed individualistic responses, than responses affirming social embeddedness and responsibility (Fowers *et al.* 1997), even though clients in an analogue study did not show any preference between counselors with a social commitment emphasis and counselors with an individualistic emphasis (Kelly and Shilo 1991). (Ironically, then, therapists who favor an individualistic approach may do so for reasons other than the preferences of individual clients.) Some therapists argue for self-actualization, self-fulfillment, and personal growth as therapy goals and as criteria by which to judge outcome. The self is the end toward which psychotherapy is properly directed. Self-interest is the client's proper focus. And, as Stiles, Shapiro, and Elliott note, the personality theorists summarized in Hall and Lindzey's (1978) classic personality text "describe psychological health as involving increases in individual variation" (Stiles *et al.* 1986: 171). And so the profoundly important, philosophically and psychologically complex concept (see Taylor 1989) of the self has been celebrated, with individual risk-taking, creativity, adventuresomeness, and individuality affirmed. As Berger notes, "self-enhancement is an ultimate goal, as opposed to self-sacrifice in the interests of enhancing others or society in general" (Berger 1982: 83). The sources of this ideology are manifold, including humanistic psychology's metaphysically rich belief in the self's "true" nature, Romanticism's fervent faith in the rich inner nature of the self, and Nietzsche's identification of "self-deification as a human being's supreme perfection" (Berkowitz 1995: 19).

But others vigorously deny the goodness of the self or, better, individualistic understandings of the self. M. B. Smith argues that "in cross-cultural perspective, American culture is really over the edge in its individualistic ethos, and the costs to people that this extreme orientation entails are increasingly visible" (M. B. Smith 1990: 530). Psychotherapy has been attacked for fostering selfishness (e.g. Wallach and Wallach: 1983[7]), navel gazing, egotism, political quietism, self-absorption, self-indulgence, a neglect of other people, and a host of other ills. Bellah, Madsen, Sullivan, Swidler, and Tipton (1985) and Cushman (1995) have argued that psychology has contributed to the "empty selves" characteristic of many in the contemporary era. Dominant forms of therapy, the former work contends, cannot provide people with the "rich and coherent selves" they want. And, in part because therapists don't engage in the serious moral dialogue required to develop rich selves, the authors ask whether "psychological sophistication has not been bought at the price of moral impoverishment" (Bellah *et al.* 1985: 139).

As early as 1968, Maslow took pains to distinguish self-actualization from selfishness (Wallach and Wallach 1983). By 1970, he acknowledged that some of his earlier work was overly individualistic. Nevertheless, mirroring the experience of other therapists and corroborating the views of critics of individualism, Doherty stated that he became aware of his having been "unwittingly promoting a moral agenda of self-interest" (Doherty 1995: 26). He asserted:

> I have seen too many parents "move on" from their children, too many spouses discard a marriage when an attractive alternative appeared, and too many individuals avoiding social responsibility under the rubric of "it's not my thing." Widespread reevaluation of the fruits of unfettered self-interest at both the psychosocial and economic levels is under way in the mid-1990s.
>
> (Doherty 1995: 10)

Distancing himself from regressive critics of therapy's emphasis on the self, Doherty advocates a progressive alternative to traditional individualism.

A growing concern for the welfare of others is thus joining therapy's traditional ideal of concern for the self. Good relational ends are affirmed, ends pertaining to family, friends, community, work, society, or humanity as a whole, as well as good environmental ends (e.g. ecological concern as therapeutic goal or positively evaluated outcome).

Some relational therapy ideals pertain to the ability of clients to interact with others effectively; the goodness of something larger than the client (e.g.

society) is emphasized in other ideals. Strupp combined both emphases when he asserted that "the purpose of therapy is to strengthen the patient's adaptive capacities, to provide whatever assistance may be necessary to enable the patient to lead a more satisfying life as a responsible citizen in our culture" (Strupp 1980: 397).

"Adaptation," a therapy ideal pertaining to the individual's relationship with others, is both praised and condemned. If viewed as conformity to a society that hampers human flourishing, adaptation is condemned, as when military therapists in Vietnam eliminated soldiers' moral qualms so they could kill again without reservation (Lifton 1976). But Wallace (1986, 1991) argues that adaptation, as employed by Freud and others, is a richer, more defensible concept. He defines it as a "creative and productive engagement with reality (akin to Freud's *Arbeiten und Leiben*) – one optimally suitable for the deeply rooted needs, desires, and aims of self, and cognizant of beloved and loving others and human and nonhuman environments" (Wallace 1991: 106).

Using less controversial terms, Jahoda (1958) and others have discussed the ability of clients to interact and communicate with others, to love, work, and play. These good ends pertain to social skills and environmental mastery, to the ability of clients to maintain good interpersonal relations.

Helping others is a more ambitious relational goal than developing effective social skills. Allport contended that one criterion for mental health is "a compassionate regard for all living creatures," including "a disposition to participate in common activities that will improve the human lot" (Allport 1960: 162). And Nicholas (1994) urged therapists to openly prefer (when not clinically contraindicated) the good ends of altruism, egalitarianism, and justice (cf. Michael 1977; Prilleltensky 1997). Doherty (1995) argued that a concern for one's community is a good therapy outcome. Therapists, he suggested, validly introduce relational considerations, like whether a particular action would hurt a client's family members. And, without claiming therapists alone can change a society, he suggested that therapists can help clients rejoin, and take seriously their responsibilities to, their communities.

Therapy stakeholders are thus increasingly affirming goals embracing both the well-being of individual clients and larger relational concerns. Feminist and multicultural therapists (Rodis and Strehorn 1997), advocates of managed care (Austad and Berman 1991b), community psychologists (Prilleltensky 1997), philosophers (Taylor 1992), those who are hermeneutically-oriented (e.g. Richardson and Guignon 1988), those articulating Jewish (Goodnick 1977) and Christian (Browning 1987) understandings of ideal human functioning, and others affirm this. Wanting to reject both self-indulgence and authoritarianism (Wallach and Wallach 1991), both selfishness and a loss of self, both the individualistic *status quo* and regressive authoritarianism (Doherty 1995), advocates affirm a concern for self *and* others.

Those unconvinced on ethical grounds that a social element should be added to therapy goals may need, on practical grounds, to introduce one: those who pay for therapy increasingly require it. Managed care advocates Austad and Berman assert, for example, that "concern for the individual *and the collective group*" is needed (Austad and Berman 1991c: viii, emphasis added).

The ideal balance between care of self and care of others is a matter of considerable disagreement. Browning (1987) argues convincingly that when Freud affirmed "love" (Fine 1990) as a therapy goal, he meant only a "cautious reciprocity": a person responds to the loving initiatives of others but does not initiate them. And so a person "loves" only when first loved, and only to the extent the person receives love. Actions benefiting others but not oneself are viewed with great suspicion. Doherty, by way of contrast, argues that "therapists since the time of Freud have overemphasized individual self-interest, giving short shrift to family and community responsibilities" (Doherty 1995: 7). The balance considered ideal is likely to vary across schools of therapy, across therapists, and across clients of the same therapist, in accord with each particular client's needs and situations.

Some therapists, especially humanistic psychologists, argue that society will benefit most when clients choose their own goals and focus on themselves. They assert that "the general good is best served by individuals' focusing on their own needs and actualization" (Wallach and Wallach 1983: 164; see Parloff 1967). That assertion rests on the metaphysical assumption that, in our harmonious universe, focusing on one's self will benefit others (Browning 1987). So strong and extensive are their metaphysical convictions about the goodness of persons and the harmonious order of the cosmos, humanistic psychologists are, in Browning's words, "at this point on equal logical footing" (ibid.: 122) with advocates of religious perspectives.

Spiritual and religious traditions posit concepts of goodness that clients, therapists, and other stakeholders employ as therapy goals or use to evaluate outcome. Jafari, for example, argued that Western therapy is inappropriate for Islamic clients because so many of its assumptions conflict with Islamic understandings of reality and Islamic ethics. "According to the Qur'an," he notes, "a life without faith is a state of spiritual non-being in which one loses touch with his/her true self (49:19)" (Jafari 1993: 335). Islam affirms, he argues, the goodness of righteous benevolence rather than (Western) self-fulfillment, the goodness of a holistic (i.e. individual and collective; mental, physical, and spiritual) rather than a materialistic outlook, the goodness of bounded rather than unbounded freedom, and the goodness of repentance rather than rationalizing guilt away. Tyler and Suan (1990) found that Native Americans were more likely to view unconventional spiritual experiences (e.g. having visions) as signs of good mental health than were Caucasian students. Schimmel (1992) explored differences and commonalities among Jewish,

Christian, and classical understandings of human nature in relation to the views of contemporary psychotherapists. Some Christian concepts of goodness mirror those of non-religious therapists; others clearly diverge. Calvinists committed to the Shorter Catechism of the Westminster Confession, for example, assert that our "chief end is to glorify God and to enjoy Him forever" (Westminster Divines 1745: 369). Browning (1987) and Jones and Butman (1991) explored the ways in which the ethical component of therapy goals among various therapeutic approaches are like, and unlike, Christian ethical traditions.

Virtues

To evaluate therapy outcome and to establish goals, some therapy stakeholders employ concepts of virtue. Maslow, for instance, asserted that the person who has completed a successful course of therapy is a "better person" (Marlow 1961: 8). And Strupp and Hadley suggested that "mentally healthy" persons have "a sound personality structure characterized by growth, development, self-actualization, integration, autonomy, environmental mastery, ability to cope with stress, reality orientation, [and] adaptation" (Strupp and Hadley 1977: 190). That is, they have those desirable and stable characteristics; they exhibit the virtue of mental health.

Other therapy stakeholders emphasize or champion other virtues. Although virtues were not the central focus of Freud's ethical thinking (Wallace 1986), several virtues are evident in his thinking: honesty (Rieff 1979; Wallace 1986), autonomy (Szasz 1965; Wallace 1986), integration and balance (Michels 1987, 1991), and the genital character (Gewirth 1956). Humanistic psychologists offered a rich array of virtues. In his discussion of the good life, for example, Rogers described the characteristics of a person in the process of becoming fully functioning: "an increasing openness to experience," "increasingly existential living," and "an increasing trust in one's organism" (Rogers 1961: 187, 188, 189). Other humanistic virtues include self-actualization, spontaneity, creativity, authenticity, expressing one's emotions, present-centeredness (Naranjo 1970), and so forth. Authenticity is a virtue emphasized by others as well, but understood in different ways. Guignon, for example, argued that authenticity "can be nothing other than a fuller and richer form of participation in the public context" (Guignon 1993: 228; see Taylor 1992). Guignon identified the following "character ideals" in Heidegger's ideal of authenticity:

> Authentic self-focusing is said to require such traits as resoluteness, steadiness, courage, and, above all, clear-sightedness about one's own life as a finite, thrown projection. It calls for integrity and a lucid openness about what is relevant to one's actions. The authentic stance toward life

makes us face up to the fact that to the extent that we are building our own lives in all we do, we are "answerable" for the choices we make.

(Guignon 1993: 232)

Nicholas (1994) argued that therapy ideally produces people who are altruistic, egalitarian, honest, just, and responsible. Doherty (1995) argued for the virtues of self-awareness, interpersonal sensitivity, moral awareness, moral courage, moral responsibility, integrity, integration, and balance. Some traditionalists no doubt view submissiveness in women as a virtue. By way of contrast, Seiden noted that feminist therapists respond with a "hearty laugh" to "the idea that a healthy woman is characterized by passivity" (Seiden 1976: 1117). Feminist therapists, of course, affirm virtues other than submissiveness and passivity.

Wolfe (1978) argues that the kind of person who emerges from successful therapy has an internal "locus of moral authority." Doherty (1995) argues for "ethical *self*-empowerment" (Doherty 1995: 54, emphasis added). And Freud clearly regarded as healthier those persons whose ethical principles are independent of religious foundations (Wallace 1986). By way of contrast, Geller argued that "far from finding direction from within, we can only find it from without" (Geller 1982: 61). And others affirming spiritual and religious traditions (Browning 1987; Goodnick 1977; Jafari 1993; Jones and Butman 1991) would concur with some form of Geller's opinion: ethical sources outside the self may be legitimate. Therapy stakeholders may thus affirm virtues like centeredness, peace, faith, hope, love, holiness, sanctification, righteousness, glorifying God, and so forth. By way of contrast, Engler (1986) and others who draw upon Eastern sources challenge the notion of the self found both in Western religious traditions and in Western non-religious traditions, arguing instead for the goal of "no-self." Some who affirm spiritual virtues see them to be harmonious with mental health (therapists' ideals are affirmed, spiritual ideals may or may not be reached by mentally healthy persons); others see spiritual virtues to be an integral part of mental health (full mental health requires those spiritual virtues).

When discussing therapy ideals, therapy stakeholders face a challenge: whether using the language of virtues, principles, or goodness, crucial terms often have multiple meanings. The self, happiness, self-exploration, maturity, identity, growth, identity, self-reflection, the individual, self-fulfillment, love, and mental health carry different meanings for different stakeholders. For example, if we assert that the "capacity for honest self-reflection" is a good therapy outcome, we may do so for a variety of reasons. As Taylor (1989) notes, we may value self-reflection in order to see the forms underlying the appearances of life (Plato), to see the order of things (Aristotle), to see God (Augustine), to gain self-mastery and control (Descartes and Locke), to discover oneself (Montaigne and Herder), or to make a personal commitment.

"Self-actualization" is also variously interpreted. The sticking point concerns *what* is actualized. As Jahoda (1958) noted, "self-destruction and crime, from petty thievery to genocide, are among the unique potentialities of the human species" (Jahoda 1958: 31; cf. Phillips, 1987, on behavior that can be justified as being "authentic"). Those potentials are not, of course, the potentials humanistic psychologists contend the "self-actualized person" actualizes. Browning (1987) notes that self-actualization theorists, in fact, make judgments about what is good, then focus on that goodness as what self-actualization produces in people. As Franck notes, those who use "self-actualization" or "self-realization" actually argue that *"certain aspects* of the self and not the entire self...ought to be actualized, namely, only those aspects of the self...considered by these psychologists to be 'good' " (Franck 1977: 9).

And so the multiple terms that therapy stakeholders use to describe therapy goals and outcome – whether principles, concepts of goodness, or virtues – have multiple meanings. One reason for those multiple meanings is the ethical theory underlying those ideals.

Therapy ideals and ethical theory

Differing ethical theories and differing philosophical assumptions produce diverse therapy ideals. And even when apparent consensus about therapy goals and evaluations of outcome exists, the reasons for affirming them may diverge. As Taylor notes, beneath the apparent consensus of those who affirm the same values we often find "various richer pictures of human nature and our predicament" (Taylor 1989: 12).

And so there is disagreement among therapy stakeholders of good will. They disagree, for example, about whether therapy ideals find their proper source within an individual, outside an individual (e.g. from science, community, or some spiritual entity), or from some combination of both (e.g. in the dialogue between therapist and client). And, because of contrasting metaphysical/ethical views, they disagree about what it means to be "properly human" (Cushman 1995: 282; see Engelhardt 1978; Parloff 1967). For example, Patterson's strongly held view is that self-actualization "is a goal that is not chosen by the therapist or the client, nor is it simply a religious or philosophical goal. It is derived from the nature of the human beings" (Patterson 1989: 171). As noted above, however, only *some* aspects of the self are actualized and only some considered good or ideal (Franck 1977), that is to say those aspects concordant with one's metaphysical and ethical convictions. Furthermore, the "nature" of human beings on which that therapy goal is based is disputed philosophically. Freud held different assumptions about human nature, and so established different therapy goals. Lear argued that because Freud believed that "love is a basic force in nature", he thought love a proper therapy goal (Lear 1990: 221). In contrast to both humanistic psychologists and Freudians, Heidegger denied that a human nature exists. Rather, he held that "we are what we make of ourselves in the course of living out our active lives"; human beings are "self-constituting beings" (Guignon 1993: 223).

Those wishing to understand the ethical character of therapy goals and outcome, and to arrive at the best possible goals and outcome, thus face the task of clarifying and justifying the ethical theory to which therapy ideals are tied. This will require choice, retrieval, or both. MacIntyre (1984) argues that we must choose between a new form of classical Aristotelian virtue theory and the liberal individualism for which Nietzsche is the most clear-sighted proponent. By way of contrast, Taylor (1992) argues that we need to retrieve and articulate the ethical theories upon which our ideals are based, acknowledging the legitimacy of each (as appropriate) and drawing upon them as sources of ethical content and motivation. Both MacIntyre and Taylor agree, however, that the reality of multiple ethical ideals must be addressed.

Addressing multiple therapy ideals

Therapists, clients, and other therapy stakeholders face a wide range of therapy goals and criteria for evaluating outcome, each tied to various ethical ideals (principles, concepts of goodness, and/or virtues). Those ideals are tied in turn to ethical theories and fundamental philosophical under-standings of human beings. How then do therapists, clients, and other therapy stakeholders choose goals, evaluate outcome, and determine which goals and outcome criterion are valid? If faced with more than one valid ideal, what should be done? If conflicts arise, how should they be addressed? To address those questions, many strategies have been proposed. In this section, I will discuss nine overlapping, often complementary strategies.

Because scientific methods have answered other psychological questions so successfully, some turn to science to determine which ideals are best, or should be selected. But as discussed in Chapter 6, science can evaluate whether a particular technique will achieve a particular result. But it cannot tell us whether that end is good, right, obligatory, or virtuous. Science can be helpful, however, in establishing goals at a middle level of abstraction. For example, if all agree that decreased depression is a good therapeutic end, empirical studies can tell us whether the middle-level goal of combating depressogenic cognitions contributes to the ultimate goal of decreased depression. But it cannot ethically evaluate that ultimate goal. Science can also provide some knowledge about human nature. It can tell us, for instance, about various human capacities. But it cannot tell us which of those capacities is ideal.

Carefully evaluating and choosing ideals is a second proposed approach to the diversity of ethical ideals. This philosophical-psychological task entails asking which ideals are good, right, and/or virtuous, and the often-more-challenging question of which are best. Some proposed goals may be rejected and certain outcomes evaluated as failures (e.g. the client whose depression worsens or who becomes "selfish" – B. E. Wolfe 1978). But a third category should be added: following Worthington's (1988) suggestion, therapy ideals can be divided into one of three categories. Ideals are located in zones of rejection, zones of toleration, and zones of affirmation. Some ideals are rejected (e.g. Bob's request that Dr Peterson tell him what to do), some tolerated (e.g. the agnostic Dr Peterson's toleration of Bob's conservative Christian ideals), and some affirmed as optimal. Therapists who aspire to be accepting and as value-free as possible require a large zone of toleration to work with the widest possible range of clients. But the influence on clients of the ideals therapists affirm and the intrinsic ethical excellence of those ideals (or lack thereof) mean therapy stakeholders also need to think clearly and well about the goals and outcomes they think *best*.

Therapy ideals can be evaluated and chosen on three levels: ideals for humankind in general, ideals for therapy in particular, and ideals for a given client at a particular point in time. An ideal appropriate for therapy in general (e.g. assertiveness) may not be appropriate for a particular client (e.g. a client whose failure to be sensitive to partners and inability to listen or compromise with others produce unsuccessful and emotionally distressing relationships). And goals that may be appropriate in general (e.g. global peace and justice) may not be an appropriate focus for a particular individual (e.g. a mentally ill client overwhelmed with stressors and obligations).

Evaluating therapy ideals is difficult for those whose training is solely in the sciences or solely in philosophy. Because I am convinced that the best evaluations draw upon both, evaluating therapy ideals is especially difficult for those prejudiced against either philosophy or psychology. Evaluating therapy ideals is also made more difficult by the *covert* character of many of therapy's ethical ideals. To make such evaluations easier, acts of retrieval are required, so we can recover the rich ethical character of therapy goals and practices, recapture the multi-faceted, multi-layered, and conceptually complex ethical meanings of terms like authenticity, autonomy, effectiveness, the general welfare, mental health, and love and work, and begin "making more palpable to [a culture's] participants what the ethic they subscribe to really involves" (Taylor 1992: 72). An especially important role will be played by therapy stakeholders who exhibit ethical articulacy (Taylor 1989, 1992), who speak and write lucidly and eloquently about therapy's ethical ideals.

A third proposal to the problem of multiple therapy ideals is to combine proposed ideals. Taylor, for instance, rejects the positions of those who contrast social concern with authenticity and self-fulfillment (which they assume produce selfishness and reinforce excessive individualism). He asserts that authenticity requires social concern, and rejects as "deviant and trivialized" (Taylor 1992: 55) those modes of authenticity that produce narcissism and self-centeredness. Other goals also combine ideals. For instance, we can imagine a goal for Bob's therapy that combines his aspirations and those of Dr Peterson: developing greater intra-psychic insight *and* clarity about his marriage. As a final example, Doherty folds self-interest as a therapy goal into a broader, more inclusive ethic of the common good, in which self-interest is "embraced and transcended" (Doherty 1995: 101).

Others who affirm more than one distinguishable therapy ideal *balance* ideals in some way. Aristotle, for example, argued for the "Golden Mean," a goal avoiding the extremes of either too little or too much of the elements of the good life (Taylor 1989). Taylor argues that a particular good end "needs to be part of a 'package,' to be sought within a life which is also aimed at other goods" (ibid.: 511). In applying this to psychology, Prilleltensky argued that psychologists should employ "complementary" values "in concert" rather than in isolation (Prilleltensky 1997: 521). And Wallace asserts that balance was Freud's "central metaphor" (Wallace 1986: 110).

Striking a balance between concern for the individual and concern for some larger social grouping is evident in the reflections on mental health by Austad and Berman (1991c), Browning (1987), Doherty (1995), Freud (Wallach and Wallach 1983; Wallace 1986), Mahoney (1991), Odell and Stewart (1993), Prilleltensky (1997), Rodis and Strehorn (1997), Veatch (1978), and others. Balancing autonomy and other ideals has also been advocated (Bellah *et al.* 1983; Callahan 1984; Freud, as interpreted by Homans 1979; Prilleltensky 1997; and Richardson 1989). And Buhler (1962) and others have maintained that health should be appropriately balanced with other ideals.

Doherty optimistically asserted that ideals can be balanced without compromising any. He argued, for example, that personal authenticity "must not be put in competition with morality" and that "there is no inherent contradiction between self-fulfillment and moral responsibility to others" (Doherty 1995: 67, 78). This is certainly true at times. But many people face choices among ideals. One's own fulfillment, for instance, may conflict with responsibilities to others. As Taylor noted, affirming multiple goods can result in "a cruel dilemma, in which the demands of fulfilment run against these other goods – one which thousands of divorcing or near-divorcing couples are living through in our time, for instance" (Taylor 1989: 511). And Veatch notes that physicians sometimes face ethical dilemmas in which one course of action "will produce the most good in total, but another course will most benefit the client" (Veatch 1978: 173). Therapists also face dilemmas. As Odell and Stewart (1993) point out, situations arise in which a particular change benefits one family member but harms another.

When faced with dilemmas among competing ethical ideals, and balance is not possible, ranking them is an alternative strategy (Taylor 1989). Stakeholders determine which ideals are most important and which are not.

Psychoanalytic theories, for instance, give priority to the individual over the collective, argues Michels (1987), a tendency which Wallach and Wallach (1983) find even more pronounced in neo-Freudian and humanistic therapeutic approaches. Mental health also has to be weighed against other ideals, such as civil liberties, justice, peace (Michels 1976), individual rights (Callahan 1988), alternative paths to happiness, and "such very different life goals as service to other persons, to the state, or to God; or the achievement of some ideal such as advancing knowledge, pursuing honor, or creating something of lasting or absolute value" (Gettner 1978: 1060). Such ranking occurs for individual clients (some clients may need to take better care of themselves; others to become less self-absorbed), as well as in general. And one therapist may consider Bob's happiness to be of paramount importance in his therapy, but another the well-being of his children.

Devoting particular attention to the most important or "superordinate" (London 1986: 9) ethical ideal is a sixth approach to addressing multiple ideals related to therapy goals and outcome. J. Michael, for instance, argued that "cultural survival" is the "primary value" held by radical behaviorists, with other values being relegated to "secondary status" (Michael 1977: 295). Taylor refers to individuals' most important ethical ideals as "hypergoods," which he defines as "goods which not only are incomparably more important than others but provide the standpoint from which these must be weighed, judged, decided about" (Taylor 1989: 63). Hypergoods are critically significant from both an ethical and a psychological perspective. Taylor argues that:

> the one highest good has a special place. It is the orientation to this which comes closest to defining my identity, and therefore my direction to this good is of unique importance to me. Whereas I naturally want to be well placed in relation to all and any of the goods I recognize and to be moving towards rather than away from them, my direction in relation to this good has a crucial importance....if I am strongly committed to a highest good in this sense I find the corresponding yes/no question utterly decisive for what I am as a person.
>
> (Taylor 1989: 63)

"Unconstrained freedom," he suggests, is "the most pervasive of all modern goods" (ibid.: 489). That and mental health, variously defined, are the hypergoods most relevant to psychotherapy.

When health functions as hypergood, it becomes *the* human value (Goldstein 1959; Monopolis *et al.* 1977), from which "all other values experienced under special conditions become comprehensible" (Goldstein 1959: 188). And so, all therapies "share a value system that accords primacy to individual self-fulfillment" (Frank 1978: 6). And Wallach and Wallach document how neo-Freudians let "psychological values preempt all others"

(Wallach and Wallach 1983: 117). Self-actualization, argues Patterson, "is, or should be, the goal of society and of all its institutions" (Patterson 1989: 171). Those assertions vividly exemplify American individualism and expressivism, whose adherents, Taylor (1989) argues, hold self-realization in such high regard that *no* goods can trump it.

But not all agree that mental health should be a hypergood. Hartmann (1960) argued that not even mental health professionals, apart from their professional activities, consider mental health to be their highest value (see also Buhler 1962). Indeed, notes Michels, some contend that ethical ideals like social justice and civil liberties "are of superordinate value." And so, "when they conflict with therapy, the therapy must retreat" (Michels 1976: 382).

Distinguishing between two forms of hypergoods may, I think, be helpful. Rescher drew a distinction between monistic *"summum bonum"* theories that seek to found a monolithic, inverted-pyramid structure of value upon one single, solitary end value to which all others are somehow means," and multivalent theories that are "polychromatic and envisage a plurality of distinct end values which, even if some are 'higher' than others, are at any rate subordinated to them in a mean–ends hierarchy" (Rescher 1969: 54). In the latter case, mental health can be regarded as a penultimate goal for those clients whose hypergood is not mental health. Achieving mental health enables them to reach the ideal they consider their highest. Therapists working with such clients will ideally employ a sufficiently flexible definition of "mental health" to facilitate reaching the goals therapy stakeholders have set.

The challenge posed by this chapter can thus be recast as one of adjudicating among the ethical ideals, and the hypergoods, of therapy's various stakeholders. When the ideals of *all* therapy stakeholders are considered, the final three approaches to multiple therapy ideals come into view, approaches to be addressed in more detail in the remaining chapters of the book.

Ongoing, extensive psychological–ethical *discourse* among all therapy stakeholders is the seventh approach to the problem of multiple therapy ideals. That, I trust, is a function this book will facilitate.

Revising the therapeutic contract to address the ethical character of therapy and *developing an improved public philosophy* that addresses the ethical character of therapy goals and outcomes – the eighth and ninth approaches – move the discussion from the level of the solitary decision maker to the level of communities and societies. Those approaches to the thorny issues of the ethical character of therapy goals and outcome will be addressed in Chapter 10.

Part V

Implications

10

Rethinking psychotherapy's location in a society

Public philosophy and social and therapeutic contracts

Because psychotherapy is an inextricably ethical endeavor – not simply the technical application of scientific findings, not simply a medical treatment to reduce psychological distress, and not simply a journey of personal growth – we need to reexamine those understandings of therapy that are based on the assumption that therapy is either value-free or inconsequentially value-laden. And so, in these final three chapters, I will explore some implications of understanding psychotherapy to be deeply and ineradicably ethical.

Suppose that Anna, a 38-year-old expectant woman, is depressed. Her morning sickness is not going away. And her husband seems preoccupied with his work, unconcerned about her, and apathetic about becoming a father to a new child. She worries about what life will be like when the baby comes. And she wonders whether she should follow the advice of her neighbor: "get rid of it, you don't need any more children." She sleeps poorly. Her appetite is diminished. And she does not feel supported by the male religious leader supposedly concerned about her well-being. (She has long belonged to a religious group whose total membership is less than one percent of the population in her society.) During a visit, her mother asks how she is doing. Anna weeps.

If the processes, goals, and outcomes of any psychotherapy Anna receives embody answers to ethical questions to a greater extent than generally believed, and if the clinical, scientific, and business contexts of therapy also carry with them certain ethical answers, then old answers to key questions about psychotherapy no longer satisfy. And so therapy stakeholders have the opportunity, and perhaps the obligation, to rethink therapy in light of its ethical character. In this chapter, I will address the role of therapy in societies, focusing on articulating and revising current implicit public philosophies and contracts (therapeutic and social) concerning therapy. This chapter primarily involves social and cultural ethics. Chapter 11, in which I will reexamine selected dimensions of professional ethics, primarily involves professional and clinical ethics. I will argue, however, that the topics addressed in both chapters are tied in important ways to fundamental questions of theoretical ethics, because answers to the issues discussed in both chapters grow out of the deepest ethical convictions and motivations of human beings. But those moral sources are too often occluded. And so, in Chapter 12, I will address how therapy stakeholders can make better ethical choices, choices that may improve the ethical character of therapy.

Although my focus in these chapters will be the implications of therapy's ethical character, some of the issues addressed represent ethical dimensions of psychotherapy which I have not yet addressed. And so these chapters will add to the portrait of the ethical character of psychotherapy which I have been developing throughout the book.

For better or worse, I will not provide anything approaching definitive or certain answers. But I hope to demonstrate that we can address in fruitful ways the vitally important questions of the ethical character of psychotherapy, doing so without resort to the "easy" solutions of relativism and absolutism.

A public philosophy for psychotherapy

By a public philosophy for psychotherapy, I mean ideas about the ideal role of therapy in society, about therapy's purpose and participants, and about its relationship with other spheres of society. Or, to paraphrase Browning, public philosophy involves discourse about, giving an account of, or providing reasons for, "the main focus of the [psychotherapy] profession and...the appropriate relation of [psychotherapy] to other regions of social life, for example, law, politics, ethics, and religion" (Browning 1991a: 18).[1]

In discussing a public philosophy relevant to Anna in the above example, I thus want to address how her society views psychotherapy: is it supported? does her government raise taxes to pay for it? does part of her (and/or her husband's) compensation package include some form of health insurance that will pay for therapy? if some party other than Anna and her family pays for it, to what extent and under what circumstances? is long-term therapy supported? with what images do those who shape Anna's society portray therapy (e.g. in the media, in written works, in religious exhortations, and so forth)? is going to a therapist shameful, acceptable, or "cool"? and, what reasons (ethical and otherwise) are given for those answers? finally, when an explicit public philosophy is absent, which answers are implicit in societal images and stories and in institutional structures and arrangements?

Answers to those questions are, of course, hotly disputed. They vary across cultures, across subcultures within pluralistic societies, and within subcultures. If Anna lives in Saudi Arabia, that nation's public philosophy regarding psychotherapy would differ from the public philosophy if she lived in Japan, Finland, Angola, or the US. Psychotherapy occupies a different location in each society.

We understand the role of therapy in a society when we get an overview of the society and see therapy's place within it – its actual place and its location relative to citizens' aspirations for it. My topographical metaphor, "the location of psychotherapy in a society," refers to the breadth of public philosophy and to public philosophy's role in describing the relationship between therapy and a society as a whole. A public philosophy for therapy addresses the relationship of psychotherapy to other professional activities, to other ways people change, to the destination(s) (good or ideal ends) toward which society wants to move, and to other dimensions of a society. As Kiesler and Morton argue, "a top-down analysis of resource allocation is necessary for responsible public policy in health and mental health care" (Kiesler and Morton 1988: 993). And Clark (1993) argues that socially responsible psychologists can function in either the micro-ethical sphere (in their relationship with clients) or the macro-ethical sphere (the realm of social policy). This movement from thinking about individual therapy clients to thinking about the broader societal level (analogous to moving from an individual view of psychopathology to a family-systems perspective) is important. A society may (and usually does) have multiple needs but may lack the resources to meet all those needs. It would be unwise, for instance, to devote large sums of governmental funding to long-term therapy for Anna's sub-clinical depression in a society in which resources are inadequate to meet basic nutritional and educational needs. A top-down analysis permits therapy stakeholders to understand that macro-ethical sphere and delineate psychotherapy's ideal location within a society.

By "public" philosophy, I mean a discussion about the public rather than private role of therapy and about the public (society-wide) implications of therapy. In the kind of public discussion (Bellah 1986) that produces an optimal public philosophy, no one's views are excluded and all stakeholders give public reasons for their views, not relying solely on their disputed basic ethical assumptions. The classic liberal in a pervasively religious society is given a voice, as is the religious minority in a pervasively secular state. Whenever full ethical agreement is not possible (and in most societies full agreements of any depth about the ethical character of therapy will be rare), a "best possible" working agreement is sought.

A public philosophy concerning psychotherapy is important for several reasons. All societies have such a philosophy – at least implicitly (M. A. Hall 1997). Articulating such philosophies facilitates their evaluation and, if necessary, their revision.

Second, although public philosophies are articulated abstractly, they have profoundly practical implications because they are translated into public policies (through the ugly, powerful, inefficient, tension-filled mechanisms of politics). Such policies deeply affect psychotherapists and their clients, for good or ill. And so a public philosophy can either contribute to good mental health in a society or its opposite. As Frank and VandenBos stated, "psychologists must be involved in policy issues so as to ensure the utilization of psychological knowledge and attention to psychological and behavioral health needs" (Frank and VandenBos 1994: 851). Of particular importance are the battles over funding for therapy, and control of that funding. Hall observes that decisions about funding are made at several levels. At the broadest level, he notes, "at the macro or global level, society must decide, whether purposefully or by default, how much of its resources to devote to the medical enterprise" (M. A. Hall 1997: 6). A society that develops an articulate, explicit public philosophy about psychotherapy's location within it will be more likely to develop a satisfactory consensus about such policy issues than one in which conflicting views are implicit.

A public philosophy for psychotherapy is also important in order to protect the autonomy and professional judgment of the psychotherapist. The psychotherapy profession needs, in Browning's words, "to protect itself and its treatments from exploitation by fashionable trends or politically ambitious powers that might like to use the increasing technical skills of contemporary psychiatry" (Browning 1991a: 20). And, one might add, to protect itself from economic powers that want to reduce expenditures for therapy, thereby preventing clients from reaching good therapy goals.

Other ethical implications of public philosophies for therapy are also important. A public philosophy for therapy that recognizes that therapy is deeply and inextricably ethical in character will be different from (and more complex than) a philosophy that assumes therapy is value-free. Because the ethical convictions held by various therapists and underlying different forms of therapy differ (at times dramatically), the *way* in which a public philosophy handles ethical differences is vitally important. If Anna is a Muslim in a predominantly secular country, its public philosophy addresses whether therapists try to conform her to a secularist mold or treat her religion more respectfully. Likewise if she is Unitarian in a society governed by fundamentalists. A public philosophy must wrestle with ethical diversity among therapists and clients and across the society as a whole. All stakeholders may applaud the diminution of Anna's depression. But they may disagree about other changes produced by therapy – changes in her views of abortion, the proper relation of husband and wife, the role of religion in her life, and so forth.

In the remainder of this chapter, I address the role of therapy in a society. I will emphasize therapy's ethical dimensions, the process of making decisions about the role of therapy in society, and the process of crafting a public philosophy in the presence of ample, deep-seated ethical diversity. Finally, I will address therapeutic and social contracts about therapy.

Ethical dimensions of the role of therapy in a society

The "traditional" role of modern psychotherapy is, of course, of very recent origin, arising in Europe and the US from a variety of sources – religious, medical, philosophical, and educational (Abbott 1988; E. M. Caplan (forthcoming); Freedheim 1992). Psychotherapists at first borrowed the social location (and legitimacy in society) of their professions. Freud, for instance, originally considered psychoanalysis a medical procedure (Strupp 1986). Psychotherapy appealed to large numbers of people, in part "because of its association with science, medicine, technology, and the romantic features of psychoanalysis" (Browning 1991b: 6). Therapy thus appealed to the ethical ideals behind both of the modern understandings of the self outlined by Taylor (1989).

Eventually, psychotherapists, professional associations, and various governmental entities collaborated to develop specialized certification and licensing procedures. Psychotherapists became professionals (if not already considered professionals) (Association of State and Provincial Psychology Boards 1996; Gorlin 1994; Hatch 1988b; Hogan 1979; Young 1987). Recognition of psychotherapists as professionals was vitally important. But, as London notes:

> our society only sanctions the practice of psychotherapy and the existence of therapeutic guilds because of a tacit assumption that the moral order to which therapists address their skills is one that ultimately benefits the social order through its treatment of the needs of individuals.
>
> (London 1986: xvi; see Meara *et al.* 1996)

That is, society sanctions psychotherapy because it benefits society.

The ethical assumptions of traditional public philosophy regarding psychotherapy were thus straightforward. Mental illness is bad. Eliminating it and producing mental health are good, both for the individuals involved and for society as a whole. Professionals effectively treat mental illness and produce mental health. And, as professionals, they abide by a code of ethics and commit themselves to the well-being of their clients. Therapists' efforts are therefore supported and they receive the public recognition and autonomy granted other professionals.

But the current picture is more complicated. Psychotherapy's social location changed when third-party payers began paying for therapy. A revised social contract entailed a (usually implicitly) revised public philosophy. Many societies are now renegotiating this contract. As the psychiatrist C. K. Aldrich put it:

> As long as Jones paid me for his psychotherapy or friendship, or however he wanted to use the time I sold him, it was none of Smith's business. But when Smith's taxes or insurance premiums began to contribute to my fee, Smith's interest in what I was doing with Jones increased. In other words, Smith now expects me to be accountable – and in terms that he can understand.
>
> (Aldrich 1975: 509)

Of particular importance is the fact that the traditional public philosophy was based, in part, on the alleged ethical neutrality of psychotherapy. As Guignon points out, "scientific endeavor from the outset has aimed at being value-free and objective" (Guignon 1993: 217). This scientific emphasis was combined with Freud's emphasis on "neutrality," Carl Rogers' emphasis on the "non-directive" nature of his therapeutic approach, and other factors to produce a deeply enshrined myth: value-free therapy.

As Michels (1991) points out, however, this claim of therapeutic neutrality "concealed" the ethical functions of therapists. I want now to address those ethical functions, all relevant to a public philosophy for psychotherapy. After discussing societal policies related to psychotherapy, I will briefly discuss some ethical ideals related to therapy, the ethical idea of the professional within a society, therapy in relationship to other spheres of society, and the role of culture.

Policies translate public philosophies concerning psychotherapy into action. As Birch and Rasmussen point out, goodness "is sometimes promoted by social arrangements and sometimes obstructed by them. But social arrangements are never neutral" (Birch and Rasmussen 1989: 91). Policies, created by governmental entities, corporations, non-profit entities, and independent business people and professionals, may be formal or informal, and explicit or implicit. Policy involves balancing what is considered ideal with perceptions of reality (which can sometimes be influenced by pertinent psychological research; see Desjarlais et al. 1995; Kiesler et al. 1991; Lorion et al. 1996; Rochefort 1989; Speer and Newman 1996). Policies relevant to therapy address which persons are licensed by governmental agencies to function independently as psychotherapists, which persons are authorized to receive payment from governments, corporations, or insurance companies, and which clients are eligible to receive reimbursed therapy (and how much of it). Policy decisions can be evaluated ethically. Hall, for instance, notes that societies "have always rationed health care resources on a massive scale, but according to irrational and unjust principles" (M. A. Hall 1997: 5). If policies in Anna's society do not permit her to obtain therapy but do permit a wealthier male neighbor to do so, de facto rationing exists, rationing that is prima facie unjust.

The task which policymakers face is made more difficult when the reality of therapist-influence on client values and psychotherapy's conflicting ethical ideals is recognized. When faced with practical decisions, about therapy with Anna or any other client, competing ethical ideals must be balanced.

One of the most challenging ethical issues pertaining to a public philosophy for therapy is whether, or under what circumstances, psychotherapy benefits society. That psychotherapy sometimes benefits a society as well as individual clients is not in dispute. But, as discussed in Chapter 7, some think the financial cost of unlimited therapy harms society. And, as discussed in Chapter 9, some think therapy can harm society because therapists convert clients to an ideology of individualism, selfishness, and political passivity. At times, we must choose between the well-being of individual therapy clients and the well-being of a society as a whole. Deciding which takes precedence is decidedly different at the societal level than at the level of a therapist and a client privately discussing therapy goals. Societies also regularly choose some balance between individual and societal well-being in their policies regarding therapy.

As discussed above, a society supports psychotherapy because it believes the pursuit of the well-being of individual clients benefits the society (London 1986; Veatch 1978). But there is a widespread (if disputed) perception that therapists are more concerned about individual well-being than the general welfare. And, indeed, therapists in the empirical investigation of Fowers, Tredinnick, and Applegate (1997) endorsed individualistic responses significantly more frequently than responses affirming social embeddedness and responsibility. This confirms an extensive literature arguing that, whatever their intentions, the *de facto* ethical influence of many therapists on clients is individualistic and therefore problematic (Cushman 1995; Doherty 1995; Lasch 1978; MacIntyre 1984; Sampson 1988; Wallach and Wallach 1983, 1990).

Albee and Ryan-Finn (1994) make a different critique of the current public philosophy concerning mental health. They argue that societies should devote far more resources to the prevention of psychological problems rather than waiting until people are impaired and in distress and then spending much more money.

In response to these criticisms (and, in some societies, to the reality of changing reimbursement systems), therapists increasingly emphasize societal as well as individual well-being. In a presidential column for the American Psychological Association's Division of Family Psychology, Silverstein argued that "if psychology is to become recognized by the public and by managed care as a major player in the mental health marketplace, we must be seen as proficient in addressing the nation's social concerns" (Silverstein 1997: 5).

Many therapists, philosophers, and cultural commentators now argue for a balance of individual and societal well-being (Callahan 1990; Cushman 1995; Doherty 1995; Gelpi 1989; Sampson 1993; Taylor 1992; Wallach and Wallach 1990). Bellah, Madsen, Sullivan, Swidler, and Tipton argue that "the goal must be nothing less than a shift from radical individualism to a notion of citizenship based on a more complex understanding of individual and social happiness" (Bellah *et al*. 1991: 107). And, in an assertion that underscores the importance of the professional nature of psychotherapy (to be discussed later in this and the following chapter), Meara, Schmidt, and Day argue that "communities grant professional autonomy to those professions that competently perform needed services and take seriously (above their own self-interests) the welfare of the individuals with whom they work and the good of the community at large" (Meara *et al*. 1996: 69).

Disagreement about ethical ideals is at the heart of the debate about a public philosophy for psychotherapy. A variety of ideals is championed. Therapists stress mental health ideals, but disagree about the ethical content of "mental health" (see Chapter 9). And even when therapists and societies agree that policies regarding therapy ought to balance a concern for the mental health of individuals and a contribution to the general welfare, citizens often disagree about the meaning of "the general welfare." Trabin and Freeman (1995) argue that business justifications, an ideal some therapists think should not interfere with decisions about therapy, should be included in social policy regarding therapy. From the perspective of evolutionary ethics, J. Michael argues that "professional activities should be primarily directed toward the development of social practices which have lasting cultural survival value" (Michael 1977: 303). Jaggar articulates ethical assumptions she believes are common to feminists: "the view that the subordination of women is morally wrong and that the moral experience of women is worthy of respect." Feminists are collectively committed, she argues, to working out "the practical and theoretical consequences of these assumptions, a commitment perhaps analogous to the projects of those who develop so-called Christian or Marxist ethics" (Jaggar 1991: 95). From a religious perspective, Browning points out that "health is only one value (albeit a highly important value) among many values by which the Western religions assess themselves" (Browning 1991a: 26). Environmental ethicists would add concern for the environment in the mix of goods a society needs to balance in formulating a public philosophy for therapy. And so, in the face of convincing claims for many ethical principles, Prilleltensky (1997) argues for a balance of ideals, a position which I also endorse. But *which* values are to be balanced and *how* they are to be balanced remain in dispute.

Some public philosophies support a broad mandate for therapists, but others advocate a narrow mandate. The issue, as Browning articulates it, is whether the mental health profession should "lead society in developing a positive view of the good society and the good person (or 'healthy' society and person), or should it confine itself to the more cautious role of caring for the mentally ill?" (Browning 1991b: 1). Cost-cutting governments, corporations, and other third-party payers tend to advocate the narrower mandate, to the dismay of many therapists and clients.

Although directly related to practical policies, public philosophies draw upon decidedly abstract philosophical assumptions. Many claim to decide such issues, not on philosophical, but on "pragmatic" grounds: "we should do whatever works." As Tillich noted, however, "most pragmatism...indulges in a hidden metaphysics" (Tillich 1959: 192). Indeed, argues Browning, a public philosophy "entails the idea that psychiatry needs in the background of its work general images of the good person and the good society" (Browning 1991a: 20), images that shape the public philosophy of the psychotherapist.

The claim that we can make valid assertions about "the good society" is disputed, of course. Indeed, modernity is characterized, MacIntyre argues, by "the thesis that questions about the good life for man or the ends of human life are to be regarded from the public standpoint as systematically unsettleable" (MacIntyre 1984: 119). Disagreement about this point deeply divides many societies and characterizes the views of some self-labeled post-modernists. In an act of retrieval, Taylor documents, however, the ways in which all contemporary thinkers (including those whom Prilleltensky (1997) labels skeptical postmodernists) draw upon four inter-related deep-seated beliefs, beliefs that are often hidden from view. These beliefs concern "not just (a) our notions of the good and (b) our understandings of the self, but also (c) the kinds of narrative in which we make sense of our lies, and (d) conceptions of society" (Taylor 1989: 105). Explicitness about those inextricably ethical beliefs, about the philosophical assumptions upon which any public philosophy draws, will, I believe, facilitate more fruitful and intellectually satisfying discussions about public philosophy.

Another important dimension of the ethical character of psychotherapy in a society is the concept of the professional. As discussed in Chapters 2 and 11, professions exist (and continue to exist) because societies agree they should, to meet particular societal needs (Bassford 1990; Michels 1991). And professionals' most fundamental principles derive, not from the profession alone, but also from the society in which they practice (Browning 1991a; Margolis 1966). In the classical understanding, professionals are highly trained people whose conduct is governed by a professional code of ethics and by a preeminent commitment to the principle of beneficence, a commitment to the well-being of others (see Hatch 1988a; Jennings *et al.* 1987). *A deep ethical core is thus intrinsic to the professional.* That means, assert Meara, Schmidt, and Day (1996), that "more is expected" in a professional relationship "than in a contractual, business relationship" (Meara *et al.* 1996: 20). Unfortunately, some economic reductionists (Chapter 7) view therapists in the latter terms, as nothing more than useful "providers" of "services" who need monitoring and control. That difference in perception of therapists, and in public philosophy, is profound. Accordingly, "we need to reappropriate the ethical meaning of professionalism, seeing it in terms not only of technical skill but of the moral contributions that professionals make to a complex society" (Bellah *et al.* 1985: 211).

Having previously addressed the relationships between psychotherapy and science, medicine, and business (Chapters 6–7), I will not discuss them further here. I do want to address one set of relationships, that between therapy and religion, a relationship relevant to Anna's depression. The history of the relationship between psychotherapy and religion is long and complex (Browning 1987; Jones 1994; Shafranske 1996), with periods of harmony and periods of tension. Psychotherapists have often been portrayed as priests,[2] supplanting with their moral authority a role previously occupied by the dying remnants of religion. Indeed, Kovacs encouraged therapists to "embrace...our essential role as secular priests" (Kovacs 1987: 16). Although it is not clear what these authors mean by "priest,"[3] they clearly envisage a greatly expanded mandate for therapists. And that is a role generally not requested by those who are religious, at odds with the wishes of many third parties paying for therapy, and falling beyond the training received by most therapists.

Undeterred by (or unaware of) the experts asserting that religion is dying, Anna and others continue to be religious. Indeed, except in Europe and some subcultures of the US, most people in the world continue to be religious, albeit at times in different ways than in the past (Hoge 1996). Although some who are religious have no interest in the kind of respectful public conversation about the role of therapy in a society (or about anything else) that I have described in this chapter, others are interested (Browning and Evison 1991; Cahill 1990; Jonsen 1994). And some (e.g. Bellah 1986; Benne 1995; Thiemann 1991) are even developing a "public theology" for the purpose. Indeed, those who want a public philosophy that is truly public (and not dogmatically anti-religious) would be likely to agree that religion "belongs in the conversation" (Bellah et al. 1991: 33).

Wallace adopts a different stance concerning the respective roles of religion and psychotherapy. In response to criticisms that therapists have undermined the moral sensitivities of their clients (and, by extension, the moral tenor of societies), he denies that therapy is "a recipe for amoral living" (Wallace 1991: 112). And he articulates the benefits of therapy. But he immediately adds an important caveat, suggesting an intimate relationship between religion and psychotherapy. Psychotherapy, he argues:

> can be a salutary counterbalance to traditional, Judeo-Christian-based ethical judgment – *but only if the clinician can count on cultural institutions to do their moral and cosmological job*. If not, then understandably patients will look to psychiatrists for meaning and morality, and getting them becomes part of the healing itself (as is explicit in the "ego lending" and "limit setting" required by some patients nowadays). Hence it is not only very difficult to rid the psychiatries of their metaphors of ultimacy and obligation, but it would perhaps be, at least for many patients in the current climate, a serious therapeutic *and* moral error to attempt to do so.
>
> (Wallace 1991: 113)

Given what Himmelfarb (1995) describes as the "demoralization of society," the optimal role of therapy in society may need rethinking.

Writing in an American context, Wallace can be reasonably sure that most "cultural institutions" are "Judeo-Christian." In other parts of the world and in subcultures not heavily influenced by that religious tradition, the relationship of culture and psychotherapy would need to take a different form. Any adequate public philosophy must grow out of that society's culture or cultures.

Deciding the role of therapy in a society

Faced with any decision, many psychotherapists turn on first impulse to science. And science can be very helpful (Kiesler *et al*. 1991; Lorion *et al*. 1996; Speer and Newman 1996), especially when we agree about a desired goal that we can measure. If we agree about what constitutes therapeutic effectiveness, for instance, scientific evidence may have clear implications for public policy and for professional ethics. Chambless and his colleagues provide this vivid example:

> To take an extreme and hypothetical example, therapists might know of only one intervention consistent with their theoretical orientation that has been empirically supported for a specific problem. Let's say research has shown it to be efficacious in 73% of the cases after a 3-year course of treatment. Are those therapists acting ethically if, because they do not read outside their own area of interest, they remain ignorant of an intervention associated with another theoretical orientation that has been repeatedly shown to be effective in 94% of the cases after a 5-week course of treatment?
>
> (Chambless *et al*. 1996: 113)

From that empirical finding, appropriate public policy would clearly follow.

Unfortunately, when public philosophies (and the public policies related to them) are discussed, the goal is often in dispute. And, as Krause and Howard note, "traditional scientific method does not concern itself with the issue of conflicting interests" (Krause and Howard 1976: 291). Indeed, Kendler (1993) argues that we cannot draw valid ethical conclusions from scientific findings alone. Policy decisions are based instead, Strupp (1986) argues, on a society's values (the ethical convictions of its members) concerning mental health. And on its values regarding other good societal ends.

Making decisions about the ethical dimensions of a public philosophy regarding therapy is similar in many ways to making any kind of ethical decision: for instance, the ethical negotiating that occurs between therapist and client concerning therapy goals and process. And so the discussions in Chapters 4, 8, and 9 (and that to come in Chapter 12) are relevant. Respectful dialogue among therapy stakeholders (Jahoda 1958; Strupp and Hadley 1977), sound ethical reasoning, drawing upon ethical traditions with an openness to new solutions, compromise, the use of multiple ideals, participants being aware of and articulating their own ethical stances, and upholding autonomy are all important.

Negotiating a *public* philosophy can be even more difficult, however, for several reasons. The range of ethical differences may be greater. And, because decisions affect an entire society, the stakes are much higher. Empirically derived findings may be more directly relevant, and so interpretation of their meaning is especially important. Hammond, Harvey, and Hastie (1992) argue that policy-makers need to take into account both the error of failing to take action when it should have been taken (e.g. a third-party payer failing to authorize additional sessions for a suicidal client) and the error of taking action when it should not have been (e.g. therapists seeing clients when they need no more sessions). To determine the proper balance between those false negative and false positive decisions is, they note, "a value question." Vested interests, however, may want society to ignore findings that do not match their point of view.

Unfortunately, no problem-solving strategy can guarantee certain answers. As Callahan points out,

> The first and most important point to make is that there exists no simple, mechanical formula, either in ethics or in policy, for devising solutions to difficult balancing and priority issues....I have constantly used terms such as "reasonable," "sensible," and "prudent" – terms of human art and judgment. I believe these to be the right terms to use, however vague and controverted they are and must remain. But that is the nature of our problem. It requires judgment, not formulas.
>
> (Callahan 1990: 160)

Because of the complexities involved, Jennings, Callahan, and Wolf link "public philosophy" and "civic discourse," describing them as "that ongoing, pluralistic conversation in a democratic society about our shared goals, our common purposes, and the nature of the good life in a just social order" (Jennings *et al.* 1987: 6). A broad perspective needs to be adopted, in part because the ways in which therapists move people toward mental health, or, better, the kind of "mental health" toward which therapists move people, profoundly affects a society. All strata of a society need to be involved, not just those who see clients, pay taxes, administer bureaucracies, and run corporations.

But a profound difficulty faces that idealistic inclusiveness: deep ethical differences divide many societies. Imposing the views of the majority on the minority will not produce a satisfactory public philosophy. And expecting everyone to live on the basis of some bland lowest common denominator, some ethical consensus that neither offends nor inspires, produces its own set of problems. And the ever-tempting "solutions" of relativism and authoritarianism will also fail us. It is to wrestling with alternative solutions to the problem of ethical diversity that I turn next.

Addressing ethical diversity

The ethical differences underlying the different conceptions of mental health and other therapy goals discussed in Chapter 9 are but part of the ethical diversity facing those designing a public philosophy for psychotherapy. Engelhardt begins the acclaimed second edition of his *Foundations of Bioethics* by acknowledging that "there is a swarm of alternative ethics ready to give rise to a babble of conflicting bioethics. This circumstance constitutes the foundational moral challenge of all health-care policy. It brings the very field of bioethics into question" (Engelhardt 1996: vii).

Competing within Anna's society may be African (Magesa 1997; Paris 1995); Buddhist (Ray 1994); classic liberal; Communist; feminist; Hindu; Marxist; materialist; Native American; neo-conservative; paleo-conservative; secular, Reformed, and Ultra-Orthodox Jewish; Roman Catholic, Orthodox, liberal, moderate, evangelical, and fundamentalist Christian; Shinto; socio-biological; Taoist; and other ethical stances. Values differ between countries and between subcultures within societies (Marsella and White 1982; Minsel *et al.* 1991; S. H. Schwartz 1994). And deep differences exist within the major Western intellectual tradition, despite superficial consensus (Taylor 1992). Of particular relevance to this book is the attack by Nietzsche (who has deeply influenced Freud and many postmodernists) on benevolence (Taylor 1989), an ethical principle central to the concept of the professional.

In response to this pluralism, various communities, such as the feminist, attempt, in Jaggar's words, "to develop distinctive ways of living and thinking that reflect fundamental normative commitments currently shared by only a limited community" (Jaggar 1991: 95). And religious communities, to the surprise of many Western intellectuals, continue to serve as a moral source for many people. As Marty points out:

> Since the Enlightenment two centuries and more ago, the instinctive projection of scholars and sages in the West was to foresee a world in which religion progressively declined. They advanced this projection by envisioning that surviving religions would be modern, progressive, friendly to mainstream science, tolerant, interactive. Students of modern religious fundamentalism instead find that there seems to be as much religion around as ever, and that the prevailing movements are closer to fundamentalisms than to modernisms.
>
> (Marty 1993: 4)

And investigations of fundamentalisms (Marty and Appleby 1991, 1992, 1993a, 1993b, 1994, 1995, 1997) make it clear that fundamentalists are patriarchal. And they are deeply concerned about such psychological-ethical issues as "gender, sexuality, intimacy, familiality, [and] the life cycle" (Marty 1993: 5). Public philosophies concerning therapy need to take into account the concerns of both feminist and fundamentalist communities, since their conflicting convictions overlap extensively with the ethical issues addressed in therapy. And many other communities exist within societies as well, including communities of religious feminists.

I do not believe that a satisfactory public philosophy can be based on *only one* of those competing options, even if it represents the convictions of the majority of the members of a society. This is true whether Anna is a Unitarian in a fundamentalist Muslim country or a devout, conservative Muslim in a Western liberal democracy. A public philosophy based solely on one ethical perspective might mean that its ethical vision would be imposed on those holding other views. And, as Engelhardt points out, there would be no difference between imposing on people "a Roman Catholic contraceptive policy" and "a Rawlsian theory of justice" (Engelhardt 1991: xiii; see Quinn 1995).

Attempts to ground ethics on an indubitably certain foundation – whether in theism, disengaged reason (which has profoundly influenced psychology through its marriage to empiricism in the scientific method), or the depths of the self (e.g. in the ethical tradition of humanistic psychologists like Rogers and Maslow) – have failed (Taylor 1989). Many believe that reason (including the efforts of Rawls 1971) has produced neither the agreement nor the certainty that many (traditionalists and postmodernists) insist that a satisfactory ethics must exhibit. "For better or worse," Smith argues, "we are stuck in a pluralistic society and world in which there is little prospect of our agreeing on first premises" (M. B. Smith 1990: 532). And those profound ethical differences have produced in the US what has been dubbed "Culture Wars," associated with political differences that are very deep (Hunter 1991).

The problem is quite real. As Engelhardt points out, "Diversity is not only engaging. Diversity with substance offends" (Engelhardt 1996: 14). And that makes developing a public philosophy regarding an inextricably ethical activity like psychotherapy very difficult indeed.

Nevertheless, several potentially fruitful approaches exist. All are disputed, of course, and the debate among bioethicists, philosophers, and political theorists is intense. But after some preliminary considerations, I will consider four potentially fruitful proposals for dealing with ethical diversity in developing a satisfactory public philosophy for therapy: a limited role for therapists, a focus on consensual ethical content for therapy, making room for a variety of approaches to therapy that meet basic standards for therapy but grow out of the particular convictions of a given ethical community, and the development of an ethic to deal with those "moral strangers" (Engelhardt 1991: xiii) whose ethical convictions are deeply at odds with one's own.

Several steps are preliminary to progress: clarifying and articulating the views of all therapy stakeholders, especially those with deeply differing ethical perspectives. This serves as a vital preface to a dialogue or "common discussion" (Bellah *et al.* 1991: 66) among those with radically different points of view. That can increase understanding and pinpoint ethical commonalities previously undetected. However, stakeholders also need to acknowledge where deep differences exist. Finally, I think it helpful to have some sense of the extant alternatives and the conflicts that exist (a map of the ethical terrain, if you will). That, of course, is a major reason I have written this book.

To deal with ethical diversity, some argue for *a tightly delineated role* for psychotherapists. Advocates of this first proposal contend that a public philosophy should involve narrowly focusing therapy on its original task – helping those with serious psychological problems so they experience less distress and function more effectively. The goal: mental health as freedom from mental illness. Michels argues, for example, that "a vital guiding principle in outlining a public philosophy for psychiatry is to maintain a clear boundary" between tasks falling within the profession's domain and those falling outside of it (Michels 1991: 72). And so he would reject the claim that therapists should "embrace" the role of priest. Indeed, he argues that the profession "should be sharply critical of those who ignore or intentionally blur that boundary in order to enhance the public credibility of their positions" (ibid.). Advocates of this view encourage therapists to minimize their ethical influence on clients, as discussed in Chapter 8. By avoiding (or adopting as neutral a stance as possible regarding) ethically controverted topics, therapists are less likely to violate rights of clients from minority ethical subcultures. Or to convert them to the ethical convictions of the therapist. And limiting the range of a therapist's actions makes it less likely that the ethical majority in a society will impose its ethical stance on persons with minority ethical viewpoints. Furthermore, therapists limit their professional actions to those for which they have competence and contract (Tjeltveit 1986). Finally, some third-party payers may espouse this tightly delineated understanding of the proper location of therapy in a society, not because of a carefully articulated, profound, or morally elevated philosophical rationale, but because it is cheaper.

Although advocates of this view claim it to be both feasible and desirable, I am less convinced than I used to be that it is either humanly or philosophically possible to draw crisp lines that delineate a narrowly ethical role for therapists. Also unanswered, of course, are the details concerning this limited role of the therapist: to which roles are the activities of the therapist to be limited? are therapists limited to the traditional individualistic, egoistic, and selfish influence on clients? or can therapists free people from mental illness in a way that balances concern for self with concern for others? As for the desirability of this proposal, advocates of the other three proposals argue that a tightly delineated role is not the best way to address ethical diversity, and the ethical character of therapy, in a public philosophy.

Consensus, properly conceived, may permit the development of a public philosophy regarding therapy that addresses the problem of ethical diversity, either completely or in part. Advocates of this second proposal assert that, even in the midst of significant ethical diversity, members of a society ought to be able to articulate a consensus, in ethical terms, of therapy's purpose. This may take the form, for example, of consensual mental health values to which the profession adheres and which actual therapy, properly conducted, exemplifies. But "consensus" is used in a variety of ways. So, let me first unpack some of the varied meanings of the term.[4] Alternative positions, and their merits, can then be discussed.

Some assume that a consensus has, or should have, only one underlying source; others assume a consensus has many sources (people of differing views agree about one issue although not agreeing about others). Advocates of the former view may assume that reason, proper rational procedure, scientific evidence, or an optimal type of dialogue will produce consensus. Reason, according to Rawls (1993), is the basic source from which an "overlapping consensus" can be built. Consensus develops from that one source; if those who disagree would align themselves with that source, they would come into harmony with the consensus. Or, to put the matter in crass terms that clearly overstate the case, "genuine consensus must come on my intellectual terms, terms I regard as rational and universally applicable."

Advocates of the view that *diverse* ethical convictions produce whatever consensus can be achieved are not sanguine that one source can produce consensus. Indeed, Rawls succeeds in obtaining a consensus, Ballard (1996) claims, by excluding concepts of good that conflict with his own understanding of liberalism. Jaggar points to the growing consensus that "reason is culturally constituted" and that "the rules of inference taken to define rational argument cannot be justified independently of social agreements about what kinds of inferential moves are acceptable." The result, she argues, is "an understanding of ethics as plural and local rather than singular and universal, grounded not in transcendent reason but rather in historically specific moral practices and traditions" (Jaggar 1991: 93). This view has two implications. First, the most substantial forms of ethics occur in particular ethical communities (which hold some views that others do not hold) rather than on universal terms (across an entire society). (Consistent with this view, some propose that forms of psychotherapy that are consistent with a local community's ethical stance become an acceptable alternative to the standard "one size fits all ethical convictions" variety of therapy. I will return shortly to that alternative for handling ethical diversity.) Second, societal consensus arises from diverse ethical sources. For example, Anna's minority religious perspective and the majority perspective in her culture may, for fundamentally different reasons, support the elimination of her depression. But those perspectives may disagree about fundamental standards of reason to adjudicate their other differences conclusively. Likewise, a classic liberal (religiously agnostic), a devout theologically moderate Christian, and a practicing Reformed Jew may all concur with Jaggar's rejection of the oppression of women, but for reasons quite different from one another, reasons based in part on metaphysical, epistemological, and ethical assumptions they do not share. Those who support particular ethical perspectives, those of local communities, may value reason. But they do not believe that reason will provide full-fledged ethical convictions of sufficient depth and richness for human flourishing. A secular public philosophy can be developed, but of necessity it must be sharply limited in scope (Engelhardt 1996).

Commentators employ a variety of metaphors to describe an ethical consensus produced by reason in contrast to other ethical perspectives. Universal ethics is contrasted with local ethics, and thin with thick. The ethical gruel produced by consensus is said to be thin, thin enough to be affirmed by consensus but insufficient to sustain and nourish people, no less permit them to flourish. Engelhardt (1991, 1996; Engelhardt and Wildes 1994) contrasts positions lacking moral content (and so of little aid in deciding therapy goals or a public philosophy for psychotherapy) with content-full ethical perspectives, those that have "moral substance." For that, argues Taylor (1989, 1992), people need ethical articulacy, articulacy concerning moral sources capable of moving people. Those who claim to hold no ethical views (or who affirm basic bioethical principles like justice and autonomy but deny holding any particular ethical theory) are said to be living off the ethical capital deposited by previous generations, to be drawing upon an ethical heritage that shaped them but which they now deny. They are, Engelhardt and Wildes (1994) argue, "covertly presupposing" a more substantive ethical stance, a stance not the product of reason alone, a stance about which there is not societal consensus. Deep moral sources, it is claimed, are necessary to provide the motivation and the content to live optimally ethical lives. The thin ethical principles derived by consensus are insufficient to move a person to understand or live the good life. They are psychologically impoverished.

The nature of any consensus that a society develops is in dispute in other ways as well. Bellah, Madsen, Sullivan, Swidler, and Tipton argue that it would be good to "create an American public philosophy less trapped in the clichés of rugged individualism and more open to an invigorating, fulfilling sense of social responsibility" (Bellah et al. 1991: 15; cf. Drane 1991). And Doherty aspires to "a new cultural ideal in which personal fulfillment will be seen as part of a seamless web of interpersonal and community bonds that nurture us and create obligations we cannot ignore and still be human" (Doherty 1995: 20). But whatever the virtues of their positions, the consensus they describe does not now exist in American society.

Various approaches to identifying an ethical consensus have been attempted. Through a process of rational analysis, Bok (1995) identified a set of common values adhered to across the world.[5] And empirical researchers have identified some areas of broad consensus concerning values related to mental health and psychotherapy (Jensen and Bergin 1988; E. W. Kelly 1995a). Engelhardt describes a form of secular humanism (which, unlike other forms of secular humanism, is not anti-religious) that entails a consensus about procedural rules for living. This "restricted moral vision" serves as a common moral language for those from differing ethical perspectives and as a "coherent statement" of the "way of life" lived by those he labels cosmopolitans (Engelhardt (1991: 125, 139). Cosmopolitans, he argues, "are men and women who have shed intensely held, content-full understandings of life, health, medicine, and death that focus on moral ultimates. Their lives are constructed around instrumental goods, not ultimate moral commitments" (ibid.: 146).

Those forms of consensus are important, especially consensus about the values affirmed by most therapists. As Michels argues, clients should be able to assume that therapists represent "a set of values defined by a professional group" (Michels 1976: 382). Identifying those values is therefore important.

Unfortunately, the usefulness of those types of consensus for developing a public philosophy for psychology may be limited, for three reasons. The mere existence of a consensus does not tell people why they should believe in those ethical convictions. *That* people believe in certain values tells us nothing about whether it is *good* they do so. Indeed, as we have seen, therapists may affirm autonomy, for example, for a variety of ethical reasons. Second, many people find such a consensus to be "too thin" intellectually, too psychologically impoverished, and too general to be of practical worth. (I will return to this issue in Chapter 12.) Finally, merely delineating a consensus provides no guidance to deal with those clients, therapists, and subgroups within a society who disagree with elements in the consensus or who hold more particular ethical views (whose convictions extend beyond, or in some way dispute, consensual ethical views), for instance, people affirming minority (dissenting) views.

Communitarians (Etzioni 1993) and others have sought to define some common vision of the public good. In doing so, they separated from classic liberals, who have traditionally believed, MacIntyre asserts, "that government within a nation-state should remain neutral between rival conceptions of the common good" (MacIntyre 1994: 302). It is not clear to me how governments can remain neutral. Indeed, if they provide funds to treat mental illness, it is surely in part because they believe that the nation's citizens, and the nation as a whole, will be better off with mentally healthy rather than mentally ill citizens. But the concern MacIntyre raises about the authoritarian dangers of an imposed "consensus" is well-taken (see Bersoff 1996). Part of the solution may be a *modest* vision of the common good, some low-level consensus. "It is good for citizens to receive effective treatment for mental illness" seems a good candidate, one that would receive wide assent and is not susceptible to authoritarian interpretations. But those holding ethical views not universally held need protection. For that and other reasons, the following two proposed solutions offer promise in helping crafters of a public philosophy for therapy to address ethical diversity well.

If ethical diversity finds concrete expression in the experiences and convictions of particular communities, *affirming forms of therapy that are in accord with particular ethical communities* stands as a third alternative for dealing with ethical diversity in a public philosophy for therapy. This is consistent with the claim that all forms of substantive ("content-full") ethics arise among those holding particular sets of ethical beliefs. As Engelhardt put it:

> there is no univocal way in general secular terms to discover a priori the meaning of health, suffering, illness, death, or the purposes of medicine. Such meaning must from a secular perspective be fashioned by actual communities and individuals in real circumstances.
>
> (Engelhardt 1991: 136)

This third proposal would require the acceptance of, or finding place for, a variety of ethical communities within the psychotherapy professions. These communities may be geographically or otherwise isolated (the Amish) or may actively interact with those holding other views. They may be intellectual communities, historical communities, or communities involving concrete relationships with other persons.

This proposal would benefit "minorities," like Anna, whose deepest convictions about life are not shared by those in her society. But it would also benefit those whose ethical convictions are widely, but not universally, held. These psychotherapy clients could recover from their psychological problems in a way that is consistent with the beliefs they hold as members of an ethical community. And those seeking a more full-orbed state of psychological flourishing could do so in a therapeutic relationship that meshes with their beliefs about ideal human functioning. Feminist clients may want to work with a therapist who is also committed to the feminist community, a community that, Jaggar suggests, is "seeking to develop distinctive ways of living and thinking that reflect fundamental normative commitments currently shared by only a limited community" (Jaggar 1991: 95). And if a potential client is concerned, like Cushman, "to collude less with contemporary capitalism and actually develop ways of treating the primary causes of psychological ills, the political and economic structures" (Cushman 1992: 58), he or she could seek a therapist, like Cushman, who shares those beliefs. With client and therapist sharing the same ethical community, the long-term result may be, as Cushman notes, "a much greater healing."

Clients and therapists would be drawing upon a variety of deeper moral sources, upon what Engelhardt calls "the post-modern pluralism of moral visions" (Engelhardt 1991: 140). This "more consistently inclusive" pragmatic pluralism (Marsden 1991: 46) could include the full range of ethical theories mentioned in this book. Engelhardt provides a non-inclusive list: "tradition, culture, and God's good grace" (Engelhardt 1991: 195).

This proposed solution to the problem of ethical diversity carries its own set of potential problems. As with any attempt to match particular types of clients with particular therapists, logistical challenges would arise, especially in sparsely populated or underserved areas. More substantive problems may arise as well. Too much ethical diversity (with as many forms of therapy as there are ethical communities) would call into question the very meaning of psychotherapy. Some basic standards for therapy (pertaining to a consensual core of therapy values) may be a solution, however.

This proposal also does not provide a solution to the person genuinely confused about ethical issues or holding few or no clear ethical convictions. In addition, professional ethical problems may also arise, especially concerning informed consent (to be discussed in Chapter 11) and the need to insure that clients who change their minds about receiving a form of therapy associated with a particular ethical community can freely withdraw from that form of therapy if they choose to do so.

But in the absence of therapy targeted to the ethical community of clients, or for those circumstances in which therapist and client, or therapist and society, have deep ethical differences, therapists and a society need to adopt *an appropriate ethic for working with "moral strangers"*. This fourth proposal to deal with ethical diversity borrows Engelhardt's felicitous terminology to refer to those whose ethical convictions are deeply at odds with our own. He uses the phrase, "to signal the relationship people have to one another when they are involved in moral controversies and do not share a concrete moral vision that provides the basis for the resolution of the controversies, but instead regard one another as acting out of fundamentally divergent moral commitments" (Engelhardt 1991: xiii).

An ethic for moral strangers is without content (Engelhardt 1991), because to introduce some content might entail imposing one's moral views on another, one of the problems related to ethical diversity that this proposal is supposed to address. But it is an ethics that provides therapists with "a way of reaching across traditions" (ibid.: 135), such as the feminist therapist encountering a fundamentalist Christian, or a staunchly pro-life Catholic therapist working with a pregnant pro-choice young adult. This ethic, closely tied to professional ethics, must include a substantial measure of tolerance and respect for the views of the moral strangers (which does not mean therapists must either agree with their views or adopt a relativist stance). And, of course, therapists must uphold the autonomy of clients.

Therapist efforts to persuade these moral strangers to adopt their own views (e.g. to convert a client concerned only with self to an ethic in which care for children plays some role) raises questions of professional ethics that were discussed in Chapter 8 and will be addressed again in Chapter 11. To surreptitiously or aggressively hawk one's own views – however noble or well intentioned those views might be – would be a clear violation of this ethic. No public philosophy for psychotherapy could countenance that trampling of client autonomy.

In summary, I have discussed four proposals to address the deep ethical diversity that bedevils efforts to construct a public philosophy for psychotherapy, a profoundly and inextricably ethical endeavor. These four proposals – a tightly delineated role for therapists, consensus, affirming forms of therapy that are in accord with a particular ethical community, and an appropriate ethic for working with "moral strangers" – all have strengths and weaknesses. Ethicists and social philosophers will continue to debate them. For the purposes of constructing a public philosophy for psychotherapy, however, we may not have to choose between them. Solutions that draw upon each and keep all four in tension may be optimal. Again, however, the design of an optimal public philosophy for a particular society is a task, not for the author of a book on ethics and values in therapy, but for members of that society.

Whatever public philosophy a society constructs, however, that philosophy finds expression in contracts related to psychotherapy.

Revised social and therapeutic contracts

Growing out of a society's public philosophy are contracts pertaining to psychotherapy. The therapeutic contract (Orlinsky 1989) addresses the relationship between therapist and client (and, if therapist and client agree, third parties that pay for some portion of the therapy). And the social contract (Michels 1991) is an agreement (usually implicit) about the location and role of psychotherapy within a society. In addition to addressing practical details (like payment and session lengths), both types of contract have an ethical quality. The therapeutic contract, Orlinsky notes, "governs the system through the normative expectations set for patients and therapists" (Orlinsky 1989: 430). And the social contract, Parloff argues, has to do with therapeutic goals, and especially therapy's ultimate goal, which reflects value judgments. That ultimate goal, he asserts, "is the principal concern of the therapist in fulfilling his [or her] contract with the patient and community" (Parloff 1967: 8).

I am using contract as a term of art, of course, because therapist and client only occasionally literally sign a contract. And those they do sign are rarely legally binding. "Social contracts" are, of course, never signed.

Both types of contract refer to generally agreed-upon understandings about the nature and role of psychotherapy. Movies, television, and books create them, with accountants, politicians, and health planners contributing as well. In addition, the writings of professional psychotherapists, and discussions between therapists and clients play a role. An absence of a dutifully signed legal document does not, however, rob these contracts of their force, because they shape expectations about therapy. When working as a family therapist on an inpatient psychiatric unit, I was struck by how often family members encouraged one another to self-disclose, often moments after I had met them: "This is the place to open up about everything. It's safe to talk about it here." Expectations about therapy were so deeply engrained in American culture that I had no need to set them forth explicitly.

The idea that contracts are with therapist, patient, *and community* (Parloff 1967) expands psychotherapy theorists' traditional emphasis on the therapeutic dyad. Although therapy has always occupied some cultural space within a society, within particular sociohistorical contexts relevant to therapy's ethical character, agreements about therapy increasingly include third parties: government entities, corporations, and various other third-party payers. As Orlinsky (1989) notes, "special complications" arise when parties other than therapist and client have a direct role in the therapeutic contract, including the *de facto* ability to end a therapeutic relationship by denying payment. In many (but not all) cases, therapists and clients invite the participation of these other entities. But those third parties, which often interact with clients and therapists through obscure bureaucracies, often fail to specify clearly the nature of the relationships among therapist, client, and the third party. This causes confusion and impedes the provision of effective therapy, which is not good.

That potentially deleterious impact of contracts is the first reason contracts are relevant to the ethical character of psychotherapy. The second is that contracts have an ethical character related to the location they assign to therapy within societies. Finally, the implicit contract governing psychotherapy may falsely promise a level of value-freedom that therapists cannot provide. And so clients may assume therapists will not make any ethical judgments about them and will not influence their values. But therapists inevitably make ethical judgments about their clients, a wide range of ethical judgments, although therapists rarely treat clients "judgmentally" and many of their ethical judgments are nonmoral rather than moral. And therapists may well influence client values (Beutler and Bergan 1991). For all those reasons, contracts regarding therapy deserve close attention.

Ideal contracts pertaining to therapy make clear what all parties can expect so they can make informed decisions about participating. If feasible, therapists and clients who disagree with the operative values of particular third-party payers should not enter into relationships with them. They have the right, of course, and perhaps the responsibility, to work within their society to insure that the kind of therapy they want is available.

With regard to the ethical character of therapy, explicit and implicit promises that therapy will be value-free are both inappropriate. Therapy's inextricably ethical character should become part of social contracts about therapy, part of the cultural consciousness about therapy, just as the idea that therapy is a safe and confidential place to talk about personal problems is now.

Given the existence of current social contracts which imply that therapy is ethically neutral and the existence of ethical diversity in societies (and among therapists), therapists often address the ethical character of therapy best of all through explicit discussion. Because therapists disagree among themselves about ethical ideals related to therapy and because their ethical ideals influence the therapy they provide, therapists actually provide a variety of "psychotherap*ies*" rather than an ethically uniform type of relationship. If, for instance, Anna's therapist has definite views on abortion that diverge from those held by Anna, the role of that therapist's ethical convictions (and likely persuasive influence) may belong in the therapeutic contract established in dialogue with Anna. As Veatch (1973) pointed out, clients appropriately trust professional judgment when agreement about goals exists, but not when disagreement is present. Given ethical diversity and the persisting belief that therapy is value-free, the therapeutic contract ideally addresses ethical issues when therapy stakeholders hold different ideas about therapy goals.

In conclusion, social contracts pertaining to therapy grow out of a society's understanding of the location of psychotherapy within it, an understanding ideally articulated in a public philosophy for psychotherapy. Therapeutic contracts grow out of implicit and explicit agreements between therapists and clients (and often third parties). Both types of contract (and public philosophies) should address the ethical character of therapy. As I have noted, however, it is often difficult to do so, especially when ample ethical diversity prevails. In the absence of clear contracts, therapists need to attend closely to the principles of professional ethics when addressing the ethical character of therapy.

11

Profession and professional ethics

Psychotherapists are professionals. Such is the affirmation of the public philosophies regarding therapy in most societies, most social and therapeutic contracts, many public policies, and most psychotherapists.

It makes a difference whether or not Anna, the depressed woman discussed in Chapter 10, turns to a professional for help. Or it *should* make a difference, because being professional implies therapist concern for clients and commitment to certain ethical standards.

In applying standards of professional ethics to the therapy Anna and others receive, however, therapy stakeholders may assume that therapy is value-free, or minimally or uncontroversially value-laden. In light of the richer understanding of the ethical character of psychotherapy now developing, some dimensions of professional ethics need rethinking, especially with regard to situations in which contested ethical issues arise in therapy, in which therapist and client hold different values (ethically understood), and in which therapist and client affirm disparate ethical theories. Anna's status as a member of minority religious group may be relevant – if her beliefs about what is good, right, and/or virtuous differ from those of her therapist or if she holds those beliefs for different reasons.

The existence of ethical diversity and the disguised nature of much of therapy's ethical character together raise another set of questions: why do professions, and individual therapists, commit themselves to a set of shared ethical principles and behaviors? and from what sources (ethical theories, personal motivations, etc.) do the full range of therapist ethical assumptions and characteristics arise? For example, for what reasons – intellectual and motivational – does Anna's therapist seek to benefit her and practice in accord with professional standards of ethics? And what is the source of the therapist's other ideas about what is good and best in life?

In this chapter, then, I will address the ethical character of being a professional, and especially a professional psychotherapist. I will address some ways in which traditional assumptions about practicing ethically may need to be reconsidered in light of therapy's deeply and indelibly ethical character. Finally, I will touch upon the psychological and intellectual sources of the professional's ethics.

Profession

When psychotherapists assert that they are professionals, they announce, they profess, they make public testimony that they possess specialized knowledge and technical skills that help people with psychological problems. But there is more. A "public declaration" of a certain sort, notes Pellegrino:

> defines a true "profession" and separates it from other occupations. The very word comes from the Latin *profiteri*, to declare aloud, to accept publicly a special way of life, one that promises that the profession can be trusted to act in other than its own interests.
>
> (Pellegrino 1989: 68)

And so more is expected of the professional than of the craftsman (Wallace 1991), the owner of a business (Meara *et al*. 1996), and the layperson.

Beneficence is the "more" that sets apart professionals, including professing psychotherapists. "The sine qua non of the professional relationship," argues W. F. May (1984: 261), is "the virtue of benevolent service." Anna's therapist, if a professional, will (with some qualifications) put Anna's interests above his or her own while providing professional services to Anna. Indeed, Pellegrino asserts that "some degree of effacement of self-interest...is morally obligatory on health professionals" (Pellegrino 1989: 58). Although critics of professionalism have questioned the extent to which professionals actually exemplify that ideal, Thompson argues that beneficence is the "core duty" of the helping professions (Thompson 1990: 105).[1] This classic emphasis has been expressed in a variety of ways. Professionals are characterized by: "service" (Raimy 1950: 19), contributions to society (Bellah *et al*. 1985), "social responsibility" (American Psychological Association 1992: 1600; K. S. Kitchener 1996a: 361), "responsibility for the whole of society" (Sullivan 1995: 11), "concern about the common good" (Meara *et al*. 1996: 8), and "special responsibilities to look out for the welfare of the client" (ibid.: 20). As Wallace put it, "By virtue of this professed vocation and the patient's suffering plea for help, a serious moral claim is made on the doctor, not merely for scientifically informed treatment, but for caring and compassion as well" (Wallace 1991: 112).

Railing angrily against this ethical core, Nietzsche and skeptical post-modernists who draw on his thinking reject benevolence. "Taking a fateful turn against the Enlightenment," notes Taylor, Nietzsche "declared benevolence the ultimate obstacle to self-affirmation" (Taylor 1989: 343). "Nietzschean professional" is thus oxymoronic: Nietzscheans disdain the beneficence that is essential to the professional. Nietzsche held that benevolence is either destructive to the professional's fulfillment, or a mask of concern covering the professional's real motivation: gaining power over others. Neo-Nietzscheans can find evidence for both claims, of course. Foucault (1965), for example, reported on malevolent displays of power masquerading as professional beneficence in *Madness and Civilization*. But to leap from "Expressions of concern for others *sometimes* mask hegemonic intent" to "*All* professionals, including therapists, who claim a commitment to their clients are really trying to control them" is a non sequitur. Rather than drawing that illogical conclusion, I think it best to understand the Nietzschean critique as a helpful cautionary tale about professional abuse of power.

Professional ethics extends far beyond a vague, general concern for clients, of course. Codes of ethics specify professional ideals and responsibilities. Although codes have sometimes focused as much on protection of profession (guild) as on the actions of professionals (e.g. Starr 1982), current codes clarify aspirational and obligatory therapist behaviors. Because professionals are members of a "moral community" (Pellegrino 1989: 69), they employ professional codes of ethics to discipline members of a profession who violate those codes. Successful lawsuits against therapists who violate current standards of ethical practice enforce the codes and give additional reason for therapists to conform to their strictures. Finally, the self-regulating tradition of professionals is reinforced when ethics codes are incorporated into the laws (and other government regulations) that govern professional licensure. Violation of the profession's ethical code can thus remove the violator from the societally sanctioned ranks of that profession.

And so psychotherapists are professionals, and professionals *qua* professionals are necessarily committed to certain ethical standards. Philosophical grounds for the ethical character of professions have been proposed as well (Camenisch 1983; Fulford 1989; Pellegrino and Thomasma 1981; W. M. Sullivan 1995). We are, however, far from agreement about those grounds. And some professions, like medicine and psychology, give far more attention to their *scientific* than to their ethical character.

Because "professional" implies ethical character and content, the idea of "A professional psychotherapist possessing neither ethical convictions nor concern for clients" is a contradiction in terms. Therapists claiming to be professionals promise to exhibit beneficence and to practice in accord with the profession's code of ethics. And that includes the ways in which they address the ethical character of therapy.

Professional ethics and the ethical character of psychotherapy

That psychotherapy has a deeply ethical character, an ethical character far broader and deeper than professional ethics, is a central claim of this book. The relevance to psychotherapy of professional ethics, of principles and virtues particular to the professionals practicing psychotherapy, needs re-examination, however, in light of the growing recognition of therapy's pervasively ethical character. I will address two issues: the tension inherent in therapists' dual commitment to clients and the general welfare, and the relevance of professional ethics to therapists' ethical influence on clients.

Commitment to clients, commitment to society

Principles of professional ethics pertain to an issue addressed by social ethicists: the tension between therapy professionals' commitment to individual clients and their commitment to society. Although codes of professional ethics mandate a focus on the person seeking services from a professional, they often stipulate a concern for the common good as well. The preamble of the American Psychological Association's (1992) code, for instance, states that the goal of applications of psychological knowledge is "to improve the condition of both the individual and society." This point is often echoed by those reflecting on the ethical principles and virtues of professionals in general (Bellah *et al.* 1985; Camenisch 1983; Doherty 1995; W. F. May 1984; Meara *et al.* 1996). As I have documented, psychotherapists tend to be deeply individualistic, focusing on clients rather than on the general welfare. Social responsibility has been the subdued note in recent professional ethics (Sullivan 1995).

Although the well-being of clients and the well-being of a society are often coterminous, conflicts occur. As Kultgen points out, "Sometimes service to patrons does indeed redound to the public good....But sometimes it does not. Patron loyalty takes priority over public interest. This pollutes the stream of professional practice at its spring" (Kultgen 1988: 4).

Conflicts between client well-being and societal well-being take a variety of forms. Pursuing the well-being of individual clients can lead to societal harm, and aiming for the general welfare can harm individual clients. Doherty argues, for instance, that a crisis in public confidence in therapists has developed in the US because of therapists' inability "to speak to the profound social and moral problems of our day" (Doherty 1995: 3). In asking, "Are therapists making these problems worse by justifying the contemporary flight from personal responsibility, moral accountability, and participatory community?" (ibid.), Doherty voices the concerns of many social critics about dominant American forms of psychotherapy. Sarason warns against those who emphasize the public interest in ways that equate public interest with the "individual and professional self-interest" of psychotherapists (Sarason 1986: 904). A different type of conflict, M. A. Hall (1997) argues, arises when professionals are expected to benefit a society by having them make decisions about health expenditures. Doing so, he asserts, compromises a central principle of professional ethics: client well-being is paramount. That is, misplaced professional concern for societal well-being can harm clients.

Balancing the twin obligations of professional ethics – to client and to society – can be accomplished in a variety of ways. Promoting individual well-being in ways that benefit society is an obvious solution, one articulated with sensitivity to client autonomy by Cushman (1995), Doherty (1995), and Gerber (1992). If three forms of therapy benefit individual clients equally – with one harming society, the second neutral, and the third benefiting society – the first is likely to be wrong, the third likely to be best. A second way to balance the professional's twin obligations is to develop goals for therapy through public philosophies and social contracts that involve all therapy stakeholders. Koocher (1994) and Veatch (1989a) suggest another approach: laypeople and professionals working together to develop codes of professional ethics emphasizing social responsibility and the public interest. May argues for an approach to being professional in which "professional privilege and loyalty to client are important but must be balanced against other societal norms" (L. May 1996: 7), an approach stressing the common good (embracing a plurality of goods) and autonomy. And Sullivan argues for revitalizing the tradition of civic professionalism so the professional takes "responsibility through one's work for ends of social importance" (Sullivan 1995: xvi).

Although they are likely components of a comprehensive solution, those proposals will not entirely eliminate the tension arising from the professional's dual allegiance to societal and client well-being. Conflict will continue because therapists, clients, and third-party payers disagree about the nature of the general welfare and the optimal way to balance the good of societies and individuals, because practices benefiting society sometimes harm individuals, and because practices benefiting individuals sometimes harm societies.

Therapists' ethical influence on clients

"Most clients come" to insight-oriented therapists, London (1986: 48) avers, "for simple cure, not knowing they may take home moral counsel." Professional ethics is relevant to such moral counsel, and to other ethical dimensions of therapy. But because the ethical character of therapy is more extensive and pervasive than once believed, rethinking how codes of ethics apply to therapy is essential. We need careful thinking about professional ethics in relationship to several ethical dimensions of therapy: conflicts between the ethical convictions of therapist and client, the empirical finding that clients sometimes adopt their therapists' values (Bergin 1991; Beutler and Bergan 1991; Kelly 1990), conflicts between the ethical convictions of therapists and third-party payers, differing therapy goals, the implicit nature of many ethical issues, ethical differences across cultural, subcultural, and religious ethical communities, and deep ethical diversity. I want to address those issues by considering two questions: how do therapists address therapy's ethical dimensions in accord with professional ethics? and, given therapy's pervasively ethical character, how can we best rethink professional ethics?

Unethical ways to handle ethical issues in therapy, discussed in connection with therapy process in Chapter 8 and ethical diversity in Chapter 10, are easily spelled out. Therapists ought neither impose their ethical convictions on clients nor claim complete value-freedom. Unethically eliminating or reducing client freedom can occur in several ways: therapists being judgmental, claiming (or implying) that clients can only improve by adopting their therapist's ethical position,[2] or addressing ethical issues in a biased manner.[3] In addition to abridging client freedom, those influence processes may result in harm to clients.

Violations of professional ethics also occur when therapists fail to provide clients with adequate information about the ethical character of therapy, violate the explicit or implicit terms of therapeutic contracts (especially when promises of ethical neutrality are made that cannot be kept), and lack the ethical competence to address ethical issues in therapy (Tjeltveit 1986). Indeed, argues Wallace, those who hold therapy "as a potentially adequate morality and *Weltanschauung*" are guilty of "medical imperialism in the worse sense of the word" (Wallace 1991: 113), a charge relevant to those who claim therapists not only do function as priests but should embrace that role.

A variety of positive proposals for handling general ethical issues in therapy has been set forth. These approaches to the ethical character of therapy overlap and often can (and perhaps should) complement one another. Indeed, overly simplistic "solutions" often cause as many problems as they solve. I will discuss, in turn, proposals that emphasize: principles and virtues of professional ethics, providing adequate information about therapy to other therapy stakeholders, dialogue among therapy stakeholders, developing and honoring agreements about therapy, and the nature of appropriate ethical influence. After stressing the practical wisdom necessary to balance those considerations in the contexts of concrete therapeutic relationships and in specific societies, I will address the need for greater awareness and more extensive education among therapy stakeholders. After reviewing some limits of professional ethics, I will revisit why – at a more fundamental level – professions and professionals affirm professional ethics, because answers at those theoretical and motivational levels can overcome some of the shortcomings of consensually developed, minimalist professional ethics, and also improve therapy's ethical character. I will address the final proposal in Chapter 12 – developing the best possible answers to the full range of ethical questions addressed in therapy.

Principles of professional ethics delineated by Meara, Schmidt, and Day (1996) include respect for autonomy, nonmaleficence, beneficence, justice, fidelity, and veracity. Therapists addressing ethical issues with clients should thus, for example, preserve and enhance client autonomy and seek to benefit them. This may mean working within a client's ethical framework (unless there are compelling reasons not to do so – like harm to the client or others) and matching clients with therapists who have similar ethical perspectives. When deep ethical differences divide therapist and client, referring clients to like-minded therapists may be in order (Odell and Stewart 1993). A therapist who despises Anna's religion, for example, should refer her to a therapist who can work effectively with her. And a religious therapist who despises a prospective client's ethical convictions should also refer. Making such referrals (matching therapist and clients on the dimension of ethical convictions) is consistent with the ethical principles of respect for client autonomy and beneficence.

Virtues befitting the role and calling of the professional therapist are also relevant, for instance, Doherty's (1995) caring, courage, and prudence. Therapists who genuinely and consistently care for clients will, for example, be more likely than therapists lacking that virtue to address ethical issues in therapy in a manner consistent with the highest standards of professional ethics.

Information about therapy, including information about its ethical character, generally benefits clients, therapists, and other therapy stakeholders. And so, in the absence of compelling reasons to withhold it, information is to be shared freely and explicitly. "It is essential," Bergin argues, "to be explicit about this valuational process [of therapy] because it always occurs, but often unwittingly" (Bergin 1991: 396–7). Feminist therapists (Feminist Therapy Institute 1990) and radical psychologists (D. R. Fox 1993), members of distinctive ethical communities, also stress providing explicit information. Therapy clients may particularly profit from information about the ethical dimensions of therapy, including potential ethical conflicts with therapists and the possibility of clients being converted to their therapists' ethical convictions. In addition, therapists and clients would benefit from clear information from third-party payers about the circumstances under which therapy will and will not be reimbursed and about the ethical convictions underlying the decisions of third-party payers. Unfortunately, some third-party payers, in accord with their business ethics, may withhold information as a "business secret."

The importance of a dialogue among therapy stakeholders about therapy goals and processes is often stressed. The ideal: therapists, clients, and third-party payers, all functioning as ethicists, conduct conversations from which clear expectations and goals develop. Such collaboration (Bergin 1991) can contribute to a positive therapeutic outcome, an outcome sought by clients and other stakeholders.

Whatever its merits in general, however, dialogue is sometimes contraindicated. When clients are psychologically vulnerable, a sustained dialogue about emotionally loaded ethical topics may harm clients, in violation of the principle of nonmaleficence. In that situation, a therapist appropriately forgoes dialogue (although dialogue respects autonomy) to benefit the client. Beneficence, respect for autonomy, and nonmaleficence thus need to be balanced.

Agreements about the nature and goals of therapy, which may arise out of such dialogues, play an important role in addressing ethical issues ethically. Clients clear about the nature of a therapeutic relationship can give informed consent to it (Braaten *et al.* 1993; Dyer and Bloch 1987; Faden and Beauchamp 1986; Lidz *et al.* 1984; Tjeltveit 1986). With clear information, therapists and clients can also give informed consent to a relationship with a third-party payer. And social contracts concerning therapy can be developed. Although, as noted in Chapter 8, completely informed consent is sometimes neither possible nor desirable (clients may be incapable of grasping information about therapy or giving consent, short-term therapy may permit little time to provide full information about therapy, and clients may be more concerned about feeling better than about the remote possibility of an ethical side-effect of therapy), when feasible and to the extent possible, clients should begin therapy agreeing with the therapist (and third-party payer, if possible) about its goals and nature. Once an agreement is established (and implicit therapeutic contracts, based on cultural and client understandings of therapy, can be assumed where explicit discussion does not occur), therapists should honor the agreement.

Therapists and clients can, in some circumstances, negotiate non-standard agreements about therapy. A therapist and client who want to address ethical issues primarily or exclusively can do so. But careful discussions need to precede such a change in roles. Unless the third-party payer concurs with the new agreement, reimbursement should not be sought. In accord with another relevant ethical principle, therapists are ethically bound to limit their practice to their areas of competence, to practices for which they have been trained. And so, a therapeutic relationship focusing on ethical issues, especially when unrelated to psychological problems, should occur only when the professional has demonstrated competence to address those issues.

Finally, the type of ethical influence which therapists exert on clients has received sustained attention, with some forms of influence viewed as ideal and others unethical. Therapists disagree about the proper scope of therapeutic influence. Proposed solutions parallel those discussed in Chapter 10 to address ethical diversity. Some argue for an ethical influence that is limited to a narrowly delineated role. Others emphasize therapist influence on ethical issues about which there is consensus. (Those, like Anna, who hold minority ethical views may not want therapists to alter those views, however.) Finally, others support ethical influence in accord with particular ethical communities, with an ethic for moral strangers, or both.

Therapists appropriately influence clients in a variety of ways. Doherty's (1995) eight-fold spectrum of ethical influence strategies, for instance, respects client autonomy, makes no claims to be ethically neutral, and requires therapist sensitivity and clinical acumen. As discussed in Chapter 8, therapists can address ethical issues without attempting to alter clients' ethical views – by consulting, teaching, acting as midwife, clarifying, engaging in dialogue, and correcting cognitive errors (Meehl 1981).

Minimizing therapist influence on the ethical dimensions of clients' lives is a proposal which many (e.g. Michels 1991) think that professional ethics requires. Therapists who want to limit their influence to the arena of their professional competence strive to minimize their influence on client ethical convictions. Although many advocates of this proposed solution recognize that complete value-freedom is impossible, they urge therapists to restrict their persuasive influence to ethical convictions consensually tied to the goal of mental health. However, the fact that any concept of mental health (including concepts of mental health consensually affirmed by most therapists) is tied to ethical assumptions – assumptions that some clients do not endorse – means therapists need to work very carefully with those holding minority ethical viewpoints. Indeed, legitimating therapist influence on mental health values may result in therapists inappropriately influencing clients to adopt a society's dominant values (tied to its understanding of "mental health"). The existence of ethical diversity thus places a burden of proof on those who attempt to influence ethical views not included in therapist–client contracts.

Ethical diversity also suggests the importance of another concept discussed in Chapter 10: professional ethics functions as an ethic for working with "moral strangers." Respect for others, minimizing ethical influence, and valuing the person's autonomy are essential. Because content-less, however, such an ethic provides no guidance to therapists who want to establish optimal therapeutic goals. Therapy with clients lacking clear goals thus tends to be shaped by implicit therapist or cultural ethical convictions. Or to drift aimlessly.

The content-full supplement to an ethics for moral strangers is this: therapists may influence client ethical convictions in accord with the ethical views of a particular ethical community. Doherty (1995) and Cushman (1995) do so, for instance. They encourage clients to consider their progressive political agendas, as do feminist therapists and therapists from particular religious communities. This, again, is appropriate only when client autonomy is preserved, clinical sensitivity employed, and informed consent obtained.

As noted above, I think that each proposal has merit in some ethical situations. To balance those, to know which is best with a given client at a given point in a therapeutic relationship in a given culture at a particular point in history, is sometimes extraordinarily difficult. No general answers, applicable always, are available. Therapists need, rather, the virtue of practical wisdom. Therapists possessing that kind of wisdom know how to think about a given situation and come up with the best possible ethical solution. They have a good sense of timing, tailor ethical influence to meet the specific needs of particular clients (Doherty 1995), and possess ethical expertise. Caplan argues that:

> expertise in both science and ethics appears to consist in part of knowing not only what theory or theories are defensible, or which moral traditions or paradigms are most defensible, but in how to pick and choose among theories and traditions to provide appropriate answers to specific problems or problematics. It should go without saying that expertise also consists of knowing when theory and tradition have nothing to offer.
>
> (Caplan 1989: 81)

Practical ethical wisdom can be developed, aided by education, dialogue with other therapists and with those who are ethically sensitive, and greater awareness. Therapists choosing to become wiser learn about their own ethical views, the views of clients, and the full range of ethical dimensions of therapy, including ethical assumptions that are implicit and that are tied to culture.

Awareness of the ethical character of psychotherapy is a prerequisite for most of the proposed solutions that I have just discussed. Parloff, Goldstein, and Iflund argued, for instance, that "the therapist must be aware of his [or her] own values" (Parloff et al. 1960: 300). To avoid imposing my values on others, I must know what my values are. Optimal awareness extends far beyond awareness of values, however. "Values" carries many connotations and many ethical dimensions of therapy are not well captured by that language. Awareness of those other ethical dimensions is important as well. To put the matter more simply, the responsible professional possesses a sophisticated ethical understanding.

Although some awareness comes through self-reflection (e.g. awareness of what an individual thinks and feels about specific issues, such as abortion), other forms of self-reflection require more concentrated educational efforts because the ethical character of therapy is by no means limited to values (understood as feelings or beliefs originated from within a person). Three levels of awareness regarding the ethical character of therapy are necessary: awareness of the therapist's own answers to ethical questions, awareness of the ethical character of therapy *qua* therapy (including its cultural location and a society's assumptions about therapy), and awareness of clients' answers to ethical questions. Pedersen and Marsella, for instance, argued that it is "the ethical responsibility of counselors and therapists to know their client's cultural values before delivering mental health services" (Pedersen and Marsella 1982: 492).

A full-fledged understanding of the ethical character of therapy is multi-dimensional: values need to be understood in psychological and ethical terms (as in the educational program implemented by Vachon and Agresti 1992), but also in terms of power. Awareness of professional ethics can be supplemented by theoretical ethics (including the full range of ethical theories), cultural ethics, social ethics, and clinical ethics. The ethical principles held by therapists and clients, and implied logically by therapy theories and procedures, can be addressed, along with the virtues possessed by, and aspired to, professionals and clients. Of particular importance is therapist awareness of the relationship between ideas about ideal psychological functioning (mental health) and other ethical ideals, because therapists who change the ethical convictions of clients often justify doing so by falsely assuming that psychological problems can only be overcome when clients adopt the ethical convictions of therapists. Knowledge of cultural, subcultural, and familial ethical convictions is often needed in order to understand clients and to work with them ethically and effectively. Finally, the vital *sources* – psychological, cultural, and intellectual – of the ethical dimensions of therapy stakeholders can be explored. To summarize, for therapists to be fully aware of the ethical character of psychotherapy, they need education about, and awareness of, the full range of ethical dimensions of therapy addressed in this book.

To optimally address the ethical character of psychotherapy requires an awareness of the shortcomings of professional ethics. Codes of professional ethics make important, but ultimately modest, contributions to therapists addressing the ethical character of psychotherapy. Although professional associations set up rules, procedures, and bureaucracies to ensure the actions of professionals conform to professional norms, "bureaucracy," as Taylor notes, "creates its own injustices and exclusions and...a great deal of suffering is not so much relieved as rendered invisible by it" (Taylor 1989: 398). Bersoff raised another critique: the current American Psychological Association (1992) ethics code is too concerned about the well-being of psychology. The code, he suggests, is "anachronistic, conservative, protective of its members, the product of political compromise, restricted in its scope, and too often unable to provide clear-cut solutions to ambiguous professional predicaments" (Bersoff 1994: 385). The minimalist code, he suggests, "builds an ethical floor but hardly urges us to reach for the ceiling." Reaching for the ceiling would surely entail what May urges: greater attention to professionals' "public obligation" (W. F. May 1984: 259).

Finally, codes of ethics usually include neither psychological nor theoretical rationales for individuals embracing them, or embracing any other ethical ideal. "Professional ethics codes cannot," Kitchener (1996a: 369) notes, "act as a conscience." And others argue that "because the Ethics Code does not argue or cite evidence but rather simply asserts, it provides no acceptable warrant for its assertions" (O'Donohue and Mangold 1996: 377). Codes of professional ethics are thus, to borrow language from Chapter 10, too thin, too content-less to nourish professionals. To sustain psychotherapy, professionals need a thicker ethical gruel, need reasons as professionals and as individuals to engage in the ethical actions and the reflection that are integral to the professional psychotherapist.

Why professional ethics?

In the absence of compelling reasons – compelling psychological reasons and compelling intellectual reasons – psychotherapists in the future may no longer affirm a profession's ethical standards. Those standards face a variety of severe challenges: skeptical questioning about "self-serving" professionals, ethical relativism (including relativistic versions of multi-culturalism and skeptical postmodernism), a retreat to the "objectivity" of science, and businesses that treat psychotherapists as mere "providers" of the business commodity labeled psychotherapy. Identifying why professions and professionals endorse professional ethical principles is thus vitally important.

Skeptics argue that professionals endorse minimal standards of professional ethics for purely pragmatic reasons: to obtain prestige, payment, and autonomy for professionals. Critics from within a profession sometimes criticize codes as well. The American Psychological Association's (1992) code, for example, has been criticized for its cautiousness (Bersoff 1994), for being based "on the unvalidated opinions and beliefs of well-intentioned colleagues with severely restricted vision" (Koocher 1994: 361), and for failing to articulate the ethical grounds on which it is based (O'Donohue and Mangold 1996). Indeed, O'Donohue and Mangold assert that the code "provides no acceptable warrant for its assertions. Epistemologically its acceptance relies upon an authoritarian appeal (Because the APA says so!) rather than upon an epistemology that recognizes the importance of defending one's claims by arguments" (ibid.: 377).

The existence of carefully delineated, lawyer-vetted rules and procedures for professional ethics committees (e.g. Ethics Committee 1996) may protect psychologists (and professional associations like the APA) from unwarranted lawsuits, ensure procedural justice for those accused of ethical violations, and sanction professionals who are found guilty of violating an ethics code. But because few people give their allegiance to bureaucracies, rules, and procedures, I suspect codes and committees inspire many psychologists to practice in a manner best characterized, not as optimally ethical, but as cautious and self-protective.

The ethical minimalism endorsed by most codes of professional ethics (and much contemporary philosophy) produces another problem. Because "we have no theory of the common good," May argues, "professionals feel relatively free to direct...power to their own ends" (W. F. May 1984: 259).

But developing an ethics code that aims for the ethical ceiling rather than towards establishing a minimally acceptable ethical floor (Bersoff 1994) is made very difficult by the neo-Nietzschean skeptical postmodernist attack on beneficence, by the deep ethical differences that divide many societies, and by other developments, including individualism and the assumption that human behavior is motivated selfishly (Wallach and Wallach 1983). In the absence of agreement about ethical theory in a society, it is profoundly difficult to follow the recommendation that "the ethical grounds of the code be explicated and defended" (O'Donohue and Mangold 1996: 376).

The absence of a compelling intellectual rationale for a profession's code of ethics is a major problem. If, as I have argued, professionalism – tied inextricably to beneficence and other ethical principles – is integral to what it means to be a psychotherapist, but the professions of psychotherapy can give no compelling reasons for affirming their ethical core, those professions are incoherent.

Given ethical diversity and the aspiration that therapy should be a universal, cross-culturally valid type of helping relationship, codes of professional ethics are necessarily built on consensus. A minimalist ethics results, one asking that therapists treat "moral strangers" justly and with respect. Although such consensual standards are important, most people do not live by ethical standards so minimal, so thin. In fact, many (most?) psychotherapists who practice ethically draw upon deeper ethical sources – deeper psychological sources and deeper intellectual sources. And so, while mandating a common core of minimal standards, professional ethics should endorse diversity regarding ethical issues falling outside the consensus, including such key issues as the reasons therapists endorse professional ethical standards, the nature of the common good, and ideal human functioning.

If professional codes of conduct cannot, as Kitchener rightly avers, function "as a conscience" for the psychotherapist, what will? "Ultimately," she notes, "the well-being of those with whom psychologists work will depend on how seriously psychologists take their ethical responsibility to treat others with care" (Kitchener 1996a: 369). Because consensual ethical standards are inadequate, professionals need to turn to deeper levels of ethics. Professionals need to draw upon local ethical communities, upon particular sets of ethical convictions that motivate and provide intellectual stimulation to therapists, that motivate them to practice as ethically as possible. They need to turn, that is, to why individual professionals and particular ethical communities affirm professional ethics and other types of ethical principles and virtues.

Manifold reasons lead communities (including professions) to take seriously ethical principles and virtues, including sources deeply interwoven into the fabric of Western thought (Taylor 1989) and in the thought of other cultures. But the curious reluctance to acknowledge and articulate moral sources in the West (Taylor 1989) and the failure of rational procedures to justify ethical claims (MacIntyre 1984) make it difficult to reflect on and articulate ethical sources. Taylor observed that benevolence has continued to be important in the West, although Westerners find it difficult to articulate why it should be so. But he asks an important question, vitally important for undergirding the ethical core of the professions: "What can sustain this continuing drive?" (Taylor 1989: 398).

Individual therapists practice ethically for a variety of reasons, including some self-serving reasons: social pressure, legal consequences, public relations, and enlightened self-interest. But there are other reasons, intellectual reasons and psychological reasons. Many psychotherapists can articulate the reasons for their convictions about what is good, right, and virtuous, reasons not derived entirely from science and reason, reasons not shared by everyone (or even the majority) within a society or a profession. Those therapists affirm professional ethics for particular ethical reasons. Other therapists, wanting better ethical answers, unclear of their ethical convictions, or both, seek out ethical dialogue and greater ethical articulacy.

Psychological reasons, growing out of an individual's moral development, cognitions, learning history, motivation, intuitions, emotions (e.g. caring), and character traits (virtues), play a role in therapists practicing ethically. Ethical action stems from ethical persons. Because professionals sometimes act in ways that do not benefit themselves, the source of their beneficence must involve powerful psychological forces. As Taylor notes, "high standards need strong sources" (Taylor 1989: 516). Professionals act to benefit others, not simply for selfish reasons but because they genuinely believe it good and right so to do, because they draw on fertile ethical sources.

I will revisit those deeper, more fundamental sources of the professional's ethical convictions and behaviors in Chapter 12. Individual (and community) sources – both intellectual and psychological – can give rise to the professional ethics that characterizes the professions conducting psychotherapy.

12

Shaping the ethical character of psychotherapy
Inevitable choices, better choices

The ethical character of psychotherapy – largely implicit, created and sustained by myriad cultural, intellectual, and practical threads that are woven into the fabric of the sciences and the professions, into the economic structures of therapy, and into contemporary images of therapy – is, in part, beyond the control of therapists, clients, third-party payers, and other therapy stakeholders. But only in part.

In this chapter, I want to address how therapy stakeholders can make better choices that influence the ethical dimensions of therapy. I want, that is, to address how therapists and other stakeholders can shape the ethical character of therapy, can make the inevitable ethical choices therapy entails, can make better choices.

Choosing in accord with professional ethics

Psychotherapists who choose to become professionals choose to limit the ethical character of the psychotherapy they provide. They limit therapy within bounds set by professional ethical standards, and constrain themselves ethically in ways other therapy stakeholders need not.

Professional ethics restricts psychotherapists to certain forms of therapy process and (to a lesser extent) to a certain range of therapy goals. The ethical principle of beneficence shapes the ethical character of therapy in a crucial manner: therapy goals should, in some way, benefit clients and/or a society, and not the therapist alone. Because clients and societies can benefit from therapy in many ways, and alternative ethical positions define "benefit" in different ways, beneficence permits ample ethical freedom to therapists. Beneficence does, however, place some limits on the goals which therapists legitimately pursue.

Principles of professional ethics constrain therapy *processes* by shaping the nature and quality of therapists' interactions with clients. Therapists are to treat clients with respect, to uphold and enhance client autonomy, to maintain confidentiality, to provide services only when competent to do so, to provide therapy in accord with the therapeutic contract, not to exploit clients sexually, and so forth. Codes of professional ethics thus serve as a form of ethics for moral strangers (Engelhardt 1991), one which professionals, by virtue of being professionals, agree to endorse.

Codes of professional ethics provide crucial, but ultimately modest, restraints on therapists' ethical choices. They do not provide reasons for therapists to affirm and live by professional ethical ideals. Lacking an intellectual and psychological rationale to affirm professional ethics, some professionals rely simply on professional consensus and enlightened self-interest. Consensus and self-interest are often insufficient, however, to motivate therapists to reach the highest ethical levels of practice. Indeed, codes tend to establish an ethical minimum, rather than helping therapists to identify, and practice in accord with, the highest possible ethical standards (Bersoff 1994). Professional codes of ethics are, as noted in Chapter 11, too thin, too intellectually and psychologically restrained, and too general to equip therapists to address the full range of ethical issues raised in therapy. Finally, professional ethics bind therapists, but not the other partners in therapeutic endeavors, the clients and the silent partners (third-party payers, taxpayers, corporations, pensioners, and others) for whom psychotherapy is important. And so professional ethics makes but a modest contribution to vigorous efforts to identify the best therapy values, specify ideal goals for clients, and to articulate the optimal role of psychotherapy in a society.

The challenge of improvement

In light of the limits of professional ethics and the reality of an ethical diversity that makes it difficult, if not impossible, to achieve substantive, content-full ethical consensus, how can the ethical character of therapy be shaped?

Conservative voices may argue there is no need to do so: "The ethical character of psychotherapy is just fine, thank you." They argue for the goodness of therapy's existing values, the impossibility of improvement, or both.

As we have seen, however, critics pose penetrating questions about the ways in which many therapists currently address therapy's ethical dimensions. In considering therapy's influence on society, for instance, Bellah, Madsen, Sullivan, Swidler, and Tipton (1985) wonder, for instance, whether "psychological sophistication has not been bought at the price of moral impoverishment" (Bellah et al. 1985: 139). They and others call for ethical improvement. They contend that therapists who address ethical issues (i.e. all therapists) can become better ethicists. And that all therapy stakeholders can choose better, richer ethical perspectives – to the benefit of therapy clients and society.

Can we make ethical progress?

"No!" assert skeptical postmodernists and advocates of logical positivist ethical theory, curious allies in opposition to careful ethical reflection. They echo what was once commonly accepted wisdom among therapists: the goal is psychotherapy that is value-free, objective, ethically neutral. When ethics needs to be involved at all, therapists were taught they ought to stick to professional codes of ethics, or to their society's consensual values. Or, if unable to do that fully, to minimize their influence on client ethical convictions.

But a growing number of voices is challenging that received wisdom, arguing that it would be good for therapists and other stakeholders to think carefully about the ethical character of therapy and to improve the ethical character of therapy. The challenge, asserts Doherty, is "to take a step beyond critique into reenvisioning psychotherapy as a moral enterprise" (Doherty 1995: 14). The issue, finally, is not whether we can conduct value-free therapy. We cannot. The issue is identifying those values, those ethical convictions, best included in particular therapy sessions and in therapy sessions in general. Beutler, for example, suggested that we may need to question "whether there are some values that may be more important for a therapist to accept than others" (Beutler 1978: 63). Drane suggested that "one has to be only a moderate rationalist" to believe that psychiatry's influence on "the ethical quality of human life…would be improved by a more thoughtful, studious, prudent, and methodical approach" (Drane 1991: 58). Likewise, Smith argued that psychologists "can do much better than is usual for us by trying…to emphasize informed, rational, disinterested, benevolent decision making" (M. B. Smith 1990: 533). And philosopher of science Laudan noted, "I suspect we all believe that some cognitive ends are preferable to others" (Laudan 1987: 29).

Taylor (1989) argues for the appropriateness of employing the "best account" we can develop. Developing a best account, he argues, requires practical reasoning. Rather than identifying some rational method by which we allegedly arrive at "certain" ethical conclusions, we compare a proposed new answer with our existing answer (or confusion). We accept the new ethical idea only if better than our existing idea. Such reasoning, Taylor argues, "aims to establish, not that some position is correct absolutely, but rather that some position is superior to some other" (Taylor 1989: 72).

Those authors share the courage to assert that one ethical position is better than another, but without claiming that that ethical position is "certain," "indubitable," "infallible," "self-evident," "absolute," or "perfect." They make ethical assertions without descending into authoritarianism. "There is a big difference," notes Prilleltensky (1997: 518), "between searching for the best moral option under a particular set of circumstances and the pursuit of a dogmatic set of rules." Similarly, we can arrive at "valid substantive ethical insights, even if they are never final or certain" (Richardson and Woolfolk 1994: 222).

In this chapter I want to explore how we can develop better ethical accounts of the full range of ethical issues in therapy. Given the ethical assumptions of many modernists (MacIntyre 1984), identifying therapy *processes* that are ethically better than others is less controversial than identifying better therapy *outcomes*. Even the logical positivist may agree that a therapy technique whose efficacy is empirically supported is better (more ethically justified) than a technique that empirical evidence suggests is ineffective or harmful. Likewise, even skeptical postmodernists might think that some forms of therapy are superior to others. For example, forms of therapy conducted by therapists who do not delude themselves (are unflinchingly honest) about their ethical ideals and their power over clients, and that promote the emancipation of clients, may be considered superior to therapy conducted by therapists who deny ethically influencing clients but, in fact, impose on clients their moral views.

Better ethical accounts of the *goals* or *outcomes* of therapy can also, I believe, be developed. For example, suppose a given therapy case has four possible outcomes: the client benefits but society is harmed, society benefits but the client is harmed, both the client and society are harmed, and both the client and society benefit. The final alternative is, I think, clearly best. A central purpose of therapy is to benefit clients. And a wide range of ethical theories and codes of professional ethics argue for the goodness of advancing the general welfare (cf. Garrison 1997; Gerber 1992; Sarason 1993). As I have documented above, many therapists and others are now arguing for forms of therapy that accomplish both aims. Mahoney, for instance, states: "I believe that the helping professions must address issues that link our individual lives and our collective responsibilities" (Mahoney 1991: 4). On those ethical accounts, then, some therapy outcomes are better than others.

Disputes about the proper balance in therapy of client and societal well-being will, I suspect, be with us always. As will other ethical controversies, such as the goodness of other therapy goals and the optimal role of therapy in a society. But my claim is not that we can solve *all* ethical problems (and definitely not that we can solve them with full rational certainty). Rather, my claim is that, when addressing the ethical character of psychotherapy, including therapy goals, we can *sometimes* develop *better* ethical answers. And so we should try.

Making better choices about the ethical character of psychotherapy

Some approaches to addressing ethical issues will, I believe, help therapy stakeholders make better choices about the ethical character of therapy, choices that undergird therapists' commitments to professional ethics, that shed light on the qualities of the ideal therapist–client relationship, and that provide insight into good (or better) therapy goals. These approaches may also lead to the wisdom that London suggests therapists should seek: "Suppose [therapists] make a virtue of necessity and ask themselves how, since their technical capacities imply a moral role anyway, they could exercise that role most wisely" (London 1986: 152–3). In this concluding section, I set forth, with broad brush, some ways I think therapists (and other therapy stakeholders) can exercise that ethical role wisely.

Ethical acuity

Therapy stakeholders who see with clarity ethical issues relevant to psychotherapy, and who see with clarity viable ethical alternatives, will tend to make ethical choices that are better than those whose ethical vision is occluded or distorted. Unless a person perceives with accuracy key ethical dimensions of a situation, unless a person faced with an ethical decision "'sizes up,' or construes ethically salient features of a situation" (Punzo 1996: 12), he or she will not make optimal ethical decisions. And without ethical acuity, people will not develop better ethical accounts of therapy.

People vary in their sensitivity to ethical issues and to the consequences of alternative actions (Rest 1984). Education can produce positive changes in that and other ethical skills (Rest 1988). And so people can improve their clarity of ethical vision.

Ethical acuity can improve, I believe, when people approach ethical issues in a balanced way, increase their knowledge of ethical alternatives, develop their ability to think ethically, and pursue the other suggestions I make in the remainder of this chapter. That enhanced ethical perceptiveness will, in turn, contribute to their ability to carry out those suggestions. And that, in turn, will contribute to improved ethical decisions about the ethical character of therapy.

Balance

Ethical approaches that balance, or hold in tension, more than one approach to the ethical character of therapy are better than those that oversimplify. They are better, for example, than ethical perspectives that promise easy answers or espouse one principle or ideal as *the* solution to *all* ethical problems. Although optimal ethical solutions to particular problems are sometimes simple, adequate ethical solutions to the full range of ethical issues that arise in therapy in general should draw upon a variety of (often complementary) ideals (Prilleltensky 1997), ideals that are, in concert, complex and tension-filled. Therapy stakeholders need to seek, and seek again, an optimal balance among approaches to ethical questions, avoiding answers that are in some way unbalanced.

When one ethical ideal acquires undue weight, unbalanced therapy outcomes can result. For example, some therapists focus solely on individual well-being and so pathologize those who devote time and energy to causes outside themselves. Doherty (1995) tells of a social activist who was repeatedly informed by his (liberal!) friends and therapists that "his social activism stems from unfinished personal business. When he takes care of his personal business, so the line goes, he will stop acting out his missionary zeal in the world" (Doherty 1995: 99). The good of resolved personal issues was not balanced by a concern for justice and societal well-being. Doherty suggests an alternative: therapy goals that respect (and even encourage) social activism along with the goal of improved psychological functioning. A balance of concern for society and individual well-being, he asserts, is a better way to shape the ethical character of therapy than traditional US individualism.

Valid claims can be made, Taylor (1989) notes, for a diversity of goods. The central goods that can be discovered through the self – disengaged reason functioning as ethical source (i.e. the ethical source upon which many scientists draw), the creative imagination that looks within the self for ethical inspiration, and the original theistic alternative (coming into a relationship with God through looking within)[1] – all shape the modern identity. In considering these and other ethical positions, he argues that:

> the trouble with most of the views that I consider inadequate, and that I want to define mine in contrast to here, is that their sympathies are too narrow. They find their way through the dilemmas of modernity by invalidating some of the crucial goods in contest....Not only are these one-sided views invalid, but many of them are not and cannot be fully, seriously, and unambivalently held by those who propound them.
>
> (Taylor 1989: 503)

Outlooks claiming that we can avoid making difficult ethical decisions (e.g. decisions "between various kinds of spiritual lobotomy and self-inflicted wounds") are, Taylor argues, "based on selective blindness" (ibid.: 520).

Tension can, and perhaps should, exist among the ethical ideals to be balanced. Taylor notes that although the various goods for which valid claims can be made "may be in conflict...they don't refute each other" (ibid.: 502). Indeed, he argues that "a complex interplay arises in which each can be at some moment strengthened by the weakness exposed in the others" (ibid.: 413). And L. Sass notes that Heidegger's hermeneutic approach represents a complex balancing of, or, perhaps better, a holding in tension of, concern for the individual self and the community: "What he prescribes is neither a straightforward merging with community, tradition, or nature nor a romantic-heroic expression of separateness and individuality" (L. A. Sass 1988: 260).

Another sort of balancing is also needed, I think, to answer well the question of how therapists optimally address the ethical character of therapy. Careful readers may have noticed that I alternately value therapists who minimize their ethical influence on clients, therapists who limit their ethical influence to the professional consensus about mental health values (values that therapists appropriately influence), and therapists who conduct therapy in concord with particular ethical communities (they consciously exert ethical influence on clients, an ethical influence that diverges from the societal or professional consensus but is consistent with the explicitly stated wishes of clients who want a form of recovery from psychological problems that is in harmony with the client's ethical ideals). Those three alternatives are, if not in conflict, at least in considerable tension with one another. I would prefer to think that my partial affirmation of each represents, not muddleheadedness, but a legitimate valuing of partial solutions to therapist influence on client values. Any of those alternatives may be most appropriate in a given situation, and all, I think, should be kept in tension when formulating the ideal role of therapy in a given society. I also hold in tension the search for better answers (*contra* relativism) and the pragmatic realization that, for the foreseeable future, deeply divergent ethical affirmations will most likely characterize almost all societies.

Balanced ethical choices also involve more than one level of discourse about ethical issues. Kurtines, Alvarez, and Azmitia (1990) argue that debates are most likely to be productive when participants are free to "move between levels of discourse, including theoretical, practical, and metatheoretical levels" (Kurtines *et al.* 1990: 294). Doherty (1995), for example, focuses more on the practical level, the level of concrete therapy sessions. This book, by contrast, emphasizes theoretical and metatheoretical issues. Those seeking the best possible ethical account of the ethical character of therapy will address all three levels. They will also take into account what Sadler and Hulgus describe as "three core aspects of the clinical encounter: problems of knowledge, ethics, and pragmatics" (Sadler and Hulgus 1992: 1315).

Finally, a sole focus on reason, including reasoning about ethical matters, can produce unbalanced, less-than-ideal ethical results. As Taylor (1989) notes, several strands of Western thought have argued that reason can be destructive, that "rational hegemony, rational control, may stifle, desiccate, repress us" (Taylor 1989: 116). And so "we stand in need of liberation" from reason. I concur with (moderate versions of) those criticisms and so I think a strictly philosophical approach is inadequate. The philosophical needs to be joined with the psychological, including the emotional. On the other hand, some people, those whose lives are controlled, not by reason, but by unchecked emotions may exhibit another kind of imbalance: emotion uncontrolled by appropriate rational self-control. Neither "being in touch with my feelings" nor "reason alone" is optimal. The best approach balances philosophical reflection with a psychology that is rich and nuanced.

An ethical character for therapy that is intellectually, psychologically, and culturally rich and nuanced

The best ethical choices are made by people who draw upon rich and nuanced ethical sources. This means, I believe, sophisticated accounts that combine, and do justice to, psychological, philosophical, and cultural complexities. Scientists devoted to the ideal of simplicity and to the tradition of the principle of parsimony may find heretical my claim that the complex is to be preferred to the simple when addressing the ethical character of therapy. But Occam's Razor, despite its benefits for science, serves the ethicist poorly, and especially therapists functioning as ethicists. Mental health, for example, is best understood as a mixed medical/psychological/ethical concept (cf. my argument in Chapter 7).

I believe that simplistic understandings produce neither adequate understandings of, nor optimal choices regarding, the ethical character of therapy. Throughout the book I have argued against simplistic intellectual understandings of ethics. Simplistic psychologies are to be avoided as well. For example, psychologies that draw upon neither psychological research nor the experience of clinicians, that ignore both science and clinical expertise, are unlikely to produce best accounts of therapy's ethical character. Some forms of the philosophy of liberal individualism, for instance, understand human beings to be what some label "absolutely free" selves (Bellah et al. 1985: 139). That simplistic psychology leads, they argue, "to the notion of an absolutely empty relationship. And this empty relationship cannot possibly sustain the richness and continuity that the therapeutically inclined themselves most want, just as they want not empty but rich and coherent selves" (ibid.: 139).

Sufficiently rich understandings of human beings do not assume that the human will alone can produce ethical behavior (Drane 1994). Rather, we need a multi-faceted psychology. Fortunately, psychologists in the post-Kohlbergian era (e.g. Kurtines and Gewirtz 1991, 1995) understand moral development and ethical decisions in increasingly complex psychological terms. J. R. Rest, for example, identified four components involved in ethical behavior: individuals "interpret the situation in terms of how one's actions affect the welfare of others," "formulate what a moral course of action would be," "select among competing value outcomes of ideals," and "execute and implement what one intends to do" (Rest 1984: 20). Virtue ethicists also use a complex, multi-faceted psychology, including human motivation, emotions, community, and ethical character (Meara et al. 1996). Ethical habits are emphasized as well. This is important because many of the deepest ethical convictions held by therapists are ingrained in their patterns of behavior. As Birch and Rasmussen point out, much practical moral reasoning is habitual, involving neither agonizing moral dilemmas between conflicting ethical ideals nor philosophical explorations of competing ethical theories. "Indeed, 'reasoning' isn't the most precise term," they note, "for what is frequently a reflexive exercise done without conscious deliberation. We don't consciously consider whether or not to hold up the clerk and empty the cash register as we pick up a gallon of milk at the store" (Birch and Rasmussen 1989: 102). Because much of the ethical character of therapy is of that mundane, unselfconscious psychological character, we need a psychology that accounts for the habitual character of therapy's ethical dimensions, along with accounting for the ethical choices therapy stakeholders make consciously.

Taylor describes some other ways in which many ethical perspectives avoid psychological complexity. Important ethical consequences follow, he argues, when we deny the complexity of what we can learn when we explore what resonates with our personal experience. "Proponents of disengaged reason or of subjective fulfilment," he observes:

> embrace those consequences gladly. There are no moral sources there to explore. Root-and-branch critics of modernity hanker after the older public orders, and they assimilate personally indexed visions to mere subjectivism. Stern moralists, too, want to contain this murky area of the personal, and tend as well to block together all its manifestations, whether subjectivist or exploratory. Morality is held to be distinct from all this, independent of it, and imperiously binding.
>
> (Taylor 1989: 512)

Strictly separating the ethical from the psychological, Taylor argues, is an error committed by some philosophers and theologians. Habermas and Hare, for instance, claim that the correct rational procedure will produce ethical knowledge. And some theologians claim we need not consult human experience because God provides us with fully satisfactory ethical knowledge. Taylor argues, however, that "a study of the modern identity ought to make one dissatisfied" with positions that claim we can ignore the psychological when we address ethical questions (ibid.: 512–13).

For Taylor, understanding the cultural and historical location of the rich psychological-philosophical "modern identity" is essential. He thus joins many others (e.g. Bellah et al. 1991; Cushman 1992, 1995; Doherty 1995) in arguing that a sophisticated understanding of culture and its role is required to develop a best account of individuals, of the ethical character of any particular therapeutic relationship, and of the ethical character of psychotherapy in general. Robinson (Robinson 1997: 675), for instance, discusses the importance of therapists recognizing the "essentially civic nature" of our humanity.

Increasing awareness of the importance of therapist sensitivity to clients from other cultures (e.g. Abe-Kim and Takeuchi 1996; Marsella and White 1982; Minsel et al. 1991; Rodis and Strehorn 1997; S. H. Schwartz 1994), including the religious and spiritual dimensions of culture (e.g. Browning 1987; Kirschner 1996; W. R. Miller (forthcoming); Richards and Bergin 1997), is, I think, leading most therapists to a more nuanced, a better, understanding of the role of culture in therapy. This makes possible better ethical accounts of therapy. And better ethical choices.

We can, however, be aware of the ethical character of other cultures but not of the ethical character of our own culture. This may be especially true of Western therapists, whose cultural contexts systematically disguise (and occasionally deny) the ethical character of therapy (see Chapters 6 and 7). And, as Browning pointed out, when practitioners are unaware of the cultural context in which they practice, "there is likely to be an exaggeration of the technical and scientific aspects of care and a blindness to" the ethical dimensions of "cultural assumptions, symbols and goals" (Browning 1976: 71). Guignon describes one way (articulated by Heidegger) in which therapists' own cultures are relevant to their ethical understanding:

> As we become initiated into the practices of our community, we soak up the tacit sense of what is important that circulates in our world. This "attunement" to shared commitments and ideals cannot be regarded simply as a matter of having certain "life-style options" on hand for our choice. For these understandings and normative commitments are definitive for the kinds of people we are. They provide us with the possibilities of assessment and aspiration that first give us an orientation toward our own lives and a window onto the world. Given that we have become the kind of people we are – people who, for example, care about children and believe in justice – there is now no way to drop these commitments without ceasing to be who we are.
>
> (Guignon 1993: 233)

The cultural character of contemporary therapy has, fortunately, been receiving increasing attention (e.g. Cushman 1995; Fancher 1995; Woolfolk 1998). Rich and nuanced understandings of culture, and of therapy, result.

Ethical alternatives

To develop better ethical accounts, for the sake of understanding and making decisions about the ethical character of psychotherapy, therapy stakeholders can explore alternative ethical approaches, to see which resonate with their own experience (Taylor 1989), to see which seem most rationally defensible, to decide which is best. Such an exploration seems especially important for psychotherapists, who are responsible for upholding professional ethical standards, to benefit others and not simply themselves. But a mere sense of obligation to those professional standards or guilt for failing to uphold them is not enough. As Taylor points out, "there is something morally corrupting, even dangerous, in sustaining the demand simply on the feeling of undischarged obligation, on guilt, or its obverse, self-satisfaction" (Taylor 1989: 516).

A wide range of ethical alternatives exists. Traditional alternatives, like classic liberal individualism and religious ethical perspectives, exist as live intellectual options alongside more recent proposals, like those bridging analytic and continental philosophical traditions and those taking seriously hermeneutic perspectives. The field of ethics in general and the narrower (but richly interdisciplinary) field of bioethics provide many resources for ethical reflection. This includes the full range of types of ethics discussed in Chapters 2 and 4 and elsewhere in this book – clinical (and applied) ethics, cultural ethics, social ethics, theoretical ethics, and virtue ethics.

I will set forth, without extensive discussion, a non-exhaustive set of four-teen alternatives, arranged in alphabetical order. I order them in that way, not to evade responsibility for categorizing them, but to emphasize the breadth of alternatives supported by intelligent, thoughtful advocates and because these ethical alternatives can be categorized in a variety of ways, all controversial. Various theorists use the same label for varying approaches, distinguish between ethical alternatives in diverse ways, and combine approaches that others differentiate. Finally, many subtypes of each ethical alternative could be set forth, especially within the hermeneutic, rational, and religious alternatives.

Casuistry, a form of clinical ethics (see Chapter 2), emphasizes the specific circumstances of a situation along with general ethical principles when making ethical decisions (Jonsen 1995). Practical, not metatheoretical, considerations are emphasized.

Classic liberal individualism emphasizes the individual decision-maker and the ideals of autonomy, justice (e.g. Rawls 1971), and procedural ethical rules. M. A. Hall (1997) contrasts it with communitarianism and MacIntyre (1984) with virtue ethics. Classical liberal individualism is relevant to ethical issues having to do with therapy process, but because it does not address the goodness of ends (MacIntyre 1984), it contributes little to (indeed, impedes) ethical discussions about therapy goals. This ethical tradi-tion has, I suspect, shaped contemporary psychotherapy more profoundly than any other. And so therapists find it difficult to engage in ethical discus-sions about therapy goals. Furthermore, its individualistic emphasis and the fact that some of its advocates deny that it is culturally-situated create what has been described as "a powerful cultural fiction that we not only can, but must, make up our deepest beliefs in the isolation of our private selves" (Bellah et al. 1985: 65).

Communitarians (Bell 1993; Etzioni 1993, 1995, 1997, 1998; Richardson and Fowers 1997) suggest that problematic ethical consequences follow from classic liberal individualism. They argue not only that we can consider the best ends for a given society, but that we should do so.

Critical psychologists engage in a more fundamental critique of psychology's ethical *status quo* (Braybrooke 1987; Fox and Prilleltensky 1997; Haan *et al.* 1985; Keat 1981; Richardson and Woolfolk 1994; E. V. Sullivan 1984). Often drawing upon Habermas and the Frankfurt School, critical psychologists argue that we should employ particular normative perspectives, including ideas about "the way a society should be, the way it should function, and the way it should be transformed" (Browning 1987: 124). They argue that allegedly "neutral and scientific social science is impossible and will inevitably be captured by the dominant ideologies of a particular culture" (ibid.: 124). Critical perspectives, like the other ethical alternatives I am discussing in this section, can be combined with other ethical approaches. Kurtines, Alvarez, and Azmitia (1990), for instance, argue for a "critical co-constructivist" approach. And Prilleltensky (1997) advocates an "emancipatory communitarianism" that combines a communitarian approach with the emphasis on autonomy found in classical liberalism and in critical psychology.

Feminist ethicists (Brown and Ballou 1994; Card 1991; Fox-Genovese 1991; Gartrell 1994; Lerman and Porter 1990; Morawski 1994; Rodis and Strehorn 1997; Sherwin 1992) argue that we best understand the ethical character of therapy from the perspective of feminism and feminist ethics.

Hermeneutic perspectives stress the inescapably ethical character of life, psychology, and psychotherapy (Browning 1987; Fowers 1993; Messer *et al.* 1988; Packer 1985a, 1985b; Richardson 1997; Spence 1982). Drawing upon continental philosophy (especially on the work of Gadamer, Heidegger, Ricoeur, and Habermas), hermeneuticists do not strive for explanations in science or ethics that take the form of "general laws" (Richardson and Woolfolk 1994: 212) or nomological explanations. They strive instead to "interpret the meaning" of human action, including moral action. Hermeneutic approaches can, Martin and Thompson (1997) assert, be combined with a neo-realist philosophy of science to create a psychology that includes, but expands upon, traditional empirical methodologies.

Narrative is stressed by hermeneutic ethicists and others (e.g. Brody 1994; Guignon 1993; MacIntyre 1984; Richardson and Woolfolk 1994; L. A. Sass 1988; Taylor 1989; Vitz 1990). They assert that we understand what is good, right, and/or virtuous through stories. And stories (including those told by therapists and clients) can have, and perhaps always have, an ethical dimension.

Naturalistic ethics (also known as sociobiological and evolutionary ethics) blends a particular set of epistemological, metaphysical, and ethical convictions (a "moral vision" – Engelhardt and Wildes 1994: 142) with scientific methods and theories to understand ethical issues and make ethical choices (e.g. Brink 1989; Flanagan 1996; Rottschaefer and Martinsen 1990; Ruse 1986; Vogeltanz and Plaud 1992; Wright 1994). The promise is to employ science and reason to ground ethics on the firm basis of nature (generally understood in terms of materialistic metaphysics). Human survival and other goods contend for the role of ultimate good, the end toward which evolution moves organisms.

Pragmatic approaches to ethics (R. A. Putnam 1991) emphasize practical consequences. Strenger and Omer assert, for example, that "to be right a construct must work," albeit work in ways that meet certain tests of coherence (Strenger and Omer 1992: 126). The ethical and metaphysical assumptions underlying pragmatic judgments (Tillich 1959; Richardson and Fowers 1994) are generally downplayed in favor of experience (R. A. Putnam 1991). A variety of ethical assumptions are held by pragmatists, ranging from the *de facto* relativism of Rorty[2] to the more substantively ethical position of William James, whose pragmatism stressed the "moral fruitfulness" of ethical alternatives (Browning 1991a: 26).

Radical psychologists (D. R. Fox 1993) argue that mainstream psychologists who adopt liberal values are coopted by an unjust *status quo*. The values of the left ought instead be adopted. Psychology's goals should be substantive rather than procedural justice and a concern for the general welfare (not just the best interest of individuals). And psychologists should be willing to make ethical claims about the goodness of particular societal ends.

Rational ethics – ethics based on reason – continues to have vigorous, thoughtful advocates (e.g. Donagan 1977; Gert 1975, 1988). Indeed, most theoretical ethics emphasizes reason to some extent. Although claims to be able to derive certain ethical knowledge through reason are less common than before, moderate rationalists (Drane 1991) still employ reason and rational dialogue in ethical discourse that has more modest aspirations than those purportedly held by champions of the Enlightenment Project (MacIntyre 1984). Indeed, Taylor (1989) argues that employing reason to address ethical issues is a major ethical source contributing to the modern identity. Reason can, of course, be combined with other ethical alternatives. Audi (1997), for instance, integrates naturalistic and rationalistic elements.

Religious ethical perspectives, varying widely in style and content, link ethics to diverse spiritual traditions and experiences. As noted elsewhere in this book, religious and spiritual perspectives, including Buddhist, Christian, Hindu, Jewish, Muslim, and others, remain live sources of ethical convictions and action for many therapists, clients, and other stakeholders. People of faith range from the anti-intellectual to the scholarly (Browning 1987; Jones and Butman 1991; Taylor 1989). Although some people are, as a matter of faith, dogmatically anti-religious,[3] Taylor notes that "in the actual life of modern culture," ethical alternatives such as "the clear vision of scientific reason, the Rousseauian or Romantic inner impulse of nature, the Kantian good will," and so forth, "have not been treated as alternatives to or seen as incompatible with religious faith" (Browning 1987: 412).

Romanticism offers its own set of ethical visions, emphasizing expressive fulfillment and the trustworthy inner impulse of a self that is tied to nature (Taylor 1989; see Kirschner 1996). As Richardson and Woolfolk note, Romantic moral philosophy "encourages us to eschew false social masks and deceits and follow the 'voice of nature' revealed in our unspoiled feelings and genuinely spontaneous impulses" (Richardson and Woolfolk 1994: 204). L. A. Sass (1988) points to a second strand of Romanticism, upon which Heidegger drew, a strand emphasizing community and tradition. The first strand of Romanticism, which maintains that reason and high moral standards harm people (Taylor 1989), tends to be emphasized by humanistic psychologists (O'Hara 1997) and certain psychoanalysts (Kirschner 1996; Strenger 1997). Accordingly, their ethical assertions tend to be nonmoral and covert.

Virtue ethicists, as discussed above, stress transformed persons and the ethical qualities they ideally exhibit (Doherty 1995; Drane 1988, 1994; Hauerwas 1995; MacIntyre 1984, 1988, 1990; W. F. May 1984; Meara *et al.* 1996; Punzo 1996; Thomas 1989). Sometimes sharply distinguished from rational approaches that emphasize principles, virtue ethics can also be seen as complementary to them. Virtue ethicists strive for a psychologically sophisticated ethics that addresses motivation, emotion, and social context.

Each of those fourteen ethical alternatives can undergird the commitment of psychotherapists to professional ethics and help therapy stakeholders to make ethical decisions about therapy process, therapy outcome, and the ideal role of psychotherapy in a society.

A particular alternative (new or old) may yet prove superior, consensually accepted by rational, intelligent people. I have not given up hope. But my best guess is that all of those ethical approaches will continue to receive support, with at least some thoughtful therapy stakeholders finding each alternative best. Public philosophies regarding therapy will thus ideally take that diversity into account. Societies should, I believe, develop a public philosophy for psychotherapy that exemplifies some form of genuine pluralism (Marsden 1991), a pluralism that permits ethical diversity falling within broad bounds and excludes only clearly harmful ethical alternatives.

Thinking

Learning to think well about ethical issues in therapy, to think carefully and critically about practical therapeutic issues and therapy in general, will benefit therapy stakeholders faced with ethical choices. Thinking well involves drawing deeply upon one (and especially more than one) of the ethical alternatives just discussed, applying ethical ideas to new situations and ideas, and critically analyzing ethical ideas.

Therapy stakeholders striving to think well would benefit from sound criteria for selecting ethical approaches, ordering principles, and making particular ethical decisions. And general epistemological criteria have been articulated. Martin and Thompson point to "conceptual adequacy, internal consistency, external coherence, utility, conceptual fruitfulness, emphatic resonance, and demonstrated empirical possibility" (Martin and Thompson 1997: 647). Rationality, comprehensiveness, simplicity, authority, and positive consequences have been proposed as well (Tjeltveit 1989). We lack a consensus about which of these criteria is best, however. Indeed, Martin and Thompson do not argue that the criteria they list will produce undeniable truth. They argue, rather, for "pluralistic and pragmatic proposals that attempt to combine, and perhaps to move beyond" those well-established criteria. In addition, particular criteria are often tied to particular ethical approaches. Advocates of rational ethics argue for rational criteria, naturalistic ethicists argue for empirical criteria (of particular kinds), and so forth. So the search for criteria, for ways to order competing values and ethical theories, is only partially helpful.

Practice in addressing ethical issues and formal educational programs (e.g. Vachon and Agresti 1992) can also help therapists to think well about ethical issues in therapy. The use of case studies in conjunction with sets of ethical principles can sharpen one's ability to perceive ethical issues, evaluate ethical alternatives, and decide on the best course of action.

Therapy stakeholders need more, however, than knowledge about ethical alternatives, criteria for ethical decision-making, practice addressing ethical issues, and training programs. We need practical wisdom, the virtue I have stressed throughout the book (see Brody 1994; Caplan 1989; Doherty 1995; Martin and Thompson 1997; Meara et al. 1996). A person with practical wisdom, or prudence, MacIntyre suggests, "knows how to exercise judgment in particular cases" (MacIntyre 1984: 154). When faced with an ethical dilemma we often seek out those who exhibit ethical wisdom. As Meehl (1981) notes, "We tend to adjust our ethical system so as to increase its coherence with" the views of those "who have engaged in extended rational ethical discussion based on extensive real and vicarious experience" (Meehl 1981: 7). Careful reflection on ethical theory does not of course guarantee practical wisdom, but those who are most wise will have thought about ethical issues broadly, deeply, and well.

Dialogue

Better ethical decisions can result from talking with others, with Meehl's (1981) ethically wise persons, with friends, with colleagues, with those who are practically minded and those who are philosophically minded, with clients, with therapists. Ethical understanding, according to Gadamer, "occurs through a process of dialogical exchange of views during which good will (a serious, honest attempt to understand) is extended to different perspectives" (Martin and Thompson 1997: 641). Dialogue of a sort can also occur, I think, with ethical ideas in works of philosophy and art, in film, in poetry, in literature.

Ethical discourse in therapy is vitally important. Properly conducted dialogue makes it more likely that therapists will address ethical issues in accord with professional ethics. Those issues are explored, Doherty argues:

> in the heart of the therapeutic dialogue, in conversations in which the therapist listens, reflects, acknowledges, questions, probes, and challenges – and in which the client is free to do the same and to develop a more integrated set of moral sensibilities.
>
> (Doherty 1995: 37)

Dialogues that are broad and dialogues that are focused can both play important roles in making ethical decisions. By broad dialogues, I mean conversations with persons holding substantially different ethical perspectives. These dialogues among moral strangers (Engelhardt 1991) can enrich, supplement, and confuse people. The person who is narrowly religious may benefit by listening to, and taking seriously, the views of those who are non-religious or who are religious in different ways. And the person who is militantly atheist may benefit by listening to, and taking seriously, the views of those who are religious, because, as Bellah, Madsen, Sullivan, Swidler, and Tipton suggest, the church "belongs in the conversation of those seeking the right answers" (Bellah *et al.* 1991: 33). In the academic world, transdisciplinary approaches may be very helpful. Rest (1988), for example, suggests drawing upon the expertise of practitioners, of those in the normative disciplines (law, moral philosophy, and theology), and of researchers in the social sciences. Jahoda wanted input from politicians and "the man in the street" as well (Jahoda 1958: 80). And Doherty (1995) suggests the dialogue should include economists and government officials, to which I would add third-party payers.

But focused dialogue within local ethical communities, communities sharing particular ethical perspectives, can also play an important role in helping therapy stakeholders to make ethical decisions. As Jaggar (1991) notes, feminists can perhaps best pursue in-depth explorations of feminist ethics with other feminists, so they need not continually revisit, for example, the question of whether women's experiences should be taken seriously and oppression opposed. They can instead explore deeply and thoroughly the implications of feminist ethics for therapy. Likewise, suppose a conservative Jewish lady takes seriously (considers binding) traditional Jewish interpretations of the Ten Commandments in thinking about the ethical character of psychotherapy. Although she would doubtless benefit from conversations with people who do not share those views (as they would with her), if she is to explore her ethical convictions deeply and well, she will need intense conversation in her local ethical community, with those who share key convictions, so she can flesh out, make deeper, and apply her ethical convictions.

Ethical articulacy

We are best equipped to make good ethical decisions when we clearly articulate our ethical convictions. After noting that therapists "already do provide moral consultation disguised as psychological consultation," Doherty (1995: 186) suggested that "we begin to do it more consciously and explicitly." We can easily articulate some therapy values (cf. Fischhoff 1991), but not others. Identifying some values (and other ethical convictions) may thus require us to engage in what Taylor (1989, 1992) calls acts of retrieval. We will need, that is, to work at making overt what is covert.

Clearly articulated ethical ideas can lead to better ethical decisions for several reasons. As discussed in Chapter 11, practicing in accord with codes of professional ethics requires therapists to be aware of their own values and, sometimes, to communicate with clients about their ethical convictions. Furthermore, as Socrates and others have argued, the examined life is worth living (Taylor 1989). Being explicit about what we think is good, right, and virtuous also helps us bring about goodness, to act rightly, and to live virtuously. As Taylor put it, "seeing good makes good" (ibid.: 454), as can be seen in Dostoyevsky, Nietzsche, and Genesis. When explicit about the ethical ideals to which a particular identity is implicitly tied, for example, we can live that identity more fully and consistently (Taylor 1989).

As feminists and ethnic minorities have made clear, liberation can take place when those whose experiences have been ignored and suppressed give voice to their experiences and beliefs, including their ethical convictions. Taylor notes that this sense of liberation by way of ethical articulation has recurred throughout the history of philosophy. Repudiating and denying ethical sources is self-stultifying. But when philosophers "recover what has been suppressed and forgotten in the conditions of experience" and articulate ethical sources, they experience "exhilaration" and "liberation" (Taylor 1989: 460).

Finally, ethical articulacy connects us with ethical sources and empowers us. In Taylor's words, "articulation can bring us closer to the good as a moral source, can give it power" (ibid.: 92). If a researcher argues eloquently for elegance and fidelity to empirical evidence in psychological theories, the researcher's commitment to those two goods may increase, and their effects on his or her life deepen. Clearly communicating a good "can help realize the good by recognizing it" (ibid.: 454). This is true as well with goods, like autonomy, to which therapists are committed. To explicitly convey to clients the goodness of autonomy may empower them and enable autonomy to function for clients as what Taylor calls a "moral source."

Unfortunately, some people cannot find adequate language, cannot find language that points convincingly to goodness. Accordingly, we may need "new languages of personal resonance to make crucial human goods alive for us again" (ibid.: 513).

Retrieving and drawing upon ethical sources

If therapy stakeholders aspire to create forms of psychotherapy with the best possible ethical character and if "high standards need strong sources" (Taylor 1989: 516), stakeholders need to identify and draw upon strong ethical sources. By sources, I mean what points us toward what is good, right, and virtuous, what helps us to become good, right, and virtuous, what ethically empowers us, "what moves us, what our lives are built around" (ibid.: 92). Clients making profound changes, therapists functioning at the highest ethical levels, and communities forging an optimal role for therapy in a community will consciously build upon such sources.

No one lacks such sources, though diverse sources exist and many people are reluctant to name the genesis of, and consciously build upon, their ethical ideas and actions. Those who want to make the best possible ethical decisions about therapy will, I am convinced, articulate and draw upon ethical sources, however.

Consistent with my stance throughout this book, I will not claim in this section to identify the best source. In fact, with Taylor (1989), I think we can and should draw upon more than one ethical source. But, with Engelhardt, I am convinced that reason alone is too anemic a source for healthy ethical functioning and that individuals will need to turn to sources whose intellectual justification requires "special premises," premises that are "not open to general rational justification" (Engelhardt 1991: xiii). Adequate ethical sources provide therapy stakeholders with content. But, "content is particular, the particular is parochial, and the parochial has moral substance" (ibid.: 140). Those drawing upon content-full ethical sources will thus draw upon *particular* ethical sources associated with particular ethical communities, local ethical communities, such as the feminist, the scientific, or the Reformed Jewish. Because these diverse ethical sources exist and individual differences should be respected, public philosophies regarding psychotherapy should be pragmatically and genuinely pluralistic.

People report drawing upon a variety of ethical sources. Bellah, Madsen, Sullivan, Swidler, and Tipton (1985) point to "the notion that one discovers one's deepest beliefs in, and through, traditions and community" (Bellah *et al.* 1985: 65). Browning notes that some think of psychology "as a practical discipline based on a critical ethic and a critical theory of society" (Browning 1987: xi). In my terms, such an "ethic" and "theory" serve as ethical sources for those psychologies. Engelhardt suggests that people seeking particular content-full moralities turn to "tradition, culture, or God's good grace" (Engelhardt 1991: 195). Communities can be ethical sources in three ways:

they can themselves serve as ethical sources, they can point to ethical sources, and they can make it easier for individuals to draw upon ethical sources. A wide range of traditions and communities exist, however, ranging from the traditions of postmodernism and classic liberal individualism to those of ancient religions still practiced. Guignon suggested that we can "find guidance" in stories about "the lives of models or exemplars drawn from history" (Guignon 1993: 234). That is, narratives can function as ethical sources. L. A. Sass (1988) pointed to the communal, the social, and the traditional, noting that those sources need not be in opposition to individuality, freedom, and critical self-reflection. Indeed, some traditions and communities strongly affirm, and even require, those ideals. Taylor pointed to a variety of ethical sources, most of which people in the West implicitly draw upon without recognizing they do so. Scientifically oriented psychologists may not, for instance, recognize their reliance on the great "power of naturalist sources" (Taylor 1989: 518). He also identified as sources "the clear vision of scientific reason," the "inner impulse of nature," the "Kantian good will," and grace (ibid.: 412). Ethical sources "may be divine, or in the world, or in the powers of the self" (ibid.: 490). Finally, ethical sources may be outside the self, but accessed through languages that resonate within people, for instance, the sources that Taylor thought held the greatest potential, the sources to which Dostoyevsky pointed.

Psychotherapy stakeholders will, no doubt, continue to draw upon a wide range of ethical sources in making decisions about the ethical character of therapy. Thoughtfully and critically retrieving and drawing upon those ethical sources is vital – for the sake of psychotherapists, for the sake of society, and for the sake of psychotherapy clients.

Notes

1 Introduction

1 I use the phrase "mental health" as a summary term for all therapy goals. Accordingly, by using it I do not intend to endorse a "medical model" understanding of psychotherapy. I use it, rather, in its broad sense of a "chapter title" (Smith 1961: 304) of a "chapter" that contains all concepts pertaining to therapy goals. In this sense, "mental health" refers to the treatment goals of both the biologically oriented psychiatrist and the non-traditional, humanistically oriented therapist.

2 See Stiles (1983), and Strupp and Hadley (1977). The latter argue that, in addition to the therapists' perspectives on therapy goals, the voices of clients and the general public need to be heard as well.

2 Ethics: challenging, inescapable questions

1 Providing less-than-fully competent therapy is not an ethical violation *per se*. Determining whether a code of professional ethics has been violated would require more information about the case.

2 Many professionals draw upon the full range of ethical considerations in making professional ethical judgments. In drawing this distinction among six types of approach to ethics, I acknowledge that the six may overlap; indeed, they should. The contrast I am drawing is between the ethics codes professionals employ (professional ethics narrowly conceived) and other approaches to ethics.

3 Philosophers (e.g. Flanagan 1991; MacIntyre 1984, 1988, 1990; Nussbaum 1994), biomedical ethicists (e.g. J. F. Drane 1988, 1994; W. F. May 1984), and theologians (e.g. Hauerwas 1995; Meilaender 1984) have recently shown increased interest in virtue ethics.

4 Cf. critiques of individualism in Hippocratic medical ethics (Veatch 1989b), in society in general (Bellah *et al.* 1985; Fox-Genovese 1991; MacIntyre 1984), and in psychology (Prilleltensky 1994; Sampson 1993; Wallach and Wallach 1983).

5 Hare-Mustin defines discourse as "a system of statements, practices, and institutional structures that share common values" (1994: 19).

6 For example, see discussions by bioethicists (Callahan 1995), philosophers (Adams 1987; Pojman 1995b), developmental psychologists (L. Kohlberg 1971), evolutionary ethicists (Campbell 1975; Wright 1994), feminists (Morawski 1994), philosophical psychologists (Bickhard 1989), and empirical researchers (Petrinovich *et al.* 1993).

3 Psychotherapists as ethicists: engaging in difficult, essential tasks

1 Veatch notes, however, that some ethical traditions "do recognize authorities in the values and normative judgments made within their traditions" (1989a: 12). In such traditions, teachers would be expected to teach the ethical perspectives of that authoritative tradition. Therapists not adhering to such a tradition may be tempted to engage in subtractive ethical influence with clients from such traditions, to be advocates of their own view and critics of those traditions.

2 Some think mental health and other therapy goals are concepts that are inextricably ethical, and so would challenge sharp distinctions between mental health and ethics. This dispute will be addressed in Chapter 9.

5 Unpacking diverse understandings of "values"

1 Taylor (1989) distinguished between two families of views: the Kantian with its emphasis on disengaged autonomy as central to morality, and the Expressivist perspective which focuses on nature as moral source.

2 Rogers (e.g. 1964) appeared to view "ought" in a wholly negative light. Maslow (1963), by way of contrast, reported that self-actualized persons have a healthy sense of "ought."

6 The intellectual contexts of psychotherapy: ethics and science

1 When I use "science" in this section, I use it as some of its advocates portray it: as an objective, value-free set of procedures that, in conjunction with data, can produce dependable knowledge. As I shall discuss later, however, sharply distinguishing ethics from science is difficult. And some deny we should.

7 The social contexts of psychotherapy: clinical practice and business

1 An important ethical issue which I will not discuss further in this chapter is that of a right to health care. Engelhardt asserts that "a basic human secular moral right to health care does not exist – not even to a 'decent minimum of health care.' Such rights must be created" (Engelhardt 1996: 375). And Brennan (1993) notes that a legal basis for a universal right to health care does not exist in the US constitution. The failure to adopt universal health care coverage in the US indicates that Americans do not believe that such a right exists, do not want to create one, or both. Or at least that they do not want to pay for it. Those who claim that such a right exists, or should be created, need to make more convincing ethical arguments to that effect, a difficult task given the (perhaps incommensurable) diversity of contemporary ethical views.

But even if we assume that a right to health care exists (as many in the world do), a second problem must be faced: the nature and extent of the health care guaranteed by that right. One way to get at that problem is to look at the goal of health care: health. A right to health care assumes the goodness of health. But what is the nature of that health, and what level of health do people have a right to receive? The right of the severely mentally ill to receive basic treatment to manage their disorders is quite different from (and easier to defend than) the right of the "worried well" or the "adventuresome seeker of personal growth" to reach therapy goals like character reconstruction or self-actualization. It is conceivable that a right to the former exists, but not a right to the latter, especially if establishing such a right causes damage to a society. The question of a right to health care may thus be tied to the ethical character of therapy goals, a topic addressed in Chapter 9.

8 Ethical dimensions of the techniques, strategies, and processes of therapy: which means to therapeutic ends?

1 Judgments of effectiveness can, of course, be made only with reference to the goals of therapy. Those ethical evaluations of therapy process thus overlap with ethical evaluations of therapy outcome.
2 The first four come from Beauchamp and Childress (1994), and the fifth from K. S. Kitchener (1984).
3 See Drane's (1994) discussion of physician virtues, and Kitchener (1996b) and Meara et al. (1996) on therapist virtues.
4 They used different methodologies to summarize research findings than did Orlinsky et al.

9 Ethical dimensions of the goals and outcome of therapy: therapy as means to which (ethics-laden) ends?

1 Family therapist Boszormenyi-Nagy (1987; Boszormenyi-Nagy and Krasner 1986; Boszormenyi-Nagy and Sparks 1984), for instance, argues that family members should be just (fair) with one another. Establishing the therapy goal that clients further social justice, addressing justice in *macro*-ethical situations (Clark 1993), is less common, however, although Cushman (1995) and Doherty (1995) clearly support clients who pursue that broader aim.
2 As noted in Chapter 1, I use this phrase as a summary term for all therapy goals, including those held by persons who would not use the term.
3 Those who have empirically or conceptually distinguished mental health values (or similar or related concepts) from moral or other values include Bergin (1985); Blatt (1964); Buhler (1962); Fine and Nichols (1980); Fromm-Reichmann (1953); Ginsburg (1950); Hartmann (1939, 1960); Haugen et al. (1991); Jensen and Bergin (1988); Katkin and Weisskopf-Joelson (1971); Kelly and Strupp (1992); Kubacki (1994); Margolis (1966); Michels (1976); Naranjo (1970); Neulinger et al. (1970); K. V. Schultz (1958); Strupp (1980); Strupp and Hadley (1977); Suan and Tyler (1990); Tjeltveit (1986); Tyler et al. (1983); Tyler et al. (1989); and Tyler and Suan (1990).

   The literature addressing the relationship of mental health/psychotherapy and values/morality/ethics is extensive. Books addressing it include Andrews (1989); Brandt and Rozin (1997); Browning (1987); Browning et al. (1990); Buhler (1962); Caplan et al. (1981); Coan (1974, 1977); Cushman (1995); Doherty (1995); Dokecki (1996); Engelhardt and Spicker (1978); Fairbairn and Fairbairn (1987); Frank and Frank (1991); Glad (1959); Hartmann (1960); Holmes and Lindley (1989); Jahoda (1958); Lakin (1988, 1991); Lear (1990); London (1986); Lowe (1976); Margolis (1966); Miller (forthcoming); Mowrer (1967); Norton (1976); Nunnally (1961); Offer and Sabshin (1966); Post (1972); Prilleltensky (1994); Rieff (1966, 1979); D. Schultz (1977); M. B. Smith (1969); Wallach and Wallach (1983); Weiner (1993); and Woolfolk (1998).

4 Ethical ideals may, of course, be evaluated in other ways. My tests are all teleological, for example. If we were drawing upon virtue ethics or deontological
normative theories, we would ask different questions when evaluating therapy
ideals.

5 Wallace notes "the tortuous complexity and ambiguity of [Freud's ethical]
thinking and attitudes" (Wallace 1986: 101). He outlines no less than twelve
"desiderata implicit and explicit in Freud's ethics" (ibid.: 118). See also Wallach
and Wallach (1983) and Browning (1987) on the tensions within Freud's
thought.

6 The Greek word "eudaimonia," usually translated as "happiness," Nussbaum
(1994) argues, is better translated as "human flourishing."

7 Cf. the special section in the *Journal of Social and Clinical Psychology*, edited by
Harvey (1985).

10 Rethinking psychotherapy's location in a society: public philosophy and social and therapeutic contracts

1 An extended discussion of the meanings of "public philosophy" (see Bellah
1986; Browning and Evison 1991; Dewey 1930; Kirschner 1993; Neuhaus
1984; Niebuhr 1944; Sandel 1996; and W. M. Sullivan 1982) is beyond the
scope of this book. I will focus here on the ethical dimension of a public philosophy rather than on the political dimension emphasized in much of that
literature. I use the term more broadly than Lippmann (1956) and do not intend
it to have a particular ideological slant, save that of an opposition to relativism,
authoritarianism, and ethical inarticulacy.

2 Drane (1991), Guignon (1993), G. S. Hall (1923, cited in Morawski 1982),
London (1964, 1986), Lowe (1976), Michels (1991), Strupp (1992), Wachtel
(1989), and Wallace (1991).

3 McNeil notes, for example, that priests in Judaism were concerned with worship
and ceremonies, not with "the principles of the good life and details of personal
conduct" (McNeil 1951: 2), which were addressed by religious leaders occu-
pying the separate role of "wise man."

4 "Consensus" carries more philosophical weight (and disguises more varied philosophical positions) than any one term perhaps ought to carry (and disguise). Cf.
Moreno (1995). This brief overview will of necessity omit many nuances from
the argument. It should be noted that contestants in this philosophical debate
often do not agree with their opponents' characterizations of their views. My use
of examples in this section should be seen, therefore, as illustrative rather than
as definitive expositions of particular authors' views.

5 Bok identified three minimalist values: "some form of positive duties regarding
mutual support, loyalty, and reciprocity"; "negative duties to refrain from
harmful action"; and "norms for at least rudimentary fairness and procedural
justice in cases of conflict regarding both positive and negative injunctions"
(Bok 1995: 13, 15, 16).

11 Profession and professional ethics

1 The extensive debates about the meaning of professionalism are beyond the
scope of this book. See Abbott (1988); Callahan (1988); Camenisch (1983);
Fulford (1989); Goldman (1980); Hatch (1988b); Jennings *et al.* (1987);
Kultgen (1988); MacNiven (1990); L. May (1996); and W. M. Sullivan (1995).

2 Roazen describes such therapists in these terms, "moral positions are taken via clinical categories without any awareness that the same categories might justify very different moral alternatives" (Roazen 1972: 202).

3 Michels stated baldly "I believe it is immoral to disguise rhetoric as therapy" (Michels 1976: 383).

12 Shaping the ethical character of psychotherapy: inevitable choices, better choices

1 These correlate, roughly, to Bellah, Madsen, Sullivan, Swidler, and Tipton's (1985) utilitarian individualism, expressive individualism, and Biblical individualism. Taylor, however, sketches the history of these "spiritual families" (1989: 502) or ethical sources within the history of Western (and especially European) thought instead of focusing on the US, points to the deep tensions between the sources, describes each source in a way that its ethical strengths are evident, and argues that the modern self contains elements of all three. He argues that whenever only one is acknowledged, the less dominant families are still present, hidden from view.

2 "It is crucial to Rorty's postmodernist view of our situation," Guignon notes, "that we see morality as nothing other than the practices a group happens to commend at a given time" (Guignon 1991: 95).

3 They illustrate Engelhardt's third sense of "secular humanism." For them, "Secular Humanism is a concrete moral vision. It is instantiated in particular moral communities that regard themselves in competition with religious sects" (Engelhardt 1991: 125). As noted in Chapter 10, those who are "secular humanist" in his other two senses of the phrase attempt to formulate ethical positions that "span and tolerate" (ibid.: 139) diverse religious and non-religious ethical claims.

References

Abbott, A. D. (1988) *The System of Professions: An Essay on the Division of Expert Labor*, Chicago, IL: University of Chicago Press.

Abe-Kim, J. S. and Takeuchi, D. T. (1996) "Cultural competence and quality of care: Issues for mental health service delivery in managed care," *Clinical Psychology: Science and Practice* 3: 273–95.

Abt, L. E. (1992) "Clinical psychology and the emergence of psychotherapy," *Professional Psychology: Research and Practice* 23: 176–8.

Adams, R. M. (1987) *The Virtue of Faith and Other Essays in Philosophical Theology*, New York: Oxford University Press.

Adleman, J. (1990) "Necessary risks and ethical constraints: Self-monitoring on values and biases," in H. Lerman and N. Porter (eds) *Feminist Ethics in Psychotherapy* (pp. 113–22), New York: Springer.

Agich, G. J. (1990) "Clinical ethics: A role theoretic look," *Social Science and Medicine* 30: 389–99.

Albee, G. W. and Ryan-Finn, K. D. (1994) "Reducing the incidence of mental disorders," in S. A. Kirk and S. D. Einbinder (eds) *Controversial Issues in Mental Health* (pp. 81–8), Boston, MA: Allyn & Bacon.

Albert. E. M. (1956) "The classification of values," *American Anthropologist* 58: 221–48.

Alderman, H. (1991) "Nietzsche, Friedrich (1844–1900)," in L. C. Becker and C. B. Becker (eds) *Encyclopedia of Ethics* (Vol. 2, pp. 903–8), New York: Garland.

Aldrich, C. K. (1975) "The long and short of psychotherapy," *Psychiatric Annals* 5: 507–12.

Allport, G. W. (1960) "Personality: Normal and abnormal," in *Personality and Social Encounter: Selected Essays* (pp. 155–68), Boston, MA: Beacon.

—— (1967) "Gordon W. Allport," in E. G. Boring and G. Lindzey (eds) *A History of Psychology in Autobiography* (Vol. 5, pp. 3–25), New York: Appleton-Century-Crofts.

American Association for Marriage and Family Therapy (1991) *Code of Ethics*, Washington, DC: Author.

American Psychiatric Association (1973) *The Principles of Medical Ethics With Annotations Especially Applicable to Psychiatry*, Washington, DC: Author; *American Journal of Psychiatry* 130: 1057–64.

—— (1993) *The Principles of Medical Ethics With Annotations Especially Applicable to Psychiatry*, Washington, DC: Author.

—— (1994) *Diagnostic and Statistical Manual of Mental Disorders* (4th edn), Washington, DC: Author.

American Psychiatric Association Committee on Religion and Psychiatry (1990) "Guidelines regarding possible conflict between psychiatrists' religious commitments and psychiatric practice," *American Journal of Psychiatry* 147: 542.

American Psychological Association (1992) "Ethical principles of psychologists and code of conduct," *American Psychologist* 47: 1597–611.

—— (1994) *Bylaws of the American Psychological Association*, Washington, DC: Author.

American Psychological Society (1988) *Bylaws*, Washington, DC: Author.

Amore, R. C. (1973) "Theravada Buddhism and psychotherapy," in R. H. Cox (ed.) *Religious Systems and Psychotherapy* (pp. 142–55), Springfield, IL: Charles C. Thomas.

Amundsen, D. W. (1995) "Medical ethics, history of: IV. Europe, A. Ancient and Medieval, 1. Greece and Rome," in W. T. Reich (ed.) *Encyclopedia of Bioethics* (2nd edn, Vol. 5, pp. 1509–16), New York: Macmillan.

Andrews, L. M. (1989) *To Thine Own Self Be True: The Relationship Between Spiritual Values and Emotional Health*, New York: Doubleday.

Annas, J. (1991) "Ethics and morality," in L. C. Becker and C. B. Becker (eds) *Encyclopedia of Ethics* (Vol. 1, pp. 329–31), New York: Garland.

Aponte, H. J. (1985) "The negotiation of values in therapy," *Family Process* 24: 323–38.

—— (1994) *Bread and Spirit: Therapy With the New Poor: Diversity of Race, Culture, and Values*, New York: W. W. Norton.

Ash, M. G. (1992) "Cultural contexts and scientific change in psychology: Kurt Lewin in Iowa," *American Psychologist* 47: 198–207.

Association of State and Provincial Psychology Boards (1996) *Professional Conduct and Discipline in Psychology*, Washington, DC: American Psychological Association.

Audi, R. (1997) *Moral Knowledge and Ethical Character*, New York: Oxford University Press.

Austad, C. S. (1996) *Is Long-term Psychotherapy Unethical? Toward a Social Ethic in an Era of Managed Care*, San Francisco, CA: Jossey-Bass.

Austad, C. S. and Berman, W. H. (1991a) "Managed health care and the evolution of psychotherapy," in C. S. Austad and W. H. Berman (eds) *Psychotherapy in Managed Health Care: The Optimal Use of Time and Resources* (pp. 3–18), Washington, DC: American Psychological Association.

—— (1991b) "Managed mental health care: Current status and future directions," in C. S. Austad and W. H. Berman (eds) *Psychotherapy in Managed Health Care: The Optimal Use of Time and Resources* (pp. 264–78), Washington, DC: American Psychological Association.

—— (1991c) "Preface," in C. S. Austad and W. H. Berman (eds) *Psychotherapy in Managed Health Care: The Optimal Use of Time and Resources* (pp. vii–x), Washington, DC: American Psychological Association.

Baier, A. (1993) "What do women want in a moral theory?" in M. J. Larrabee (ed.) *An Ethic of Care* (pp. 19–32), New York: Routledge.

Ballard, B. W. (1996) "Quasi-Hegelian utopias," *Journal of Value Inquiry* 30: 1–4.

Ballou, M. (1990) "Clients' rights, values, and context," in H. Lerman and N. Porter (eds) *Feminist Ethics in Psychotherapy* (pp. 239–47), New York: Springer.

Bandura, A. (1969) *Principles of Behavior Modification*, New York: Holt, Rinehart & Winston.

Baritz, L. (1960) *The Servants of Power: A History of the Use of Social Science in American Industry*, Middletown, CT: Wesleyan University Press.

Barlow, D. H. (1996) "The effectiveness of psychotherapy: Science and policy," *Clinical Psychology: Science and Practice* 3: 236–40.

Bassford, H. A. (1990) "The basis of medical ethics," in D. MacNiven (ed.) *Moral Expertise: Studies in Practical and Professional Ethics* (pp. 128–43), London: Routledge.

Batson, C. D. (1990) "How social an animal? The human capacity for caring," *American Psychologist* 45: 336–46.

Bauman, Z. (1993) *Postmodern Ethics*, Oxford: Blackwell.

—— (1995) *Life in Fragments: Essays in Postmodern Morality*, Oxford: Blackwell.

Baylis, F. (1989) "Persons with moral expertise and moral experts: Wherein lies the difference?" in B. Hoffmaster, B. Freedman, and G. Fraser (eds) *Clinical Ethics: Theory and Practice* (pp. 89–99), London: Routledge.

Beauchamp, T. L. and Childress, J. F. (1994) *Principles of Biomedical Ethics* (4th edn), New York: Oxford University Press.

Bell, D. (1993) *Communitarianism and Its Critics*, Oxford: Oxford University Press.

Bellah, R. (1986) "Public philosophy and public theology," in L. S. Rouner (ed.) *Civil Religion and Political Theology* (pp. 79–97), Notre Dame, IN: University of Notre Dame Press.

Bellah, R. N., Haan, N., Rabinow, P., and Sullivan, W. M. (1983) "Introduction," in N. Haan, R. N. Bellah, P. Rabinow, and W. M. Sullivan (eds) *Social Science as Moral Inquiry* (pp. 1–18), New York: Columbia University Press.

Bellah, R. N., Madsen, R., Sullivan, W. M., Swidler, A., and Tipton, S. M. (1985) *Habits of the Heart: Individualism and Commitment in American Life*, New York: Harper & Row.

—— (1991) *The Good Society*, New York: Knopf.

Benedict, R. (1934) "Anthropology and the abnormal," *Journal of General Psychology* 10: 59–82.

Benne, R. (1995) *The Paradoxical Vision: A Public Theology for the Twenty-first Century*, Minneapolis, MN: Fortress.

Berger, M. (1982) "Ethics and the therapeutic relationship: Patient rights and therapist responsibilities," in M. Rosenbaum (ed.) *Ethics and Values in Psychotherapy: A Guidebook* (pp. 67–95), New York: Free Press.

Bergin, A. E. (1980a) "Behavior therapy and ethical relativism: Time for clarity," *Journal of Consulting and Clinical Psychology* 48: 11–13.

—— (1980b) "Psychotherapy and religious values," *Journal of Consulting and Clinical Psychology* 48: 95–105.

—— (1985) "Proposed values for guiding and evaluating counseling and psychotherapy," *Counseling and Values* 29: 99–116.

—— (1991) "Values and religious issues in psychotherapy and mental health," *American Psychologist* 46: 394–403.

Berkowitz, P. (1995) *Nietzsche: The Ethics of an Immoralist*, Cambridge, MA: Harvard University Press.

Bersoff, D. N. (1994) "Explicit ambiguity: The 1992 ethics code as an oxymoron," *Professional Psychology: Research and Practice* 25: 382–7.

—— (1995) *Ethical Conflicts in Psychology*, Washington, DC: American Psychological Association.

—— (1996) "The virtue of principle ethics," *The Counseling Psychologist* 24: 86–91.

Beutler, L. E. (1970) "Predicting outcomes of psychotherapy on the basis of social judgment theory," (Doctoral dissertation, University of Nebraska) *Dissertation Abstracts International* 31: 2272B (University Microfilms No. 70–17,702).

—— (1978) "Discussion," *Counseling and Values* 23: 60–4.

—— (1979) "Values, beliefs, religion and the persuasive influence of psychotherapy," *Psychotherapy: Theory, Research and Practice* 16: 432–40.

—— (1981) "Convergence in counseling and psychotherapy: A current look," *Clinical Psychology Review* 1: 79–101.

—— (1989) "Psychotherapy and religious values: An update," paper presented at the annual meeting of the American Psychological Association, New Orleans, LA (August).

—— (1995) "The germ theory myth and the myth of outcome homogeneity," *Psychotherapy* 32: 489–94.

Beutler, L. E. and Bergan, J. (1991) "Value change in counseling and psychotherapy: A search for scientific credibility," *Journal of Counseling Psychology* 38: 16–24.

Beutler, L. E. and Clarkin, J. F. (1990) *Systematic Treatment Selection: Toward Targeted Therapeutic Interventions*, New York: Brunner/Mazel.

Beutler, L. E. and Harwood, T. M. (1995) "Prescriptive therapies," *Applied and Preventive Psychology* 4: 89–100.

Beutler, L. E., Machado, P. P. P., and Neufeldt, S. A. (1994) "Therapist variables," in A. E. Bergin and S. L. Garfield (eds) *Handbook of Psychotherapy and Behavior Change* (4th edn, pp. 229–69), New York: Wiley.

Bickhard, M. (1989) "Ethical psychotherapy and psychotherapy as ethics: A response to Perrez," *New Ideas in Psychology* 7: 159–64.

Birch, B. C. and Rasmussen, L. L. (1989) *Bible and Ethics in the Christian Life* (2nd edn), Minneapolis, MN: Augsburg.

Blackstone, W. T. (1975) "The American Psychological Association code of ethics for research involving human participants: An appraisal," *Southern Journal of Philosophy* 13: 407–18.

Blanck, R. R. and DeLeon, P. H. (1996) "Managed care: Strongly conflicting views," *Professional Psychology* 27: 323–4.

Blatt, S. J. (1964) "An attempt to define mental health," *Journal of Consulting Psychology* 28: 146–53.

Bok, S. (1995) *Common Values*, Columbia, MO: University of Missouri Press.

Boszormenyi-Nagy, I. (1987) *Foundations of Contextual Therapy*, New York: Brunner/Mazel.

Boszormenyi-Nagy, I. and Krasner, B. R. (1986) *Between Give and Take: A Guide to Contextual Therapy*, New York: Brunner/Mazel.

Boszormenyi-Nagy, I. and Sparks, G. M. (1984) *Invisible Loyalties: Reciprocity in Intergenerational Family Therapy* (2nd edn), New York: Harper & Row.

Boyd-Franklin, N. (1989) *Black Families in Therapy: A Multisystems Approach*, New York: Guilford.

Braaten, E. B., Otto, S., and Handelsman, M. M. (1993) "What do people want to know about psychotherapy?" *Psychotherapy* 30: 565–70.

Braithwaite, V. A. and Scott, W. A. (1991) "Values," in J. R. Robinson, P. R. Shaver, and L. S. Wrightsman (eds) *Measures of Personality and Social Psychological Attitudes* (pp. 661–753), San Diego, CA: Academic Press.

Brandt, A. M. and Rozin, P. (eds) (1997) *Morality and Health*, New York: Routledge.

Braybrooke, D. (1987) *Philosophy of Social Science*, Englewood Cliffs, NJ: Prentice-Hall.

Brennan, T. A. (1993) "An ethical perspective on health care insurance reform," *American Journal of Law and Medicine* 19: 37–74.

Brink, D. O. (1989) *Moral Realism and the Foundation of Ethics*, New York: Cambridge University Press.

Brody, H. (1989) "Applied ethics: Don't change the subject," in B. Hoffmaster, B. Freedman, and G. Fraser (eds) *Clinical Ethics: Theory and Practice* (pp. 183–200), London: Routledge.

—— (1994) "The four principles and narrative ethics," in R. Gillon (ed.) *Principles of Health Care Ethics* (pp. 207–15), Chichester (England): Wiley.

Broskowski, A. (1991) "Current mental health care environments: Why managed care is necessary," *Professional Psychology: Research and Practice* 22: 6–14.

Brown, H. C. (1914) "The thirteenth annual meeting of the American Philosophical Association," *Journal of Philosophy, Psychology and Scientific Methods* 11: 57–67.

Brown, L. S. and Ballou, M. (eds) (1994) *Personality and Psychopathology: Feminist Reappraisals*, New York: Guilford.

Browning, D. (1982) "The estrangement of pastoral care from ethics," in S. Kepnes and D. Tracy (eds) *The Challenge of Psychology to Faith* (pp. 10–17), New York: Seabury.

Browning, D. S. (1976) *The Moral Context of Pastoral Care*, Philadelphia, PA: Westminster.

—— (1987) *Religious Thought and the Modern Psychologies: A Critical Conversation in the Theology of Culture*, Philadelphia, PA: Fortress.

—— (1991a) "A public philosophy for psychiatry: A view from theology," in D. S. Browning and I. S. Evison (eds) *Does Psychiatry Need a Public Philosophy?* (pp. 13–28), Chicago, IL: Nelson-Hall.

—— (1991b) "Introduction," in D. S. Browning and I. S. Evison (eds) *Does Psychiatry Need a Public Philosophy?* (pp. 1–12), Chicago, IL: Nelson-Hall.

Browning, D. S. and Evison, I. S. (eds) (1991) *Does Psychiatry Need a Public Philosophy?* Chicago, IL: Nelson-Hall.

Browning, D. S., Jobe, T., and Evison, I. S. (1990) *Religious and Ethical Factors in Psychiatric Practice*, Chicago, IL: Nelson-Hall.

Bryson, G. (1932) "The emergence of the social sciences from moral philosophy," *International Journal of Ethics* 42: 304–23.

Buber, M. (1970) *I and Thou*, trans. W. Kaufmann, New York: Scribner's (original work published in 1922).

Buhler, C. (1962) *Values in Psychotherapy*, New York: Free Press.

Burnham, J. C. (1974) "The struggle between physicians and paramedical personnel in American psychiatry, 1917–1941," *Journal of the History of Medical and Allied Sciences* 29: 93–106.

Burns, D. D. (1980) *Feeling Good: The New Mood Therapy*, New York: New American Library.

Cahill, L. S. (1990) "Can theology have a role in 'public' bioethical discourse?" *Hastings Center Report* Supplement (July/August): 10–14.

Callahan, D. (1981) "Minimalist ethics," *Hastings Center Report* 11: 19–25.

—— (1984) "Autonomy: A moral good, not a moral obsession," *Hastings Center Report* 14: 40–2.

—— (1988) "Beyond individualism: Bioethics and the common good" [Interview], *Second Opinion* 9: 52–69.

—— (1990) *What Kind of Life: The Limits of Medical Progress*, New York: Simon & Schuster.

—— (1995) "Bioethics," in W. T. Reich (ed.) *Encyclopedia of Bioethics* (2nd edn, Vol. 1, pp. 247–56), New York: Macmillan.

Camenisch, P. F. (1983) *Grounding Professional Ethics in a Pluralistic Society*, New York: Haven.

Camfield, T. (1973) "The professionalization of American psychology," *Journal of the History of the Behavioral Sciences* 9: 66–75.

Campbell, D. T. (1975) "On the conflicts between biological and social evolution and between psychology and moral tradition," *American Psychologist* 30: 1103–26.

Canter, M. B., Bennett, B. E., Jones, S. E., and Nagy, T. F. (1994) *Ethics for Psychologists: A Commentary on the APA Ethics Code*, Washington, DC: American Psychological Association.

Caplan, A. L. (1989) "Moral experts and moral expertise: Do either exist?" in B. Hoffmaster, B. Freedman, and G. Fraser (eds) *Clinical Ethics: Theory and Practice* (pp. 59–87), Clifton, NJ: Humana Press.

Caplan, A. L., Engelhardt, H. T., Jr, and McCartney, J. J. (eds) (1981) *Concepts of Health and Disease: Interdisciplinary Perspectives*, Reading, MA: Addison-Wesley.

Caplan, E. (1998, forthcoming) *Mind Games: American Culture and the Birth of Psychotherapy*, Berkeley, CA: University of California Press.

Card, C. (ed.) (1991) *Feminist Ethics*, Lawrence, KS: University Press of Kansas.

Carroll, M. A., Schneider, H. G., and Wesley, G. R. (1985) *Ethics in the Practice of Psychology*, Englewood Cliffs, NJ: Prentice-Hall.

Cartwright, S. A. (1981) "Report on the diseases and physical peculiarities of the Negro race," in A. L. Caplan, H. T. Engelhardt, Jr, and J. J. McCartney (eds) *Concepts of Health and Disease: Interdisciplinary Perspectives* (pp. 305–25), Reading, MA: Addison-Wesley (original report published in 1851).

Cattell, R. B. (1972) *A New Morality From Science: Beyondism*, New York: Pergamon.

Chambless, D. L., Sanderson, W. C., Shoham, V., Johnson, S. B., Pope, K. S., Crits-Cristoph, P., Baker, M., Johnson, B., Woody, S. R., Sue, S., Beutler, L., Williams, D. A., and McCurry, S. (1996) "An update on empirically validated therapies," *The Clinical Psychologist* 49 (Spring): 5–14.

Christopher, J. C. (1996) "Counseling's inescapable moral visions," *Journal of Counseling and Development* 75: 17–25.

Clark, C. R. (1993) "Social responsibility ethics: Doing right, doing good, doing well," *Ethics and Behavior* 3: 303–27.

Clouser, K. D. (1989) "Ethical theory and applied ethics: Reflections on connections," in B. Hoffmaster, B. Freedman, and G. Fraser (eds) *Clinical Ethics: Theory and Practice* (pp. 161–81), London: Routledge.

Coan, R. W. (1974) *The Optimal Personality: An Empirical and Theoretical Analysis*, New York: Columbia University Press.

—— (1977) *Hero, Artist, Sage, or Saint? A Survey of Views on What Is Variously Called Mental Health, Normality, Maturity, Self-actualization, and Human Fulfillment*, New York: Columbia University Press.

Consoli, A. J. (1996) "Psychotherapists' personal and mental health values according to their theoretical/professional orientation," *Revista Interamericana de Psicologia/Interamerican Journal of Psychology* 30: 59–83.

Consoli, A. J. and Beutler, L. E. (1996) "Valores y psicoterapia," *Argentine Journal of Clinical Psychology* 5: 17–35.

Corey, G., Corey, M. S., and Callanan, P. (1990) "Role of group leader's values in group counseling," *Journal for Specialists in Group Work* 15: 68–74.

—— (1993) *Issues and Ethics in the Helping Professions* (4th edn), Pacific Grove, CA: Brooks/Cole.

Cournand, A. (1977) "The code of the scientist and its relationship to ethics," *Science* 198: 699–705.

Crittenden, J. (1992) *Beyond Individualism: Reconstituting the Liberal Self*, New York: Oxford University Press.

Cummings, N. A. (1992) "Professional psychology's 50-year centennial," *American Psychologist* 47: 845–6.

Cushman, P. (1992) "Psychotherapy to 1992: A historically situated interpretation," in D. K. Freedheim (ed.) *History of Psychotherapy: A Century of Change* (pp. 21–64), Washington, DC: American Psychological Association.

—— (1993) "Psychotherapy as moral discourse," *Journal of Theoretical and Philosophical Psychology* 13: 103–13.

—— (1995) *Constructing the Self, Constructing America: Studies in the Cultural History of Psychotherapy*, New York: Addison-Wesley.

Daniels, N. (1979) "Wide reflective equilibrium and theory acceptance in ethics," *Journal of Philosophy* 76: 256–82.

Davis, K. (1989) "[Response to Jonsson]," *Health Care Financing Review: Annual Supplement* 11: 104–7.

DeCarvalho, R. J. (1989) "Contributions to the history of psychology: 62: Carl Rogers' naturalistic system of ethics," *Psychological Reports* 65: 1155–62.

—— (1991) *The Founders of Humanistic Psychology*, New York: Praeger.

Deigh, J. (ed.) (1992) *Ethics and Personality: Essays in Moral Psychology*, Chicago, IL: University of Chicago Press.

Department of Health and Human Services (1991) *DHHS Regulations for the Protection of Human Subjects* (45 CFR 46), June 18.

Desjarlais, R., Eisenberg, L., Good, B., and Kleinman, A. (1995) *World Mental Health: Problems and Priorities in Low-income Countries*, New York: Oxford University Press.

Detmer, D. (1989) "Heidegger and Nietzsche on 'thinking in values,'" *Journal of Value Inquiry* 23: 275–83.

Dewey, J. (1920) *Reconstruction in Philosophy*, New York: Henry Holt.

—— (1930) *Individualism Old and New*, New York: Putnam.

Dickson, P. (1994) "Freedom as the source of all value," *The Personalist Forum* 10: 15–28.

Doherty, W. J. (1995) *Soul Searching: Why Psychotherapy Must Promote Moral Responsibility*, New York: Basic Books/HarperCollins.

Dokecki, P. R. (1996) *The Tragi-comic Professional: Basic Considerations for Ethical Reflective-generative Practice*, Pittsburgh, PA: Duquesne University Press.

Donagan, A. (1977) *The Theory of Morality*, Chicago, IL: University of Chicago Press.

Drane, J. F. (1982) "Ethics and psychotherapy: A philosophical perspective," in M. Rosenbaum (ed.) *Ethics and Values in Psychotherapy: A Guidebook* (pp. 15–50), New York: Free Press.

—— (1988) *Becoming a Good Doctor: The Place of Virtue and Character in Medical Ethics*, Kansas City, MO: Sheed & Ward.

—— (1991) "Doctors as priests: Providing a social ethics for a secular culture," in D. S. Browning and I. S. Evison (eds) *Does Psychiatry Need a Public Philosophy?* (pp. 40–60), Chicago, IL: Nelson-Hall.

—— (1994) "Character and the moral life: A virtue approach to biomedical ethics," in E. R. DuBose, R. P. Hamel, and L. J. O'Connell (eds) *A Matter of Principles?: Ferment in U.S. Bioethics* (pp. 284–309), Valley Forge, PA: Trinity.

Dreikurs, R. (1967) "Psychotherapy as correction of faulty social values," in O. H. Mowrer (ed.) *Morality and Mental Health* (pp. 98–103), Chicago, IL: Rand McNally.

Dukes, W. (1955) "Psychological studies of values," *Psychological Bulletin* 52: 24–50.

Dwairy, M. and Van Sickle, T. D. (1996) "Western psychotherapy in traditional Arabic societies," *Clinical Psychology Review* 16: 231–49.

Dyer, A. R. (1988) *Ethics and Psychiatry: Toward Professional Definition*, Washington, DC: American Psychiatric Press.

Dyer, A. R. and Bloch, S. (1987) "Informed consent and the psychiatric patient," *Journal of Medical Ethics* 13: 12–16.

Edel, A. (1986) "Ethical theory and moral practice: On the terms of their relation," in J. P. DeMarco and R. M. Fox (eds) *New Directions in Ethics* (pp. 317–35), New York: Routledge & Kegan Paul.

—— (1988) "The concept of value and its travels in twentieth-century America," in M. G. Murphey and I. Berg (eds) *Values and Value Theory in Twentieth-century America: Essays in Honor of Elizabeth Flower* (pp. 12–36), Philadelphia, PA: Temple University Press.

—— (1991) "Nature and ethics," in L. C. Becker and C. B. Becker (eds) *Encyclopedia of Ethics* (Vol. 2, pp. 890–4), New York: Garland.

Eisenberg, L. (1986) "Health care: For patients or for profits," *American Journal of Psychiatry* 143: 1015–19.

Elliott, R. (1991) "Five dimensions of therapy process," *Psychotherapy Research* 1: 92–103.

Elliott, R. and Anderson, C. (1994) "Simplicity and complexity in psychotherapy research," in R. L. Russell (ed.) *Reassessing Psychotherapy Research* (pp. 65–113), New York: Guilford.

Ellis, A. (1978) "Atheism: A cure for neurosis," *American Atheist* 20: 10–13.

—— (1987a) "A sadly neglected cognitive element in depression," *Cognitive Therapy and Research* 11: 121–46.

—— (1987b) "Integrative developments in Rational-Emotive Therapy (RET)," *Journal of Integrative and Eclectic Psychotherapy* 6: 470–9.

Ellis, A. and Bernard, M. E. (1985) "What is rational-emotive therapy?" in A. Ellis and M. Bernard (eds) *Clinical Applications of Rational-Emotional Therapy* (pp. 1–30), New York: Plenum.

Elshtain, J. B. (1995) "Ethics: Social and political theories," in W. T. Reich (ed.) *Encyclopedia of Bioethics* (2nd edn, Vol. 2, pp. 748–58), New York: Macmillan.

Engelhardt, H. T., Jr (1973) "Psychotherapy as meta-ethics," *Psychiatry* 36: 440–5.

—— (1974) "The disease of masturbation: Values and the concept of disease," *Bulletin of the History of Medicine* 48: 234–48.

—— (1978) "Introduction," in H. T. Engelhardt, Jr and S. F. Spicker (eds) *Mental Health: Philosophical Perspectives* (pp. vii–xxii), Dordrecht (The Netherlands): D. Reidel.

—— (1991) *Bioethics and Secular Humanism: The Search for a Common Morality*, Philadelphia, PA: Trinity.

—— (1996) *The Foundations of Bioethics* (2nd edn), New York: Oxford University Press.

Engelhardt, H. T., Jr and Spicker, S. F. (eds) (1978) *Mental Health: Philosophical Perspectives*, Dordrecht (The Netherlands): D. Reidel.

Engelhardt, H. T., Jr and Wildes, K. W. (1994) "The four principles of health care ethics and post-modernity: Why a Libertarian interpretation is unavoidable," in R. Gillon (ed.) *Principles of Health Care Ethics* (pp. 135–47), Chichester (England): Wiley.

Engler, J. (1986) "Therapeutic aims in psychotherapy and meditation," in K. Wilber, J. Engler, and D. Brown (eds) *Transformations of Consciousness* (pp. 17–51), Boston, MA: New Science Library.

Erikson, E. H. (1963) *Childhood and Society* (2nd edn), New York: W. W. Norton.

Ethics Committee (1996) "Rules and Procedures: Ethics Committee of the American Psychological Association," *American Psychologist* 51: 529–48.

Etzioni, A. (1993) *The Spirit of Community: Rights, Responsibilities, and the Communitarian Agenda*, New York: Crown.

—— (ed.) (1995) *Rights and the Common Good: The Communitarian Perspective*, New York: St. Martin's Press.

—— (1997) *The New Golden Rule: Morality and Community in a Democratic Society*, New York: Basic Books.

—— (ed.) (1998) *The Essential Communitarian Reader*, Lanham, MD: Rowman & Littlefield.

Evans, R. B. (1984) "The origins of American academic psychology," in J. Brozek (ed.) *Explorations in the History of Psychology in the United States* (pp. 17–60), Lewisburg, PA: Bucknell University Press.

Facione, P. A., Scherer, D., and Attig, T. (1991) *Ethics and Society* (2nd edn), Englewood Cliffs, NJ: Prentice-Hall.

Faden, R. and Beauchamp, T. (1986) *Informed Consent: History, Theory and Implementation*, New York: Oxford University Press.

Fairbairn, S. and Fairbairn, G. (eds) (1987) *Psychology, Ethics, and Change*, London: Routledge & Kegan Paul.

Fancher, R. T. (1995) *Cultures of Healing: Correcting the Image of American Mental Health Care*, New York: W. H. Freeman.

Faust, D. and Meehl, P. E. (1992) "Using scientific methods to resolve questions in the history and philosophy of science: Some illustrations," *Behavior Therapy* 23: 195–211.

Fava, J. L., Velicer, W. F., and Prochaska, J. O. (1995) "Applying the transtheoretical model to a representative sample of smokers," *Addictive Behaviors* 20: 189–203.

Fay, J. W. (1939) *American Psychology Before William James*, New Brunswick, NJ: Rutgers University Press.

Feminist Therapy Institute (1990) "Feminist Therapy Institute code of ethics," in H. Lerman and N. Porter (eds) *Feminist Ethics in Psychotherapy* (pp. 37–40), New York: Springer (original work published in 1987).

Fine, H. J. and Nichols, R. C. (1980) "Gestalt therapy: Some aspects of self-support, independence, and responsibility," *Psychotherapy: Theory, Research and Practice* 17: 124–35.

Fine, R. (1990) *Love and Work: The Value System of Psychoanalysis*, New York: Continuum.

Finney, J. W., Riley, A. W., and Cataldo, M. R. (1991) "Psychology in primary health care: Effects of brief targeted therapy on children's medical care utilization," *Journal of Pediatric Psychology* 16: 447–57.

Fischhoff, B. (1991) "Value elicitation: Is there anything in there?" *American Psychologist* 46: 835–47.

Fishbein, M. and Ajzen, I. (1975) *Belief, Attitude, Intention, and Behavior: An Introduction to Theory and Research*, Reading, MA: Addison-Wesley.

Flanagan, O. (1991) *Varieties of Moral Personality: Ethics and Psychological Realism*, Cambridge, MA: Harvard University Press.

—— (1996) *Self Expressions: Mind, Morals, and the Meaning of Life*, New York: Oxford University Press.

Flanagan, O. and Rorty, A. O. (eds) (1990) *Identity, Character, and Morality: Essays in Moral Psychology*, Cambridge, MA: MIT Press.

Fletcher, J. C. and Brody, H. (1995) "Clinical ethics: Elements and methodologies," in W. T. Reich (ed.) *Encyclopedia of Bioethics* (2nd edn, Vol. 1, pp. 399–404), New York: Macmillan.

Follette, W. C., Bach, P. A., and Follette, V. M. (1993) "A behavior-analytic view of psychological health," *Behavior Analyst* 16: 303–16.

Fossum, M. A. and Mason, M. J. (1986) *Facing Shame: Families in Recovery*, New York: W. W. Norton.

Foucault, M. (1965) *Madness and Civilization: A History of Insanity in the Age of Reason*, trans. R. Howard, New York: Pantheon.

Fowers, B. J. (1993) "Psychology as public philosophy: An illustration of the moral dimension of psychology with marital research," *Journal of Theoretical and Philosophical Psychology* 13: 124–36.

Fowers, B. J., Tredinnick, M., and Applegate, B. (1997) "Individualism and counseling: An empirical investigation of the prevalence of individualistic values in psychologists' responses to case vignettes," *Counseling and Values* 41: 204–18.

Fox, D. R. (1993) "Psychological jurisprudence and radical social change," *American Psychologist* 48: 234–41.

Fox, D. and Prilleltensky, I. (eds) (1997) *Critical Psychology: An Introduction*, London: Sage.

Fox, R. E. (1995) "The rape of psychotherapy," *Professional Psychology: Research and Practice* 26: 147–55.

Fox-Genovese, E. (1991) *Feminism Without Illusions: A Critique of Individualism*, Chapel Hill, NC: University of North Carolina Press.

Franck, I. (1977) "Self-realization as ethical norm: A critique," *Philosophical Forum* 9 (Fall): 1–25.

Frank, J. D. (1973) *Persuasion and Healing: A Comparative Study of Psychotherapy* (2nd edn), Baltimore, MD: Johns Hopkins University Press.

—— (1978) *The Human Predicament*, New York: Schocken.

Frank, J. D. and Frank, J. B. (1991) *Persuasion and Healing: A Comparative Study of Psychotherapy* (3rd edn), Baltimore, MD: Johns Hopkins University Press.

Frank, R. G. (1993) "Health-care reform: An introduction" *American Psychologist* 48: 258–60.

Frank, R. G. and VandenBos, G. R. (1994) "Health care reform: The 1993–1994 evolution," *American Psychologist* 49: 851–4.

Frankena, W. K. (1967) "Value and valuation," in P. Edwards (ed.) *Encyclopedia of Philosophy* (Vol. 8, pp. 229–32), New York: Macmillan.

—— (1973) *Ethics* (2nd edn), Englewood Cliffs, NJ: Prentice-Hall.

—— (1976) "The concept of morality," in K. E. Goodpaster (ed.) *Perspectives on Morality: Essays by William K. Frankena* (pp. 125–32), Notre Dame, IN: University of Notre Dame Press.

Franklin, G. (1990) "The multiple meanings of neutrality," *Journal of the American Psychoanalytic Association* 36: 195–219.

Fraser, G. (1989) "Introduction," in B. Hoffmaster, B. Freedman, and G. Fraser (eds) *Clinical Ethics: Theory and Practice* (pp. 1–5), Clifton, NJ: Humana Press.

Freedheim, D. K. (ed.) (1992) *History of Psychotherapy: A Century of Change*, Washington, DC: American Psychological Association.

Freedman, B. (1978) "A meta-ethics for professional morality," *Ethics* 89: 1–19.

Freud, S. (1958) "Recommendations to physicians practicing psychoanalysis," in J. Strachey (ed.) *The Standard Edition of the Complete Psychological Works of Sigmund Freud* (Vol. 12, pp. 111–20), London: Hogarth Press (original work published in 1912).

—— (1959) " 'Civilized' sexual morality and modern nervous illness," in J. Strachey (ed.) *The Standard Edition of the Complete Psychological Works of Sigmund Freud* (Vol. 9, pp. 181–204), London: Hogarth Press (original work published in 1908).

—— (1961) "Civilization and its discontents," in J. Strachey (ed.) *The Standard Edition of the Complete Psychological Works of Sigmund Freud* (Vol. 21, pp. 57–146), London: Hogarth Press (original work published in 1930).

Freud, S. and Pfister, O. R. (1963) *Psychoanalysis and Faith: The Letters of Sigmund Freud and Oskar Pfister*, ed. H. Meng and E. L. Freud, trans. E. Mosbacher, New York: Basic Books.

Friedman, M. (1991) "The social self and the partiality debates," in C. Card (ed.) *Feminist Ethics* (pp. 161–79), Lawrence, KS: University Press of Kansas.

Fromm-Reichmann, F. (1953) *Principles of Intensive Psychotherapy*, London: George Allen & Unwin.

Frondizi, R. (1963) *What Is Value?*, trans. S. Lipp, La Salle, IL: Open Court.

Fulford, K. W. M. (1989) *Moral Theory and Medical Practice*, Cambridge: Cambridge University Press.

Gamwell, L. and Tomes, N. (1995) *Madness in America: Cultural and Medical Perceptions of Mental Illness Before 1914*, Binghamton, NY: Binghamton University Art Museum.

Garfield, S. L. (1974) "Values: An issue in psychotherapy: Comments on a case study," *Journal of Abnormal Psychology* 83: 202–3.

Garfield, S. L. and Bergin, A. E. (eds) (1986) *Handbook of Psychotherapy and Behavior Change* (3rd edn), New York: Wiley.

Garrison, A. (1997) "Adaptationism, mental health, and therapeutic outcome," *Psychotherapy* 34: 107–14.

Gartrell, N. K. (ed.) (1994) *Bringing Ethics Alive: Feminist Ethics in Psychotherapy Practice*, Binghamton, NY: Harrington Park Press.

Gaus, G. F. (1990) *Value and Justification: The Foundation of Liberal Theory*, New York: Cambridge University Press.

Geller, L. (1982) "The failure of self-actualization theory: A critique of Carl Rogers and Abraham Maslow," *Journal of Humanistic Psychology* 22: 56–73.

Gelpi, D. L. (ed.) (1989) *Beyond Individualism: Toward a Retrieval of Moral Discourse in America*, Notre Dame, IN: University of Notre Dame Press.

Gerber, L. A. (1992) "Integrating political–societal concerns in psychotherapy," in S. Staub and P. Green (eds) *Psychology and Social Responsibility: Facing Global Challenges* (pp. 165–81), New York: New York University Press.

Gert, B. (1975) *The Moral Rules: A New Rational Foundation for Morality* (2nd edn), New York: Harper & Row.

—— (1988) *Morality: A New Justification of the Moral Rules*, New York: Oxford University Press.

Gesell, A., Goddard, H. H., and Wallin, J. E. W. (1919) "The field of clinical psychology as an applied science," *Journal of Applied Psychology* 3: 81–95.

Gettner, A. (1978) "Mental health in competition with other values," in W. T. Reich (ed.) *Encyclopedia of Bioethics* (2nd edn, Vol. 3, pp. 1059–64), New York: Macmillan.

Gewirth, A. (1956) "Psychoanalysis or ethics – mental or moral health?" *Christian Register* 135: 12–13, 30–1.

—— (1986) "The problem of specificity in evolutionary ethics," *Biology and Philosophy* 1: 297–305.

Gillon, R. (ed.) (1994) *Principles of Health Care Ethics*, Chichester (England): Wiley.

Ginsburg, S. W. (1950) "Values and the psychiatrist," *American Journal of Orthopsychiatry* 20: 466–78.

Glad, D. D. (1959) *Operational Values in Psychotherapy*, New York: Oxford University Press.

Glasser, W. (1965) *Reality Therapy: A New Approach to Psychiatry*, New York: Harper & Row.

Goldman, A. H. (1980) *The Moral Foundations of Professional Ethics*, Totowa, NJ: Rowman & Littlefield.

Goldstein, K. (1959) "Health as value," in A. H. Maslow (ed.) *New Knowledge in Human Values* (pp. 178–88), New York: Harper & Row.

Goode, W. J. (1960) "Encroachment, charlatanism, and the emerging profession: Psychology, sociology, and medicine," *American Sociological Review* 25: 902–14.

Goodnick, B. (1977) "Mental health from the Jewish standpoint," *Journal of Religion and Health* 16: 110–15.

Gorlin, R. A. (ed.) (1994) *Codes of Professional Responsibility* (3rd edn), Washington, DC: Bureau of National Affairs.

Gorsuch, R. L. (1984) "R. B. Cattell: An integration of psychology and ethics," *Multivariate Analysis* 19: 209–20.

Graber, G. C. and Thomasma, D. C. (1989) *Theory and Practice in Medical Ethics*, New York: Continuum.

Graham, L. R. (1981) *Between Science and Values*, New York: Columbia University Press.

Grawe, K., Donati, R., and Bernauer, F. (1996) *Psychotherapy in Transition: From Speculation to Science*, trans. German Translation Service, Seattle, WA: Hogrefe & Huber.

Grob, G. N. (1994) *The Mad Among Us: A History of the Care of America's Mentally Ill*, New York: Free Press.

Guignon, C. B. (1991) "Pragmatism or hermeneutics? Epistemology after foundationalism," in J. Bohman, D. Hile, and R. Schusterman (eds) *The Interpretive Turn: Philosophy, Science, Culture* (pp. 81–101), Ithaca, NY: Cornell University Press.

—— (1993) "Authenticity, moral values, and psychotherapy," in C. B. Guignon (ed.) *Cambridge Companion to Heidegger* (pp. 215–39), Cambridge: Cambridge University Press.

Haan, N., Aerts, E., and Cooper, B. A. B. (1985) *On Moral Grounds: The Search for Practical Morality*, New York: New York University Press.

Haan, N., Bellah, R. N., Rabinow, P., and Sullivan, W. M. (eds) (1983) *Social Science as Moral Inquiry*, New York: Columbia University Press.

Haas, L. J. and Malouf, J. L. (1995) *Keeping up the Good Work: A Practitioner's Guide to Mental Health Ethics* (2nd edn), Sarasota, FL: Professional Resource Exchange.

Hale, N. G., Jr (1971) *Freud and the Americans: The Beginnings of Psychoanalysis in the United States, 1876–1917*, New York: Oxford University Press.

—— (1995) *The Rise and Crisis of Psychoanalysis in the United States: Freud and the Americans, 1917–1985*, New York: Oxford University Press.

Hall, C. S. and Lindzey, G. (1978) *Theories of Personality* (3rd edn), New York: Wiley.

Hall, G. S. (1894) "On the history of American college textbooks and teaching in logic, ethics, psychology, and allied subjects," *Proceedings of the American Antiquarian Society* 9: 137–74.

—— (1923) *Life and Confessions of a Psychologist*, New York: Appleton.

Hall, M. A. (1997) *Making Medical Spending Decisions: The Law, Ethics, and Economics of Rationing Mechanisms*, New York: Oxford University Press.

Hammond, K. R., Harvey, L. O., and Hastie, R. (1992) "Making better use of scientific knowledge: Separating truth from justice," *Psychological Science* 3: 80–7.

Handelsman, M. M., Kemper, M. B., Kesson-Craig, P., McLain, J., and Johnsrud, C. (1986) "Use, content, and readability of written informed consent forms for treatment," *Professional Psychology: Research and Practice* 17: 514–18.

Handy, R. (1969) *Value Theory and the Behavioral Sciences*, Springfield, IL: Charles C. Thomas.

—— (1970) *The Measurement of Values: Behavioral Science and Philosophical Approaches*, St. Louis, MO: W. H. Green.

Hare-Mustin, R. T. (1994) "Discourses in the mirrored room: A postmodern analysis of therapy," *Family Process* 33: 19–35.

Hare-Mustin, R. T., Marecek, J., Kaplan, A. G., and Liss-Levinson, N. (1979) "Rights of clients, responsibilities of therapists," *American Psychologist* 34: 3–16.

Hartmann, H. (1939) "Psycho-analysis and the concept of health," *International Journal of Psycho-Analysis* 20: 308–21.

—— (1960) *Psychoanalysis and Moral Values*, New York: International Universities Press.

Harvey, J. H. (1985) "Editorial preface," *Journal of Social and Clinical Psychology* 3: 1.

Hatch, N. O. (1988a) "Introduction: The professions in a democratic culture," in N. O. Hatch (ed.) *The Professions in American History* (pp. 1–13), Notre Dame, IN: University of Notre Dame Press.

—— (ed.) (1988b) *The Professions in American History*, Notre Dame, IN: University of Notre Dame Press.

Hauerwas, S. (1995) "Virtue and character," in W. T. Reich (ed.) *Encyclopedia of Bioethics* (2nd edn, Vol. 5, pp. 2525–32), New York: Macmillan.

Haugen, M. L., Tyler, J. D., and Clark, J. A. (1991) "Mental health values of psychotherapists: How psychologists, psychiatrists, psychoanalysts, and social workers conceptualize good mental health," *Counseling and Values* 36: 24–36.

Hayes, S. C., Follette, V. M., Dawes, R. M., and Grady, K. E. (eds) (1995) *Scientific Standards of Psychological Practice*, Reno, NV: Context Press.

Hays, R. B. (1996) *The Moral Vision of the New Testament*, San Francisco, CA: HarperSanFrancisco.

Heatherton, T. F. and Weinberger, J. L. (1994) *Can Personality Change?* Washington, DC: American Psychological Association.

Heller, T. C., Sosna, M., and Wellbery, D. E. (eds) (1986) *Reconstructing Individualism: Autonomy, Individuality, and the Self in Western Thought*, Stanford, CA: Stanford University Press.

Hermans, H. J. M., Kempen, H. J. G., and van Loon, R. J. P. (1992) "The dialogical self: Beyond individualism and rationalism," *American Psychologist* 47: 23–33.

Herron, W. G., Javier, R. A., Primavera, L. H., and Schultz, C. L. (1994) "The cost of psychotherapy," *Professional Psychology: Research and Practice* 25: 106–10.

Higham, J. (1979) "The matrix of specialization," in A. Oleson and J. Voss (eds) *The Organization of Knowledge in Modern American, 1860–1920* (pp. 3–18), Baltimore, MD: Johns Hopkins University Press.

Hill, C. E. (1994) "From an experimental to an exploratory naturalistic approach to studying psychotherapy process," in R. L. Russell (ed.) *Reassessing Psychotherapy Research* (pp. 144–65), New York: Guilford.

Himmelfarb, G. (1995) *The De-moralization of Society: From Victorian Virtues to Modern Values*, New York: Knopf.

Hoagland, S. L. (1991) "Some thoughts about 'caring,'" in C. Card (ed.) *Feminist Ethics* (pp. 246–63), Lawrence, KS: University Press of Kansas.

Hobbs, N. (1948) "The development of a code of ethical standards for psychology," *American Psychologist* 3: 80–4.

Hoffman, J. C. (1979) *Ethical Confrontation in Counseling*, Chicago, IL: University of Chicago Press.

Hofstadter, R. and Metzger, W. P. (1955) *The Development of Academic Freedom in the United States*, New York: Columbia University Press.

Hogan, D. B. (1979) *The Regulation of Psychotherapists: A Study in the Philosophy and Practice of Professional Regulation*, Cambridge, MA: Ballinger.

Hoge, D. R. (1996) "Religion in America: The demographics of belief and affiliation," in E. P. Shafranske (ed.) *Religion and the Clinical Practice of Psychology* (pp. 21–41), Washington, DC: American Psychological Association.

Holifield, E. B. (1983) *A History of Pastoral Care in America: From Salvation to Self-realization*, Nashville, TN: Abingdon.

Holmes, A. F. (1984) *Ethics: Approaching Moral Decisions*, Downers Grove, IL: Inter-Varsity.

Holmes, J. and Lindley, R. (1989) *The Values of Psychotherapy*, Oxford: Oxford University Press.

Homans, P. (1979) "The case of Freud and Carl Rogers," in A. R. Buss (ed.) *Psychology in Social Context* (pp. 367–93), New York: Irvington.

Hood, R. W., Jr, Spilka, B., Hunsberger, B., and Gorsuch, R. L. (1996) *The Psychology of Religion: An Empirical Approach* (2nd edn), New York: Guilford.

Horney, K. (1950) *Neurosis and Human Growth*, New York: W. W. Norton.

Horvath, A. O. and Greenberg, L. S. (eds) (1994) *The Working Alliance: Theory, Research, and Practice*, New York: Wiley.

Howard, G. S. (1985) "The role of values in the science of psychology," *American Psychologist* 40: 255–65.

Hull, C. L. (1944) "Value, valuation and natural science methodology," *Philosophy of Science* 11: 125–41.

Hunter, J. D. (1991) *Culture Wars: The Struggle to Define America*, New York: Basic Books.

Imber, S. D., Glanz, L. M., Elkin, I., Sotsky, S. M., Boyer, J. L., and Leber, W. R. (1986) "Ethical issues in psychotherapy research: Problems in a collaborative clinical trials study," *American Psychologist* 41: 137–46.

Jacobs, L. (1978) "The relationship between religion and ethics in Jewish thought," in M. M. Kellner (ed.) *Contemporary Jewish Ethics* (pp. 41–57), New York: Sanhedrin Press.

Jafari, M. F. (1993) "Counseling values and objectives: A comparison of Western and Islamic perspectives," *The American Journal of Islamic Social Studies* 3: 326–39.

Jaggar, A. M. (1991) "Feminist ethics: Projects, problems, prospects," in C. Card (ed.) *Feminist Ethics* (pp. 78–104), Lawrence, KS: University Press of Kansas.

Jahoda, M. (1958) *Current Concepts of Positive Mental Health*, New York: Basic Books.

James, W. (1978) *The Varieties of Religious Experience*, Garden City, NY: Doubleday (original work published in 1902).

Jennings, B., Callahan, D., and Wolf, S. M. (1987) "The professions: Public interest and common good," *Hastings Center Report* 17: 3–10.

Jensen, J. P. and Bergin, A. E. (1988) "Mental health values of professional therapists: A national interdisciplinary survey," *Professional Psychology: Research and Practice* 19: 290–7.

Johnson, J. P. (1967) "The fact–value question in early modern value theory," *Journal of Value Inquiry* 1: 64–71.

Johnson, M. (1993) *Moral Imagination: Implications of Cognitive Science for Ethics*, Chicago, IL: University of Chicago Press.

Johnson, P. E. (1995) *Reason in the Balance: The Case Against Naturalism in Science, Law and Education*, Downers Grove, IL: InterVarsity.

Jones, S. L. (1994) "A constructive relationship for religion with the science and profession of psychology," *American Psychologist* 49: 184–99.

Jones, S. L. and Butman, R. E. (1991) *Modern Psychotherapies: A Comprehensive Christian Appraisal*, Downers Grove, IL: InterVarsity.

Jonsen, A. R. (1994) "Theological ethics, moral philosophy, and public moral discourse," *Kennedy Institute of Ethics Journal* 4 (March): 1–11.

—— (1995) "Casuistry," in W. T. Reich (ed.) *Encyclopedia of Bioethics* (2nd edn, Vol. 1, pp. 344–50), New York: Macmillan.

Jonsen, A. R., Siegler, M., and Winslade, W. J. (1992) *Clinical Ethics: A Practical Approach to Ethical Decisions in Clinical Medicine* (3rd edn), New York: McGraw-Hill.

Jordan, A. E. and Meara, N. M. (1990) "Ethics and the professional practice of the psychologist: The role of virtues and principles," *Professional Psychology: Research and Practice* 21: 107–14.

Kahneman, D. and Tversky, A. (1984) "Choices, values, and frames," *American Psychologist* 39: 341–50.

Karasu, T. B. (1980) "The ethics of psychotherapy," *American Journal of Psychiatry* 137: 1502–12.

Karon, B. P. (1995) "Provision of psychotherapy under managed health care: A growing crisis and national nightmare. Special section: Managed care and health policy," *Professional Psychology: Research and Practice* 26: 5–9.

Katkin, S. and Weisskopf-Joelson, E. (1971) "Relationship between professed values and emotional adjustment of college students," *Psychological Reports* 28: 523–8.

Kaufman, G. (1992) *Shame: The Power of Caring* (3rd edn), Rochester, VT: Schenkman.

—— (1996) *The Psychology of Shame: Theory and Treatment of Shame-based Syndromes* (2nd edn), New York: Springer.

Kaufmann, W. (1967) "Nietzsche, Friedrich," in P. Edwards (ed.) *Encyclopedia of Philosophy* (Vol. 5, pp. 504–14), New York: Macmillan.

Kazdin, A. E. (1996) "Validated treatments: Multiple perspectives and issues – Introduction to the Series," *Clinical Psychology: Science and Practice* 3: 216–17.

Keat, R. (1981) *The Politics of Social Theory: Habermas, Freud and the Critique of Positivism*, Chicago, IL: University of Chicago Press.

Kellner, M. M. (1978) "The structure of Jewish ethics," in M. M. Kellner (ed.) *Contemporary Jewish Ethics* (pp. 3–18), New York: Sanhedrin Press.

Kelly, E. L. (1947) "Clinical psychology," in W. Dennis, B. F. Skinner, R. R. Sears, E. L. Kelly, C. Rogers, J. C. Flanagan, C. T. Morgan, and R. Lifetree, *Current Trends in Psychology* (pp. 75–108), Pittsburgh, PA: University of Pittsburgh Press.

Kelly, E. W., Jr (1995a) "Counselor values: A national survey," *Journal of Counseling and Development* 73: 648–53.

—— (1995b) *Spirituality and Religion in Counseling and Psychotherapy: Diversity in Theory and Practice*, Alexandria, VA: American Counseling Association.

Kelly, E. W. Jr and Shilo, A. M. (1991) "Effects of individualistic and social commitment emphases on clients' perceptions of counselors," *Professional Psychology: Research and Practice* 22: 144–8.

Kelly, T. A. (1990) "The role of values in psychotherapy: A critical review of process and outcome effects," *Clinical Psychology Review* 10: 171–86.

Kelly, T. A. and Strupp, H. H. (1992) "Patient and therapist values in psychotherapy: Perceived changes, assimilation, similarity, and outcome," *Journal of Consulting and Clinical Psychology* 60: 34–40.

Kendall, P. C. and Chambless, D. L. (eds) (1998) "Special section: Empirically supported psychological therapies," *Journal of Consulting and Clinical Psychology* 66: 3–167.

Kendler, H. H. (1989) "The Iowa tradition," *American Psychologist* 44: 1124–32.

—— (1992) "Ethics and science: A psychological perspective," in W. M. Kurtines, M. Azmitia, and J. L. Gewirtz (eds) *The Role of Values in Psychology and Human Development* (pp. 131–60), New York: Wiley.

—— (1993) "Psychology and the ethics of social policy," *American Psychologist* 48: 1046–53.

Kiesler, C. A. and Morton, T. L. (1988) "Psychology and public policy in the 'health care revolution,'" *American Psychologist* 43: 993–1003.

Kiesler, C. A., Simpkins, C. G., and Morton, T. L. (1991) "Research issues in mental health policy," in M. Hersen, A. E. Kazdin, and A. S. Bellack (eds) *The Clinical Psychology Handbook* (2nd edn, pp. 78–101), New York: Pergamon.

Kirschner, S. R. (1993) "Inescapable moralities: Psychology as public philosophy," *Journal of Theoretical and Philosophical Psychology* 13: 87–9.

—— (1996) *The Religious and Romantic Origins of Psychoanalysis: Individuation and Integration in Post-Freudian Theory*, New York: Cambridge University Press.

—— (1997) "Between idealization and denigration: Recent revisionist approaches to the history of psychoanalysis," *Theory and Psychology* 7: 263–8.

Kitchener, K. S. (1984) "Intuition, critical evaluation and ethical principles: The foundation for ethical decisions in counseling psychology," *The Counseling Psychologist* 12: 43–55.

—— (1986) "Teaching applied ethics in counselor education: An integration of psychological processes and philosophical analysis," *Journal of Counseling and Development* 64: 306–10.

—— (1996a) "Professional codes of ethics and ongoing moral problems in psychology," in W. O'Donohue and R. F. Kitchener (eds) *The Philosophy of Psychology* (pp. 361–70), London: Sage.

—— (1996b) "Reconceptualizing Responsibilities to Students: A Feminist Perspective," paper presented at the annual meeting of the American Psychological Association, Toronto, Canada (August).

Kitchener, R. F. (1980a) "Ethical relativism and behavior therapy," *Journal of Consulting and Clinical Psychology* 48: 1–7.

—— (1980b) "Ethical relativism, ethical naturalism, and behavior therapy," *Journal of Consulting and Clinical Psychology* 48: 14–16.

Kitcher, P. (1985) *Vaulting Ambition: Sociobiology and the Quest for Human Nature*, Cambridge, MA: MIT Press.

Kitwood, T. (1990) *Concern for Others*, London: Routledge.

Klein, J. (1992) "Whose family? Who makes the choices? Whose values?" *Newsweek* June 8: 18–22.

Kluckhohn, C. (1951) "Values and value-orientations in the theory of action," in T. Parsons and E. A. Shils (eds) *Toward a General Theory of Action* (pp. 388–433), Cambridge, MA: Harvard University Press.

Knapp, M. (ed.) (1995) *The Economic Evaluation of Mental Health Care*, Aldershot (England): Arena.

Knutson, D. J., Fowles, J. B., Finch, M., McGee, J., Dahms, N., Kind, E. A., and Adlis, S. (1996) "Employer-specific versus community-wide report cards: Is there a difference?" *Health Care Financing Review* 18: 111–25.

Koch, S. (1969) "Value properties: Their significance for psychology, axiology, and science," in M. Greene (ed.) *The Anatomy of Knowledge* (pp. 119–48), London: Routledge & Kegan Paul.

—— (1981) "The nature and limits of psychological knowledge: Lessons of a century qua 'science,'" *American Psychologist* 36: 257–69.

Koch, S. and Leary, D. E. (eds) (1992) *A Century of Psychology as Science* (revised edn), Washington, DC: American Psychological Association.

Kockelmans, J. (1991) "History of Western ethics: 11. Twentieth-century continental, part I," in L. C. Becker and C. B. Becker (eds) *Encyclopedia of Ethics* (Vol. 1, pp. 522–8), New York: Garland.

Kohlberg, L. (1971) "From is to ought: How to commit the naturalistic fallacy and get away with it in the study of moral development," in T. Mischel (ed.) *Cognitive Development and Epistemology* (pp. 151–235), New York: Academic Press.

Kohlenberg, R. J. (1974) "Treatment of a homosexual pedophiliac using in vivo desensitization: A case study," *Journal of Abnormal Psychology* 83: 192–5.

Koocher, G. R. (1994) "The commerce of professional psychology and the new ethics code," *Professional Psychology: Research and Practice* 25: 355–61.

Kovacs, A. L. (1987) "Psychology as a 'health service' profession," *Psychotherapy Bulletin* 22 (Winter): 13–16.

Kovel, J. (1980) "The American mental health industry," in D. Ingleby (ed.) *Critical Psychiatry: The Politics of Mental Health* (pp. 72–101), New York: Random House.

Krause, M. S. and Howard, K. I. (1976) "Program evaluation in the public interest: A new research methodology," *Community Mental Health Journal* 12: 291–300.

Kristiansen, C. M. and Zanna, M. P. (1994) "The rhetorical use of values to justify social and intergroup attitudes," *Journal of Social Issues* 50: 47–65.

Kubacki, S. R. (1994) "Applying Habermas's theory of communicative action to values in psychotherapy," *Psychotherapy* 31: 463–77.

Kubacki, S. R. and Gluck, J. P. (1993) "Relating values and methods in psychodynamic and cognitive–behavioral therapy," paper presented at the annual meeting of the American Psychological Association, Toronto, Canada (August).

Kultgen, J. H. (1988) *Ethics and Professionalism*, Philadelphia, PA: University of Pennsylvania Press.

Kurtines, W. M., Alvarez, M., and Azmitia, M. (1990) "Science and morality: The role of values in science and the scientific study of moral phenomenon," *Psychological Bulletin* 107: 283–95.

Kurtines, W. M. and Gewirtz, J. L. (eds) (1991) *Handbook of Moral Behavior and Development* (3 Vols), Hillsdale, NJ: Erlbaum.

—— (eds) (1995) *Moral Development: An Introduction*, Boston, MA: Allyn & Bacon.

Ladd, J. (1978) "The task of ethics," in W. T. Reich (ed.) *Encyclopedia of Bioethics* (2nd edn, Vol. 1, pp. 400–7), New York: Macmillan.

Lakin, M. (1988) *Ethical Issues in the Psychotherapies*, New York: Oxford University Press.

—— (1991) *Coping With Ethical Dilemmas in Psychotherapy*, New York: Pergamon.

Lambert, M. J. (1983) "Introduction to assessment of psychotherapy outcome: Historical perspective and current issues," in M. J. Lambert, E. R. Christensen, and S. S. DeJulio (eds) *The Assessment of Psychotherapy Outcome* (pp. 3–32), New York: Wiley.

—— (1989) "The individual therapist's contribution to psychotherapy process and outcome," *Clinical Psychology Review* 9: 469–85.

Lambert, M. J. and Hill, C. E. (1994) "Assessing psychotherapy outcomes and process," in A. E. Bergin and S. L. Garfield (eds) *Handbook of Psychotherapy and Behavior Change* (4th edn, pp. 72–113), New York: Wiley.

Lasch, C. (1978) *The Culture of Narcissism*, New York: W. W. Norton.

Laudan, L. (1984) *Science and Values: The Aims of Science and Their Role in Scientific Debate*, Berkeley, CA: University of California Press.

—— (1987) "Progress or rationality? The prospects for normative naturalism," *American Philosophical Quarterly* 24: 19–31.

Leahey, T. H. (1987a) *A History of Psychology: Main Currents in Psychological Thought* (2nd edn), Englewood Cliffs, NJ: Prentice-Hall.

—— (1987b) "Psychology and the problem of moral authority," paper presented at the annual meeting of the American Psychological Association, New York (August).

—— (1992) *A History of Psychology: Main Currents in Psychological Thought* (3rd edn), Englewood Cliffs, NJ: Prentice-Hall.

—— (1997) *A History of Psychology: Main Currents in Psychological Thought* (4th edn), Englewood Cliffs, NJ: Prentice-Hall.

Lear, J. (1990) *Love and Its Place in Nature: A Philosophical Interpretation of Freudian Psychoanalysis*, New York: Farrar, Straus & Giroux.

Leary, D. E. (1980) "The intentions and heritage of Descartes and Locke: Toward a recognition of the moral basis of modern psychology," *Journal of General Psychology* 102: 283–310.

Lerman, H. and Porter, N. (eds) (1990) *Feminist Ethics in Psychotherapy*, New York: Springer.

Levine, M. and Levine, A. (1970) *A Social History of Helping Services: Clinic, Court, School, and Community*, New York: Appleton-Century-Crofts.

Levitin, T. (1973) "Values," in J. P. Robinson and P. R. Shaver (eds) *Measures of Social Psychological Attitudes* (revised edn, pp. 489–585), Ann Arbor, MI: Institute for Social Research.

Lichtenstein, A. (1978) "Does Jewish tradition recognize an ethic independent of Halaka?" in M. M. Kellner (ed.) *Contemporary Jewish Ethics* (pp. 102–23), New York: Sanhedrin Press.

Lidz, C. W., Meisel, A., Zernbavel, E., Carter, M., Sestak, R. M., and Roth, L. H. (1984) *Informed Consent: A Study of Decisionmaking in Psychiatry*, New York: Guilford.

Lifton, R. J. (1976) "Advocacy and corruption in the healing professions," *International Review of Psycho-analysis* 3: 385–98.

Lippmann, W. (1956) *The Public Philosophy*, New York: Mentor.

London, P. (1964) *The Modes and Morals of Psychotherapy*, New York: Holt, Rinehart & Winston.

—— (1986) *The Modes and Morals of Psychotherapy* (2nd edn), Washington, DC: Hemisphere.

Long, E. L., Jr (1967) *A Survey of Christian Ethics*, New York: Oxford University Press.

—— (1982) *A Survey of Recent Christian Ethics*, New York: Oxford University Press.

Longino, H. E. (1990) *Science as Social Knowledge: Values and Objectivity in Scientific Inquiry*, Princeton, NJ: Princeton University Press.

Lorion, R. P., Iscoe, I., DeLeon, P. H., and VandenBos, G. R. (eds) (1996) *Psychology and Public Policy: Balancing Public Service and Professional Need*, Washington, DC: American Psychological Association.

Lovinger, R. J. (1984) *Working With Religious Issues in Therapy*, New York: J. Aronson.

—— (1996) "Considering the religious dimension in assessment and treatment," in E. P. Shafranske (ed.) *Religion and the Clinical Practice of Psychology* (pp. 327–64), Washington, DC: American Psychological Association.

Lowe, C. M. (1976) *Value Orientations in Counseling and Psychotherapy: The Meanings of Mental Health* (2nd edn), Cranston, RI: Carroll Press.

McAlister, L. L. (1982) *The Development of Franz Brentano's Ethics*, Amsterdam: Rodopi.

McClure, G. and Tyler, F. (1967) "Role of values in the study of values," *Journal of General Psychology* 77: 217–35.

McFall, R. M. (1991) "Manifesto for a science of clinical psychology," *The Clinical Psychologist* 44: 75–88.

McGovern, T. V., Furumoto, L., Halpern, D. F., Kimble, G. A., and McKeachie, W. J. (1991) "Liberal education, study in depth, and the arts and sciences major: Psychology," *American Psychologist* 46: 598–605.

McGuire, T. G. (1992) "Research on economics and mental health: The past and future prospects," in R. G. Frank and W. G. Manning, Jr (eds) *Economics and Mental Health* (pp. 1–14), Baltimore, MD: Johns Hopkins University Press.

MacIntyre, A. (1966) *A Short History of Ethics*, New York: Macmillan.

—— (1984) *After Virtue* (revised edn), Notre Dame, IN: University of Notre Dame Press.

—— (1988) *Whose Justice? Which Rationality?* Notre Dame, IN: University of Notre Dame.

—— (1990) *Three Rival Versions of Moral Enquiry: Encyclopaedia, Genealogy, and Tradition*, Notre Dame, IN: University of Notre Dame.

—— (1994) "A partial response to my critics," in J. Horton and S. Mendus (eds) *After MacIntyre: Critical Perspectives on the Work of Alasdair MacIntyre* (pp. 83–304), Notre Dame, IN: University of Notre Dame Press.

Macklin, R. (1982) *Man, Mind, and Morality: The Ethics of Behavior Control*, Englewood Cliffs, NJ: Prentice-Hall.

—— (1989) "Ethical theory and applied ethics," in B. Hoffmaster, B. Freedman, and G. Fraser (eds) *Clinical Ethics: Theory and Practice* (pp. 101–24), Clifton, NJ: Humana.

McNeil, J. (1951) *A History of the Cure of Souls*, New York: Harper & Row.

MacNiven, D. (ed.) (1990) *Moral Expertise: Studies in Practical and Professional Ethics*, London: Routledge.

Magesa, L. (1997) *African Religion: The Moral Traditions of Abundant Life*, Maryknoll, NY: Orbis.

Maher, B. (1991) "A personal history of clinical psychology," in M. Hersen, A. E. Kazdin, and A. S. Bellack (eds) *Clinical Psychology Handbook* (2nd edn, pp. 3–25), New York: Pergamon.

Mahoney, M. J. (1991) *Human Change Processes: The Scientific Foundations of Psychotherapy*, New York: Basic Books.

Maimonides, M. (1975a) "Guide of the perplexed," in *Ethical Writings of Maimonides* (pp. 129–54), trans. R. L. Weiss and C. E. Butterworth, New York: New York University Press (original work published in the 12th century).

—— (1975b) "On the management of health," in *Ethical Writings of Maimonides* (pp. 105–11), trans. R. L. Weiss and C. E. Butterworth, New York: New York University Press (original work published in the 12th century).

Mansbridge, J. J. (ed.) (1990) *Beyond Self-interest*, Chicago, IL: University of Chicago Press.

Margolin, G. (1982) "Ethical and legal considerations in marital and family therapy," *American Psychologist* 37: 788–801.

Margolis, J. (1966) *Psychotherapy and Morality: A Study of Two Concepts*, New York: Random House.

Marsden, G. M. (1991) "The soul of the American university," *First Things* 9 (January): 34–47.

Marsella, A. J. and White, G. M. (eds) (1982) *Cultural Conceptions of Mental Health and Therapy*, Dordrecht (The Netherlands): D. Reidel.

Martin, J. (1995) "Against scientism in psychological counselling and therapy," *Canadian Journal of Counselling* 29: 287–307.

Martin, J. and Thompson, J. (1997) "Between scientism and relativism: Phenomenology, hermeneutics and the new realism," *Theory and Psychology* 7: 629–52.

Marty, M. E. (1983) *Health and Medicine in the Lutheran Tradition*, New York: Crossroad.

—— (1993) "Fundamentalism and the scholars," *The Key Reporter* 58 (Spring): 1, 3–6.

Marty, M. E. and Appleby, R. S. (eds) (1991) *Fundamentalisms Observed*, Chicago, IL: University of Chicago Press.

—— (eds) (1992) *The Glory and the Power: The Fundamentalist Challenge to the Modern World*, Boston, MA: Beacon.

—— (eds) (1993a) *Fundamentalisms and Society: Reclaiming the Sciences, the Family, and Education*, Chicago, IL: University of Chicago Press.

—— (eds) (1993b) *Fundamentalisms and the State: Remaking Polities, Economies, and Militance*, Chicago, IL: University of Chicago Press.

—— (eds) (1994) *Accounting for Fundamentalisms: The Dynamic Character of Movements*, Chicago, IL: University of Chicago Press.

—— (eds) (1995) *Fundamentalisms Comprehended*, Chicago, IL: University of Chicago Press.

—— (eds) (1997) *Religion, Ethnicity, and Self-identity: Nations in Turmoil*, Hanover, NH: University Press of New England.

Maslow, A. H. (1956) "Self-actualizing people: A study of psychological health," in C. E. Moustakas (ed.) *The Self: Explorations in Personal Growth* (pp. 160–94), New York: Harper & Row.

—— (1961) "Eupsychia: The good society," *Journal of Humanistic Psychology* 1: 1–11.

—— (1963) "Fusions of facts and values," *American Journal of Psychoanalysis* 23: 117–31.

—— (1968) *Toward a Psychology of Being* (2nd edn), Princeton, NJ: Van Nostrand.

—— (1970) *Religions, Values, and Peak-experiences* (2nd edn), New York: Viking.

—— (1987) *Motivation and Personality* (3rd edn), New York: Harper & Row.

May, L. (1996) *The Socially Responsive Self: Social Theory and Professional Ethics*, Chicago, IL: University of Chicago Press.

May, L., Friedman, M., and Clark, A. (eds) (1995) *Mind and Morals: Essays on Ethics and Cognitive Science*, Cambridge, MA: MIT Press.

May, R. (1953) "Historical and philosophical presuppositions for understanding therapy," in O. H. Mowrer (ed.) *Psychotherapy: Theory and Research* (pp. 9–43), New York: Roland.

May, W. F. (1984) "The virtues in a professional setting," *Soundings* 67: 245–66.

Meara, N. M., Schmidt, L. D., and Day, J. D. (1996) "Principles and virtues: A foundation for ethical decisions, policies, and character," *The Counseling Psychologist* 24: 4–77.

Meehl, P. E. (1959) "Some technical and axiological problems in the therapeutic handling of religious and valuational material," *Journal of Counseling Psychology* 6: 255–9.

—— (1970) "Psychology and the criminal law," *University of Richmond Law Review* 5: 1–30.

—— (1981) "Ethical criticism in value clarification: Correcting cognitive errors within the client's – not the therapist's – framework," *Rational Living* 16: 3–9.

—— (1989) "Paul E. Meehl," in G. Lindzey (ed.) *A History of Psychology in Autobiography* (Vol. 8, pp. 336–89), Stanford, CA: Stanford University Press.

—— (1997) "Credentialed persons, credentialed knowledge," *Clinical Psychology: Science and Practice* 4: 91–8.

Meehl, P. E. and McClosky, H. (1947) "Ethical and political aspects of applied psychology," *Journal of Abnormal and Social Psychology* 42: 91–8.

Meilaender, G. C. (1984) *The Theory and Practice of Virtue*, Notre Dame, IN: University of Notre Dame Press.

Menninger, K. A. (1943) "Clinical psychology in the psychiatric clinic," *Bulletin of the Menninger Clinic* 7: 89–92.

Merriam-Webster's Collegiate Dictionary (1993) Springfield, MA: Merriam-Webster.

Messer, S. B., Sass, L. A., and Woolfolk, R. L. (eds) (1988) *Hermeneutics and Psychological Theory*, New Brunswick, NJ: Rutgers University Press.

Michael, J. (1977) "Radical behaviorism as a way of life," in J. E. Krapfl and E. A. Vargas (eds) *Behaviorism and Ethics* (pp. 293–303), Kalamazoo, MI: Behaviordelia.

Michels, R. (1976) "Professional ethics and social values," *International Review of Psycho-analysis* 3: 377–84.

—— (1987) "Psychiatry: Where medicine, psychology, and ethics meet," *Second Opinion* 6: 35–48.

—— (1991) "Psychiatry: Where medicine, psychology, and ethics meet," in D. S. Browning and I. S. Evison (eds) *Does Psychiatry Need a Public Philosophy?* (pp. 61–73), Chicago, IL: Nelson-Hall.

Midgley, M. (1978) *Beast and Man: The Roots of Human Nature*, Ithaca, NY: Cornell University Press.

Miller, I. J. (1996) "Managed care is harmful to outpatient mental health services: A call for accountability," *Professional Psychology* 27: 349–63.

Miller, J. G. (1946) "Clinical psychology in the Veterans Administration," *American Psychologist* 1: 181–9.

Miller, R. B. (1983) "A call to armchairs," *Psychotherapy: Theory, Research and Practice* 20: 208–19.

Miller, R. W. (1991) "Moral realism," in L. C. Becker and C. B. Becker (eds) *Encyclopedia of Ethics* (Vol. 2, pp. 847–52), New York: Garland.

Miller, W. R. (ed.) (forthcoming) *Integrating Spirituality in Treatment: Resources for Practitioners*, Washington, DC: American Psychological Association.

Minsel, B., Becker, P., and Korchin, S. (1991) "A cross-cultural view of positive mental health," *Journal of Cross-cultural Psychology* 22: 157–81.

Moffic, H. S. (ed.) (1997) *The Ethical Way: Challenges and Solutions for Managed Behavioral Healthcare*, San Francisco, CA: Jossey-Bass.

Monopolis, S., Moraitis, J., Kouvaris, M., and Galanopoulou, P. (1977) "Health as a human value," *Transnational Mental Health Research Newsletter* 19: 5–9.

Moore, D. L. (1992) "The Veterans Administration and the training program in psychology," in D. K. Freedheim (ed.) *History of Psychotherapy: A Century of Change* (pp. 776–800), Washington, DC: American Psychological Association.

Moore, T. V. (1944) "A century of psychology in its relationship to American psychiatry," in American Psychiatric Association (ed.) *One Hundred Years of American Psychiatry* (pp. 443–77), New York: Columbia University Press.

Morawski, J. G. (1982) "Assessing psychology's moral heritage through our neglected utopias," *American Psychologist* 37: 1082–95.

—— (1994) *Practicing Feminisms, Reconstructing Psychology: Notes on a Liminal Science*, Ann Arbor, MI: University of Michigan Press.

Moreno, J. D. (1995) *Deciding Together: Bioethics and Moral Consensus*, New York: Oxford University Press.

Mouw, R. J. (1990) *The God Who Commands*, Notre Dame, IN: University of Notre Dame Press.

Mowrer, O. H. (ed.) (1967) *Morality and Mental Health*, Chicago, IL: Rand McNally.

Nagy, T. F. (1994) "The Ethical Principles of Psychologists and Code of Conduct (1992 revision)," in R. J. Corsini (ed.) *Encyclopedia of Psychology* (2nd edn, Vol. 1, pp. 504–8), New York: Wiley.

Naranjo, C. (1970) "Present-centeredness: Technique, prescription, and ideal," in J. Fagan and I. L. Shepherd (eds) *Gestalt Therapy Now: Theory/techniques/applications* (pp. 47–69), New York: Harper.

Nathan, P. E. and Gorman, J. M. (eds) (1998) *A Guide to Treatments That Work*, New York: Oxford University Press.

National Association of Social Workers (1993) *Code of Ethics*, Washington, DC: Author.

Neimeyer, R. A. (1993) "An appraisal of constructivist psychotherapies," *Journal of Consulting and Clinical Psychology* 61: 221–34.

Nerlich, G. (1989) *Values and Valuing: Speculations on the Ethical Life of Persons*, Oxford: Clarendon Press.

Neuhaus, R. J. (1984) *The Naked Public Square: Religion and Democracy in America*, Grand Rapids, MI: Eerdmans.

Neulinger, J., Schillinger, M., Stein, M. I., and Welkowitz, J. (1970) "Perceptions of the optimally integrated person as a function of therapists' characteristics," *Perceptual and Motor Skills* 30: 375–84.

Newman, F. L., DeLiberty, R., Hodges, K., McGrew, J., and Tejeda, M. (1997) *The Hoosier Assurance Plan: Report on Research/implementation Strategy and Assessment Instruments to Support Level of Care Determination*, July 29, unpublished report, Florida International University.

Nicholas, M. (1994) *The Mystery of Goodness and the Positive Moral Consequences of Psychotherapy*, New York: W. W. Norton.

Niebuhr, R. (1944) *The Children of Light and the Children of Darkness*, New York: Scribner's.

Nietzsche, F. (1909) "The will to power: An attempted transvaluation of all values," in O. Levy (ed.) *The Complete Works of Friedrich Nietzsche* (Vol. 14, Book 1), trans. A. M. Ludovici, New York: Macmillan.

Noddings, N. (1984) *Caring: A Feminist Approach to Ethics and Moral Education*, Berkeley, CA: University of California Press.

Norcross, J. C. (1995) "Dispelling the Dodo bird verdict and the exclusivity myth in psychotherapy," *Psychotherapy* 32: 500–4.

Norton, D. L. (1976) *Personal Destinies: A Philosophy of Ethical Individualism*, Princeton, NJ: Princeton University Press.

Nunnally, J. (1961) *Popular Conceptions of Mental Health*, New York: Holt, Rinehart & Winston.

Nussbaum, M. (1994) *The Therapy of Desire: Theory and Practice in Hellenistic Ethics*, Princeton, NJ: Princeton University Press.

Odell, M. and Stewart, S. P. (1993) "Ethical issues associated with client values conversion and therapist value agendas in family therapy," *Family Relations* 42: 128–33.

O'Donnell, J. M. (1985) *The Origins of Behaviorism: American Psychology, 1870–1920*, New York: New York University Press.

O'Donohue, W. (1989) "The (even) bolder model: The clinical psychologist as meta-physician-scientist-practitioner," *American Psychologist* 44: 1460–8.

O'Donohue, W. and Mangold, R. (1996) "A critical examination of the Ethical Principles of Psychologists and Code of Conduct," in W. O'Donohue and R. F. Kitchener (eds) *The Philosophy of Psychology* (pp. 371–80), London: Sage.

Offer, D. and Sabshin, D. (1966) *Normality: Theoretical and Clinical Concepts of Mental Health*, New York: Basic Books.

O'Hara, M. (1997) "Emancipatory therapeutic practice in a turbulent transmodern era: A work of retrieval," *Journal of Humanistic Psychology* 37: 7–13.

Orlinsky, D. E. (1989) "Researchers' images of psychotherapy: Their origins and influence on research," *Clinical Psychology Review* 9: 413–41.

Orlinsky, D. E., Grawe, K., and Parks, B. K. (1994) "Process and outcome in psychotherapy – noch einmal," in A. E. Bergin and S. L. Garfield (eds) *Handbook of Psychotherapy and Behavior Change* (4th edn, pp. 270–376), New York: Wiley.

Orlinsky, D. E. and Howard, K. I. (1978) "The relation of process to outcome in psychotherapy," in. S. L. Garfield and A. E. Bergin (eds) *Handbook of Psychotherapy and Behavior Change: An Empirical Analysis* (2nd edn, pp. 283–329), New York: Wiley.

Ozar, D. T. (1995) "Profession and professional ethics," in W. T. Reich (ed.) *Encyclopedia of Bioethics* (2nd edn, Vol. 4, pp. 2103–11), New York: Macmillan.

Packer, M. J. (1985a) "Hermeneutic inquiry in the study of human conduct," *American Psychologist* 40: 1081–93.

—— (1985b) *The Structure of Moral Action: A Hermeneutic Study of Moral Conduct*, Basel (Switzerland): Karger.

Paris, P. J. (1995) *The Spirituality of African Peoples: The Search for a Common Moral Discourse*, Minneapolis, MN: Fortress.

Parloff, M. B. (1967) "Goals in psychotherapy: Mediating and ultimate," in A. R. Mahrer (ed.) *The Goals of Psychotherapy* (pp. 5–19), New York: Appleton-Century-Crofts.

Parloff, M. B., Goldstein, N., and Iflund, B. (1960) "Communication of values and therapeutic change," *Archives of General Psychiatry* 2: 300–4.

Pascal, B. (1958) *Pensées*, trans. W. F. Trotter, New York: E. P. Dutton, (original work published in 1670).

Patterson, C. H. (1989) "Values in counseling and psychotherapy," *Counseling and Values* 33: 164–76.

Pedersen, P. B. and Marsella, A. J. (1982) "The ethical crisis for cross-cultural counseling and therapy," *Professional Psychology* 13: 492–500.

Pellegrino, E. D. (1989) "Character, virtue, and self-interest in the ethics of the professions," *Journal of Contemporary Health Policy and Law* 5: 53–73.

Pellegrino, E. D. and Thomasma, D. C. (1981) *A Philosophical Basis of Medical Practice: Toward a Theory and Ethic of the Healing Professions*, New York: Oxford University Press.

Peperzak, A. (1986) "Values: Subjective – objective," *Journal of Value Inquiry* 20: 71–80.

Pepper, S. C. (1950) "A brief history of general theory of value," in V. Ferm (ed.) *A History of Philosophical Systems* (pp. 493–503), New York: Philosophical Library.

Perrez, M. (1989a) "Psychotherapeutic knowledge in a prescientific state or founded on an ethico-ontological discourse on human relationship? A reply to Kanfer, Fischer, and Bickhard," *New Ideas in Psychology* 7: 165–71.

—— (1989b) "Psychotherapeutic methods between scientific foundation and everyday knowledge," *New Ideas in Psychology* 7: 133–45.

Perry, R. B. (1914) "The definition of value," *Journal of Philosophy, Psychology and Scientific Methods* 11: 141–62.

—— (1943) "James the psychologist – as a philosopher sees him," *Psychological Record* 50: 122–4.

—— (1954) *Realms of Value: A Critique of Human Civilization*, Cambridge, MA: Harvard University Press.

Petrinovich, L., O'Neill, P., and Jorgensen, M. (1993) "An empirical study of moral intuitions: Toward an evolutionary ethics," *Journal of Personality and Social Psychology* 64: 467–78.

Phillips, L. D. (1987) "Authenticity or morality?" in R. B. Kruschwitz and R. C. Roberts (eds) *The Virtues: Contemporary Essays on Moral Character* (pp. 22–35), Belmont, CA: Wadsworth.

Pilgrim, D. and Treacher, A. (1992) *Clinical Psychology Observed*, London: Routledge.

Piore, M. J. (1995) *Beyond Individualism*, Cambridge, MA: Harvard University Press.

Platts, M. de B. (1991) *Moral Realities: An Essay in Philosophical Psychology*, London: Routledge.

Pojman, L. P. (ed.) (1995a) *Ethical Theory: Classical and Contemporary Readings* (2nd edn), Belmont, CA: Wadsworth.

—— (1995b) *Ethics: Discovering Right and Wrong* (2nd edn), Belmont, CA: Wadsworth.

Popper, K. R. (1976) "The logic of the social sciences: First contribution to the symposium," in T. W. Adorno, H. Albert, R. Dahrendorf, J. Habermas, H. Pilot, and K. R. Popper, *The Positivist Dispute in German Sociology* (pp. 87–104), London: Heinemann (original work published 1962).

Post, S. C. (ed.) (1972) *Moral Values and the Superego Concept in Psychoanalysis*, New York: International Universities Press.

Practitioner Focus (1989) 3 (2): 7 – "Court approves settlement of psychoanalytic suit."

Prilleltensky, I. (1994) *The Morals and Politics of Psychology: Psychological Discourse and the Status Quo*, Albany, NY: State University of New York Press.

—— (1997) "Values, assumptions and practices: Assessing the moral implications of psychological discourse and action," *American Psychologist* 52: 517–35.

Prochaska, J. O. and DiClemente, C. C. (1994) *The Transtheoretical Approach: Crossing Traditional Boundaries of Therapy*, Melbourne, FL: Krieger.

Prochaska, J. O., DiClemente, C. C., and Norcross, J. C. (1992) "In search of how people change: Applications to addictive behaviors," *American Psychologist* 47: 1102–14.

Prochaska, J. O. and Norcross, J. C. (1994) *Systems of Psychotherapy: A Transtheoretical Analysis* (3rd edn), Pacific Grove, CA: Brooks/Cole.

Proctor, R. N. (1991) *Value-free Science? Purity and Power in Modern Knowledge*, Cambridge, MA: Harvard University Press.

Punzo, V. A. (1996) "After Kohlberg: Virtue ethics and the recovery of the moral self," *Philosophical Psychology* 9: 7–23.

Putnam, H. (1993) "Objectivity and the science–ethics distinction," in M. Nussbaum and A. Sen (eds) *The Quality of Life* (pp. 143–57), Oxford: Oxford University Press.

Putnam, R. A. (1991) "Pragmatism," in L. C. Becker and C. B. Becker (eds) *Encyclopedia of Ethics* (Vol. 2, pp. 1002–5), New York: Garland.

Quinn, P. L. (1978) *Divine Commands and Moral Requirements*, Oxford: Oxford University Press.

—— (1995) "Political liberalisms and their exclusions of the religious," *Proceedings and Addresses of the American Philosophical Association* 69: 35–56.

Raimy, V. C. (1950) *Training in Clinical Psychology*, New York: Prentice-Hall.

Rambo, L. R. (1980) "Ethics, evolution, and the psychology of William James," *Journal of the History of the Behavioral Sciences* 16: 50–7.

Ramsey, P. (1971) "The ethics of a cottage industry in an age of community and research medicine," *New England Journal of Medicine* 284: 700–6.

Rawls, J. (1971) *A Theory of Justice*, Cambridge, MA: Harvard University Press.

—— (1980) "Kantian constructivism in moral theory," *Journal of Philosophy* 77: 515–72.

—— (1993) *Political Liberalism*, New York: Columbia University Press.

Ray, R. A. (1994). *Buddhist Saints in India: A Study in Buddhist Values and Orientations*. New York: Oxford University Press.

Redick, R. W., Witkin, M. A., Atay, J. E., and Manderscheid, R. W. (1992) "Specialty mental health system characteristics," in Center for Mental Health Services and National Institute of Mental Health, R. W. Manderscheid and M. A. Sonnenschein (eds) *Mental Health, United States, 1992* (pp. 1–141), Washington, DC: Superintendent of Documents, US Government Printing Office. DHHS Pub No. (SMA) 92–1942.

Regier, D. A., Narrow, W. E., Rae, D. S., Manderscheid, R. W., Locke, B. Z., and Goodwin, F. K. (1993) "The de facto US mental and addictive disorders service system: Epidemiological catchment area prospective 1-year prevalence rates of disorders and services," *Archives of General Psychiatry* 50: 85–94.

Reich, W. T. (ed.) (1995a) *Encyclopedia of Bioethics* (2nd edn, Vols 1–5), New York: Macmillan.

Reich, W. T. (1995b) "Introduction," in W. T. Reich (ed.) *Encyclopedia of Bioethics* (2nd edn, Vol. 1, pp. xix–xxxii), New York: Macmillan.

Reisman, J. M. (1976) *A History of Clinical Psychology* (revised edn), New York: Irvington-Halsted.

Rescher, N. (1969) *Introduction to Value Theory*, Englewood Cliffs, NJ: Prentice-Hall.

Rest, J. R. (1984) "Research on moral development: Implications for training counseling psychologists," *The Counseling Psychologist* 12: 19–29.

—— (1988) "Can ethics be taught in professional schools? The psychological research," *Easier Said Than Done* (Winter): 22–6.

Richards, P. S. and Bergin, A. E. (1997) *A Spiritual Strategy for Counseling and Psychotherapy*, Washington, DC: American Psychological Association.

Richards, P. S., Rector, J. M., and Tjeltveit, A. C. (forthcoming) "Values, spirituality, and psychotherapy," in W. Miller (ed.) *Integrating Spirituality in Treatment: Resources for Practitioners*, Washington, DC: American Psychological Association.

Richardson, F. C. (1989) "Freedom and commitment in modern psychotherapy," *Journal of Integrative and Eclectic Psychotherapy* 8: 303–19.

—— (1995) "Beyond relativism? Psychology and the moral dimension [Review of *Social Discourse and Moral Judgment*]," *Theory and Psychology* 5: 316–18.

—— (1997) "Overcoming fragmentation in psychology: A hermeneutic approach," paper presented at the annual meeting of the American Psychological Association, Chicago (August).

Richardson, F. C. and Fowers, B. J. (1994) "Beyond scientism and constructionism," paper presented at the annual meeting of the American Psychological Association, Los Angeles (August).

—— (1997) "Psychology, psychotherapy, and contemporary communitarian thought," paper presented at the annual meeting of the American Psychological Association, Chicago (August).

Richardson, F. C. and Guignon, C. B. (1988) "Individualism and social interest," *Journal of Individual Psychology* 44: 13–29.

Richardson, F. C. and Woolfolk, R. L. (1994) "Social theory and values: A hermeneutic perspective," *Theory and Psychology* 4: 199–226.

Rieff, P. (1959) *Freud: The Mind of the Moralist*, New York: Viking.

—— (1966) *The Triumph of the Therapeutic: Uses of Faith After Freud*, New York: Harper & Row.

—— (1979) *Freud: The Mind of the Moralist* (3rd edn), Chicago, IL: University of Chicago Press.

Riley, G. (ed.) (1974) *Values, Objectivity, and the Social Sciences*, Reading, MA: Addison-Wesley.

Roazen, P. (1972) "The impact of psychoanalysis on values," in S. C. Post (ed.) *Moral Values and the Superego Concept in Psychoanalysis* (pp. 197–204), New York: International Universities Press.

Robinson, D. N. (1981) *An Intellectual History of Psychology* (revised edn), New York: Macmillan.

—— (1985) *Philosophy of Psychology*, New York: Columbia University Press.

—— (1997) "Therapy as theory and as civics," *Theory and Psychology* 7: 675–81.

Rochefort, D. A. (ed.) (1989) *Handbook on Mental Health Policy in the United States*, New York: Greenwood.

Rodis, P. T. and Strehorn, K. C. (1997) "Ethical issues for counseling in the post-modern era: Feminist psychology and multicultural therapy (MCT)," *Journal of Theoretical and Philosophical Psychology* 17: 13–31.

Rogers, C. R. (1951) *Client-centered Therapy: Its Current Practice, Implications, and Theory*, Boston, MA: Houghton Mifflin.

—— (1961) *On Becoming a Person*, Boston, MA: Houghton Mifflin.

—— (1964) "Toward a modern approach to values: The valuing process in the mature person," *Journal of Abnormal and Social Psychology* 68: 160–7.

Rokeach, M. (1973) *The Nature of Human Values*, New York: Free Press.

—— (ed.) (1979) *Understanding Human Values: Individual and Societal*, New York: Free Press.

Rosenau, P. M. (1992) *Post-modernism and the Social Sciences: Insights, Inroads, and Intrusions*, Princeton, NJ: Princeton University Press.

Rosenberg, C. (1979) "Toward an ecology of knowledge: On discipline, context, and history," in A. Oleson and J. Voss (eds) *The Organization of Knowledge in Modern America, 1860–1920* (pp. 440–55), Baltimore, MD: Johns Hopkins University Press.

Rosenthal, D. (1955) "Changes in some moral values following psychotherapy," *Journal of Consulting Psychology* 19: 431–6.

Rosenthal, P. (1984) *Words and Values: Some Leading Words and Where They Lead Us*, New York: Oxford University Press.

Ross, D. (1979) "The development of the social sciences," in A. Oleson and J. Voss (eds) *The Organization of Knowledge in Modern America, 1860–1920* (pp. 107–38), Baltimore, MD: Johns Hopkins University Press.

Roth, A. and Fonagy, P. (1996) *What Works for Whom? A Critical Review of Psychotherapy*, New York: Guilford.

Rottschaefer, W. A. and Martinsen, D. (1990) "Taking Darwin seriously: An alternative to Michael Ruse's Darwinian metaethics," *Biology and Philosophy* 5: 149–73.

Routh, D. (1994) *Clinical Psychology Since 1917*, New York: Plenum.

Ruble, D. N., Costanzo, P. R., and Oliveri, M. E. (eds) (1992) *The Social Psychology of Mental Health: Basic Mechanisms and Applications*, New York: Guilford.

Ruddick, W. and Finn, W. (1985) "Objections to hospital philosophers," *Journal of Medical Ethics* 11: 42–6.

Ruse, M. (1986) *Taking Darwin Seriously*, Oxford: Blackwell.

Sadler, J. Z. and Hulgus, Y. F. (1992) "Clinical problem solving and the bio-psychosocial model," *American Journal of Psychiatry* 149: 1315–23.

Salmon, J. W. (ed.) (1990) *The Corporate Transformation of Health Care: Part 1: Issues and Directions*, Amityville, NY: Baywood.

Saltzman, N. and Norcross, J. C. (eds) (1990) *Therapy Wars: Controversy and Convergence*, San Francisco, CA: Jossey-Bass.

Sampson, E. E. (1988) "The debate on individualism: Indigenous psychologies of the individual and their role in personal and societal functioning," *American Psychologist* 43: 15–22.

—— (1993) *Celebrating the Other: A Dialogic Account of Human Nature*, Boulder, CO: Westview.

Sandel, M. (1996) *Democracy's Discontent: America in Search of a Public Philosophy*, Cambridge, MA: Harvard University Press.

Sanderson, W. C. and Woody, S. (1995) *Manuals for Empirically Validated Treatments: A Project of the Task Force on Psychological Interventions*, Oklahoma City, OK: Division of Clinical Psychology, American Psychological Association.

Sarason, S. B. (1981) "An asocial psychology and a misdirected clinical psychology," *American Psychologist* 36: 827–36.

—— (1986) "And what is the public interest?" *American Psychologist* 41: 899–905.

—— (1993) "American psychology and the needs for transcendence and community," *American Journal of Community Psychology* 21: 185–202.

Sass, H. M. (1988) "Introduction," in H. M. Sass and R. U. Massey (eds) *Health Care Systems: Moral Conflicts in European and American Public Policy* (pp. ix–ixx), Dordrecht (The Netherlands): Kluwer.

Sass, H. M. and Massey, R. U. (eds) (1988) *Health Care Systems: Moral Conflicts in European and American Public Policy*, Dordrecht (The Netherlands): Kluwer.

Sass, L. A. (1988) "Humanism, hermeneutics, and the concept of the subject," in S. B. Messer, L. A. Sass, and R. L. Woolfolk (eds) *Hermeneutics and Psychological Theory* (pp. 222–71), New Brunswick, NJ: Rutgers University Press.

Schacht, R. (1991) "History of Western ethics: 10. Nineteenth-century continental," in L. C. Becker and C. B. Becker (eds) *Encyclopedia of Ethics* (Vol. 1, pp. 515–22), New York: Garland.

Schimmel, S. (1992) *The Seven Deadly Sins: Jewish, Christian, and Classical Reflections on Human Nature*, New York: Free Press.

Schmidt, G. P. (1930) *The Old Time College President*, New York: Columbia University Press.

Schofield, W. (1986) *Psychotherapy: The Purchase of Friendship* (2nd edn), New Brunswick, NJ: Transaction Books (original work published in 1964).

Schroeder, W. R. (1991) "History of Western ethics: 11. Twentieth-century continental, part II," in L. C. Becker and C. B. Becker (eds) *Encyclopedia of Ethics* (Vol. 1, pp. 528–36), New York: Garland.

Schultz, K. V. (1958) "The psychologically healthy person: A study in identification and prediction," *Journal of Clinical Psychology* 14: 112–17.

Schultz, D. (1977) *Growth Psychology: Models of the Healthy Personality*, New York: Van Nostrand Reinhold.

Schwartz, B. (1986) *The Battle for Human Nature: Science, Morality and Modern Life*, New York: W. W. Norton.

—— (1990) "The creation and destruction of value," *American Psychologist* 45: 7–15.

Schwartz, S. H. (1992) "Universals in the content and structure of values: Theoretical advances and empirical tests in 20 countries," in M. P. Zanna (ed.) *Advances in Experimental Psychology* (Vol. 25, pp. 1–65), San Diego, CA: Academic Press.

—— (1994) "Beyond individualism/collectivism: New cultural dimensions of values," in U. Kim, H. C. Triandis, Ç. Kagitçibasi, S. Choi, and G. Yoon (eds) *Individualism and Collectivism: Theory, Method, and Applications* (pp. 85–119), Thousand Oaks, CA: Sage.

Schwartz, S. H. and Bilsky, W. (1990) "Toward a theory of the universal content and structure of values: Extensions and cross-cultural replications," *Journal of Personality and Social Psychology* 58: 878–91.

Schwehn, J. and Schau, C. G. (1990) "Psychotherapy as a process of value stabilization," *Counseling and Values* 35: 24–30.

Seashore, C. E. (1942) *Pioneering in Psychology*, Iowa City, IA: University of Iowa Press.

Sechrest, L. (1992) "The past future of clinical psychology: A reflection on Woodworth (1937)," *Journal of Consulting and Clinical Psychology* 60: 18–23.

Seiden, A. (1976) "Overview: Research on the psychology of women. II. Women in families, work and psychotherapy," *American Journal of Psychiatry* 133: 1111–23.

Seligman, C. and Katz, A. N. (1996) "The dynamics of value systems," in C. Seligman, J. M. Olson, and M. P. Zanna (eds) *The Psychology of Values: The Ontario Symposium* (Vol. 8, pp. 53–75), Mahwah, NJ: Lawrence Erlbaum.

Seligman, M. E. P. (1996) "The pitfalls of managed care," *The Pennsylvania Psychologist Update* 56 (April): 5, 7.

Sensenig, A. L., Heffler, S. K., and Donham, C. S. (1997) "Hospital, employment, and price indicators for the health care industry: Third quarter 1996" *Health Care Financing Review*, 18: 231–73.

Sexton, V. S. (1965) "Clinical psychology: An historical survey," *Genetic Psychology Monographs* 72: 401–34.

—— (1978) "American psychology and philosophy, 1876–1976: Alienation and reconciliation," *Journal of General Psychology* 99: 3–18.

Shafranske, E. P. (ed.) (1996) *Religion and the Clinical Practice of Psychology*, Washington, DC: American Psychological Association.

Shafranske, E. P. and Malony, H. N. (1996) "Religion and the clinical practice of psychology: A case for inclusion," in E. P. Shafranske (ed.) *Religion and the Clinical Practice of Psychology* (pp. 561–86), Washington, DC: American Psychological Association.

Shapiro, D. A., Harper, H., Startup, M., Reynolds, S., Bird, D., and Suokas, A. (1994) "The high-water mark of the drug metaphor: A meta-analytic critique of process-outcome research," in R. L. Russell (ed.) *Reassessing Psychotherapy Research* (pp. 1–35), New York: Guilford.

Sherman, N. (1989) *The Fabric of Character: Aristotle's Theory of Virtue*, Oxford: Clarendon Press.

Sherwin, S. (1992) *No Longer Patient: Feminist Ethics and Health Care*, Philadelphia, PA: Temple University Press.

Shweder, R. A. (1990) "In defense of moral realism: Reply to Gabennesch," *Child Development* 61: 2060–7.

Sieber, J. E. (1992) *Planning Ethically Responsible Research: A Guide for Students and Internal Review Boards*, Newbury Park, CA: Sage.

Silverstein, L. (1997) "President's message: A strategy for survival vs. a strategy for liberation," *The Family Psychologist* 13 (Summer): 1, 4–5.

Singer, P. (1981) *The Expanding Circle*, New York: Farrar, Straus & Giroux.

Sinnott-Armstrong, W. and Timmons, M. (eds) (1996) *Moral Knowledge? New Readings in Moral Epistemology*, New York: Oxford University Press.

Skinner, B. F. (1948) *Walden Two*, New York: Macmillan.

—— (1971) *Beyond Freedom and Dignity*, New York: Knopf.

—— (1972) "A lecture on 'having' a poem," in B. F. Skinner, *Cumulative Record: A Selection of Papers* (3rd edn, pp. 345–55), New York: Appleton-Century-Crofts.

Skolimowski, H. K. (1975) "Commentary," in N. H. Steneck (ed.) *Science and Society: Past, Present, and Future* (pp. 124–34), Ann Arbor, MI: University of Michigan Press.

Slote, M. (1995) "Ethics: Task of ethics," in W. T. Reich (ed.) *Encyclopedia of Bioethics* (2nd edn, Vol. 2, pp. 720–7), New York: Macmillan.

Smith, E. (ed.) (1997) *Integrity and change: Mental health in the marketplace*, London: Routledge.

Smith, M. B. (1961) " 'Mental health' reconsidered: A special case of the problem of values in psychology," *American Psychologist* 16: 299–306.

—— (1969) *Social Psychology and Human Values: Selected Essays*, Chicago, IL: Aldine.

—— (1990) "Psychology in the public interest: What have we done? What can we do?" *American Psychologist* 45: 530–6.

—— (1994) "Selfhood at risk: Postmodern perils and the perils of postmodernism," *American Psychologist* 49: 405–11.

Smith, M. B. and Anderson, J. W. (1989) "Henry A. Murray (1893–1988) [obituary]," *American Psychologist* 44: 1153–4.

Snyder, C. R. and Forsyth, D. R. (eds) (1991) *Handbook of Social and Clinical Psychology: The Health Perspective*, New York: Pergamon.

Speer, D. C. and Newman, F. L. (1996) "Mental health services outcome evaluation," *Clinical Psychology: Science & Practice* 3: 105–29.

Spence, D. P. (1982) *Narrative Truth and Historical Truth: Meaning and Interpretation in Psychoanalysis*, New York: W. W. Norton.

Sprague, E. (1967) "Moral sense," in P. Edwards (ed.) *Encyclopedia of Philosophy* (Vol. 5, pp. 385–7), New York: Macmillan.

Spranger, E. (1928) *Types of Men: The Psychology and Ethics of Personality*, trans. P. J. W. Pigors, New York: Johnson (1966 reprint).

Stam, H. J. (1993) "Is there anything beyond the ideological critique of individualism?" in H. J. Stam, W. Thorngage, L. P. Mos, and B. Kaplan (eds) *Recent Trends in Theoretical Psychology* (Vol. 3, 143–51), New York: Springer-Verlag.

Starr, P. (1982) *The Social Transformation of American Medicine: The Rise of a Sovereign Profession and the Making of a Vast Industry*, New York: Basic Books.

Steere, J. (1984) *Ethics in Clinical Psychology*, New York: Oxford University Press.

Steininger, M. (1979) "Objectivity and value judgments in the psychologies of E. L. Thorndike and W. McDougall," *Journal of the History of the Behavioral Sciences* 15: 263–81.

Stevenson, L. and Byerly, H. (1995) *The Many Faces of Science: An Introduction to Scientists, Values, and Society*, Boulder, CO: Westview.

Stiles, W. B. (1983) "Normality, diversity, and psychotherapy," *Psychotherapy: Theory, Research and Practice* 20: 183–9.

Stiles, W. B., Shapiro, D. A., and Barkham, M. (1993) "Research directions for psychotherapy integration: A roundtable," in J. C. Norcross (ed.) "Research directions for psychotherapy integration: A roundtable," *Journal of Psychotherapy Integration* 3: 91–131.

Stiles, W. B., Shapiro, D. A., and Elliott, R. (1986) "Are all psychotherapies equivalent?" *American Psychologist* 41: 165–80.

Stiles, W. B., Shapiro, D. A., and Harper, H. (1994) "Finding the way from process to outcome: Blind alleys and unmarked trails," in R. L. Russell (ed.) *Reassessing Psychotherapy Research* (pp. 36–64), New York: Guilford.

Stout, J. (1988) *Ethics After Babel: The Languages of Morals and Their Discontents*, Boston, MA: Beacon.

Strenger, C. (1997) "Further remarks on the classic and the romantic visions in psychoanalysis: Klein, Winnicott, and ethics," *Psychoanalysis and Contemporary Thought* 20: 207–43.

Strenger, C. and Omer, H. (1992) "Pluralistic criteria for psychotherapy: An alternative to sectarianism, anarchy, and Utopian integration," *American Journal of Psychotherapy* 46: 111–30.

Strong, S. R. (1978) "Social psychological approach to psychotherapy research," in S. L. Garfield and A. E. Bergin (eds) *Handbook of Psychotherapy and Behavior Change: An Empirical Analysis* (2nd edn, 101–35), New York: Wiley.

Strupp, H. H. (1974) "Some observations on the fallacy of value-free psychotherapy and the empty organism: Comments on a case study," *Journal of Abnormal Psychology* 83: 199–201.

—— (1980) "Humanism and psychotherapy: A personal statement of the therapist's essential values," *Psychotherapy: Theory, Research and Practice* 17: 396–400.

—— (1986) "Psychotherapy: Research, practice, and public policy (how to avoid dead ends)," *American Psychologist* 41: 120–30.

—— (1992) "Overview: Psychotherapy research," in D. K. Freedheim (ed.) *History of Psychotherapy: A Century of Change* (pp. 307–8), Washington, DC: American Psychological Association.

Strupp, H. H. and Hadley, S. W. (1977) "A tripartite model of mental health and therapeutic outcomes with special reference to negative effects in psychotherapy," *American Psychologist* 32: 187–96.

Suan, L. V. and Tyler, J. D. (1990) "Mental health values and preference for mental health resources of Japanese-American and Caucasian-American students," *Professional Psychology: Research and Practice* 21: 291–6.

Sullivan, E. V. (1984) *A Critical Psychology: Interpretation of the Personal World*, New York: Plenum.

Sullivan, W. M. (1982) *Reconstructing Public Philosophy*, Berkeley, CA: University of California Press.

—— (1995) *Work and Integrity: The Crisis and Promise of Professionalism in America*, New York: HarperBusiness.

Suppe, F. (1977) *The Structure of Scientific Theories* (2nd edn), Urbana, IL: University of Illinois Press.

Szasz, T. S. (1965) *The Ethics of Psychoanalysis*, New York: Basic Books.

—— (1974) *The Myth of Mental Illness: Foundations of a Theory of Personal Conduct* (revised edn), New York: Harper & Row.

Talley, P. F., Strupp, H. H., and Butler, S. F. (1994) *Psychotherapy Research and Practice: Bridging the Gap*, New York: Basic Books.

Task Force on Promotion and Dissemination of Psychological Procedures (1995) "Training in and dissemination of empirically-validated psychological treatments: Report and recommendations," *The Clinical Psychologist* 48: 3–23.

Taylor, C. (1989) *Sources of the Self: The Making of the Modern Identity*, Cambridge, MA: Harvard University Press.

—— (1992) *The Ethics of Authenticity*, Cambridge, MA: Harvard University Press.

Thackray, A. and Mendelsohn, E. (eds) (1974) *Science and Values*, Atlantic Highlands, NJ: Humanities Press.

Thiemann, R. (1991) *Constructing a Public Theology: The Church in a Pluralistic Culture*, Louisville, KY: Westminster/John Knox.

Thomas, L. (1989) *Living Morally: A Psychology of Moral Character*, Philadelphia, PA: Temple University Press.

Thompson, A. (1990) *Guide to Ethical Practice in Psychotherapy*, New York: Wiley.

Tillich, P. (1959) "Is a science of values possible?" in A. Maslow (ed.) *New Knowledge in Human Values* (pp. 189–96), New York: Harper.

Tisdale, J. R. (1961) "Psychological Value Theory and Research: 1930–1960," (Doctoral dissertation) *Dissertation Abstracts* 22: 1244.

Tjeltveit, A. C. (1986) "The ethics of value conversion in psychotherapy: Appropriate and inappropriate therapist influence on client values," *Clinical Psychology Review* 6: 515–37.

—— (1989) "The ubiquity of models of human beings in psychotherapy: The need for rigorous reflection," *Psychotherapy* 26: 1–10.

Tjeltveit, A. C., Fiordalisi, A. M., and Smith, C. (1996) "Relationships among mental health values and various dimensions of religiousness," *Journal of Social and Clinical Psychology* 15: 364–77.

Toulmin, S. E. (1950) *An Examination of the Place of Reason in Ethics*, London: Cambridge University Press.

—— (1975) "The twin moralities of science," in N. H. Steneck (ed.) *Science and Society: Past, Present, and Future* (pp. 111–24), Ann Arbor, MI: University of Michigan Press.

—— (1978) "Psychic health, mental clarity, self-knowledge and other virtues," in H. T. Engelhardt, Jr, and S. F. Spicker (eds) *Mental Health: Philosophical Perspectives* (pp. 55–70), Dordrecht (The Netherlands): D. Reidel.

Toulmin, S. and Leary, D. E. (1992) "The cult of empiricism, and beyond," in S. Koch and D. E. Leary (eds) *A Century of Psychology as Science* (pp. 594–617), Washington, DC: American Psychological Association.

Trabin, T. and Freeman, M. A. (1995) *Managed Behavioral Healthcare: History, Models, Strategic Challenges and Future Course*, San Francisco, CA: Jossey-Bass.

Truax, C. B. (1966) "Reinforcement and nonreinforcement in Rogerian psychotherapy," *Journal of Abnormal Psychology* 71: 1–9.

Tugendat, E. (1990) "The necessity for cooperation between philosophical and empirical research in the clarification of the meaning of the moral 'ought,'" in T. E. Wren (ed.) *The Moral Domain: Essays in the Ongoing Discussion Between Philosophy and the Social Sciences* (pp. 3–14), Cambridge, MA: MIT Press.

Tyler, J. D., Clark, J. A., Olson, D., Klapp, D. A., and Cheloha, R. S. (1983) "Measuring mental health values," *Counseling and Values* 27: 20–30.

Tyler, J. D., Clark, J. A., and Wittenstrom, R. C. (1989) "Mental health values and response to alcoholism treatment," *Counseling and Values* 33: 204–16.

Tyler, J. D. and Suan, L. V. (1990) "Mental health values differences between Native American and Caucasian American college students," *Journal of Rural Community Psychology* 11: 17–29.

Vachon, D. O. and Agresti, A. A. (1992) "A training proposal to help mental health professionals clarify and manage implicit values in the counseling process," *Professional Psychology: Research and Practice* 23: 509–14.

VandenBos, G. R., Cummings, N. A., and DeLeon, P. H. (1992) "A century of psychotherapy: Economic and environmental influences," in D. K. Freedheim (ed.) *History of Psychotherapy: A Century of Change* (pp. 65–102), Washington, DC: American Psychological Association.

VandenBos, G. R. and DeLeon, P. H. (1988) "The use of psychotherapy to improve physical health," *Psychotherapy* 25: 335–43.

Varma, V. K. (1988) "Culture, personality and psychotherapy," *International Journal of Social Psychiatry* 34: 142–9.

Veatch, R. M. (1973) "Generalization of expertise," *Hastings Center Report* 1: 29–40.

—— (1978) "Codes of medical ethics: Ethical analysis," in W. T. Reich (ed.) *Encyclopedia of Bioethics* (2nd edn, Vol. 1, pp. 172–80), New York: Macmillan.

—— (1989a) "Clinical ethics, applied ethics, and theory," in B. Hoffmaster, B. Freedman, and G. Fraser (eds) *Clinical Ethics: Theory and Practice* (pp. 7–25), Clifton, NJ: Humana.

—— (1989b) "Medical ethics: Its implications for the development of professional ethics," in C. T. Mitchell (ed.) *Values in Teaching and Professional Ethics* (pp. 37–51), Macon, GA: Mercer University Press.

Vernon, P. E. and Allport, G. W. (1931) "A test for personal values," *Journal of Abnormal and Social Psychology* 26: 231–48.

Vitz, P. C. (1990) "The use of stories in moral development: New psychological reasons for an old education method," *American Psychologist* 45: 709–20.

Vogeltanz, N. D. and Plaud, J. J. (1992) "On the goodness of Skinner's system of naturalistic ethics in solving basic value conflicts," *Psychological Record* 42: 457–68.

Wachtel, P. L. (1989) "The social significance of psychotherapy," in L. Simek-Downing (ed.) *International Psychotherapy: Theories, Research, and Cross-cultural Implications* (pp. 45–55), New York: Praeger.

Wakefield, J. C. (1992a) "Disorder as harmful dysfunction: A conceptual critique of DSM-III-R's definition of mental disorder," *Psychological Review* 99: 232–47.

—— (1992b) "The concept of mental disorder: On the boundary between biological facts and social values," *American Psychologist* 47: 373–88.

—— (1997) "Normal inability versus pathological disability: Why Ossorio's definition of mental disorder is not sufficient," *Clinical Psychology: Science and Practice* 4: 249–58.

Wallace, E. R., IV (1986) "Freud as ethicist," in P. Stepansky (ed.) *Freud, Appraisals and Reappraisals: Contributions to Freud Studies* (pp. 83–141), Hillsdale, NJ: Analytic Press.

—— (1991) "Psychiatry: The healing amphibian," in D. S. Browning and I. S. Evison (eds) *Does Psychiatry Need a Public Philosophy?* (pp. 74–120), Chicago, IL: Nelson-Hall.

Wallach, M. A. and Wallach, L. (1983) *Psychology's Sanction for Selfishness: The Error of Egoism in Theory and Therapy*, San Francisco, CA: W. H. Freeman.

—— (1990) *Rethinking Goodness*, Albany, NY: State University of New York Press.

Wallerstein, R. S. (1976) "Introduction to symposium on 'Ethics, Moral values and psychological interventions,'" *International Review of Psycho-analysis* 3: 369–72.

Walsh, R. A. (1995) "The study of values in psychotherapy: A critique and call for an alternative method," *Psychotherapy Research* 5: 313–26.

Waterman, A. S. (1984) *The Psychology of Individualism*, New York: Praeger.

—— (1988) "On the uses of psychological theory and research in the process of ethical inquiry," *Psychological Bulletin* 103: 283–98.

Watson, J. B. (1924) *Behaviorism*, New York: W. W. Norton.

Watson, R. I. (1954) *Psychology as a Profession*, Garden City, NY: Doubleday.

Weiner, N. O. (1993) *The Harmony of the Soul: Mental Health and Moral Virtue Reconsidered*, Albany, NY: State University of New York Press.

Weisskopf-Joelson, E. (1980) "The enfant terrible of psychotherapy," *Psychotherapy: Theory, Research and Practice* 17: 459–66.

Wendorf, D. J. and Wendorf, R. J. (1985) "A systematic view of family therapy ethics," *Family Process* 24: 443–53.

Werkmeister, W. H. (1970) *Historical Spectrum of Value Theories: Vol. 1: The German Group*, Lincoln, NE: Johnsen.

—— (1973) *Historical Spectrum of Value Theories: Vol. 2: The Anglo-American Group*, Lincoln, NE: Johnsen.

Westminster Divines (1745) "The shorter catechism agreed upon by the Assembly of Divines of Westminster with the assistance of the Commissions from the Church of Scotland," in *A Compendium of the Westminster Confession of Faith and the Shorter and Longer Catechism* (pp. 367–410), Philadelphia, PA: Benjamin Franklin (original work published in 1648).

Wig, N. N. (1990) "Indian concepts of mental health," *International Journal of Mental Health* 18: 71–80.

Williams, A. (1994) "Economics, society and health care ethics," in R. Gillon (ed.) *Principles of Health Care Ethics* (pp. 829–42), Chichester (England): Wiley.

Williams, R. M., Jr (1979) "Change and stability in values and value systems: A sociological perspective," in M. Rokeach (ed.) *Understanding Human Values: Individual and Societal* (pp. 15–46), New York: Free Press.

Wilson, W. J. and Nye, F. I. (1966) *Some Methodological Problems in the Empirical Study of Values* (Washington Agricultural Experiment Station, Bulletin 672), Pullman, WA: Washington State University.

Wolfe, A. (1989) *Whose Keeper? Social Science and Moral Obligation*, Berkeley, CA: University of California Press.

Wolfe, B. E. (1978) "Moral transformations in psychotherapy," *Counseling and Values* 23: 43–9.

Wolman, B. B. (ed.) (1965) *Handbook of Clinical Psychology*, New York: McGraw-Hill.

Wong, D. B. (1991) "Moral relativism," in L. C. Becker and C. B. Becker (eds) *Encyclopedia of Ethics* (Vol. 2, pp. 856–9), New York: Garland.

Woodworth, R. S. (1937) "The future of clinical psychology," *Journal of Consulting Psychology* 1: 4–5.

Woolfolk, R. L. (1998) *Cure of Souls: Science, Values and Psychotherapy*, San Francisco, CA: Jossey-Bass.

World Health Organization (1981) "Constitution," in A. L. Caplan, H. T. Engelhardt, Jr, and J. J. McCartney (eds) *Concepts of Health and Disease: Interdisciplinary Perspectives* (pp. 83–4), Reading, MA: Addison-Wesley (original work published in 1958).

Worthington, E. L., Jr (1988) "Understanding the values of religious clients: A model and its application to counseling," *Journal of Counseling Psychology* 35: 166–74.

Wren, T. E. (ed.) (1990) *The Moral Domain: Essays in the Ongoing Discussion Between Philosophy and the Social Sciences*, Cambridge, MA: MIT Press.

Wright, R. (1994) *The Moral Animal: The New Science of Evolutionary Psychology*, New York: Pantheon.

Wulff, D. M. (1996) "The psychology of religion: An overview," in E. P. Shafranske (ed.) *Religion and the Clinical Practice of Psychology* (pp. 43–70), Washington, DC: American Psychological Association.

Yates, B. T. (1995) "Cost-effectiveness analysis, cost-benefit analysis, and beyond: Evolving models for the scientist-manager-practitioner," *Clinical Psychology: Science and Practice* 2: 385–98.

Young, S. D. (1987) *The Rule of Experts: Occupational Licensing in America*, Washington, DC: Cato Institute.

Index